THE
MISTRESSES
OF
CLIVEDEN

Natalie Livingstone was born and raised in London. She graduated with a first-class degree in history from Christ's College, Cambridge in 1998. She began her career as a feature writer at the *Daily Express* and now contributes to *Tatler*, *Harper's Bazaar*, US *Vogue*, *Elle*, *The Times* and the *Mail on Sunday*. Natalie lives in London with her husband and two children.

Praise for *The Mistresses of Cliveden*

'Natalie Livingstone has written an utterly fascinating and completely beguiling account of three centuries of high living, high politics, and high drama at one of Britain's most famous stately homes. A page turner from start to finish, *The Mistresses of Cliveden* perfectly illustrates why social history rules the shelves; it's history with all the good stuff left in.'
Amanda Foreman, author of *Georgiana, Duchess of Devonshire*

'A wonderful voyage through the fascinating history of Cliveden - this is a brilliant book full of gripping personalities and beautiful detail.'
Kate Williams, author of *Becoming Queen* and *Josephine*

'Chronicled with scholarship, readability, wit and a fine eye for telling detail.'
Evening Standard

THE MISTRESSES OF CLIVEDEN

THREE CENTURIES OF SCANDAL, POWER AND INTRIGUE

NATALIE LIVINGSTONE

arrow books

3 5 7 9 10 8 6 4 2

Arrow Books
20 Vauxhall Bridge Road
London SW1V 2SA

Arrow Books is part of the Penguin Random House group
of companies whose addresses can be found at
global.penguinrandomhouse.com.

Penguin
Random House
UK

First published by Hutchinson in 2015
First published in Great Britain by Penguin Random House in 2015

www.penguin.co.uk

A CIP catalogue record for this book is available from the British Library

ISBN 9780099594727

Typeset in 11/15 pt Granjon
Jouve (UK), Milton Keynes
Printed and bound by Clays Ltd, St Ives plc

For Ian, Grace and Alice

CONTENTS

CAST OF CHARACTERS

Characters who appear in more than one part are listed under their first appearance.

PART I

ANNA MARIA TALBOT (née Brudenell), Countess of SHREWSBURY, 1642–1702. Married Francis Talbot, 11th Earl of Shrewsbury, and had an affair with George Villiers, 2nd Duke of Buckingham. With Mary Villiers, the first mistress of Cliveden.

FRANCIS TALBOT, 11th Earl of SHREWSBURY, 1623–68. Husband of Anna Maria Talbot, died following a duel with George Villiers, 2nd Duke of Buckingham.

GEORGE VILLIERS, 2nd Duke of BUCKINGHAM, 1628–87. Husband of Mary Villiers, lover of Anna Maria Talbot, and creator of Cliveden.

CHARLES TALBOT, Duke of SHREWSBURY, 1660–1718. Politician; son of Anna Maria and Francis Talbot.

MARY VILLIERS (née Fairfax), 1638–1704. Wife of George Villiers, 2nd Duke of Buckingham; with Anna Maria Talbot, the first mistress of Cliveden.

CHARLES II, King of England, Scotland and Ireland from 1660–85.

BARBARA PALMER (née VILLIERS), Duchess of Cleveland.

ELEANOR 'NELL' GWYN.

MISTRESSES OF CHARLES II

JAMES, Duke of YORK (James II from 1685–88). Younger brother of Charles II.

JOHN DRYDEN. Writer, and artistic rival of the 2nd Duke of Buckingham.

HENRY BENNET, 1st Earl of ARLINGTON. Statesman, and political rival of the 2nd Duke of Buckingham.

SAMUEL PEPYS. Diarist.

WILLIAM WINDE. Architect to the 2nd Duke of Buckingham.

PART II

ELIZABETH VILLIERS (married name HAMILTON), Countess of Orkney, 1657–1733. Lover of William of Orange (later William III); married George Hamilton, Earl of Orkney in 1695. Mistress of Cliveden from 1696 to 1733.

GEORGE HAMILTON, Earl of ORKNEY, 1666–1737. Soldier; husband of Elizabeth Villiers.

LADY ANNE, 2nd Countess of ORKNEY, 1700–77. Eldest surviving daughter of Elizabeth and George Hamilton; married William O'Brien.

LADY FRANCES.

LADY HENRIETTA.

DAUGHTERS OF ELIZABETH AND GEORGE HAMILTON

WILLIAM of ORANGE (William III from 1689–1702). Husband of Mary Stuart; deposer of James II in the 'Glorious Revolution' of 1688.

ANNE HAMILTON, *suo jure* 3rd Duchess of HAMILTON, 1632–1716. Wife of William Douglas, 1st Earl of Selkirk; mother of George Hamilton, 1st Earl of Orkney.

JAMES HAMILTON, 4th Duke of HAMILTON and 1st Duke of Brandon, 1658–1712. Eldest son of Anne Hamilton and William Douglas; elder brother of George Hamilton, 1st Earl of Orkney.

PRINCESS MARY, 1662–94. Wife of William of Orange (later William III). Ruled as Queen Mary II from 1689–1694.

PRINCESS ANNE, 1665–1714. Ruled as Queen Anne from 1702–1714.

DAUGHTERS OF JAMES II

SARAH CHURCHILL (née JENNINGS), Duchess of MARLBOROUGH, 1660–1744. Politician; wife of John Churchill, 1st Duke of Marlborough.

JOHN CHURCHILL, 1st Duke of MARLBOROUGH, 1650–1722. Army officer and politician; husband of Sarah Churchill, Duchess of Marlborough.

JONATHAN SWIFT. Writer, and Dean of St Patrick's in Dublin; friend of Elizabeth, Countess of Orkney.

SIDNEY GODOLPHIN, 1st Earl of GODOLPHIN. Politician, overthrown in Robert Harley's coup of 1710.

ROBERT HARLEY, 1st Earl of OXFORD. Politician, and sometime ally of Elizabeth Villiers.

THOMAS ARCHER. Architect to the Earl of Orkney.

LADY MARY WORTLEY MONTAGU. Writer.

PART III

AUGUSTA, Princess of WALES (Princess AUGUSTA of SAXE-GOTHA), 1719–72. Mistress of Cliveden 1738–51; married Frederick, Prince of Wales in 1736.

FREDERICK, Prince of WALES, 1707–51. Eldest son (and heir) of George II and his consort Queen Caroline, and husband of Augusta, Princess of Wales.

PRINCESS AUGUSTA, 1737–1813.

PRINCE GEORGE (later GEORGE III), 1738–1820.

PRINCE EDWARD (later Duke of York and Albany), 1739–67.

PRINCESS ELIZABETH, 1741–59.

PRINCE WILLIAM HENRY (later Duke of Gloucester and Edinburgh), 1743–1805.

CHILDREN OF FREDERICK AND AUGUSTA

GEORGE II, 1683–1760. King of Great Britain and Ireland 1727–60. Father of Frederick, Prince of Wales; husband of Caroline of Ansbach.

QUEEN CAROLINE (Caroline of Brandenburg-Ansbach), 1683–1737. Mother of Frederick, Prince of Wales; wife of George II.

Lady JANE HAMILTON. Mistress of Frederick, Prince of Wales, and sister-in-law of George Hamilton, 1st Earl of Orkney.

JOHN HERVEY, 2nd Baron HERVEY, 1696–1743. Courtier and memoirist; favourite of Queen Caroline.

Prince WILLIAM, Duke of CUMBERLAND. Soldier, and brother of Frederick, Prince of Wales.

JOHN STUART, 3rd Earl of BUTE. Tutor to Prince George.

WILLIAM KENT. Designer to the Prince and Princess of Wales.

PART IV

HARRIET GEORGIANA LEVESON-GOWER (née Howard), Duchess of SUTHERLAND, 1806–68. Married her cousin, George Leveson-Gower, in 1823. Mistress of Cliveden from 1849 to 1868.

GEORGE LEVESON-GOWER, 2nd Duke of SUTHERLAND, 1786–1861. Husband of Harriet, Duchess of Sutherland.

GEORGE GRANVILLE LEVESON-GOWER, 1st Duke of SUTHERLAND, 1758–1833. Husband of Elizabeth; father of George Leveson-Gower, 2nd Duke of Sutherland.

ELIZABETH LEVESON-GOWER, Duchess of SUTHERLAND (and *suo jure* 19th Countess of Sutherland), 1765–1839. Wife of George Granville Leveson-Gower; mother of George Leveson-Gower, 2nd Duke of Sutherland.

LADY ELIZABETH GEORGIANA, 1824–78.

LADY EVELYN, 1825–69.

LADY CAROLINE, 1827–87.

LORD GEORGE GRANVILLE WILLIAM (succeeded as 3rd Duke of Sutherland), 1828–92.

CHILDREN OF HARRIET AND GEORGE LEVESON-GOWER

CAST OF CHARACTERS

LADY BLANCHE JULIA, 1830–32.

LORD FREDERICK GEORGE, 1832–54.

LADY CONSTANCE GERTRUDE, 1834–80.

LADY VICTORIA, 1838–39.

LORD ALBERT, 1843–74.

LORD RONALD CHARLES, 1845–1916.

LADY ALEXANDRINA ('Aline'), 1848–49.

CHILDREN OF HARRIET AND GEORGE LEVESON-GOWER

QUEEN VICTORIA (Alexandrina Victoria), 1819–1901.
Queen of the United Kingdom of Great Britain and Ireland
from 1837–1901; friend of Harriet, Duchess of Sutherland,
who served for many years as her Mistress of the Robes.

WILLIAM GLADSTONE. Politician, and friend of Harriet,
Duchess of Sutherland.

CHARLES BARRY. Architect to the Sutherlands.

HUGH LUPUS GROSVENOR, 1st Duke of WESTMINSTER,
1825–99. Married Constance Sutherland-Leveson-Gower in 1852;
two years after Constance's death in 1880, he remarried, to
Katherine Caroline Cavendish.

PART V

NANCY ASTOR (née Langhorne), Viscountess ASTOR, 1879–
1964. Mistress of Cliveden from 1906 to 1952. Married Robert
Gould Shaw in 1897 and divorced him in 1903; married Waldorf
Astor in 1906.

WALDORF ASTOR, 2nd Viscount ASTOR, 1879–1952. Second
husband of Nancy Astor.

ROBERT GOULD SHAW, 1871–1930. First husband of Nancy
Astor.

BOBBIE SHAW (Robert Gould Shaw), 1898–1970. Eldest son of
Nancy Astor, and her only child with Robert Shaw.

CAST OF CHARACTERS

BILL (William Waldorf Astor II), 1907–1966.

WISSIE (Nancy Phyllis Louise Astor),
1909–1975.

DAVID (Francis David Langhorne Astor),
1912–2001.

MICHAEL (Michael Langhorne Astor),
1916–1980.

JAKIE (John Jacob Astor VII), 1918–2000.

CHILDREN OF
NANCY AND
WALDORF ASTOR

NANCY WITCHER KEENE LANGHORNE, 'NANAIRE',
1848–1903. Mother of Nancy Astor; wife of Chillie Langhorne.

CHISWELL DABNEY LANGHORNE, 'CHILLIE', 1843–1919.
Father of Nancy Astor; husband of Nanaire.

WILLIAM WALDORF ASTOR, 1st Viscount ASTOR, 1848–
1919. Father of Waldorf Astor.

LIZZIE, 1865–1916.

IRENE, 1873–1956.

PHYLLIS, 1880–1937.

NORA, 1889–1955.

NANCY ASTOR'S
SISTERS

BOB BRAND (Robert Henry Brand), Baron BRAND, 1878–1963.
Married to Phyllis Brand; public servant and banker, and friend of
Nancy Astor.

PHILIP KERR, 11th Marquess of LOTHIAN, 1882–1940. Politician
and diplomat; close friend of Nancy Astor.

ROSINA (ROSE) HARRISON. Nancy Astor's maid.

ETTIE GRENFELL, Lady DESBOROUGH. The Astors'
neighbour at Taplow Court.

STEPHEN WARD. Society osteopath and friend of Bill Astor.

CHRISTINE KEELER. Model and showgirl.

JACK PROFUMO (John Dennis Profumo). Conservative politician.

TIMELINE

TIMELINE

1688	The Glorious Revolution: William of Orange invades England, deposing James II and becoming William III
1689	ELIZABETH returns to England
	William III and Mary II become co-regents
1694	Queen Mary dies; her dying wish is that William end his affair with ELIZABETH
1695	ELIZABETH given Irish lands by William III; marries George Hamilton, Earl of Orkney
1696	The Earl of Orkney buys Cliveden
1700	ELIZABETH stripped of her Irish lands by Parliament
1701–1714	War of the Spanish Succession, in which the Earl of Orkney and the Duke of Marlborough fight
1702	ANNA MARIA dies
	William III dies; Anne becomes queen
1704	Battle of Blenheim (part of the War of the Spanish Succession), in which Marlborough distinguishes himself
1706	Thomas Archer begins renovating Cliveden for the Orkneys
	Battle of Ramillies (part of the War of the Spanish Succession), in which Orkney leads a charge across the Petite Ghee
1707	The Act of Union joins the crowns and parliaments of Scotland and England
1712	Archer's renovation of Cliveden complete
1714	Queen Anne dies; George I becomes king
1717	George I's first visit to Cliveden
1719	PRINCESS AUGUSTA OF SAXE-GOTHA born
1727	Giacomo Leoni's Blenheim Pavilion built at Cliveden
	George II succeeds his father as king

1729	Queen Caroline and her son Frederick, Prince of Wales visit Cliveden
1733	ELIZABETH dies
1735	Leoni's Octagon Temple built at Cliveden
1736	AUGUSTA marries Frederick, son of George II
1737	Earl of Orkney dies and Cliveden passes to Anne, 2nd Countess of Orkney
	AUGUSTA and Frederick lease Cliveden
1738	AUGUSTA gives birth to George William Frederick, later George III
1740	'Rule, Britannia!' performed at Cliveden
1745	Bonnie Prince Charlie lands in Scotland; Jacobite Rebellion
1746	Battle of Culloden
1751	Frederick dies; Anne, Countess of Orkney, regains possession of Cliveden
1760	George II dies; succeeded by AUGUSTA's son George III
1772	AUGUSTA dies
1795	Cliveden burns down; the ruins become popular among tourists interested in Gothic sites
1806	HARRIET HOWARD born
1813	Architect Peter Nicholson commissioned to design a tea room by the Thames at Cliveden; George Devey would later develop the tea room into Spring Cottage
1813–1821	Highland Clearances in Sutherland
1821	Cliveden is sold at auction
1823	HARRIET marries George Gower, 2nd Duke of Sutherland

TIMELINE

TIMELINE

1893	William Waldorf Astor buys Cliveden
1895	National Trust established
1897	NANCY marries Bob Shaw
1903	NANCY divorces Bob Shaw
1906	NANCY marries Waldorf Astor; Waldorf and NANCY given Cliveden as a wedding present; NANCY redesigns the garden and the interior
1914–1918	First World War; hospital built at Cliveden
1918	Representation of the People Act extends the vote to women aged 30 and over
1919	NANCY becomes the first female MP to take her seat
1937	*The Week* runs the Cliveden Set story
1939–1945	Second World War; new hospital built at Cliveden
1942	Waldorf approaches the National Trust about the donation of Cliveden
1945	NANCY resigns from Parliament
1952	Waldorf dies; NANCY gives Cliveden to their son Bill
1961	Jack Profumo meets Christine Keeler at Cliveden beside the newly built swimming pool
1963	Profumo Affair becomes a public scandal
1964	NANCY dies and is buried next to Waldorf at Cliveden
1966	Bill Astor dies of a heart attack. The Astors vacate Cliveden
1969–1983	Stanford University leases Cliveden from the National Trust for use as an overseas campus
1970	Bobbie Shaw commits suicide
1985	Lease acquired by the Von Essen hotel group
2012	Lease acquired by Ian Livingstone of London and Regional Properties to run as a hotel

INTRODUCTION

On the sultry night of 8 July 1961, the 19-year-old showgirl Christine Keeler was in the swimming pool at Cliveden when she heard voices approaching from the terrace. She had been larking about with her friend Stephen Ward (who rented a cottage at the foot of the estate), a law student called Noel Howard-Jones, and a pretty young hitch-hiker whom the three of them had picked up on the drive down from London. Usually Ward asked permission to use the pool from the estate's owner Bill Astor, but tonight Bill was occupied by a more sober dinner party in the main house. The pool was tucked away in a walled garden on the west side of the property, so the group thought nothing of going for an impromptu swim without giving Astor prior warning. The party grew raucous, and at some point Keeler shed her swimsuit in a bet.

Up at the main house, the company at dinner included Field Marshal Ayub Khan, president of Pakistan, John Profumo, secretary of state for war, and his film-star wife Valerie. The hosts were Bill Astor, who had inherited the house from his parents Waldorf and Nancy, and Bill's wife Bronwen. After dinner, the hosts decided to take advantage of the balmy night and suggested a stroll down to the swimming pool to show off a newly installed bronze statue of their son riding a dolphin. What the guests actually saw, as they rounded the corner into the walled garden, was the lithe form of Christine Keeler, lifting herself from the pool and dashing across the patio, her feet making damp prints on the terracotta tiles. Profumo wasted no time in asking Bill for an introduction.

Late that night Keeler returned to London to pick up a couple more of Ward's girlfriends, and the next morning they were all driven back to Cliveden by the Russian naval attaché and intelligence officer Yevgeny Ivanov. The group spent a lazy Sunday by Bill Astor's pool, where Ivanov challenged Profumo to a swimming race. Just before Keeler left that evening, Profumo, who according to Ivanov had been 'flirting outrageously' with the young girl, asked for her contact details.[1] Ivanov drove Christine back to Ward's flat where, the Soviet attaché would later claim, they slept together. Two days later, Profumo tracked Keeler down and arranged to meet her while his wife Valerie was visiting his Warwickshire constituency. It marked the beginning of a tepid, half-hearted liaison, which Keeler – who once cooked them sausages before they had sex in front of the television – described as 'a very, very well-mannered screw of convenience'.[2]

The weekend at Cliveden was the first act in a drama that would bring down a government and change the course of British history. The apparent *ménage à trois* between the minister of war, a Soviet spy and a good-time girl made Cliveden synonymous with scandal in the collective consciousness of an entire generation.

But the outraged headlines and lurid scoops of the Profumo Affair – as it came to be known – were nothing new. During its dawn in the 1660s as much as its twilight in the 1960s, Cliveden was an emblem of elite misbehaviour and intrigue. Indeed the 350-year history of the house began when a powerful politician decided to build a secluded mansion in which to enjoy his affair with an ambitious courtesan not much older than Keeler. The courtesan was Anna Maria, Countess of Shrewsbury, and the politician George Villiers, Duke of Buckingham, a childhood friend of Charles II and one of the wealthiest men in England. When Buckingham bought Cliveden in the 1660s, it comprised two modest hunting lodges set within 400 acres of land. Over the following decade, he transformed it, landscaping the gardens and constructing a magnificent house as a monument to his scandalous affair with the countess.

The estate sits just 5 miles upriver from Windsor Castle and fewer than 30 from the Palace of Westminster in London, a privileged location that would be crucial to the lives of its residents. Its outlines have changed little since the 17th century, and, then as now, Cliveden is one of England's most breathtaking landmarks. To the south-west, the grounds overlook the Thames from the tall chalk cliffs that give the site its name – over the centuries it has also been spelt Cliefden, Clifden, and Cliffden. Further north, the cliffs, which are densely planted with oak, beech, ash and chestnut, dip into a hollow, and the gardens trail like skirts down to the water. At the top of these gardens, at the end of a long parterre, and raised to an even more imperious height by an arcaded terrace, stands the house itself, an elaborate Italianate mansion, flanked by two wings and approached by road from the north, down a long gravel drive.

In April 2012 Cliveden became central to my life when my husband acquired the property. When it came into our possession it was no longer a private residence – Cliveden had been reincarnated as a university and a hospital, and latterly run as a hotel. But amid its faded charms there were clues everywhere to the past lives of the estate, most noticeably in the portraits of the house's former mistresses.

In the great hall hangs a portrait of Anna Maria, the original inspiration for the house, a courtesan much maligned in her own time and misunderstood by subsequent generations. Carved into the staircase is Elizabeth, Countess of Orkney, a formidable intellect, power-broker and long-time lover to Britain's conqueror of 1688, William III. Augusta of Saxe-Gotha, the queen that Britain was promised and then denied in the middle of the 18th century, is immortalised in a painting over the grand staircase, while the fourth mistress, Harriet, Duchess of Sutherland, a glittering society hostess and the closest confidante of Queen Victoria, presides over the dining room. Finally, hanging beside the fireplace in the great hall is John Singer Sargent's portrait of Nancy Astor – Cliveden's last great mistress, Britain's first female Member of Parliament, and one of the most controversial and colourful women in British political history.

The struggles and sacrifices of these women, their juggling of outer image and inner life, are familiar and universal. Their privileges, however, were extraordinary. It is from their elite viewpoint that this book narrates the tumultuous events of the last three centuries: Restoration and Glorious Revolution, aristocratic rise and fall, two world wars and the Cold War. Along the way there are tales of fanaticism and fashion, of censorship, disease, slavery and the unlikely correlation between gardening and warfare.

As well as being a story about women and power, this book is also the biography of a house. Conceived by Stuart aristocracy, Cliveden later served as a counter-court during the power struggles of the Hanoverian dynasty, and in the 19th century became a crucible for a new brand of liberal politics, while continuing to offer a safe haven for royalty. With the decline of aristocratic wealth, it was one of the first houses to be bought up by American money, and in the later 20th and 21st centuries, it has become part of a new commercial order in which my husband and I – Jewish and self-made – play our part. Throughout the narrative Cliveden itself remains central – the constant character and a defining presence in the lives of all these women. For more than three centuries, the house provided opportunity and authority to women; in return, successive mistresses shaped the house, transforming both its architectural appearance and its social role.

While these women's biographies reflect the gender politics of their times, their story is not a simple one of progress towards emancipation and equality. Nancy, in the 20th century, was more financially reliant on her husband than Elizabeth Villiers was in the 17th. In the early 19th century Harriet, Duchess of Sutherland, watched from the balcony of the Lords as an act passed into law that would formally prevent women from participating in parliamentary elections – a privilege that had been enjoyed by women burgesses in the Tudor period. The life of each mistress is a dance of progress and reaction, of old and new. In this way, the biographies are not dissimilar from the house itself, where past and present are woven together: where 20th-century wiring runs underground along 16th-century tunnels, service bells from the 19th century hang from the wall above Wi-Fi boxes, and a swimming pool from the 1950s sits within a garden landscaped in the 1700s.

On the opposite side of the house to the pool, between the main block and the east wing, lies an unusual monument from the early 20th century that commemorates an event from the late 17th. Carved into the grass, inlaid in brickwork, is a rapier with an elegant handle, the sort a gentleman would have used in a duel. Alongside it lies a date: 1668.

It is a monument to the day on which a duel was fought between two of the most powerful people in the land, the Duke of Buckingham and the Earl of Shrewsbury. They were fighting for one woman – Anna Maria – Shrewsbury's wife and Buckingham's lover. The duel was to the death. Buckingham killed Shrewsbury and claimed Anna Maria as his prize. She became the first mistress of this great house, and it is to her that I turn to begin my story.

PART I

ANNA MARIA

1642-1702

THE DUEL

I n the thin light of a January morning, the Duke of Buckingham galloped towards Barn Elms, the appointed site
for the duel he had so long awaited. In springtime and
summer, revellers flocked to Barn Elms with their bottles, baskets and chairs, recorded the diarist Samuel Pepys, 'to sup
under the trees, by the waterside', but in winter the ground
next to the Thames was frozen and deserted. Nevertheless,
there was still activity on the river.[1] Nearby Putney was famous
for its fishery and was also the point at which travellers going
west from London disembarked from the ferry and continued
by coach.[2] The harried cries of watermen and the shouts of
fishermen returning from dawn trips filled the air as Buckingham neared his destination.

The grounds of the old manor of Barn Elms lay on a curve
in the river just west of Putney. The land was divided into
narrow agricultural plots – some open, others fenced off by
walls or hedgerows. Pepys recorded that the duel took place in
a 'close', meaning a yard next to a building or an enclosed
field – somewhere screened off from passers-by.[3]

But as his horse's hoofs thundered along the icy riverbank,

Buckingham's thoughts lay on a more distant turf. Anna Maria, the woman who had provoked the duel, was 270 miles away, in self-imposed exile in a convent in France. Nine years before, in 1659, Anna Maria Brudenell had married Francis Talbot, 11th Earl of Shrewsbury, but the union had been an unhappy one. He was 36, a wealthy but sedate landowner; she was a pleasure-loving 16-year-old already conscious of her seductive charms. Anna Maria kept a series of lovers but Shrewsbury turned a blind eye, making himself a laughing stock at court. During a trip to York in 1666, she began a new affair, this time with the flamboyant courtier George Villiers, 2nd Duke of Buckingham, and the following summer sexual rivalry between him and another of her paramours, the hot-headed rake Henry Killigrew, exploded in a violent scuffle.[4] This very public fracas made it abundantly clear that Anna Maria had been serially unfaithful, and Shrewsbury's failure to challenge either man to a duel was seen as a dereliction of his role as a noble husband. Anna Maria fled to France in shame.

Amid reports that Buckingham was actually hiding Anna Maria in England, Shrewsbury at last summoned the courage to defend his marriage and his name. He challenged Buckingham to a duel and the duke eagerly accepted. Anna Maria exerted an extraordinary hold over a great number of men but she quite simply possessed the duke. 'Love is like Moses' serpent,' he lamented in his commonplace book, 'it devours all the rest.'[5]

Pepys reported that King Charles II had tried to dissuade Buckingham from fighting the duel but the message was never received.[6] Even if it had been delivered, Buckingham would probably have taken little heed of the king's wishes. Charles II was more like his brother than his monarch. Buckingham's father, also George Villiers, had been made a duke by Charles I and, when Villiers senior was assassinated in 1628, the king took the Buckingham children into his household. Young George became a close friend of the future king and many of Charles's happiest childhood memories involved Buckingham. The pair spent their student days at Cambridge University and their names appear side by side in the records of matriculation at Trinity College.[7] Buckingham felt little obligation to defer to the king, while Charles tended to turn a blind eye to Buckingham's reckless conduct.

Unknown to Shrewsbury, Buckingham had another reason to be riding to Barn Elms that January day in 1668. Shortly after the start of his affair with Anna Maria, Buckingham had viewed a magnificent estate next to the Thames. The site, then owned by the Manfield family, was within easy boating distance of London and included two hunting lodges set in 160 acres of arable land and woods. The estate was known as Cliveden, or Cliffden, after the chalk cliffs that rose above the river. From the lodges the ground dropped sharply towards the Thames, and on the far side of the river flooded water meadows and open land spread out for miles beyond. There had once been a well-stocked deer park on the site and Buckingham knew he could restore the estate to its former glory. He intended to replace the lodge with a large house that would boast the best views in the kingdom.

Buckingham bought Cliveden with the pleasures of the flesh at the forefront of his mind. This, he fantasised, would be his grand love nest with Anna Maria, a place for them to freely indulge in their affair – hunting by day, dancing by night. It was Buckingham's obsession with Anna Maria and his dream of a gilded life with her at Cliveden that led him to accept Shrewsbury's challenge.

Buckingham's fight with Shrewsbury was not to be an impulsive brawl of the sort seen every night across London's streets and taverns, but a carefully calibrated episode of violence. Although there had been medieval precedents for settling disputes through combat, the duel of honour was essentially a Renaissance invention, imported from Italy. Duelling formalised conflicts between aristocrats, replacing cycles of revenge, usually romantic in nature, with a single, rule-bound encounter. Its outcome served to resolve and annul any other grievances. The duel was part of a new court culture, which placed heavy emphasis on civility and courtesy; when these principles were ignored, duelling provided a means of redress. In the 1660s, after the monarchy was restored, duels became more common and attracted significant public interest and press comment, even if the participants lacked any kind of celebrity status.[8] Charles II did issue an anti-duelling proclamation in 1660: 'It is become too frequent,' this stated, 'especially with Persons of quality, under a vain pretence of Honour, to take upon them to be the Revengers of their private quarrels, by Duel and single Combat.'[9] In reality, however, Charles II had no moral objection to the culture of romantic fighting, and in the absence of effective legislation from Parliament, duels were judged on a case-by-case basis.

A duel was conventionally initiated with a challenge from the aggrieved party, whose complaint could be anything from the monumental to the trivial. The philosopher Thomas Hobbes wrote that men fought duels 'for trifles, as a word, a smile, a different opinion, and any other sign of undervalue in their Kindred, their Friend, their Nation, their Profession or their Name'.[10] Even if a challenge were accepted, the duel itself could be avoided, either by one of the parties backing down or by a third party intervening. When a fight did take place, the duellists were each required to select two men as 'seconds'. In earlier times the seconds had merely an auxiliary role, carrying weapons and arbitrating, but by the 1660s it had become fashionable for them to engage at the same time as the main combatants – turning the duel into a ritualised piece of gang violence. Nominally, the aim was to prove one's honour by exposing oneself to danger, not to kill the opponent, but inevitably some duels ended in serious injury or death.

Fired up by the occasion and all it signified for him, Buckingham arrived at Barn Elms early. He had already dismounted, stripped off his riding cape and put on his duelling gloves by the time Shrewsbury arrived at the close. The duke's seconds were his friend Sir Robert Holmes and the accomplished fencing master Sir John Jenkins. Shrewsbury had picked Sir John Talbot, a soldier, and Bernard Howard, a son of the Earl of Arundel.[11] The combatants lined up opposite each other and stared across the frozen earth in tense expectation. This would be no token contest: the stakes were too high. At the agreed signal, all six engaged at once. Bernard Howard, Shrewsbury's second, ran furiously at Jenkins, killing him instantly. On Buckingham's other flank, his cause was more successful: Holmes severed John Talbot's arm, leaving Buckingham and

Shrewsbury to fight alone. The rivals squared up, their breath pluming white in the cold air, the ghost of Anna Maria between them. Their contest was over in seconds. Shrewsbury launched himself first, finally intent on proving himself a man. But Buckingham parried the attack, feinted and then straightened his arm. His sword pierced Shrewsbury's right breast and came out through his shoulder. As Buckingham withdrew his weapon, Shrewsbury fell to the ground, blood pulsing from his wound. His manservant stripped off his bloodied shirt, hastily bandaged his chest and carried him to a house in nearby Chelsea. It was five days before Shrewsbury could be safely moved to Arundel House in the Strand to recuperate. Buckingham, meanwhile, suffered little more than a scratch.[12]

For a while, it seemed that Shrewsbury would make a full recovery. Newsletters from London reported the opinion of surgeons, that 'his wound doth now well digest, and . . . his spitting blood was a good sign of his recovery',[13] and Pepys was told by his apothecary that 'Lord Shrewsbury is likely to do well'.[14] However, in the first week of March 1668, Shrewsbury deteriorated suddenly and inexplicably and he died on 16 March. The doctor's report concluded that 'his heart had grown very flaccid, and his liver and entrails much discoloured and decayed'.[15] 'Seven of the most eminent of physicians and three surgeons' examined the body and stated that Shrewsbury's death had nothing to do with his duelling wound, which was 'well, and fairly cured'.[16] The verdict was important for Buckingham as it relieved him of direct responsibility for the death, but it seems unlikely that the wound had nothing to do with Shrewsbury's deterioration.

Now free to return from France, in public Anna Maria would have to adopt the demeanour of a grieving widow. In private, however, she and Buckingham were determined to begin a life of hedonism together on the banks of the Thames. Even though these pleasures would in fact elude them, Anna Maria and Buckingham, easily caricatured as a whore and a rake, were a pair of 'star-crossed lovers' who inaugurated Cliveden as a place of beauty, luxury, love and intrigue.

Chapter 2

'BEDS OF JEWELS AND
RICH MINES OF GOLD'

Six months before Anna Maria married the Earl of Shrewsbury, the diarist Rachel Newport tartly wrote that Shrewsbury was 'in motion to two sisters . . . the elder being unhandsome and crooked, the younger tolerable; it is thought he will not have the elder'.[1] Newport was one of many women whose jealousy was aroused by Anna Maria. With cheeks unblemished by smallpox and chestnut hair curled into tight ringlets over her forehead, her features, although not those of a delicate beauty, were striking. Contemporary depictions show a woman with large, heavy-lidded eyes, an elegant, well-defined nose, and, just below her chin, a 'soggiogaia' – a little swelling of extra flesh that was considered attractive among Restoration aristocrats. At the nape of her neck she would sometimes have sported two small curled locks of hair, known as 'heartbreakers'.

Born on 25 March 1642 to Robert Brudenell, 2nd Earl of Cardigan, and his second wife, Anne Savage, Anna Maria had grown up in a period of political and religious turmoil. Continental Europe had been wracked by religious wars, as the Protestant Reformation struggled for hearts and minds, land

and power with the Catholic Counter-Reformation. England had itself undergone a prolonged and difficult transformation from Catholic to Protestant nation in the 16th century and debate over doctrine – especially the extent of the religious toleration – continued to rage throughout the 17th century. Like Shrewsbury, Anna Maria's family were prominent Catholics – a faith viewed in Protestant England not only as theological error, but also as a dangerous political force. Catholics owed their allegiance to the Pope in Rome in religious matters and it was felt that this undermined the politico-religious authority claimed by the monarch as head of the Church of England. Moreover, the papacy claimed the right to depose 'ungodly' princes, and was backed by the military might of the Holy Roman Empire. Talk of Catholic plots – both real and fictitious – abounded. English Catholics risked persecution for their faith and, before Anna Maria was born, her family had already been charged with recusancy, the failure to attend worship in the Anglican Church.[2]

Just months after Anna Maria's birth, England descended into a chaotic period of civil war that pitted the king, Charles I, and his Royalist supporters against the Parliamentarian forces who believed that Charles's monarchy of personal rule had descended into tyranny. The conflict lasted almost eight years. On 30 January 1649, when Anna Maria was six years old, the king was executed at the command of a radical Parliamentarian minority. This horrified most English people – Royalist and Parliamentarian alike. To kill a king, it was said, was next to killing God. One of those who signed the death warrant was Oliver Cromwell. He became the leader of the new regime, first as head of the Council of State that ruled in what was known as the Commonwealth period, and later as the first holder of the office of Lord Protector, which afforded him greater personal power. Cromwell eventually died in 1658, a few months before Anna Maria's wedding. His son Richard Cromwell proved an inept successor and so the monarchy was restored in May 1660, in the person of the beheaded king's son, Charles II. Anna Maria came of age in the wake of the Restoration.

Her wedding to Shrewsbury was an arranged match, bringing together two Catholic families and offering her status, security and wealth. Shrewsbury, a widower 20 years her senior, would never ignite her passion. The epithalamium – a poem in celebration of a marriage – included an appeal to Hymen, the Greek god of wedding ceremonies:

> May Hymen's torch burn clear as your Desires
> Lighted in heaven with pure Promethean fires . . .
> Fit for a Husband who hath practised Love
> Whose Beds of Jewels and rich mines of Gold
> Are lodged within, to be enjoyed, not told.[3]

Shrewsbury did bring 'rich mines of gold' to the marriage, in the form of his sizeable estates, but although married previously, he was far from practised in the 'art of love'. At the age of 36, he was staid, sombre and reserved. After the Restoration, he shunned the decadence of Charles II's court, devoting himself instead to managing his land. He brought a daughter, Mary, from his first marriage, and on 24 July 1660, when Anna

Maria was 17, she gave birth to the couple's first son, Charles. Although they were to have a second son, Jake, it was Anna Maria's relationship with Charles, Shrewsbury's heir, which would in time define her future. Soon after his birth, Anna Maria began to evince an interest in dancing and music and drifted into the frenetic social whirl of Restoration society. After a straitened and often traumatic childhood during the Civil War and the puritanism of the Protectorate, she was ready to throw herself into the new culture of hedonism. If Buckingham was fascinated by the culture of the duel, Anna Maria was captivated by the role of the mistress.

After his father was executed, Charles II had spent some of his exile at the French court of Louis XIV, whose mistresses were well known. At the Restoration, French fashion, culture and music became prevalent at the English court. The musician Louis Grabu was brought over from France and appointed 'Composer to His Majesty's Musique', the French style for ornamental interior design became popular in aristocratic households and, during the first five years of the monarchy, lace coats became more elaborate and sleeves more voluminous in imitation of the French mode.[4] Along with these other Francophile imports came the cult of the mistress. Like most court fashions, the trend for mistress-keeping arose in imitation of the monarch's own behaviour. Charles II had married Catherine of Braganza in 1662, but the match did not prevent the king from courting other women: he already had a number of other lovers and, while he and Catherine were on their honeymoon, his mistress Barbara Villiers (a cousin of Buckingham's) gave birth to their second child at Hampton Court Palace.[5] In

Whitehall, the king was supplied with young women by the redoubtable team of William Chiffinch, Page of the Royal Bedchamber, and his wife. Using bribery, blackmail and flattery, the Chiffinches sourced royal mistresses from the streets of London, from the stage, and from within the court itself. Although the paramours of Charles II did not have the quasi-constitutional powers of their Continental counterparts, they were given wealth and titles and could contribute – albeit informally – to political debate. Villiers's apartments in Whitehall, which were maintained by the government and included an aviary, doubled up as a political arena where both office and reputation could be made and broken. She was given land in Ireland, conferred the title of Duchess of Cleveland and endowed with sufficient resources and influence to deliver patronage of her own.

Mistresses were not only able to attain political influence – they also stood to gain widespread popularity. Many of the lovers of Charles II became national celebrities in their own right. A healthy market sprang up for woodcuts and mezzotints depicting this elite tribe of women. Those looking for images of the king's most famous mistresses such as Nell Gwyn and Barbara Villiers had at least a dozen different prints to choose from, and portraits of the less famous courtesans still enjoyed successive editions, at a price of at least six pence.[6] Court mistresses were not forbidden from enjoying their popularity, and the more successful ones kept lovers of their own. Barbara Villiers, whose insatiable sexual appetite became the stuff of legend, stood out in this regard. Villiers counted the playwright William Wycherley, Jacob the rope-dancer, and the actor Cardonnell Goodman among her exotic and energetic coterie of bedfellows.

There was a tension between the sexual availability of these women and the way they were portrayed in contemporary art, often as saints, penitents or goddesses. Barbara Villiers was herself painted as Mary Magdalene, and as St Agnes the shepherdess, the patron saint of virgins. Sir John Reresby described her as 'the finest woman of her age'.[7] Samuel Pepys, who bought a copy of her portrait, was mesmerised by the sight of her smocks and pretty linen petticoats drying in the Privy Garden: 'Did me good to look on them', he wrote in his diary.[8] Pepys exemplified the way in which court mistresses were at the same time idealised for their beauty and disparaged for their moral frailty when, reflecting on her disrespectful behaviour towards her husband, he commented, 'for her beauty I am willing to construe all this for the best and to pity her wherein it is to her hurt, though I know she is a whore'.[9] This mix of desire and contempt was not simply a product of Pepys's sexually tortured mind. The same celebrity that inspired penny ballads, woodcuts and mezzotints could also inspire downright hostility, and even public disorder. The first significant political riots of Charles's reign centred on London's brothels, haunts of many courtiers, and symbols of the sexual corruption that was supposedly abetted by the monarch himself.[10] However much power and wealth and celebrity a mistress enjoyed, and however effectively she revenged herself against aggressors at court, in the public arena she was still 'a whore'. Her reputation, for good and for ill, depended on her sexuality.

Anna Maria quickly learned that the way to achieve recognition within the court was to wield her sexual power. She understood how her beauty and allure could be harnessed to further her personal fortunes and political influence. Embarking on numerous affairs, she soon became notorious to the extent that court satirists even cast aspersions on the integrity of her mother, the upright Lady Anne Brudenell. One poem depicted her as having experienced a sort of Damascene conversion to vice and pimping.

> Brudenell was long innocent,
> But for the time she has misspent,
> She'll make amends hereafter.
> Who can do more,
> Than play the whore,
> And pimp too for her daughter?[11]

A rivalry developed between Anna Maria and Nell Gwyn. On one occasion, Anna Maria was denied an invitation to a house-warming party hosted by Nell, who quipped that 'One whore at a time is enough for his Majesty'.[12] A contemporary recorded with incredulity the cult-like behaviour displayed by men who had become infatuated with Anna Maria: 'there are three or four gentlemen wearing an ounce of her hair made into bracelets, and no person finds any fault'.[13] She was also the cause of many duels, some of them fatal. 'I would wager she might have a man killed for her every day', wrote Anthony Hamilton in his *Memoirs of Count Grammont*, 'and she would only hold her head the higher for it.'[14]

Chapter 3

'HE CAME, HE SAW AND CONQUERED'

When the Civil War broke out in 1642, Buckingham was 16 and his brother Francis 15. Given the family's close connections to the Crown, they naturally signed up to fight for the Royalist cause but, fearing for their lives, Charles I sent them abroad, and for the next few years they lived in Italy and France, 'in as great state as some of those sovereign princes'.[1] In Rome and Florence, they received tuition from some of the most remarkable thinkers of the time, including Thomas Hobbes – although Buckingham clearly did not acquire his mentor's distaste for duelling. But the brothers could not bear to stay away from England and, six years after leaving home, they returned to fight. Francis lost his life in a skirmish near Kingston in 1648 and Buckingham fled once more to the Continent, this time to Charles II's court in exile in Holland. Parliament offered him a pardon and an opportunity to keep his estates if he returned to the country within 40 days, but he decided to stay with the king, sacrificing his vast estates in London, Rutland, Essex, Lincolnshire, Leicestershire, Nottingham, Buckinghamshire and Yorkshire. He was received with 'great grace and kindness' by Charles, though without the income from his lands, he was forced to sell some of his father's paintings in order to finance his lifestyle.[2]

When Charles I was executed in 1649, Buckingham was officially branded a traitor and banished, but nevertheless he returned to England again in 1657. With the country still under the control of Cromwell and the Parliamentarians, he disguised himself in various extravagant costumes in order to escape recognition. Buckingham set up a stage at Charing Cross and, donning some days a wizard's mask and others a hat with a fox's tail, performed his satirical ballads to passing crowds, who were unaware that this lowly busker had practically shared a cradle with the Stuart prince.[3] During this time Buckingham nurtured his talent for performance, showmanship and satire – skills that would make him an invaluable addition to court life in the Restoration.

A letter by the spy Colonel Bamfield reported Buckingham's presence in England and conjectured that he was 'about some desperate design, either for some rising in the City or some attempt upon the Protector's person'.[4] In fact, Buckingham's reasons for staying in England were not so seditious. He was determined to reclaim his sequestered land. His estates had been given to Sir Thomas Fairfax, Cromwell's one-time commander-in-chief. The total value amounted to £10,000 in cash and lands worth £4,000 a year.[5] He resolved to seduce the 'spiritless but amiable' Mary Fairfax, daughter and heir of the former Parliamentarian leader. Theirs was to be a strangely complex relationship – and one that also shaped the life of Anna Maria.

Fairfax doted on his daughter, whom he called 'Little Moll', but his military service had entailed long absences from home.[6] Mary was left in the care of her mother, Anne, a plain and deeply pious woman, whose childhood in Holland had encouraged her Presbyterian religious beliefs. Partly because she was not as charming as other ladies of her status, partly because of her open Presbyterianism, and partly because she was widely considered to have ideas above her station, Anne was unpopular at the Cromwellian court. A further source of tension was the fate of the king. Though committed to the Parliamentarian cause, Thomas Fairfax felt profoundly uneasy about the trial of Charles I. In this, Fairfax sided with the majority of Parliamentarians, who believed they were fighting against the tyranny of a particular ruler rather than the fundamental evil of monarchy itself. He refused to take his seat beside his more radical contemporaries, Cromwell among them, as a judge at Charles's trial and was horrified when the king was executed. His wife is said to have shouted from the public gallery, 'Oliver Cromwell is a traitor'.[7]

In the wake of the trial, Fairfax abandoned politics and the family spent most of their time at their favourite house, picturesque Nun Appleton, built on the ruins of a former nunnery in North Yorkshire. There Mary enjoyed an unusual childhood for an aristocratic girl. She was not only Fairfax's daughter but also his heir. Aged 12, Mary began to receive instruction from a private tutor, as though she were a boy. Her teacher, Andrew Marvell, was to become one of the most noted poets and political writers of the later 17th century. While at Nun Appleton he taught Mary languages, as well as writing his own poetry inspired by the house and its owners.

Though clever, Mary did not possess great charm, and the rumours of her likely union with Buckingham only reinforced the general opinion that the Fairfax women were relentless social climbers. Yet Mary was not an entirely unattractive prospect for Buckingham: she was pleasant, intelligent and sensible, in addition to being a means by which the duke could regain his lost estates.

Although banns had already been published for Mary's marriage to the Earl of Chesterfield, Buckingham quickly won over both Mary and her parents. Dressed in the Continental fashion, tall, athletic and well-built, he was 'extremely handsome' and well aware of it. He also went to great lengths to endear himself to Mary, writing to Lady Fairfax of the 'excess of that respect and devotion I shall ever bear Mistress [Mary] Fairfax whom if my fortune were in any way proportionable to my affections I should have the impudence to pretend to deserve at least as much as any other body whatsoever, since I am sure it is impossible to love or honour anything more than I truly do her.'[8] In another letter to one of Mary's servants, the duke claimed that just 'one minutes conversation' with 'that deare Mistresse of yours' would 'settle me in a condition not to envy the happiest man living'.[9] Genuine or contrived in sentiment, Buckingham's letters had the desired effect. Mary always, even at the height of the duke's affair with Anna Maria, adored her husband. Mary's cousin Brian Fairfax wryly observed:

> The young lady could not resist his charms . . .
> All his trouble in wooing was,
> He came, he saw and conquered.[10]

The marriage took place on 15 September 1657 at Bolton Percy Church in Yorkshire. The poet Abraham Cowley was Buckingham's best man, also composing the epithalamium to celebrate the match. The service was presided over by Mr Vere Harcourt, who, overawed by the duke, claimed that he 'saw God' in Buckingham's face.[11] But not everyone was supportive of the marriage. Buckingham's transparent attempts to seize back his assets incurred the wrath of Cromwell's government. Lord Fairfax pleaded in person against the incarceration of his son-in-law, but the Council resolved to send him to the Tower. He was finally released in February 1659, on a £20,000 security from his father-in-law.

Although the marriage had been prompted by necessity, it was a more affectionate and understanding union than that of Anna Maria and Shrewsbury. Buckingham developed a deep regard for Mary over the course of the courtship. In a poem he composed to her he wrote, 'That till my Eyes first gaz'd on you, I ne'er beheld that thing I could adore'.[12] He also became fond of Mary's father, Thomas Fairfax, and would write an epitaph on his death in 1671. Mutual affection, unevenly distributed though it was, explains much of Mary's behaviour towards her husband and his lover in the ensuing years.

With his marriage secure and his childhood friend Charles II restored to the throne, Buckingham's fortunes soared. His estates were returned, he was appointed a Gentleman of the King's Bedchamber, admitted to the Privy Council, and was chosen to carry the orb at the coronation. From entertaining street crowds at Charing Cross, Buckingham was now one of the biggest landowners in the kingdom. The strength of his childhood bond with the king gave him a special licence to act provocatively at court, safe in the knowledge that even if he temporarily fell from favour, their friendship was resilient. Buckingham became one of Charles's most dissolute and charismatic courtiers.

The Restoration court spawned its own flamboyant culture. This was both a reaction to the puritanical austerity of the Commonwealth and Protectorate periods, and an imitation of the hedonistic practices of Continental courts where many Royalists had spent their exile. Among the features of this culture was a new approach to sex and gender, epitomised by the sexually licentious figure of the rake. It was a commonplace of biblical, medieval and Renaissance thought that lust was the result of intellectual weakness and frailty. Women had been viewed as particularly susceptible to this weakness – perhaps the archetype of this was Milton's 'credulous' Eve, who in succumbing to the advances of Satan introduced sin to the world. During the 17th century there was a growing recognition that men were equally susceptible. Rakes at the court of Charles II self-consciously inverted the notion of lust as weakness, instead embracing sexual libertinism as a mark of masculine identity.

Even among this libertine culture, however, Buckingham's behaviour was remarkable. His habits attracted wonder and criticism in equal measure. Samuel Butler, a poet and satirist, wrote:

The Duke of Bucks is one that has studied the whole body of vice. His parts are disproportionate to the whole, and, like a monster, he has more of some and less of others, than he should have . . . His appetite to his pleasures is diseased and crazy . . . Perpetual surfeits of pleasure have filled his mind with bad and vicious humours, (as well as his body with a nursery of diseases) . . . He is as inconstant as the moon which he lives under.[13]

Butler may have described Buckingham as a monster, but the duke did have many redeeming and beguiling qualities. Another trait held to be desirable among Restoration courtiers was 'wit', a profoundly masculine virtue, which encompassed not only humour, but also originality and charisma. Among other factors, wit was the hallmark of being an accomplished writer, something to which many courtiers aspired. Inevitably, not everyone achieved literary distinction, and the court – not to mention the country as a whole – was full of would-be writers penning dismal verses that attempted rakish style. This contest between 'truewits' and 'witwoulds' became itself a subject for raillery and amusement.

Buckingham expressed his wit in his plays, as well as in his repertoire of anecdotes, sketches and impersonations. He could not help mimicking powerful and pompous figures at court, and it was often said that he would rather lose a friend than a jest. His skit on Lord Chancellor Clarendon was particularly popular: hanging from his belt a pair of bellows that represented the Great Seal in its case of woven silk, Buckingham puffed out his belly and limped forward with pursed lip and withering eye, venting high-pitched lamentations on the declining standards of government. He entertained friends and lovers with stories and songs, many of which he had memorised during his time as a ballad-monger. During his seduction of court beauty Frances Stuart, who famously resisted the advances of Charles II, he often visited her apartment and built high castles out of cards for her amusement.

Buckingham undoubtedly had a voracious appetite for pleasure and comedy, but he was not simply a court jester. The glassworks he owned in London used the latest technology to produce looking glasses 'far larger and better than any that come from Venice', as well as 'huge vases of metal as cleare, ponderous and thick as chrystal'.[14] He also nurtured an enthusiasm for the experimental philosophy known as the 'new science' and was an original Fellow of the Royal Society, which was established to encourage knowledge of the natural world through observation and experiment, and to provide a forum for scientific discussion. During the early years of the Society, the king had wanted to examine every mathematical invention submitted for patenting, and had sent messages enquiring why, for instance, some plants contracted to the touch, and some ant eggs were larger than the ant that produced them. Many subjects now considered fantastical or occult were considered fit for scientific investigation: Buckingham researched alchemy and contributed a 'unicorn's horn' to the Society for verification. He was also fascinated by astrology, a fixation that would later be exploited by his political opponents to damage his relationship with the king.

But no astrologer could have foretold the profound impact that meeting Anna Maria in 1666 would have on Buckingham. ''Tis you alone, that can my heart subdue / To you alone it shall always be true!' he wrote to her.[15] Poor, devoted Mary was sidelined. Buckingham wrote in his commonplace book:

'Wives we choose for our posterity, mistresses for ourselves, marriage is the greatest solitude, for it makes two but one and prohibits us from all others'.[16] But the duke was determined not to be 'prohibited' by marriage from 'all others' – and one above all. He ordered clothes from Paris for himself and his new paramour. He also employed a Parisian musician to serenade her. The diarist John Evelyn recorded seeing Buckingham with his crowd of fiddlers at the races, and Samuel Butler said of him that 'his ears are perpetually drilled with a fiddlestick'.[17]

The affair with Anna Maria also brought out Buckingham's belligerent streak. Friends and courtiers noticed that he drew his sword at the slightest provocation, over political as well as romantic disputes. One instance of this was his quarrel with the Marquis of Dorchester, which occasioned one of his several duelling challenges of the 1660s. The two had long been political enemies and their rivalry flared up at the Canary Conference, a trade meeting between the Lords and the Commons in the Painted Chamber in the Palace of Westminster. Buckingham deliberately provoked the marquis by rudely elbowing him during a debate. 'Are you uneasy, Dorchester?' Buckingham taunted. Dorchester rose to the bait and launched into an angry tirade against the duke. 'I am a better man than you,' Buckingham retorted, and with this, he lurched across the table, ripped off Dorchester's hat, grabbed his periwig, and held him in a throttle position. The Lord Chamberlain was forced to intervene, and both men were ordered to the Tower. The incident was debated in the House of Lords, where Buckingham was branded a 'delinquent'.[18]

On 20 July 1667, Buckingham took a box at the Duke of York's Theatre in Lincoln's Inn Fields, and decided to bring along both Anna Maria and Mary. At the time of its construction, the theatre was the most technologically advanced in London, boasting state-of-the-art machinery to facilitate scene changes.[19] The stage and auditorium were illuminated by candles, as well as innovative oil-lamp footlights, and refreshments were provided by 'orange women', some of whom were attractions in their own right. But on the night of the theatre trip, it seems that all eyes were on Anna Maria. A letter written by the Countess Dowager of Roscommon, who was present at the theatre, reported that Anna Maria was 'with child'.[20] It is impossible to verify whether or not this is true, but there are no records of her giving birth at any point that year, so if she was pregnant with either Shrewsbury or Buckingham's child, she must have suffered a miscarriage.

Unfortunately, Henry Killigrew, an old flame of Anna Maria's, was sitting in the adjacent box. Unable to contain his anger, Killigrew hurled abuse at the duke. Buckingham made a valiant effort to contain his temper, but Killigrew continued his goadings. Eventually, Killigrew climbed into Buckingham's box, struck him with a sheathed sword, and clambered away around the dress circle, disrupting the entire performance. Theatregoers were accustomed to disturbances in the stalls of the theatre, but a fracas in the boxes, which were largely occupied by aristocrats, was more unusual. Incensed by Killigrew's conduct, Buckingham pursued his rival through the boxes. By the time he caught up with him in the foyer, Buckingham's periwig had fallen off, and his cropped hair was shockingly exposed. Buckingham snatched Killigrew's sword and furiously kicked him, until he begged for his life.[21]

Buckingham was publicly praised for his conduct. The Countess Dowager of Roscommon thought he had carried himself 'as became a man of honour' and Pepys agreed that 'he did carry himself very innocently and well'.[22] Anna Maria's position was more problematic. It was widely assumed that Shrewsbury would now finally fight for his wife's honour but he still held back.

The power of a high-society mistress was derived from the lust and favour of men and they were vulnerable to scorn and ridicule when private passions turned into public scandal. In the dead of night the mortified Anna Maria summoned her trusted maid Mrs Daliston, left letters to her parents and husband, and fled court society for an English Catholic convent at Pontoise, north-west of Paris.[23] The journey was long and gruelling – a day-long crossing from Dover to Calais, overnight in an insalubrious French inn and then a long and bumpy coach journey.[24] Anna Maria arrived at the convent exhausted yet still burning with anger.

Anna Maria would spend six months in seclusion at Pontoise. She was unaware that her flight had finally pushed the timid Shrewsbury to challenge her lover to a duel, and ignorant of the encounter they had arranged for Barn Elms. Ignorant, that is, until a letter arrived informing her of the death of her husband.

Chapter 4

A LONDON LOVE TRIANGLE

Anna Maria returned to England in May 1668, two months after Shrewsbury's death. But her future had in part been determined before she arrived.

In his will of 10 March, Anna Maria's husband had placed their three children under the guardianship of four men: the Earl of Cardigan, Anna Maria's father; Mervyn Tuchett, the children's uncle; William Talbot of Wittington, a kinsman of the Talbot family; and Gilbert Crouch, the family lawyer.[1] Relations between the guardians and Anna Maria were strained from the outset, and they were intent on denying her access to her sons. The children had spent their early childhood at the Talbot family seat of Grafton in Worcestershire, but following their father's death were moved to the house of their uncle Tuchett in Southcote, Berkshire.[2] Even though Anna Maria's father was among the guardians of her children, the Talbot faction dominated, and Tuchett was determined to prevent Charles, as heir to his father's earldom, from seeing any members of the Brudenell family. As Charles matured into a young man and grew in self-awareness, he would become cognisant of this dynamic and seek to challenge it.

Perhaps if Anna Maria had chosen to end her affair with Buckingham, there might have been some hope of a rapprochement with the Talbots, but she chose amorous passion over maternal responsibility and did nothing to contest the arrangements. By modern standards, her failure to fight for her children seems callous, but our judgement should be tempered by late 17th-century aristocratic conventions, which encouraged emotional distance between mother and child. Babies were frequently sent out to wet nurses for the first 12 to 18 months of their lives, and were then cared for mainly by nurses, governesses and tutors, before leaving home to attend boarding school some time between the ages of 7 and 14. But even in this cultural context, Anna Maria's absence from her children's lives was remarkable: her sons felt abandoned and later she herself would mourn her choice. Anna Maria was a woman of extremes. She threw herself wholeheartedly into her life with Buckingham – a life in which her children were to have no part.

Yet life with Buckingham was not simple either. The months prior to Anna Maria's return had been challenging for Buckingham because of public comment on the duel. His immediate anxieties were short-lived – on 27 January Charles II issued a pardon, allowing Buckingham to reappear at court.[3] Four days later, he was back at the Duke of York's Theatre, where the original scuffle with Killigrew had taken place, for the first night of his friend George Etherege's comedy *She Would If She Could*.[4] The heavy rain forced audience members to remain in the auditorium after the performance, and Pepys observed Buckingham in high spirits, speaking animatedly with the playwright.[5] But Shrewsbury's death re-ignited public controversy over duelling, and lobbyists exerted pressure on the king to act more forcefully against the practice. Charles responded with a statement that henceforth, 'on no pretence whatsoever any pardon shall ... be granted to any person whatsoever for killing of any man in a duel ... but that the course of law shall wholly take place in all such cases'.[6] It was a half-hearted attempt to placate critics of duelling while ensuring that Buckingham would be exempt from prosecution.

The City of London was just beginning to be rebuilt after the Great Fire of 1666. During the three days the fire raged, Charles II, fearing a full-scale riot or rebellion, arranged for bread to be brought to the city, and established 'safe markets' around the edge of the city, guarded by militia. Buckingham was involved in raising troops for this purpose, and wrote to his deputy lieutenants requesting that they 'immediately summon all the militia under my command to be in arms with all speed imaginable'.[7] The Great Fire incinerated 13,200 houses, and consumed an area a mile and a half in length and half a mile in breadth, rendering the city unrecognisable.[8] Evelyn recalled 'clambering over heaps of yet smoking rubbish, and frequently mistaking where I was'.[9] The conflagration became so hot that it melted iron gates and bars in the prisons, and left water boiling in the fountains. Throughout this wasted landscape, dark clouds of smoke emerged from subterranean cellars, wells and dungeons. Many Londoners who had lost their homes moved elsewhere in the country, or emigrated to America, though some continued to live in the ruins of their old properties.

One of the most noticeable changes wrought by the fire on the skyline of the city was the gutting of the old medieval cathedral of St Paul's, which, although not entirely destroyed, was reduced to a skeleton. The ruins were unstable, and Pepys recalled how 'the very sight of the stones falling from the top of the steeple do make me seasick'.[10] The rebuilding of the city proceeded intermittently and well into the 1670s large areas remained in ruins. The resurrection of St Paul's was not assigned to Christopher Wren until June 1669 and the old edifice was still standing as late as 1674. Without a doubt, in the eight months between Anna Maria's departure to Pontoise and her return to London in May 1668, no significant reconstruction would have taken place.

Before outrage had died down over the duel, Buckingham provoked further controversy by inviting Anna Maria to live with him. Buckingham's two main London residences – Wallingford House and York House – were upriver in Westminster, on Whitehall and the Strand respectively, and both were untouched by the fire. The first duke of Buckingham bought Wallingford House in the early 1620s, and George himself had been born there in 1627. The first Duke held the post of Lord High Admiral and hosted many meetings at the house, giving his son early exposure to political life. Seven years after the first duke's assassination his widow, Catherine Manners, married the prominent Catholic, Lord Dunluce, and the couple made Wallingford their home. The house had also played a small part in the political upheavals of the mid-17th century: it was the meeting place of the Wallingford House Party, an army faction that eventually overthrew the short-lived protectorate of Oliver Cromwell's son, Richard, paving the way for Charles II's return to power.

Buckingham's second and much larger London property was York House, which had been built for his father in the 1620s. The only part of the house remaining today is the Buckingham Watergate, which was the riverside entrance to the mansion. Due to the construction of the Thames embankment in the 19th century, the gate is now some distance from the river it was built to serve, and stands marooned at the edge of Victoria Embankment Gardens, east of Charing Cross Station. The Villiers coat of arms features above the gate's central arch.

York House was built in the Italianate style popularised by Inigo Jones during the reign of Charles I. The painter Peter Paul Rubens had been a guest in 1629 and had given Buckingham's father important works, some of which were among those that Buckingham sold in Amsterdam to finance his upkeep during his exile. The house had also been the site of infamous and dissolute court parties. At a party in 1627 attended by King Charles and his wife Henrietta Maria, guests were invited to dress up as vices and virtues; the first duke of Buckingham appeared dressed as envy, 'with divers open-mouthed dogs heads representing the people's barking'.[11] The most notable feature of the property was the magnificent garden, in which a number of Italianate statues were exhibited.

Either house would have been a beautiful home for Anna Maria. But right from the start it was clear that she would be sharing it not only with Buckingham but also with Mary. Divorce was impossible: wife and mistress would have to live together with the man each loved in a bizarre *ménage à trois*.

This was a particularly uncomfortable arrangement for Mary. According to the Vicomtesse de Longueville, Buckingham's wife had become 'a little round crumpled woman', utterly devoted to her husband, and delusional about their original courtship, attributing only sincere motives to his advances.[12] Though she had previously been magnanimous to Buckingham's lovers, the prospect of having to share him and his homes with Anna Maria was too much for her to bear. She was humiliated and angered by this arrangement. Besides being personally affronted, she would also have taken exception to the flouting of mourning convention, which showed deep disrespect for the late earl.

When Mary expressed her horror at the prospect of living with Anna Maria, according to Pepys Buckingham retorted, 'Why Madam, I did think so, and therefore have ordered your coach to be ready, to carry you to your father's.'[13] A heartbroken Mary backed down, and was forced to accept this uncomfortable way of life. It seems that she shut her eyes to Buckingham's infidelity; Brian Fairfax wrote that she 'patiently bore those faults in him which she could not remedy'.[14] For Mary, the relationship with Anna Maria was Buckingham's most egregious error, but even this was not so great a betrayal as to diminish the affection she felt for her husband. She was forced to look on as Buckingham and Anna Maria cultivated the kind of relationship that she had never been able to nurture in ten years of marriage. In time, she and Anna Maria would become friends, and the painful love triangle of the late 1660s would mature into a singular and relatively peaceful domestic arrangement.

The reunion of Anna Maria and Buckingham provided fertile ground for the imagination, both for contemporaries and for later commentators. One perpetual myth that prevailed in 19th-century histories of the Restoration was based on a claim of Lord Peterborough's that after Shrewsbury's fall 'the Duke slept with her [Anna Maria] in his bloodied shirt'.[15] Given that there were four intervening months between the duel and the reunion, it seems unlikely that Buckingham still would have had Shrewsbury's blood on his clothes for their first night back together. Nevertheless, stories such as this ensured that Anna Maria came to enjoy a reputation on a par with those of the royal mistresses, including Nell Gwyn and Louise de Kéroualle, as one of the most licentious, wicked women in Restoration history.

Anna's Maria's bloodlust may have become embellished over time, but the extent to which she revelled in her role as Buckingham's mistress is indisputable. She embraced the part completely, imbuing her daily routine with drama and glamour of regal proportions. On occasions when she was entertaining guests, she began the day with the theatrical ceremony of a 'levee'. This morning ritual, which involved aristocrats receiving visitors in their dressing rooms, had been imported from France to the English court by Charles II, and had transformed getting up into an elaborate spectacle. Like Louise de Kéroualle, Anna Maria admitted men as well as women into her dressing room.

In order to receive guests, Anna Maria had to ensure she looked her best. Beauty rituals in the 17th century required much planning and preparation. Cleansing and moisturising was a time-consuming affair. Every evening in the kitchens, fat from a puppy dog was boiled in water to prepare a beautifying emulsion for the face, while gloves fashioned from chicken skin and lined with almond paste and egg yolk were worn overnight to keep hands smooth. In the dressing rooms, the odour of the skins would have been overpowered by the smell of Hungary water, and perfumes such as red chypre, which was rose scented. Anna Maria's dressing table would have been crammed with tonics, powders and creams: there was pomatum, a scented oil to dress her hair; ceruse, a powdery foundation which would be mixed on a palette with egg white and applied to the skin with a damp cloth; and rouge, which was made from an acacia shellac, to be dabbed on dampened cheeks. There was also a fashion for women gluing black taffeta spots onto their faces, on the cheek or next to the mouth.[16]

To affirm her status as a high-society mistress, Anna Maria commissioned a portrait by Sir Peter Lely, the most sought-after painter at the Restoration court. Many important courtiers of the time sat for Lely, who was known for his idealistic depictions of female beauty. Although he often painted his female subjects as saints or goddesses – Nell Gwyn, Charles II's mistress, was depicted as Venus – Anna Maria was painted in a loose morning garment and her signature pearls. Something of her vibrant personality comes across in her expression, but because Lely's paintings were always rather generic, he fails to fully capture her enigmatic charm. The portrait still hangs in Cliveden today.

Court mistresses were given licence to enjoy many entertainments from which courtiers' wives, including Mary, were excluded, and Anna Maria quickly developed a reputation as one of London's most dazzling and daring social luminaries. She and Buckingham turned 'day into night and night into day' with their 12-hour party marathons.[17] The couple were particularly fond of attending masquerade balls. The vizard – a black velvet mask – might be worn in any number of public places, such as the theatre or park, but it came to be most closely associated with the masquerade ball, a type of party popular-ised by the king and court. Though masquerades were beloved of fashionable society, they were also a source of great fear and moral anxiety, due to the lewd and disorderly behaviour that was 'released' when revellers' identities were disguised. The London papers abounded with stories about challenges and assaults at masquerades: perhaps the most sensational of these came in February 1671 when it emerged that the killers of Peter Vernell, a beadle who was murdered after a masked ball in Lincoln's Inn Fields, were not thugs or lowlifes, but Viscount Dunbar, the Duke of Monmouth and the Duke of Albemarle.

Anna Maria was in her element at a masquerade. One can imagine her enrobed in a silk mantua laced with ribbons and richly adorned with gold brocade, scanning the room through the eyes of her black velvet mask, contemplating what oppor-tunities for mischief lay ahead. Dainty Fidget, a character in William Wycherley's play *The Country Wife*, expressed the sexual freedom women were able to enjoy once their faces were hidden: 'women are least masked when they have their velvet vizard on'.[18] This was one iteration of a popular witti-cism of the time: that a masked face was barer than a bare one.

In her capacity as Buckingham's mistress, Anna Maria also

attended many banquets. Charles II was a great fan of French cooking and had summoned the Gallic masterchef François Pierre de la Varenne to court. Varenne favoured herbs and pepper over spices, and moved away from the sweet palette that had since Tudor times dominated aristocratic cooking. The rich savoury flavours of ragouts, soups and French sauces became de rigueur. Elaborate fricassees combined a myriad of ingredients: pigeons, peepers, lamb, sweetbread, hard-boiled eggs, bone marrow, and even tortoise started making appearances at noble tables. Great emphasis was placed on the presentation of food; a huge variety of dishes were required to be 'landscaped' across the dining table. The most spectacular act in this gastronomic drama was the entrée, in which platters were arranged in a geometric order, the large and substantial surrounded by the small and delicate. Bone-marrow fritters, rissoles, stewed stuffed tongues, steamed bass, poached salmon, peacock, quail, and game pies adorned the table; sparkling French wines, including champagne, which had recently been imported for the first time, were liberally dispensed. Many guests brought along their own servants, who walked to and fro around the table ferrying their masters' preferred food – asking for a dish to be passed personally was virtually impossible on such a heavily laden table. Since the Restoration, the sweet course had more often been known by its French name, *dessert*. Crystal jellies flavoured and perfumed with rose water, sugar, ginger and nutmeg glittered, while extravagant mountains of fruit threatened to eclipse diners' views of each other across the table. Tarts and pies, their pastry tops cut with Euclidean precision, were brought out ceremoniously and arranged in interlocking patterns along the table. Society hostesses often became competitive about the content and presentation of their events. Many hired professional napkin folders to transform starched fabric into fanciful pleats, elaborate scallop shells, and even the family coat of arms.[19]

Despite immersing herself in revelry, Anna Maria remained vigilant on the subject of her honour. Henry Killigrew returned from Paris in 1668 an unreformed character. While abroad, he had been convicted of rape and was only spared the death sentence at the behest of the French Queen Mother.[20] On his arrival back in London, he was still aggrieved by the relationship between Anna Maria and Buckingham and continued to harass his former lover. According to the memoirs of Count Grammont, 'he let loose all his abusive eloquence against her ladyship. He attacked her with the most bitter invectives from head to foot: he drew a frightful picture of her conduct, and turned all her personal charms . . . into defects'.[21] Killigrew was warned several times to desist, but, as had happened at the theatre in the summer of 1667, he continued his slanderous attacks until they provoked a violent response.

On the night of 16 May 1669, Anna Maria wreaked her revenge. Killigrew had been at the apartments of the Duke of York in St James's Park and had fallen into a drunken sleep in his coach en route to his house at Turnham Green, when he passed a black mourning coach, drawn by six horses, at the side of the road. Four footmen, armed with knives and cudgels, leapt forth, stopped his coach, broke inside and stabbed him repeatedly. The French ambassador, Charles Colbert, recalled Killigrew's bloody fate: 'he was awoke by the thrust of a sword, which pierced his neck and came out at the shoulder. Before he could cry out he was flung from the vehicle and stabbed in three other places'.[22] In other accounts, Killigrew suffered nine wounds and was left bleeding at the roadside. The mourning coach was unmistakably Anna Maria's. Once again, blood had been spilt in the name of her honour.[23]

Wild rumours spread about the extent of her malice: some people suggested she had been at the duel at Barn Elms dressed as a pageboy, and had taken great pleasure in watching her husband stabbed; others whispered that she had brought her two young sons along as spectators to the brutal attack on Henry Killigrew.[24] The next year Friar Nicholas Cross dedicated his work *The Cynosura*, a religious tract on the subject of penitence, to the 'Countess of Shrewsbury' and urged her to return to the 'Christian vertues' of 'humility, purity, temperance'. 'Fear not to take up the arms of penance,' he wrote, 'they will not blemish your fair hand, but prove your advantage in what posture so ever you stand with your dear Creatour'.[25] To the same extent as Barbara Villiers some years earlier, Anna Maria's name had become synonymous with the vices of lust and violence.

An investigation was launched into the incident, and once again, Buckingham was willing to put his own career and reputation at risk to defend Anna Maria, maintaining to the king that, although she was responsible for the attack, murder was never her intention. The Duke of York, a political opponent of Buckingham's, confided to Pepys that the duke's allegiance to Anna Maria might 'cost him his life in the Lords'.[26] Though at the time this may have been mere hyperbole, later in the decade York would be proved right.

Buckingham's declining favour with the king, for whom the duke was becoming something of a liability, would provide unexpected inspiration for his building project at Cliveden. In late July 1670, he was sent to France to represent Charles II at the funeral of his sister, who had been married to the Duc d'Orléans, brother of Louis XIV. Buckingham believed that the political purpose of his visit was to negotiate a treaty between England and France, but in fact the secret and deeply controversial Treaty of Dover, an agreement in which Charles pledged to publicly convert to Catholicism as part of a new alliance between the two countries, had been signed on 22 May without Buckingham's knowledge. Despite this political deception, Buckingham was inspired by Versailles. A sumptuous play was performed for him, with music provided by 300 instrumentalists, and a choir of 100 women and 100 eunuchs. Ballets and banquets followed, and the visit culminated in the French king presenting Buckingham with a sword and belt set with pearls and diamonds.[27] Buckingham returned to England enchanted by French showmanship and the scale of their entertainments. He wanted this lavish style to be replicated at his country pleasure palace, Cliveden, whose terraced gardens would bear a striking resemblance to those of Versailles.

During Buckingham's time in France, an unlikely alliance had formed between his wife and his mistress; the tensions between Anna Maria and Mary Fairfax had dissipated. Perhaps Mary had come to feel something bordering on affection for the woman with whom she shared such close quarters. Or else she had grown accustomed to their peculiar love triangle. By the summer of 1670, Anna Maria was pregnant again and, in a show of remarkable emotional strength, Mary had made it her mission to care for and support her. Indeed the pair, growing frustrated with Buckingham's prolonged absence, conceived a plan to meet him in Calais. They set sail for France but bad weather forced them back into port at Margate. They ended up staying together in Dover, awaiting Buckingham's return.[28]

In late February 1671, Anna Maria gave birth to Buckingham's son. Despite the nascent bond between Anna Maria and Mary, this must have been a source of great sadness to Mary, who bore Buckingham no heirs over the course of their marriage. The baby was christened George Villiers, after his father, and Charles II was persuaded to act as godfather. Tragically, the child died just a few days after the christening. On 12 March Buckingham arranged for him to be buried, 'with all solemnities' and under his second title of Earl of Coventry, in the Villiers family vault at Westminster Abbey.[29]

Illegitimate children were not uncommon and the birth of Anna Maria's child would have caused nothing more than idle gossip had it been handled discreetly. The king had always taken an active interest in the children of his own mistresses – his eldest illegitimate son, James, lived at court, while his two children by Catherine Pegge were set up in a house in Pall Mall. Royal bastards were not treated dissimilarly from legitimate children, and were often given titles and almost always well provided for. But this was an exclusively royal prerogative and aristocrats who had children outside marriage were not expected to confer on them familial privileges. By unilaterally bestowing a title on little George and burying him in the family vault, Buckingham was assuming for himself royal powers, and for this he was widely condemned. It was a particularly sensitive issue, as Buckingham had previously been accused of harbouring hubristic aspirations – Pepys had recorded the duke's alleged desire to overthrow the king and Parliament, and seize the crown for himself.[30]

Buckingham, of course, viewed his actions as a tribute to his son and to Anna Maria and not a bid for princely power. As was so often the case with the duke, his political judgement had been clouded by personal passion and it had not occurred to him that the burial would appear seditious in its intent. The controversy over the burial would rear its head again a decade later when Buckingham was fighting for his political survival.

Chapter 5

THE DRAMA OF POLITICS

After three years of living with Anna Maria, Mary had come to accept her husband's mistress as a mainstay of her life. Even though she was still very much in love with Buckingham, Mary acknowledged that her feelings were not reciprocated. She had made the decision to embrace the object of Buckingham's passion and remained silent on the subject of her own loneliness. Anna Maria, meanwhile, was grateful for Mary's continued support and encouragement. She felt considerable pity for Mary, who was unable to transfer her affection from her husband to another man. Buckingham, for his part, had expected Mary to rebel against his relationship with Anna Maria, a sentiment he expressed in his dialogue *The Militant Couple*: '[if a husband] violates the original contract it is as natural for wives as for subject to rebel'.[1] Although all his sexual desire for his wife had dissipated, Buckingham admired Mary's stoicism and always retained a platonic affection for her. Both he and Anna Maria would go to great trouble to make Mary feel welcome at Cliveden: the gates of their river-side mansion would always be open to her. In 1670, however, the grand house at Cliveden was yet to be built, and from

January that year the three of them lived together in a set of apartments in the Cockpit, an extension to Whitehall Palace.[2]

Yet Mary was not reduced to an anonymous or solitary life. Buckingham may have loved Anna Maria in Mary's place, but Mary was still his wife and enjoyed all the material trappings that this entailed. She was, said the Vicomtesse de Longueville, 'very fond of finery', adorning her dresses with luxurious, if rather unfashionable, gold lace cuffs and heavy jewels.[3] These added to Mary's faintly absurd appearance, but at least gave her a modicum of pleasure. Her marriage had also secured for Mary a position as one of the foremost noblewomen in the country, after Queen Catherine and the Duchess of York. Indeed she was known to greatly enjoy the company of the queen, with whom she attended balls and played games.

Even when his currency at court was low, Buckingham used his writing to express his political opinions. Of his many plays *The Rehearsal*, first staged in 1671 and published anonymously a year later, is the most enduring. *The Rehearsal* was a satire on the heroic drama, a genre of play popular with Restoration audiences. Heroic dramas were written in rhyming couplets and formal language, which often verged on the bombastic. Typically, these plays were set in exotic or historic locations such as Ancient Rome, Babylon or Peru. The plots were epic, entailing conquests, sieges and clashes of civilisations, and the characters usually grand and powerful – protagonists included Alexander the Great, Cleopatra and Moctezuma, the Aztec emperor. Common themes were love, honour and divided allegiance.[4] The main advocate of the form was the poet John Dryden, who invented the term 'heroic drama' to describe his play *The Conquest of Granada* (1670), which dramatised the conflict between Islam and Christianity during the fall of Moorish Spain.

Buckingham found the pomp and pretension of the genre objectionable and its scale risible. He particularly took exception to the classical rhyming couplets in which Dryden wrote. In *The Rehearsal* two gentlemen, Mr Smith and Mr Johnson, watch with increasing scorn and incredulity the preposterous new work by the playwright Mr Bayes. The action of the play-within-the-play encompasses a sequence of absurd mock-heroic episodes: two characters challenge each other to a duel on the grounds that they do not love the same woman; a company of soldiers kill each other, then stand up and perform a dance, with limited success; the playwright attempts to demonstrate the moves, but falls flat on his face, breaking his nose.

The first performance of *The Rehearsal* took place on 7 December 1671 at the Drury Lane Theatre. By this time Buckingham had returned to London following a period of mourning in the country for his lost son and, having sold York House, was living at Wallingford House with Anna Maria and Mary. The duchess enjoyed a comfortable but quiet life, while Buckingham and Anna Maria's lives continued in an endless whirl of social activity. The poet Edward Waller recalled one night of revelry with the couple that lasted until four in the morning and was forced to decline an invitation for the following night, writing to his wife that 'such hours cannot be kept'.[5]

The Drury Lane Theatre was managed by the King's Company, which was one of two licensed theatre companies in London and run by Thomas Killigrew, father of the loutish

Henry. On the night of a play, Drury Lane was always crammed with coaches. Access to the theatre was down narrow passages between the surrounding buildings, an architectural flaw that would have resulted in significant congestion and particularly irked Pepys.

On the first night of *The Rehearsal* Buckingham positioned Dryden in an adjacent box to his, so that he could enjoy the playwright's reaction to the work.[6] Their artistic differences had played themselves out in a long-running personal feud that dated back to 1667, when Buckingham and Dryden had staged plays at the same time: *The Chances* and *Secret Love* respectively.[7] In the epilogue to *The Chances*, Buckingham poked fun at Dryden's pomposity: 'The end of plays should be to entertain / And not to keep the auditors in pain'. A year later, Dryden retaliated in a prologue, accusing Buckingham, who had adapted *The Chances* from an existing play by John Fletcher, of 'robbing the dead'. Dryden's continued acclaim only spurred Buckingham on in his literary endeavours.

The protagonist of *The Rehearsal*, Mr Bayes, was played by the celebrated comic actor John Lacy, who was favourite of Charles II and had been responsible for spotting the talent of 14-year-old orange-seller Nell Gwyn, who went on to be an acclaimed actress before becoming long-term mistress to the king. For the first performance of Buckingham's play, Lacy's Mr Bayes was dressed in Dryden's signature black velvet. Dryden later retaliated in his poem *Absalom and Achitophel*, which depicted the central political players of the time – Thomas Clifford, 1st Baron Clifford of Chudleigh; Henry Bennet, 1st Earl of Arlington; Buckingham; Anthony Ashley Cooper, 1st Baron

Ashley; and John Maitland, 1st Duke of Lauderdale – in the guise of biblical characters. Buckingham's character was reflected in the frivolous Zimri, a dilettante with erroneous opinions and a debauched lifestyle:

> Stiff in opinions, always in the wrong;
> Was everything by starts, and nothing long:
> But in the course of one revolving moon,
> Was chemist, fiddler, statesman, and buffoon:
> Then all for women, painting, rhyming, drinking;
> Besides ten thousand freaks that died in thinking.
> Blest madman, who could every hour employ,
> With something new to wish, or to enjoy![8]

By the time Dryden penned *Absalom*, his wrath had been simmering for ten years; sitting across from Buckingham on the opening night, he remained taciturn. *The Rehearsal* concluded with a vigorous jig, and an epilogue that called for an end to heroic drama: 'Let's have, at least, once in our lives, a time / When we may hear some reason, not all rhyme / We have this ten years felt its influence / Pray, let this prove a year of prose and sense.'

The character of Bayes was not only a parody of Dryden, but was also inspired by another of Buckingham's rivals, Lord Arlington, secretary of state of the southern office (in the 17th century, the position was divided geographically). Years earlier, Buckingham and Arlington had formed a temporary alliance to ensure the political ruin of the Lord Chancellor, the 1st Earl of Clarendon. With Clarendon forced into exile, a new political arrangement evolved. Whereas English monarchs had previously taken counsel from a single, favourite minister, Clarendon was replaced by several influential advisers. These were Clifford, Ashley, Buckingham, Arlington and Lauderdale, the elite political group who came to be known by the acronym the 'Cabal'. Although popular perception of the Cabal was of a unified coterie surrounding the king, it in fact comprised disparate members with clashing political agendas that surfaced in the wake of Clarendon's removal from power. The greatest of these rivalries was between Buckingham and Arlington.

Arlington cut a powerful figure at court. He was a formidable linguist and a good political tactician; a strip of black tape covering a wound on his nose served as a reminder of his loyal service during the Civil War. Like many courtiers, he was jealous of Buckingham's close relationship with Charles II, which gave the duke an influence disproportionate to his political position. In 1667, Arlington exploited Buckingham's association with the astrologer John Heydon in order to damage his relationship with the king. Heydon was a controversial mystic who had a reputation for treasonous pursuits and had previously been accused of trying to break Buckingham out of the Tower of London with the help of a gang of disgruntled sailors. Heydon, branded a plotter, was a liability to Buckingham. During a search of Heydon's Tower Hill lodgings, Arlington claimed to have discovered a treasonous horoscope commissioned by Buckingham, which predicted the date of the king's death. Using this evidence, Arlington embarked on a mission to disgrace his rival.

Arlington's smear campaign proved successful in so far as

Buckingham was sent to the Tower. Conditions at the Tower were better than most other prisons, and many held there were guilty of religious or political crimes. In some instances, incarceration at the Tower was the prelude to execution, but others were detained there indeterminately, or 'at the King's pleasure'. Buckingham's stay was unlikely to last more than a few months, and gave the London public an opportunity to express their support for him. As Buckingham coached across London, he was cheered by the traders and the city merchants who championed him as a man of the people. He even stopped off on the way to dine with companions at the Sun Tavern in Bishop's Gate. The meal was a debauched affair and Pepys recorded that the duke was 'mighty merry, and sent word to the Lieutenant of the Tower that he would come to him as soon as he had dined'.[9] A large crowd gathered outside the tavern and, after eating and drinking his fill, Buckingham appeared on the balcony to acknowledge the cheers. Following his release in July 1667, the feud continued.

Bayes's blundering attempts to direct his unruly troupe of actors were widely interpreted as a parody of Arlington's political delusions and his credibility at court collapsed. Aspiring wits strutted about court with black patches on their noses to mimic Arlington's disfigurement and later printed editions of *The Rehearsal* depicted the central protagonist with a black patch on his nose.

As *The Rehearsal* opened to cheering crowds, it seemed that Buckingham's fortunes were once again ascending. The time to set his plans for Cliveden into motion had arrived.

Chapter 6

CONCEPTION

The most convenient way to travel from London to Cliveden in 1671 was by boat along the River Thames. The Thames west of London had traditionally been a stronghold of royal power. During the early stages of the English Civil Wars, large sections of the river had been held by the Royalists, and when Charles I's government was banished from London in 1642, Oxford became the temporary royal capital. At the Restoration, there was much pomp and ceremony to signify the return of royal power to the river; in August 1662, Charles II was rowed from Hampton Court in a flotilla that self-consciously imitated the great Tudor pageants that had occurred on the Thames. But despite these regal associations, most of the traffic on the river was not so refined. The Thames was the main east–west thoroughfare in the south of England and estimates of the number of watermen working on the river at the end of the 17th century range up to 40,000.[1] On top of these there were many 'bargees', who lived and worked on large brightly coloured barges, some of which had riverscapes painted on the sides, as well as boats carrying all kinds of cargo, and ferries crossing between the riverbanks.

Travelling upriver from the royal palace at Hampton Court, a 17th-century vessel would pass between Shepperton shore and the town of Weybridge, before winding around Chertsey, where Buckingham's friend Abraham Cowley went to escape the crowds and vice of the capital, only to die an early death while out gathering hay. The vessel would then pass beneath Windsor Castle, situated on its precipitous knoll of chalk, and Dorney Court, where the first English pineapple was grown in the 1660s (the gardener John Rose later presented it to Charles II). Moving west along the river, the average size and draught of boats got smaller: as they decreased in size the boats were known as 'western barges', 'trows', and 'worsers'. Boats operating at the western reaches of the river had to be shallow and highly manoeuvrable, and it was said of the Thames barges that they could sail anywhere after a heavy dew.[2]

Further upriver, just beyond Maidenhead, the Thames was bordered on its east side by a cliff of 140 feet. The woods that stood along the top of the cliff were all that remained of the primeval forest that once covered the Thames Valley south of the Chiltern Hills. Except for the woods, the land along this stretch of the Thames was, by the 17th century, quite bare. John Evelyn described it as 'wretchedly barren . . . producing nothing but fern'.[3] Buckingham's house at Cliveden would be built at the north end of the cliff, with the Thames and the Cookham floodplain to the west, and a wooded hollow to the south and east.

In order to build a house in this position an enormous platform needed to be created, which would have involved excavating massive amounts of earth. The house was to stand in the centre of this platform, surrounded by a vast terrace. It was an unusual design. Many of Buckingham's peers were somewhat perplexed by Cliveden's location. The contemporary preference was for a sheltered setting close to water, or a house situated in the middle of a hillside with space for gardens below and plantations above.[4] Instead Buckingham planned to build his house on the highest ground, forgoing shelter for an all-encompassing view of the Buckinghamshire countryside. Buckingham's decision to build a country house in such a unique location was not just a question of style or design. On a symbolic level, a 17th-century country house was an index of status and expressed the genealogy, political power, prestige and character of its owner. Buckingham sought to communicate something of his worldliness and education in his choice of an Italianate design for Cliveden, and the Villiers coat of arms was to feature prominently around the house.

Political uncertainty and continued fears about confiscation of property meant that only ten country houses were built in the 1660s, but during the following decade construction picked up, and Cliveden was one of 19 new-build country houses of the 1670s. Among the other members of the court nobility who built houses during this decade was Arlington, Buckingham's political foe. It was not only members of the peerage who expressed their stature in this way. During the last third of the 17th century an increasing proportion of country houses were built by wealthy professionals and merchants. Country-house builders of the 1680s included the slave trader Ferdinando Gorges, and Henry Parker, who built Honington Hall in Warwickshire with profits made trading English cloth for currants, wine and cotton wool in the Levant.[5] Buckingham was determined that his project would rival not only the plans of entrepreneurs and aristocrats, but those of the king himself: at the time Charles was undertaking extravagant building programmes at Richmond, Whitehall, Greenwich and Kensington, designed and overseen by Sir Christopher Wren.

Such undertakings were extremely expensive and the future of Buckingham's Cliveden was not fully secure. The duke was not renowned for his ability to manage money. Like most aristocrats of the time, Buckingham had inherited many estates, some of which he leased for a profit. According to the system of primogeniture, land passed from the father to the eldest son. Buckingham's father had not been born into landed wealth but had been given estates by James I and Charles I; however, the greatest part of the second duke's substance came through his maternal grandfather, the 4th Earl of Rutland, from whom he inherited substantial groupings of land in Rutland and Yorkshire. Estimates of the value of Buckingham's estates varied widely. Writing to Charles II in 1660, Buckingham had guessed his rent roll to be about £30,000 a year, just under £2.5 million in today's money; Pepys assessed it more conservatively, at £19,600; and a report by his trustees, who managed his finances from 1671 onwards, calculated that if his mortgaged lands were recovered and all his lands were leased, he would receive an annual rent yield of £17,951.[6]

Buckingham's decision to establish a trust to manage his assets was motivated, at least in part, by political anxiety. It had not escaped him that his trip to Versailles had been a fool's mission and a sign that his favour with the king was waning.

Clarendon's prosecution for treason following his fall set a dangerous precedent for deposed courtiers to face serious legal charges. One of the consequences of a felony conviction such as treason was the forfeiture of estates to the Crown. Having narrowly escaped charges of treason during the Heydon affair, the risks of this must have weighed heavily on Buckingham's mind. One way of securing assets against confiscation in the event of such a prosecution was to arrange for them to be held under a Declaration of Trust. Although the legal status of trusts was unclear at the time of the Restoration in 1660, a widely discussed legal case in 1669 had reinforced their status as bulwarks against the confiscation of assets by the Crown.[7] It is likely that an awareness of his fragile political position informed Buckingham's decision to visit the London bank of Clayton and Morris in Austin Friars, just north of the junction between Throgmorton Street and Threadneedle Street, in 1671.

From 1671 until Buckingham's death in 1687, Robert Clayton and John Morris, along with four other trustees, controlled the duke's estates. They inherited a badly managed portfolio. After the Restoration Buckingham's estates were managed by Mr Braythwaite, a republican whom Buckingham found entertaining, but who was extravagant and untrustworthy, later siding with his employer's enemies during the Heydon affair. In 1668, Braythwaite was succeeded by Edward Christian, who falsified accounts in order to line his own pockets and stole from the duke's ready cash. He was eventually dismissed by the trustees in 1673, but by this time Christian had wreaked significant damage on Buckingham's finances.[8] The unfortunate succession of accountants provided more fodder for Dryden, whose Zimri was 'Beggar'd by fools whom still he found too late / He had his jest, and they had his estate.'[9] To make matters worse, Buckingham had accumulated huge debts and was paying interest rates as high as 18 per cent on his borrowings. On 24 August 1672, in a desperate bid to save his beloved glassworks from his creditors, Buckingham signed a deed gifting it and 'all the stock at Vauxhall' to Anna Maria,[10] but his plan failed. A year later, Buckingham's glassworks were put up for sale at £4,000.[11]

The first step taken by the trustees in order to improve the condition of Buckingham's finances was to increase rents on his lands so that they reflected the value of the properties, and the next step was to consolidate his debts in loans with an interest rate of no more than 6 per cent.[12] Their aim was to enable him to meet his regular expenses, to grant him £5,000 a year allowance and to mitigate for extraordinary expenses such as the building of the house at Cliveden. But even after the trustees' initial measures had been taken, Buckingham's estates still failed to yield sufficient funds to achieve these ends and, between 1674 and 1678, Clayton and Morris sold off large groups of the duke's estates in Lincolnshire, Leicestershire, Buckinghamshire and London, raising £101,238.[13] As these properties were being sold off, new investment opportunities arose: in 1672 the company of Royal Adventurers Trading To Africa was re-established as the Royal African Company, with a charter that included the right to sell slaves. The company benefited from close ties with Charles II and his successor James II, and was popular among aristocratic investors. Buckingham was an early subscriber.[14]

Most of the documents from Buckingham's time at Cliveden were destroyed in a fire in the 18th century, but up until now, it has always been assumed that Buckingham started building the main house at Cliveden when he acquired the land in 1666. However, a previously unexamined document at the National Archives shows that construction of the house did not actually begin until a decade later. The account of John Goodchild, who was employed to oversee the work at Cliveden, indicates that the site for the house was only surveyed in August 1676, when 'Buckingham did employ the Orator [legal representative] to view the said site and to draw up a plot on which said house should be built.'[15]

In the decade before the main house was built, there was still accommodation on the estate, in the form of two old hunting lodges where Anna Maria and Buckingham enjoyed many jaunts. But Buckingham had always imagined the site would become something much more than a hunting estate. On a practical level, Cliveden was intended as a replacement for Buckingham's London mansion, York House, and was to play the same role in entertaining royalty, ambassadors and other guests of political significance. Without an impressive residence in which to entertain these dignitaries on the scale expected of an aristocratic host, he risked losing social and political standing.

But most importantly, Buckingham wanted to create in Cliveden a palace for his continuing affair with Anna Maria. By the early 1670s Buckingham's close friends had begun to call Anna Maria 'the Duchess', while dutiful Mary had been relegated to the status of 'Duchess-Dowager'.[16] The estate was to be a haven where Buckingham and Anna Maria could receive guests, throw parties, and indulge their love of hunting. Even after his relationship with the duke and duchess collapsed and he became embroiled in an acrimonious legal dispute with them, John Goodchild was still willing to concede that Cliveden 'was very Romantic'.[17] Anyone who has taken in the view from the back of the house, along the parterre and down the wooded cliffs to the river, can be in no doubt that Cliveden was built by a man in love.

With so much at stake, Buckingham had to pick an architect with the imagination to understand his vision and the expertise to execute it. Captain William Winde was the ideal candidate for his pioneering project. In the 17th century there was no formal programme of architectural training, so Winde's work experience was varied. He had worked with the Anglo-Dutch architect Sir Balthazar Gerbier, who remodelled York House for Buckingham's father and curated the first duke's art collection, and had also spent much time at Versailles, where he cultivated an interest in formal gardening and an appreciation of French building craft. He also had engineering expertise – while working in the military, he had assisted with the fortification of Gravesend Reach on the banks of the Thames. No doubt his experiences building this embankment would be useful in creating a stable platform for the house at Cliveden. Buckingham and Anna Maria would also have been familiar with Winde's work at Ashdown House, owned by the bawdy courtier the Earl of Craven. Ashdown, built in the Dutch-classical style, stood three storeys high atop the Berkshire Downs. Like Cliveden, the estate at Ashdown had striking views and had been designed for the purposes of hunting and entertaining.[18]

Buckingham and Anna Maria shared a clear vision for Cliveden. Their house was to be a single block built of brick with four storeys and a hipped roof. At the back of the house a double staircase, flanked by 26 arches, would lead down from the terrace to the gardens, a full storey below.[19] Guests would enter through an impressive hall, the central feature of which was to be a sweeping staircase, the mark of any truly fashionable home. John Evelyn would later remark that the staircase at Cliveden was 'for its materials singular'.[20] Two doors would lead out from the hall: one into a parlour, through which one could access the withdrawing room, where the men could retreat after dinner and smoke tobacco; the other into a salon, where the women could take tea. On the first floor would be bedchambers, closets and guest accommodation, and a great chamber, where all the lavish entertainments would take place. The second floor was to be taken up by a long gallery providing space to walk and exercise. This would be the ideal space to display Buckingham's art collection, including, in pride of place, the Lely portrait of Anna Maria. Servants were to be quartered on the top floor. Careful consideration had been given to the layout of the bedrooms. A state bedchamber in the south-east corner of the ground floor was to be a public room where Buckingham would receive guests from his bed. Adjacent to this would be a magnificent boudoir in which Anna Maria would hold her levees.

While Anna Maria planned for her life in the country, verses about her continued to circulate at court. In November

1673, the Duke of York's second bride arrived in England from Italy, surrounded by a vast entourage of 'signiors'. One poet, most likely Buckingham's friend the Earl of Rochester, wrote a satirical ballad about one fictional member of the Italian party, 'Signior Dildo'. A whole stanza of the satire was dedicated to Anna Maria. It dredged up old allegations, and predicted, in typically lewd terms, her future abandonment:

> The countess o'th'Cockpit (who knows not her name?
> She's famous in story for a killing dame),
> When all her lovers forsake her, I trow,
> She'll then be contented with Signior Dildo.[21]

Anna Maria and Buckingham would be separated, but it wouldn't be a desertion. The couple's world was about to be torn apart by forces beyond their control.

Chapter 7

BETRAYALS

Charles Talbot felt cruelly abandoned by his mother. He was eight years old when Anna Maria had gone to live with Buckingham, choosing her lover over her sons. Now a young man of 14, Charles had come to understand and resent the events surrounding her departure. His trustees, who had long been hostile to Anna Maria, harnessed this sense of betrayal for their own purposes. On 7 January 1674, they presented a petition to the House of Lords, stating that Charles 'becomes every day more and more sensible of the deplorable death of his father, and of the dishonour caused to his family by the wicked and scandalous life led by George, Duke of Buckingham, with Anna Maria, Countess of Shrewsbury'.[1] The petitioners claimed they would not have complained 'had the offenders employed the usual care to cover their guilt and shame, or had they given any outward show of remorse or amendment'. Instead, they said, the couple 'ostentatiously persist in their shameless course of life, in defiance of the laws of God and man'. Being branded a shameless woman must have humiliated Anna Maria, but more hurtful still was the reference the petition made to her dead child, 'buried in the Abbey church at Westminster, with all the solemnities under the title of the Earl of Coventry'. The petitioners pleaded with the House to 'take the honour of [Charles Talbot] the orphan peer under their protection'.

The petition also had serious political ramifications for Buckingham. Among the measures demanded to protect young Charles's honour was the removal of Buckingham from 'the king's presence, and from his Employment'.[2] The duke's political position had incurred further damage since 1671. Parliament held him responsible for the French treaty that had bound England into the protracted disaster of the most recent conflict with the Dutch. Clarendon's career had been ruined by the Second Dutch War, and now Buckingham's credibility had been seriously damaged by the Third. Before Parliament opened, Buckingham had resorted to meeting MPs individually, endeavouring to win their favour and transfer their hostility onto his old foe, Lord Arlington. But his transparent attempts to canvass support had been noted. On 2 January 1674, Sir Gilbert Talbot, a brother of Anna Maria's deceased husband, had written to Sir Joseph Williamson, describing Buckingham's manoeuvres:

> [H]e hath so personally courted all the Members in town, the debauchees by drinking with them, the sober by grave and serious discourses, the pious by receiving the sacrament at Westminster, that he thinketh he hath gained a strong party of friends . . . his greatest endeavor with all men (next to the clearing of his own innocence) is to characterize the Lord Arlington for the most pernitious person in his Majestyes Counsailes.[3]

Talbot's letter also confirmed that the petition was the cul-
mination of a larger political plan. 'I hope we shall spoil his
designe,' he wrote, 'for we have a petition to be presented
against him in the Lords House for the death of the Earl of
Shrewsbury and the scandalous cohabitation with his wife'.
Buckingham was outraged that his private life had been
brought into the public domain in such a brutal and humiliating manner.

But matters were only to get worse. As Buckingham set
about composing a riposte to be delivered in the Lords, he, along
with Arlington, became the subject of serious charges in the
Commons. Various kinds of political misconduct were alleged
to have been perpetrated by Buckingham, but the matter of
greatest concern was his close relationship with the French,
which had for a long time been seen as treacherous. Buckingham was now in the unenviable position of having to defend
himself to both houses.

His performance failed to impress the Commons, who
voted to request his removal from offices held at the royal
pleasure, and exclusion from the 'Royal Presence and Coun-
cils'. The same day, the House of Lords debated the Talbot
petition. Mary Villiers was deeply distressed by the public
humiliation: Lord Conway reported that she was 'crying and
tearing herself'. But even so she offered Anna Maria and Buckingham her unwavering support, soliciting on behalf of both
her husband and his lover.[4] Self-sacrifice was at the core of her
being, and her capacity to express it within this love triangle
was seemingly endless. Anna Maria's father, the Earl of Cardigan, also tried to diffuse the anger of the Lords, citing a letter

he had received from his daughter, in which she admitted to doing wrong and 'begged she might not be made desperate'.[5]

Buckingham's woes in the Lords and Commons may not have taken on such monumental significance had the king been willing to intervene on his behalf. But Charles II had finally tired of his old childhood friend. The range and severity of the charges raised during cross-examination in the Commons made it clear that Buckingham was a political liability and could not be trusted to handle any affairs of state. The king assented to the Commons' request that the duke be stripped of his positions on the Privy Council, the Council for Trade and Plantations, and the Admiralty Commission, as well as losing his Lord Lieutenancy of the West Riding. In a desperate letter to Charles, Buckingham revealed the extent of his personal suffering, recalling their shared childhood and the sacrifices he had made for his friend and monarch:

Consider, I beseech you, that I had the honour to be bred up with your majesty from a child; that I lost my estate for running from Cambridge, where I was a student, to serve Your Majesty and your Father, at Oxford, when I was not thought of age sufficient to bear arms, and for that reason was sent away from thence to travel. That after the end of the wars, returning into England and having my whole estate restored to me by the Parliament, without composition, a few weeks after my return, there happening to be a design laid to take up arms for Your Majesty, my brother and I engaged in it, and in the engagement he was killed.

That after this the Parliament voted my pardon in case

I would return within forty days; that I being concealed in London, chose rather, with the hazard of my life, to wait upon Your Majesty in the Fleet, where I found you, than to stay, possessed of my estates upon condition of having nothing more to do with Your Majesty's fortunes: . . . I humbly ask Your Majesty's pardon for this trouble I have given you, and beg of you to believe that nothing shall ever separate me from my duty and allegiance to Your Majesty; as I cannot despair but that one day Your Majesty will find the difference between those that truly love you and those that serve you only for private ends of their own. [6]

The letter had little impact. Of his own volition, Charles removed Buckingham from the Chancellorship of the University of Cambridge, and launched an investigation into his financial conduct as Master of the Horse. Buckingham's political career lay in ruins, but worse was still to come.

On 5 February, the debate in the Lords was resumed and the House resolved – in a move that would be unthinkable in modern society – that Buckingham and Anna Maria be forced to separate. They were ordered 'not to converse or cohabit for the future' and to 'enter into security by recognizance to the king in £10,000 each'.[7] Anna Maria moved out of the house she had shared with Buckingham and Mary. Buckingham was beleaguered and humiliated, and worst of all, his dream of a life with Anna Maria at Cliveden lay in ruins.

Chapter 8

'YOUR MOST UNHAPPY MOTHER'

Perhaps for the first time, Anna Maria began to question the choices she had made. She understood that young Charles's guardians had significant influence over his behaviour and hoped that reconciliation with the Talbots would give her a chance to mend her fractured relationship with her son. While Charles may have judged Anna Maria severely for her conduct with Buckingham and her involvement in his father's death, he retained a sentimental attachment to his mother. He longed to see her, but had to negotiate the difficult family dynamics. The Talbots were resolute that Charles should have as little contact as possible with any relations of Anna Maria and had discouraged him from visiting his grandfather, Robert Brudenell, or his aunt, the Countess of Westmorland. Sensing that the young earl was anxious to see his mother, John Talbot made arrangements to send Charles away to enjoy the distractions of Paris with his tutor.[1]

Anna Maria was frustrated by the Talbots' intransigence and decided to appeal to her son directly. In a letter, one of the few surviving documents written in her hand, she conveyed her wish to see Charles so that she could: 'express to [Charles] (by the assistance of God's holy spirit) the true sense of my former errors and sorrow for those high provocations and injuries done to your deceased father now with God, whose excellent virtues I hope you will ever imitate'.[2] She lamented the years that had been wasted, chastised herself for her failure to appreciate her husband – only too late, she wrote, had she realised that Shrewsbury was 'a blessing given me by heaven greater than I knew how to prize' and conveyed her 'firme resolutions for the future never to err' as she had done in the past.[3]

In the final paragraph of her letter, Anna Maria deferred to Charles's evident moral fastidiousness by offering to renounce any of her company of which he disapproved. 'I am informed that you have taken umbrage at some women which have and some that do resort to me,' she wrote, 'I do hereby promise you I will neither see converse nor correspond with either Mrs Knight or any other men or women that you shall disapprove of.' She concluded with a vow that she would obey Charles as a wife was expected to obey a husband: 'I will make haste after you into France to put my self into such a retirement that you will not be displeased at and which may afford me a better life than that of your most unhappy mother.' Anna Maria's final sentence contains two crossings-out that show she had originally intended to sign off as 'your most unfortunate Shrewsbury'.

While some historians have seen Anna Maria's letter as evidence of her contrition and part of a clear-cut morality tale in which a shamed woman acknowledged her sin and begged forgiveness, the reality is more nuanced. Anna Maria may have come to deeply regret her behaviour and clearly longed to see her son, but she also would have been acutely aware that the thawing of relations with the Talbots was essential for her future. The Talbots had confiscated Anna Maria's jointure before she returned from France in 1668, and since then Buckingham had provided her not only with a place to live, but also with an allowance. Now that the couple had been forced to separate, she would again find herself in straitened circumstances. The king assisted her with an annual pension of £1,600, but she would need further financial support from the Talbots.[4] An emotional chameleon, she quickly adapted to her changed circumstances, describing Buckingham as 'the unhappy author of my injuries' in her letter to Charles. In doing this and expressing sadness about her treatment of Shrewsbury, she was beginning to create some much-needed distance between herself and her old lover.

By the autumn of 1674, Anna Maria had returned to the convent in Pontoise, while Charles was staying in a pension near the college of Navarre, where he was to study. Away from the controlling influence of John Talbot, they began to spend time together. Although Charles recognised that he had yet to come to terms with his abandonment, he was eager to get to know his mother and believed that she had suffered enough for her transgressions. In a letter to his guardian, Talbot, he wrote: 'I will be as kind to her as any child can be to a mother . . . I do assure she has gone through a part of purgatory since she came hither.'[5] He craved his mother's attention and resented the presence of others. After one visit during which Anna Maria's time was divided between him and his grandfather,

Charles noted his frustration with the situation: 'I wish with all my soule my Grand Father was with you in England that I might have my mother to myself '.[6]

Charles's letters to his guardian during this period record Anna Maria's attempts to make amends. He noted presents of a diamond ring and a pair of silver candlesticks, but saw her changed attitude as far more important, and felt that Anna Maria was finally behaving towards him as a mother should: 'Her kindness and behaviour is such that all the world, as well as myself, ought to be satisfied'.[7] He often visited her at Pontoise and read to her letters from London. On one occasion, certain that he had come across an anecdote about his mother's scandalous behaviour, he broke off reading aloud. Anna Maria, sensing the subject of the letter, fell to her knees crying and begged his forgiveness.[8] She confessed that she had formerly done very ill, but said that for the future all she desired from Charles was that he should be kind to her, as she believed she deserved.[9] It seems that, despite their difficult history, Anna Maria and Charles managed to develop an understanding in the months that followed. In June 1675, Anna Maria went to see Charles in his lodgings and the pair visited the 'house and the waterworks' at Versailles, the palace that had done so much to inspire Cliveden. Recounting the trip to his guardian, Charles again noted his mother's 'kindness . . . and sorrow for what is past'.[10]

Anna Maria had finally established a close, loving relationship with her son. She would never be able to reclaim those lost years of his childhood, but she had shown Charles the extent of her regret and her resolve to behave respectably. We can assume that a similar reconciliation was achieved with her younger son, Jake. This renewed connection with the Talbot family provided Anna Maria not only with emotional comfort but also with some political and financial stability, as Charles was Shrewsbury's heir. Her next aim was to orchestrate her return to England and reception at court. She asked Charles to convey her desire for forgiveness to the Talbot family, hoping that their support would smooth her transition back to society. She was a woman who usually got what she wanted, and, early in 1677, she was received back at court. Her reputation had not diminished during her absence, and she appeared in court satires as a jilted, inveterate, disease-ridden wench. One poem, circulated in 1679, imagined her and a succession of other 'Ladies of the Town' applying to buy the role of king's mistress from the Duchess of Portsmouth. The poet implies that Anna Maria had previously given the king venereal disease that she had contracted from Richard Talbot, one of her husband's relatives, and casts the Earl of Danby as her pimp:

> Shrewsbury offered for the place,
> All she had gotten from his grace;
> She knew his ways and could comply,
> With all decays of lechery;
> Had often licked his amorous sceptre,
> Until the jaded stallion leapt her;
> But long ago had the mishap,
> To give the King Dick Talbot's clap.
> Though for her all was said that can be,
> By her drudge the Earl of Danby,

She was dismissed with scorn and told,
Where a tall page was to be sold.[11]

Meanwhile Buckingham, the 'jaded stallion', was left to lay the first bricks of his palace at Cliveden, without the woman for whom it had been conceived.

Chapter 9

CONSTRUCTION

D espite, or perhaps because of his heartbreak, Buckingham made it his mission to oversee every aspect of the construction of Cliveden. The first phase involved the redistribution of large volumes of earth from the north to the south of the site in order to create the 433-foot platform on which the house would be built. Scores of labourers lumbered to and fro with their wheelbarrows. Brian Fairfax, who became Buckingham's agent and later biographer, compared the audacious plans for Cliveden's foundations to the Capitol in Rome, which was perched on a precipitous rock. He quoted Cicero to suggest that Cliveden, like the Capitol, had 'insanae substructiones' (crazy foundations).[1]

The main structure of the house was made of brick, which, prior to industrial methods, took months to craft. Each brick had been painstakingly made – earth had been dug up the previous autumn, left over winter in the frost, and then formed in an open-frame mould before being fired in a kiln. The early stages progressed rapidly, and although work on the estate – which Winde had designed in accordance with Buckingham's original vision – carried through into the following decade, a habitable building was in place by 1678. In the spring of that year, beds, soft furnishings and wall hangings were already being put in place, and shortly after, the house was ready to receive guests. Among the early visitors was one of the king's mistresses, Louise de Kéroualle, whom Buckingham entertained in an effort to improve relations with Charles.[2]

From the late 1670s until the mid-1680s, Buckingham continued to add to the existing house and develop the surrounding land. Barges laden with stone and timber regularly docked at the riverside, while carts piled high with building supplies arrived from nearby towns like Cippenham and Lullebrook, as well as from further afield. Winches were used to haul heavy materials up the steep incline from the river to the house. Woodcutters had been employed to clear an avenue through the woods and, elsewhere, other trees were trained to create shaded walkways. Buckingham had cherry trees planted and also created a vineyard, which he later surrounded with hedges to protect it from winds on the exposed hillside. In the newly constructed parts of the house, doors were being hung, walls panelled, windows framed with fir wood. In the roof of the house, plumbers laboured on the water cistern.[3]

Buckingham's project required the services of a number of different craftsmen. To sculpt a series of 'statues bigger than the life', which would stand in the centre of each of the 26 alcoves beneath the terrace, he employed Edward Pierce, a mason and stone-carver who had worked with Sir Christopher Wren on the rebuilding of London churches in the aftermath of the Great Fire of London.[4] The father-and-son team of Jonathan and Edward Wilcox, who had also worked with Wren in the building of St James's Church, Piccadilly, were appointed as carpenters. Edward Gouge, whose work was considered to be the best in the country, was brought in to create the plasterwork that covered the ceilings, and John Bellingham, who described himself as 'expert in the art or mystery of making looking-glass plates', was engaged to make mirrors for the house.[5] Most extravagantly, Buckingham summoned the Flemish painter Jan Siberechts to England to create local landscapes to adorn the walls of the house. Siberechts took four years to complete his task and his work at Cliveden earned him several further commissions from English nobles.

Strong and brilliant colours adorned the house – there was an abundance of purple, gold, emerald green and crimson. One 'closet' – which at the time meant 'study' – was hung with gilt leather. Fabrics such as velvet, silk and brocade were used to line the walls of the grander bedrooms, and the sleeping quarters of the staff were furnished with flock beds and coloured rugs. Flemish tapestries, Oriental rugs and marquetry furniture were all popular decorations in the decades after the Restoration. Such ornamentations would have reflected well Buckingham's flamboyant personal style. But all of these items came at a cost.

Buckingham, of course, took little account of expense during the building works. In 1677, a year after construction started, he wrote to the king that 'a little mistake in my builders at Cliveden may cost me above £10,000 because I shall certainly pull it down again if it be not to my own mind'.[6] Soon after, Buckingham was able to live in the house. By default, Mary had become the first mistress of Cliveden. The couple employed a full retinue of staff, including a number of footmen, stable-hands, a coach driver, a cook, and an usher of the hall called Jasper Eaton. Edward Manfield, from whom Buckingham had bought the estate, was kept on as gentleman of the duke's horses on a board wage of £100, and his wife was paid to help with the interior decoration.[7]

The great hall was the centre of the social activities of the house, and among Jasper Eaton's duties would have been waiting on Buckingham and Mary's guests. Entertaining was built into the fabric of the house. Beneath the great parlour, Buckingham had built a domed chamber, joined to the garden by an anteroom that could be accessed through an arch in the middle of the terrace. It was also joined to the ground floor by a brick staircase. The room, known as the Sounding Chamber, had been designed so that music played would be transmitted upstairs into the hall without diminishment or distortion. The acoustics work just as well today as they did in the 17th century: a radio played in the room can be heard upstairs in the main hall with perfect clarity.

Music was a large part of Restoration culture, and in building a sounding room at Cliveden, Buckingham equipped himself to compete with the grand entertainments at court. Charles II often commissioned recitals of the music of his favourite composer, Giacomo Carissimi, and brought a range of virtuoso performers from the Continent, including a troupe of Italian opera singers, whom he paid £200 each – four times the salary of an ordinary court musician. Buckingham's musical interests were not exclusively Continental. During his turn as a street entertainer in Commonwealth London, he had become familiar with a variety of ballads and he admired folk tunes as well as arias.

Although Buckingham entertained in the 1680s, the surviving accounts give the impression that his lifestyle was not as decadent as it had been at the start of his affair with Anna Maria. Accounts from Cliveden include infrequent bills of up to £366 on meat, whereas the Clayton and Morris accounts of the 1660s record several bills of £500 a time or more to butchers and poulterers (the equivalent of over £40,000 in today's money). Surviving records show that while Mary took charge of the more mundane aspects of domestic chores, purchasing butter, cream and whey, Buckingham concerned himself with procuring more lavish goods: one bill to tradeswoman Jane Scarf for 'Oranges, Lemmons, Apples & Oysters and all manner of herbs & flavours' amounted to £239.19.11 (£20,000 in today's money).[8] But it was clear that Buckingham's money worries had done something to curb his spending. Perhaps Mary also proved a sobering influence during her time as mistress of Cliveden.

Meanwhile, Cliveden's lost chatelaine had begun her life anew. Buckingham's loss of Anna Maria became irreversible on 23 June 1677 when she married Captain George Rodney Bridges. The duke fell into an oubliette of misery. *The Lost Mistress*, a poem he wrote around this time, expresses his despair at losing Anna Maria, in the form of a pastoral lament spoken by the spurned shepherd, Strephon: 'She had the power to make my bliss or woe / And has given my heart its mortal blow'. He also claimed that he would rather suffer than think poorly of Anna Maria: 'My suffering heart can all Relief refuse, / Rather than her, it did adore, accuse'. The poem also suggests the extent of Buckingham's indifference to Mary, and her failure to console him in the absence of Anna Maria. 'I have no Hope, no second comfort left . . . I lov'd not at a rate to love again . . . No Change can Ease for my sick Heart prepare / Widow'd to hope, and wedded to Despair.'[9]

Unsurprisingly, in view of the sentiments expressed in the poem, by this time Mary and Buckingham were living virtually separate lives and their daily routines at Cliveden did not intersect. Mary had some responsibilities in running the estate – 20 cows were kept for her use at the estate dairy at Cippenham – but it seems that the shame of being an unwanted wife may finally have become too great for her to bear. Mary's health started to suffer. A bill of £20 to the apothecary Moses Bratch documents the purchase of 'Physic by my Lady's order' and another, to Henry Cleaver, the purchase of 'spirits for my Lady's use'.[10]

Buckingham, meanwhile, immersed himself in his studies and in spite of his own sporadic ill-health, he continued to hunt. Some 30 horses, 36 hounds and 16 whelps were kept on the estate and, judging by a payment to Andrew Smith, who was given £5.10 shillings 'for potting venison', it appears that the duke may still have had some success at his favourite sport.[11]

The hunting grounds had been remodelled since Buckingham had hunted there with Anna Maria when he first acquired the land in the 1660s. Before the 17th century, deer parks had formed a separate and adjacent part of country estates, connecting to a hunting lodge rather than the main house. Cliveden had been built with hunting in mind, so it was only natural that the house would connect directly to the deer park; this had been achieved by the construction of an 'august and stately' avenue leading from the mansion, through the formal gardens, and into the woods. Such avenues, which had appeared 100 years earlier in Italian Renaissance landscaping, were fashionable at the time: during the 1670s, they were planted at Hyde Park, Buxted and Audley End.[12]

The formal gardens were an integral feature of Winde's design for Cliveden, spreading out along the great artificial platform to the south of the mansion, and descending towards the river in terraces linked by a succession of steps.[13] The grand villas of Italy, where he had spent so much time in his youth, had made an indelible mark on Buckingham's architectural predilections, and guests commented on the similarity between Cliveden's southern façade and cascading gardens and the front of the Villa Aldobrandini in Frascati, just east of Rome.[14]

Despite breaking with convention in terms of its location, Cliveden was remarkably on trend in terms of its garden design. The house's position on an exposed hilltop gave the formal gardens an arresting view. In Tudor and early Stuart houses, which were conventionally built on lower, flatter land, there had been a fashion for special viewing mounts, which gave visitors the opportunity to appreciate the intricate planning of gardens from a high vantage point. At Hampton Court, Henry VIII had used 250,000 bricks to construct an enormous elevation overlooking the entire garden.[15] Buckingham's choice of site cannily provided a natural viewing mount south of the mansion. From here it was possible to see the village of Maidenhead, the river and the deer park to the east. But the mesmerising view was now a painful reminder of everything he had hoped for.

In the years following his split from Anna Maria, at the same time as supervising building works, Buckingham tried to distract himself by re-entering the political fray with renewed vigour. In 1675 he returned to Parliament, now determined to cause disruption to Charles II and his government. The Lord High Treasurer, Thomas Osborne, Earl of Danby, was a vociferous opponent of both Catholic and Protestant nonconformity, while Buckingham was an advocate of broad toleration, and Buckingham threw himself into this principled cause. In October he spoke in the Lords requesting leave to introduce a bill for the toleration of Protestant nonconformists. In expectation that new elections would produce a Parliament more supportive of his bill, Buckingham also lobbied for the dissolution of Parliament. He was unsuccessful and, without new elections to reorganise Parliament, Danby managed to get the bill defeated by two votes.

By 1677, Parliament was divided between the Country Party, which included Buckingham, Ashley, now Earl of Shaftesbury, and their supporters, and the Court Party, who supported Danby and the king. The most committed members of the Country Party formed the Green Ribbon Club, a private club that met at the King's Head Tavern at the corner of Fleet

Street and Chancery Lane. The club was notorious for its radical politics – their green badge was an old Leveller symbol from the Civil War – as well as the informality of their meetings: they convened without hats or swords, smoked long clay pipes, and often removed their periwigs.

From this culture of debate and opposition emerged two political parties. The Tories included many Parliamentarians who had previously been allied to the Court Party. Their principles were traditionalist and conservative, they tended to exhibit High Anglican religious beliefs and they were sympathetic to the idea of a strong monarch. Their opponents, the Whigs, evolved from the Country Party that Buckingham had known in the 1670s. They were fearful and suspicious of absolute monarchy and most of them were in favour of greater toleration for Christian minorities. The conflict between these factions was to dictate politics for decades to come.

But Buckingham's personal experience of fractured English politics was soon to come to an end. His involvement in the Green Ribbon Club and continued agitation for the dissolution of Parliament intensified the wrath of Charles. After one particularly forceful speech to the Lords, in which Buckingham made a thinly veiled suggestion that a rebellion might occur if a new Parliament was not called, the House decreed that he should issue a formal apology. Buckingham steadfastly refused and in May 1677 was sent, yet again, to the Tower. His health had been slowly deteriorating and he pleaded to be taken there by coach rather than boat, fearing the damp would worsen his condition. It was a stark contrast to Buckingham's journey to the Tower in 1667, when crowds had gathered to cheer him on. A decade later the streets were empty. Buckingham's appeal to the people too had waned.

It was clear that, during this period, Cliveden preoccupied Buckingham. After several weeks in the Tower, he wrote to Charles begging for temporary release to visit his riverside mansion and inspect the ongoing building works there. He was let out for two days on 22 June, given temporary release in July and formally freed in August. His incarceration had served its purpose. Following his release, Buckingham ceased to antagonise the Court Party. He made a formal apology to the House of Lords and set about mending relations with Charles. It is unlikely that his view on Protestant dissenters had changed, but from the late 1670s onwards, Buckingham's appetite for politics waned. In 1679 Shaftesbury and other members of the Country Party began lobbying for the exclusion of Charles's Catholic brother, James, Duke of York, from the royal succession, in favour of the king's illegitimate son, the Duke of Monmouth. It was a hugely controversial plan, which would lead to a decade of crisis, and bring the labels Whig (for supporters of exclusion) and Tory (for opponents) into popular usage. Buckingham, sapped of his vigour, did not contribute to the parliamentary debates. His failure to stand up for the cause discredited him in the eyes of the Country Party, and was damningly invoked by Dryden at the climax of his passage satirising Buckingham as Zimri. The duke's caprice, suggested Dryden, led him to betray the Protestant cause, leaving Monmouth (Absalom) and Shaftesbury (Achitophel) to lead the fight against a Catholic succession.

He laughed himself from court; then sought relief,
By forming parties, but could ne'er be chief;
For, spite of him, the weight of business fell
On Absalom, and wise Achitophel;
Thus, wicked but in will, of means bereft,
He left not faction, but of that was left.

Chapter 10

THE LOST MISTRESS

The final scandal of the duke's life unfolded in 1680 when his opponents conspired to accuse him of the capital crime of sodomy. The plot was probably instigated either by Danby or Edward Christian, the corrupt former manager of Buckingham's estates. Two Irishmen claimed that Buckingham had committed sodomy with a woman called Sarah Harwood and then forced her to flee to France. The case was brought before Sir William Waller, Justice of the Peace, but the grand jury found that the evidence against Buckingham was inadequate. Although Buckingham's accusers were subsequently put on trial and found guilty of conspiring to defame the duke, the incident had already further eroded his reputation. The coronation of James II in 1685 was Buckingham's final public appearance. With the death of Charles, he no longer held a position of privilege at the English court and there was no reason for him to remain within easy reach of London and Windsor any more.

Worn down and stripped of his honours, Buckingham retired to Helmsley Castle in Yorkshire. In April 1687, he caught a chill while out fox hunting. He was put to bed in one of his tenants' houses in the marketplace at Kirkby Moorside. His condition grew worse and, on 16 April, the man who had been raised in the cradle with the king died alone among strangers.

While Buckingham died a broken man, Anna Maria had successfully reinvented herself as a respectable wife. Her financial support enabled her new husband, George Rodney Brydges, to become active in politics. She paid £4,500 to buy him a position as Groom of the Bedchamber and it was almost certainly through her influence that he was appointed to the Staffordshire Lieutenancy in 1680. Later, backed by Charles Talbot, he developed influential connections in the Whig Party, a move that would have aligned him with his wife's former lover. He was also noted for his involvement in the management of Irish estates and his role in the inquiry into the corrupt affairs of the East India Company, which paved the way for the impeachment of Lord Danby at the end of 1695. The pair remained married for 25 years until Anna Maria's death in 1702, at the age of 60.

History has not been kind to Buckingham and Anna Maria. Writers at the time and subsequent historians have viewed the duke's life as a simple morality tale, the story of a degenerate's decline and fall; Buckingham has been entered into the annals of history as emblematic of all that was louche, excessive and immoral in the Restoration court. Alexander Pope's depiction of his death in his *Moral Essays* encouraged the perception of a once-mighty figure who through his arrogance, lust and stupidity, lost his fortune and died in squalor, left with only the jewelled insignia of the Order of the Garter as a reminder of his life of splendour:

In the worst inn's room, with mat half-hung,
The floors of plaster, and the walls of dung,
On once a flock-bed, but repaired with straw,
With tape-tied curtains, never meant to draw,
The George and Garter dangling from that bed
Where tawdry yellow strove with dirty red,
Great Villiers lies – alas! How changed from him,
That life of pleasure and that soul of whim![1]

It is true that Buckingham viewed both his own life and his loss of Anna Maria as tragic, writing in his commonplace book, 'in those mighty volumes of the stars / There's writ no sadder story than my fate'.[2] However, to dismiss George Villiers, Duke of Buckingham as an incompetent reprobate, who got his just deserts, is to ignore the complexities, talents and vision of the man. Buckingham may have been a remorseless pleasure-seeker but he also made valuable contributions to art and culture. His play *The Rehearsal* had a big impact on the London stage for over a century – between 1674 and 1777 there were at least 156 revivals, the most recent being by the American Shakespeare Center in 2012. Buckingham's decision to create a trust to manage his finances was originally seen as further evidence of his inability to manage his excessive spending, but was actually part of a complex strategy to protect his lands in a time of political uncertainty. The fact that his wealth was held in trust, along with the neatness of Pope's narrative, and the immediate circumstances of his death, have led to a widespread misconception that he died in poverty: in fact, the duke died a wealthy man, and his estates were sold off after his death not to satisfy his creditors – most of whom had already been paid – but because he died intestate and without legal heirs.[3]

Anna Maria has been treated even more harshly. Her affair with Buckingham made her notorious within her lifetime. In annotations to his copy of Nicholas Cross's *Cynosura*, Thomas Barlow, the Bishop of Lincoln and a contemporary of Anna Maria's, identified her as a 'whore'.[4] Other contemporary commentators characterised her as lustful, greedy and Machiavellian. One Restoration reader added Anna Maria's name to the title in their copy of the Jacobean play *The Insatiate Countess*, so that it became 'the Insatiate Countess of Shrewsbury'.[5]

The relative lack of surviving letters or manuscripts documenting Anna Maria's experience and opinions has made her an easy target for moralising and caricature. The vilification of Anna Maria reached its apotheosis in late Victorian times. In her biography of Buckingham, Lady Winifred Burghclere depicted Anna Maria as a monstrous creature:

In an age of scandalous depravity, Anna Maria Brudenell, Countess of Shrewsbury, achieved an evil pre-eminence. Reared amidst the turbulence of civil factions, she had imbibed none of that wholesome terror of the law, which often curbs the impulses of the conscienceless; while, though born and bred a Roman Catholic, no ghostly menace, no dread of death and judgement, could check the primeval vigour of her natural instincts. Even in that coarse and blood-stained time, she seems an anachronism, and we seek her fellows rather in the Rome of the Caesars than in the Court of the laughter-loving Charles.[6]

But perhaps instead of seeing Anna Maria as a wanton woman with an insatiable lust for blood and sex, we can understand her as an arch pragmatist, trying to negotiate her way in a competitive court culture where women had little independent material power. She was dazzled by the glittering prizes offered by a life as Buckingham's mistress. It is a sad irony that she was never able to fully enjoy Cliveden, the greatest prize of all, which Buckingham had the vision to create for her in a previously bare landscape. She will always be the lost mistress of Cliveden.

PART II
ELIZABETH
1657-1733

Chapter 1

FROM RICHMOND to 'ROYAL WHORE'

Unlike Anna Maria, Elizabeth Villiers was never lauded for her beauty. Her distinguishing feature was a severe squint in her left eye; a contemporary described her as being 'crookedly built' and contrasted the 'jerky' manner in which she walked with the swan-like gait considered desirable.[1] But her sharp intelligence, compassion and social dexterity more than compensated for her lacklustre appearance. She excelled in conversation and was, according to Jonathan Swift, 'the wisest woman I ever saw',[2] while her natural instinct for politics made her the confidante of many leading figures of the time. In his long poem *The Progress of Beauty*, Lord Lansdowne lauded Elizabeth, who was 'for wisdom and deep judgement fam'd'.[3] In short, she offers a very different conception of feminine power from the first mistress of Cliveden.

Elizabeth was born in 1657, the eldest daughter of Frances and Sir Edward Villiers. Frances Villiers was governess to the children of James, Duke of York, Charles II's brother and heir. After the Restoration, Sir Edward Villiers was appointed estate keeper at Richmond Palace, one of the duke's residences.[4] The position involved looking after the park, lodges and game as well as the wardrobe and garden of the palace, which dated back to the reign of Henry VII. Elizabeth and her five sisters spent a carefree childhood in the charmingly dilapidated red-brick buildings of the old royal residence.

In 1669, the Duke of York underwent a crisis of conscience and sought comfort in the arms of the Catholic Church. Over the next few years it became widespread knowledge that he had converted to Catholicism. He was eventually forced to admit this publicly by the Test Act of 1673, which required public office holders to take an oath repudiating papism. When James refused to comply, he was forced to resign from his position as Lord Admiral. At a time when popular English wisdom associated Protestantism with political liberty and Catholicism with tyranny, James's papish predilections sparked fears that he would turn the country into a Catholic state along the lines of absolutist France. In order to prevent the duke's two daughters Mary and Anne from succumbing to the corrosive influence of their father's religion, Charles II relocated them from St James's Palace to Richmond, where they were put into the care of Elizabeth's parents, Edward and Frances Villiers.[5] By this point Elizabeth was in her early teens. Like George Villiers, Duke of Buckingham, her second cousin once removed, she would spend her formative years in the intimate company of royalty. There seems to be a royal thread running through the fabric of Cliveden's history.

Mary, who would later become Mary II, was highly strung and even at a young age intensely concerned with questions of religion and morality. In Richmond Palace in the early 1670s, neither she nor Elizabeth Villiers could have imagined the tortuous romantic liaisons that would later divide them. The royal nursery was an environment dominated by women and the atmosphere at Richmond resembled that of a refined sleepover. Besides the princesses, Elizabeth and her sisters were educated with other daughters of the aristocracy. The wide age range in the nursery resulted in an emotional hierarchy in which older girls would care for the younger ones, but they were all equally mischievous: the girls would often ask their art teacher, the dwarf Richard Gibson, to smuggle out notes to their friends living nearby.[6] Her years at Richmond equipped Elizabeth with two immensely important attributes – a strong female sensibility and a sense of ease in the company of royalty. These were skills that would serve her well in the next phase of her life.

Although the Richmond set were schooled in French and arithmetic, the primary focus of their education was the acquisition of feminine accomplishments – drawing, playing music, dancing – and the teachings of the Church of England, in which they were instructed by Henry Compton, Bishop of Oxford and then London, and the chaplain Edward Lake.[7] While Elizabeth distinguished herself academically, her sister Anne found the lessons more challenging. Anne was considered the prettiest Villiers sister; she was also the most sensitive, and found it hard growing up in Elizabeth's shadow. This set up a dynamic of sibling rivalry that would intensify as the girls matured. In reality Anne's perception of her sister's educational accomplishment was inflated, for despite growing up in a royal nursery and having obvious intellectual gifts, Elizabeth did not receive the education she deserved. By the end of the 17th century, the broad humanist curriculum prescribed to both sexes during the Tudor period had disappeared and literacy was no longer considered a priority in female education.

The sisterly spirit at Richmond Palace also extended to girls in the surrounding area. Nearby in Kew lived the four daughters of Samuel Fortrey, and through the Fortreys, Elizabeth was introduced to the beautiful and charismatic Sarah Jennings, with whom she would later have a volatile and competitive relationship.[8] Meanwhile, the princesses Mary and Anne developed a particular attachment to Frances Apsley, daughter of Sir Allen Apsley, the Treasurer of the Duke of York's household. Written correspondence between Frances and Mary started around 1675, when the former was 22 and the latter 13. The princess's passionate avowals went far beyond the sentiments ordinarily expressed by female friends. The language of her letters was quite remarkable. 'My dearest dear husband,' she wrote, 'my much loved husband . . . How I dote on you, oh, I am in raptures of sweet amaze, when I think of you I am in ecstasy'. On another occasion, she confessed that she loved Frances 'with a flame more lasting than the vestals' fire . . . with a love that ne'er was known by man; I have for you excess of friendship, more of love than any woman can for woman.'[9] Whether or not Mary's attachment was sexual or platonic, the sheer force of her admiration for Frances highlights the value she placed on female kinship. Anne also developed strong feelings for Frances, and this became a source of tension between the sisters for a while. After she was moved away from Richmond, Mary never again had such an obsession with a member of her own sex; in Anne's case, her attraction to Frances Apsley was a precursor to future infatuations with women.[10]

Adult responsibilities came early in the 17th century and the years of girlish glee at Richmond were brought to a premature end when in 1677, at the age of 15, Mary was married. Charles II, concerned that the monarchy was in jeopardy due to his brother's evident Catholicism, had arranged a shrewd alliance, matching his niece Mary to his Dutch nephew, Prince William III of Orange, a celebrated Protestant and the living incarnation of resistance to Catholic tyranny. Mary was second in line to the throne and the marriage would ensure Protestant succession provided James remained childless. The pair would live together in the Dutch Republic. Mary asked Elizabeth, as well as her sisters Catherine and Anne and their mother Frances, to join her retinue. Elizabeth was appointed to the coveted position of maid of honour.

The marriage between William and Mary was a sombre private affair, held on 4 November 1677 in Mary's bedchamber at St James's Palace. Only their closest relatives were present; along with Henry Compton, who was officiating, and Hans William Bentinck, the Prince of Orange's best man. The bride wept frequently in the lead-up to the ceremony – they were not tears of joy.[11] Emotionally charged at the best of times, Mary was terrified of leaving her native England and travelling to an alien land with a man she barely knew. The role of guardian of Protestant succession in England was an onerous responsibility to rest on the slight shoulders of a 15-year-old girl. To make matters worse, William was twice Mary's age and anything but an Adonis. He had a long, hooked and rather crooked nose, and legs that were too short for the rest of his body. Mary, who at 5 feet 11 inches was unusually tall, towered half a foot over him. William's manner failed to compensate for these physical flaws – formal and aloof, he was socially graceless and found it impossible to put others at ease.

Mary's impending departure to the Dutch Republic was accelerated by news, a few days later, that her sister Anne had contracted smallpox. Soon Lady Frances, Elizabeth's mother, had also succumbed to the disease. Fearful that his new wife would fall prey to the illness, William decided to leave for Holland as soon as possible. Lady Frances could not accompany her daughters because she was contagious, and was too unwell to travel regardless. When the wind changed on 19 November, the party boarded a barge at Whitehall steps and then the yacht *Mary* at Erith, a port further down the Thames. Elizabeth and her sisters were forced to leave their mother in England on the point of death. They were never to see her again.

Elizabeth endured a punishing crossing to Holland. While contending with seasickness, homesickness and grief about her mother, she was also responsible for the pastoral care of the anxious Princess Mary. From the start, the journey was beset by problems. The sea was so unpredictable that the travellers were forced to land at Sheerness, before starting their journey again when the weather improved.[12] It was eventually decided that William and Mary should travel in separate ships, but when the yachts finally reached the Dutch coast, they found the River Maas blocked by ice floes. If they waited for the Maas to clear the wind might blow them back to England, so they anchored off the small fishing village of Ter Heyde. Elizabeth, Mary and the rest of the girls all piled into a small rowing boat and were taken ashore.[13] No doubt they would have been struck, as were other English travellers, by the bleak, flat land-scape with its silty inlets and poldered farmlands. At 20 years old Elizabeth Villiers had been wrenched from the uterine safety of Richmond, cast out to sea, and deposited in a land that, though England's neighbour, was entirely foreign and inhospitable.

The Dutch Republic had a complex and bloody history. The territory had previously been ruled by the Habsburg Crown as part of the larger Spanish Netherlands, but in 1568, the Habsburgs had been ejected by popular Protestant rebellion. Thirteen years later, the rebellion culminated in the northern part of the Spanish Netherlands becoming the Republic of the Seven United Netherlands, or the Dutch Republic. Conflict between the Republic and the Habsburg Crown had raged on for generations in the Eighty Years War, which only ended in 1648 with the Peace of Munster. Spanish brutality during the prolonged war had created a lasting anti-Catholic feeling and spawned various legends of resistance and fortitude around which Dutch national identity had been constructed.

The Republic consisted of seven relatively autonomous provinces, presided over by a central assembly, the States General, and an elected ruler, the stadtholder. Though each province was in theory empowered to choose its own stadt-holder, after the initial stadtholderate of William I, the role became closely associated with the House of Orange, which came to form an effective dynasty of rulers. There were signifi-cant disagreements about how powerful the role of stadtholder should be. The centralising rule of William II provoked much dissent among those who wanted to limit the power of the stadtholder and, after his sudden death in 1650, five of the seven provinces voted to eschew the role altogether, opting instead to be governed by the less powerful figure of Grand Pensionary. For 22 years, this office was occupied by the republican Johan de Witt, Holland's answer to Oliver Cromwell.

Johan de Witt's rule was brought to a bloody end in 1672. This was Holland's *rampjaar* or 'disaster year', in which England and France, recently allied by the Secret Treaty of Dover, mounted a vicious onslaught against Holland by land and sea. The crisis increased public support for the House of Orange, who were associated with the successful defence of the Republic against the Habsburg Crown during the Eighty Years War. De Witt was butchered by an Orangist militia, and his body torn up by a mob on the flagstones of the Buitenhof, a public square in The Hague. William took the opportunity to seize power as stadtholder, styling himself as the defender of the liberties of the nation. Despite such domestic upheavals, the power and prosperity of the Dutch Republic continued to increase. While other states such as Britain, France, and Spain had been weakened by their own bouts of civil strife, the Dutch Republic had boomed, becoming the centre of a global empire.

If Elizabeth Villiers found the transition to life in a new country challenging, the prospect of becoming first lady of this Republic was frankly overwhelming for Mary. Her fear and anxiety would have undoubtedly been exacerbated by English prejudice against the Dutch. The typical Dutchman of English popular imagination was an uncouth, obese slob, drunk on gin and lighting the next pipe with the smouldering remains of the last. The Dutch practice of building polders to defend and reclaim land from the sea was the source of another commonplace insult: that the Dutch were amphibian creatures, inhabitants of a watery land of infirm structure. The Andrew Marvell poem *The Character of Holland*, which was written for Cromwell in 1651 and republished during subsequent Dutch wars, featured a classic expression of this slur: 'Holland, that scarce deserves the name of land / As but th'off-scouring of the British sand . . . / This indigested vomit of the sea / Fell to the Dutch by just propriety.'[14]

Mary spent her first few months in Holland living in the Palace of Honselaarsdijk, only a short journey from The Hague, which was the location of the Orangist Court and the States General. Honselaarsdyck was an austere grey stone building constructed around a central courtyard and surrounded by a formal garden. It was isolated, with ornamental water separating the garden from the village beyond. The interior of the house was imposing – the upstairs gallery had windows reaching to the ground, pilastered walls, a gilded ceiling and a chimney piece by Rubens of Diana with a hound, a lion and a tiger. In the great gallery, the coving was decorated with groups of figures on balconies, playing music or occupying themselves with domestic tasks.[15] The formality and seclusion of Honselaarsdyck made Mary yearn for the cosy informality of Richmond. Early in her marriage, she suffered a succession of miscarriages, which only intensified her misery. The wives of rulers were under extreme pressure to produce an heir and the distress of a miscarriage must have been made even worse by the weight of expectation.

William's new wife was introduced to the people of The

Hague on 14 December 1677. Church bells rang and guns were fired as they drove towards the city in a gilded coach drawn by six piebald horses, and in the evening, fireworks were let off. The day finished with feasting, and a commemorative medal was struck with a portrait of William on one side and Mary on the other. But despite all the festivities, William of Orange was also already suffering under the strain of the marriage. Not only was he frustrated by his wife's inability to produce an heir, but he quickly realised that their union would not provide him with the emotional and intellectual sustenance he needed. William was a serious man, whose temperament and health did not sit easily with his position as stadtholder. He suffered from chronic attacks of asthma and a hacking cough, which flared up in crowded rooms, especially when they were candlelit as was then the norm. He disliked the pomp and ceremony associated with court life. The 12-year age gap between the couple made conversation difficult and highlighted Mary's immaturity and emotional volatility. This was particularly difficult for William, who seems to have sought out an almost motherly attention from his lovers. It is hardly surprising, therefore, that he was drawn into an extramarital dalliance with a mature, emotionally balanced grown-up: Elizabeth Villiers.

The Villiers sisters had prospered at the Dutch court. The pious and sensitive Anne had married William Bentinck and become a close confidante of Mary. Catherine had become the wife of the Marquis de Puissars, an exiled Huguenot, and was established in a suite of rooms at the Binnenhof, the meeting place for the States General. Elizabeth, meanwhile, had carved out a reputation for herself as a witty conversationalist and practical, clear-headed thinker: William expected the maids of honour to act as unofficial intelligence agents, and with her engaging manner, Elizabeth excelled at picking up nuggets of information from visiting envoys. Already there were complaints that the Villiers family wielded too much influence at court, which intensified, during the visit of the Duke of Monmouth in January 1685, when it became evident that William and Elizabeth were having an affair.

Though the Whigs had been defeated on the issue of exclusion, Monmouth remained an icon of the alternative Protestant succession. He was forced to leave England, and arrived in Brabant in May 1684. Charles immediately asked William not to receive Monmouth or allow him any military honours, but William and Mary liked their cousin, and believed his assurance that he had no ambition to be King of England.[16] The Orange court welcomed him wholeheartedly, throwing lavish entertainments in his honour. Despite his disdain for festivities, William attended several evening parties with his wife and her ladies.

It was during celebrations in The Hague in 1685 that courtiers observed the frisson between William and the maid of honour, whose strabismus had earned her the cruel nickname 'Squinting Betty'. Indeed, the Prince of Orange was so captivated by Betty that he barely noticed the intimacy of his wife's relationship with Monmouth, which was becoming a scandal. William usually did not allow Mary any private visits from either men or women, but the French ambassador reported that the Prince of Orange, 'the most jealous of men living', seemed unperturbed by 'all those airs of gallantry' between Monmouth and Mary.[17] Rumours began to circulate that William was more relaxed than usual because his own attentions were occupied by Elizabeth Villiers.

Mary's suspicions about the nature of her husband's relationship with Elizabeth were encouraged by her nurse Mrs Langford, and her childhood friend Anne Trelawney. William had been staying up late in recent months, claiming to be working at his correspondence; one evening, after pretending to go to bed, Mary waited on the back stairs that led to the apartments of the maids of honour. At two o'clock in the morning, William emerged from the ladies' quarters to be ambushed by his wife. Enraged and shamed by the indignity of being outsmarted, he embarked on a witch-hunt to hold accountable those who had incited Mary. Mrs Langford and Anne Trelawney were soon discovered, and in the course of the investigation it also transpired that Mary's chaplain Dr Covell had been reporting Elizabeth's movements to Bevil Skelton, James II's ambassador at The Hague. When William ordered Covell's letters to be intercepted and deciphered, they turned out to contain stories about William, Mary and Elizabeth.[18] The affair had become the subject of international gossip. For a private, introspective man like William this was mortifying.

Confirmation of her husband's infidelity was one thing, but for Mary to discover that William had been cavorting with Elizabeth, her old childhood friend and maid of honour, was a devastating blow. The girl who had once casually remarked that men were programmed to grow weary of their wives and 'look for misses as soon as they can get them' was now forced to confront the harsh reality of having a husband who had done just that.[19] 'I do not now mourn a dead lover, but a false one,' she wrote to Frances Apsley, adding that she had 'never known sorrow until now.'[20] Burning with the fury of betrayal, Mary ordered Elizabeth back to England.

Elizabeth arrived back home to a hostile reception from her father, who was enraged that she had tarnished her reputation and ruined her marriage prospects. He insisted she return to Holland immediately and beg forgiveness, and Elizabeth had little choice but to comply with his wishes. Back in the Dutch Republic, her first port of call was The Hague, where she implored her sister Anne to take her in. But Anne, appalled by the affair, remained staunchly loyal to Mary and refused to speak to her sister.[21] It was a crushing snub to Elizabeth; she eventually took refuge with her other sister, Catherine de Puissars.[22]

Disgraced, spurned by her family, and forced out of court society, Elizabeth appeared to have little chance of recovering her position. However, events in England would conspire to reverse her fortunes. Charles II died in February 1685, and in April James II was crowned. The cataclysmic events of his reign would place 'Squinting Betty' at the centre of political negotiations that would lead her to wealth, status and, ultimately, Cliveden.

Chapter 2

THE END OF THE AFFAIR

Two months after the coronation of James II, the Duke of Monmouth landed in Lyme Regis in Dorset with the intention of seizing power from the new Catholic monarch. The insurrection failed to rally the necessary public support and swiftly collapsed. Monmouth was beheaded on Tower Hill by the executioner Jack Ketch, who was infamous for his botched jobs, and took five hacks to remove the rebel duke's head from his body. It appeared that there was no popular appetite for regime change in the months after James's coronation. The king had come to the throne at the age of 52, which was elderly by the standards of the time. His two heirs, Anne and Mary, were veritable poster children of Protestantism, and it seemed inevitable that once James's reign had come to an end, England would again be presided over by a Protestant monarch.

But initially there was no reason to suppose that such a transition was imminent. At first it seemed that despite his own religious convictions, James would be a moderate ruler. One of his early acts was to promise the Archbishop of Canterbury that he 'would undertake nothing against the religion which is established by law'. In the first two years of his reign, Catholicism was informally tolerated – people were no longer prosecuted for recusancy (failure to attend Anglican worship) and were allowed to take Mass within their own homes – but in April 1687, this arrangement was formalised in the Declaration of Indulgence, which also abolished religious oaths for those taking government office. For the Church of England, which had long enjoyed protected status, toleration of this kind was seen as an act of aggression. Soon, symbols of Catholic practice – monks and nuns walking in the streets in their habits, bell-ringing for Mass and public processions on high holy days – were once again visible in the streets of England. Catholic officers were able to return to the army and navy, and rumours that formal relations with Rome were to be re-opened gathered pace. The visible Catholicisation of England aroused parliamentary concern and popular hysteria. Fears took hold that James's real ambition was to establish 'himself into a Supremacy and Absoluteness over the Law' so that he could 'subvert the established Religion, and set up Popery'.[1]

The situation was made worse by the news, on 23 December 1687, that the queen was 'with issue'. If the child were a boy he would become heir apparent ahead of Mary or Anne, and would guarantee a Catholic succession. On the day appointed for celebration of the pregnancy, only two of the Oxford colleges rang their bells; libels circulated, alleging that the pregnancy was fabricated, and that someone else's child would be smuggled into the royal household in a bedpan. The king was 'extreamly displeased' to find one such libel lodged behind the mirror in his bedchamber.[2]

James failed to listen to the voices of dissent and reissued the Indulgence, this time requiring clergy to read it out to their congregations. When seven bishops objected, he responded furiously and indicted them in Westminster on charges of seditious libel and diminishing regal authority. On 30 June when the jury returned a verdict of 'not guilty', James did not take heed of the applause inside and outside the courtroom. That night bonfires were lit across London, especially outside the doors of known Catholics, who were later forced to pay for the damage. Anti-Catholic sentiment was reaching boiling point and yet the king, apparently unaware of the potential consequences, refused to modify his policies.

James's heir, a healthy baby boy, was born on 10 June 1688 and later baptised with Roman rites as James Francis Edward Stuart. When news of the birth reached the Dutch Republic, it was met with anger and dismay. A stable Catholic succession in England via James and his son would bypass Mary and her consort William, the erstwhile heirs to the throne. In Amsterdam, crowds threw stones at the English consulate. For William, the notion of an English Catholic state, which would inevitably ally with France, evoked memories of the *rampjaar* when the Republic had nearly been obliterated. He could not risk such a crippling union forming again, especially when he had married Mary partly to militate against a repetition of the Treaty of Dover.

The prospect of an uninterrupted Catholic succession spurred seven noblemen, whom Whig historians would later mythologise as 'The Seven', into action. In an unprecedented move, they invited William of Orange to intervene in England in order to uphold the Church of England against Catholic tyranny. Among the famous 'Seven' who issued the invitation to William was none other than Anna Maria's son, Charles Talbot, the Earl of Shrewsbury.

Charles Talbot's life had taken an unpredictable turn since his rapprochement with his mother Anna Maria in Paris. At the Lincoln's Inn Chapel, on 4 May 1679, he had attended Anglican service, thereby making public his conversion to Protestantism. Although his decision was expedient – the 1678 Test Act required peers to take an oath of loyalty to the Church of England and if Shrewsbury had remained a Catholic he would not have been able to take his seat in the Lords – he handled the transition with characteristic sincerity, discussing the theological implications with his Talbot relatives and with Dr John Tillotson, who later became Archbishop of Canterbury. Talbot embraced his new faith with the fervour of a convert. When James II was crowned and Anglicanism suddenly became an impediment to a military or political career, Talbot stuck resolutely to his new religious convictions. By 1687 he was in contact with William of Orange, and hosting meetings of the opposition to James II at his house in London. A year later, he showed the strength of his principles by mortgaging his estates to raise money for William of Orange, and joining the prince in the Republic.

On 1 November 1688, a Dutch armada comprising 500 ships, 15,000 highly trained troops, and a further 9,000 crew sailed from Hellevoetsluis. William organised the ships in a flotilla 25 deep, 'stretching the whole fleet in a line, from Dover to Calais.'[3] Despite their meticulous planning and sheer force of numbers, the Dutch remained at the mercy of the mercurial winds, and on previous attempts to sail had blown back into harbour; this time, the wind had more Protestant sympathies. On 5 November 1688, William made landfall at Torbay. The banner of his frigate *Den Briel* was emblazoned with the slogan 'For liberty and the Protestant religion', and beneath these words was the motto of the House of Orange: 'I will persevere'.[4]

William's landing may have looked impressive, but his first experience on English soil could not have been less regal. He disembarked at Braxton, a run-down village on the coast of Devon. In his diary, William's secretary Constantijn Huygens described the 'poorly constructed houses, built of that inferior stone which this entire coast and the land adjacent to it are made of'. Huygens passed his first night in England at the Crowned Rose Tavern where he drank a glass of cider, ate 'an exceptionally leathery fricassee of mutton' and slept on a mattress on the floor of a bedroom occupied by Lord Coote. The soldiers in the bar downstairs raged and fought all night.[5] It was a humble introduction to the land his master would soon rule.

Most of William's troops were mercenaries: there were regiments from the Dutch Republic, England, Germany, Switzerland, Sweden and Lapland, as well as 200 black soldiers from the colony of Surinam in South America.[6] As the army marched towards London, its numbers were increased by English volunteers. Well-wishers gathered along the streets shouting 'God bless you', and giving the Orange army fruit and mead.[7] Understanding that his success depended on winning English hearts and minds, William went to great lengths to present himself as a great liberator who had delivered the nation from the clutches of Catholicism. He processed into Exeter riding a white horse, a plume of white feathers on his head, 42 footmen running alongside him. One hundred gentlemen and pages followed, some of them supporting a banner that read 'God and the Protestant religion'. The trappings of his cavalcade were cannily symbolic; the white horse was an allusion to one of John the Apostle's visions recorded in the Book of Revelation: 'I saw, and behold, a white horse: and he that sat on him had a bow; And a crown was given to him, and he went forth conquering, and to conquer.'[8]

The march wasn't all pomp and ceremony. William also took the opportunity to do some sightseeing. As the army progressed from Henley to Windsor, William and Huygens took a slight detour along the south bank of the Thames. The weather was glorious and Huygens recorded seeing 'the world's most beautiful views' along the way.[9] Riding beneath Cliveden, they were enamoured by the same vista that had captured the imagination of the Duke of Buckingham 20 years previously. In the afternoon, William stayed behind in Maidenhead to remove a pebble from the shoe of his horse, and Huygens continued by himself. He ended up lost and riding through water that came up to his horse's belly. 'I could find no one to ask directions,' he recalled in his diary, 'because all the people had gone to the street where His Highness was scheduled to make his procession.'[10]

While William was taking in the English landscape, King James, unprepared, disorientated and lacking in any viable strategy, finally realised that the crown was slipping from his grasp. His support base was growing smaller by the day – even members of his own family and commanders at the head of his troops were defecting. He was devastated when his younger daughter Lady Anne switched her allegiance to the House of Orange, and dumbfounded to learn that his most trusted general, John Churchill, had betrayed him to join the conquering Dutchman. Desperate and disheartened, James resolved to flee the capital, but before he left he demanded that the Great Seal – the stamp used by the king to authorise government business – be brought to him. As he fled by boat from White-hall Palace to Vauxhall, he dropped the Seal into the Thames. It was a final gesture of defiance. Eventually he made an igno-minious escape to France. On 18 December, William entered London in a blaze of glory. Some supporters festooned them-selves in orange ribbons, while others proudly held up oranges on sticks. One onlooker recounted that 'an orange woman without Ludgate gave diverse baskets full of oranges to the Prince's officers and soldiers as they marched by'.[11] The favour-ite fruit of Restoration theatregoers was having a political moment.

In late January a Convention Parliament was called, and arguments put forward on how to settle the future of the king-dom. Radical Whigs argued for a limited monarchy, while Tories favoured either restoring James upon certain terms, or a regency. After lengthy debates the Convention determined that James II had abdicated, and passed a resolution in favour of crowning William and Mary jointly. On 13 February the pair were proclaimed king and queen 'in front of Whitehall with trumpets and drums'.[12] At their coronation, before the crowns were set on their heads, a reading of the Declaration of Rights passed by the Convention took place. So this was to be constitutional monarchy, learning the lessons that Charles I and James II had failed to heed. It was a momentous occasion for the Whigs, the advocates of a balance of power between Crown and Parliament. Charles Talbot was among those who had argued for the co-regency, and was subsequently appointed to William's first privy council, as secretary of state for the southern department.

Elizabeth returned to England in January 1689, at the same time as Mary, and took up residence near Kensington Palace. A tragic event had brought the shamed maid of honour and the petulant princess to a mutual understanding. Shortly before William set sail for England, Elizabeth's sister Anne had become gravely ill. On the day before the landing, her condition deteriorated and Mary was summoned to her deathbed. Severely distressed by the thought of leaving her five children, the youngest of whom was nine years old, Anne asked the princess to step in as guardian. Mary obliged and promised not to leave Anne's side. At about ten o'clock in the evening of 20 November, Anne was barely breathing; her two sisters, her children and many of her husband's relations were keeping vigil in anticipation of the end. For some time now, Anne and Elizabeth had been estranged. Conscious of this, Elizabeth was standing apart from the rest, trying to remain inconspicuous. Then Mary, who had been bending over the dying woman, turned to Elizabeth and told her to come and make peace with Anne. Elizabeth knelt by her bedside and begged forgiveness. Barely had the sisters been reconciled when Anne passed away.[13]

Elizabeth was grateful to Mary for this kind gesture. Mary had matured during her years in the Dutch Republic: her bitterness towards her husband and his mistress had subsided and her feelings were no longer so raw. Once the pair were settled in England, relations between William and Mary were aided by their role as co-regents. Despite a rocky start to the marriage, they established a warm working partnership grounded in mutual respect, understanding and a shared interest in the future of England and the Dutch Republic.

Unfortunately for Mary, her more tolerant disposition did not induce any remorse in William and Elizabeth – rather they took the opportunity to continue their affair with renewed enthusiasm. Soon after the coronation of the new monarchs, the affair was once again the subject of speculation and hearsay. It was rumoured that Sarah Jennings had secured her husband's appointment by cancelling a large gambling debt owed to her by Elizabeth, and pamphlet writers produced scurrilous accounts of the royal tryst.[14]

In the Jacobite pamphlet *A Dialogue between K. W. and Benting*, Elizabeth appears as a foul-mouthed, contemptuous shrew. The dialogue imagines a bawdy interaction between King William, Elizabeth Villiers and Bentinck (whom William ennobled in 1689 as Earl of Portland). It begins with William asking Bentinck to fetch him his mistress, 'the witty slut' Elizabeth Villiers, 'for diversion'. Elizabeth is unwilling to oblige and suggests that Bentinck perform the service himself: 'Go, te[ll] that shameless Buggering, Sodomitical Rascal your King, that I scorn to come near such a Beast; nor ought any Woman to come at him, unless it were to scratch out his

Eyes, or serve him,' she says. The pamphlet was one contribution to a large body of prurient literature about William. The idea that the king slept with men was a commonplace of both pamphlets and general court gossip and Bentinck was frequently cited as a sexual partner. When Swift read much later in a history book that William 'had no vice, but of one sort, in which he was very cautious and secret', he commented in the margin, 'It was of two sorts – male and female – in the former he was neither cautious nor secret.'[15] Although William undoubtedly felt more at ease in the company of men, there is no conclusive evidence that this preference was sexual. The Prince of Orange was a different animal entirely from Charles and James. While the Stuart brothers, Charles in particular, were guided by passion, William was measured and logical. Even his relationship with Elizabeth was grounded in a meeting of the minds and mutual companionship, not simply pleasures of the flesh.

The culture of the Orange court likewise reflected William's restrained, sometimes ascetic personality, a counterpoint to Charles's flamboyance and sexual permissiveness. While it remained common practice to indulge in extramarital affairs, the nature of the man–mistress relationship underwent a seismic shift. Instead of being openly paraded at court like an ornamental decoration, Elizabeth was expected to conduct her relationship with William discreetly, away from public view. This culture trickled down from the top and resulted in other court mistresses maintaining a lower public profile: when the Dutch nobleman Johan van Dorp and the officer Seger van Zoutelande brought their mistresses to dine at Hampton

Court, Huygens recorded it in his diary with a scandalised tone, writing that they 'sat in public with their whores at the general dining table'.[16]

Another factor influencing this cultural shift was the co-regency. Whereas the protests of Charles's wife Catherine of Braganza could be overlooked by courtiers because she was merely queen consort, it was important that Mary's dignity be upheld. A pious and morally anxious figure, Mary was a strong advocate of restraint in every sphere of life. She severely reprimanded her lady-in-waiting Eleanor Franklin for calling her lover 'husband' before their actual marriage, and when Mary Villiers – Elizabeth's sister – gave birth just two months into her marriage to William O'Brien, the queen closely interrogated her.[17] As her reign progressed, Mary became even more committed to promoting what she perceived to be 'moral improvement'. During William's absence in the summer of 1692, she issued proclamations 'for the more reverent observation of the Sabbath and against swearing and profanity', and sent directives to magistrates urging severity against drunkenness.[18] In this environment of moral fastidiousness, it would have been improper and insulting for William to flaunt his mistress.

In 1694, the queen, who had taken great care of her health – she was famed for her daily walks between her palaces at Whitehall and Kensington – caught smallpox. By December that year she was dying. She summoned Archbishop Tenison and with her final breath entreated him to persuade William to end his affair with Elizabeth. The queen died shortly after midnight on 28 December and the bereaved William collapsed at her bedside, begging forgiveness. He resolved to break off all contact with his lover. William Whiston recorded the episode in his memoirs:

> There was a Court Lady, the Lady Villers, with whom it was well known King William had been too familiar. Upon the Queen's Death, the new Archbishop, whether as desired by the Queen before her death, or of his own voluntary Motion, I do not know; took the freedom after his Loss of so excellent a Wife, to represent to him, the great Injury he had done that excellent Wife by his Adultery with the Lady Villers. The King took it well, and did not deny his Crime, but faithfully promised the Archbishop he would have no more to do with her. Which resolution I believe he kept.[19]

An alternative story suggests that Mary left William a letter admonishing him for 'some irregularity in his conduct' and pleading with him for the 'sake of her immortal soul' to part with Elizabeth.[20] No such letter survives, but the story is not entirely implausible. Whatever the specifics, William did indeed break all contact with Elizabeth. But he had no intention of leaving his mistress of fifteen years destitute. He set about fixing a deal that would guarantee her wealth and status beyond her wildest dreams.

Chapter 3

FAVOURS

On 25 April 1695, Elizabeth Villiers became one of the wealthiest women in England. In recognition of 'the favours she had conferred on him', William granted his former lover a 135-acre estate in Knockingen, Ireland, and all the Irish castles, manors and towns that had previously belonged to King James.[1] Ireland had been the last stronghold of the deposed king, but following William's decisive victory in the Battle of the Boyne in July 1690, James had once again fled to the Continent, this time for good; William had marched into Dublin unopposed and arrogated the former king's estates for his own use. Elizabeth's endowment was worth £26,000 per year – around the same amount that the Duke of Buckingham's rent roll had been in the 1660s. At a time when the public purse was severely in debt, for William to dispense these valuable lands to court favourites rather than apply them to the public interest was bound to cause national outrage. Public and Parliament alike were furious, and the grants were derided mercilessly in the popular press.

After the 1691 Treaty of Limerick brought peace to Ireland, William redeployed the English army to the Continent to support the Dutch against their perennially aggressive neigh-bour, the Spanish Netherlands. The decision engendered a serious political divide in William's first ministry, which was a coalition of Whigs and Tories. Both parties had regarded the war in Ireland as a strategic imperative, but while interven-tionist Whigs saw it as a crusade in defence of European liberty, many Tories had reservations about sending troops abroad, advocating a defensive 'blue water' policy that would rely on the strength of the English navy. As the war dragged on, the Tory line gathered support both in Parliament and within William's ministry. The king returned from the 1693 campaign season feeling betrayed by domestic politics, and determined to re-establish his government on a more firmly Whiggish footing.

To facilitate this, he turned to his old friend Charles Talbot, the Earl of Shrewsbury. Shrewsbury's initial stint as secretary of state had been brief – after several failed attempts to return his seals of office, he had eventually managed to resign in June 1690, little more than a year after his appointment. Neverthe-less, he was still influential within the Whig 'Junto' – the group of four nobles who effectively managed the Whig Party in Par-liament. This made him the ideal candidate to replace the Tory secretary of state, the Earl of Nottingham. William was aware that Shrewsbury would be reluctant to return to political office. During a protracted correspondence over his resignation in 1689–90, Shrewsbury had written to the king explaining that he 'never solicited for, but rather accepted [the position of sec-retary of state] with fear and trembling, being all my life sensible to my own inabilities'.[2]

Determined to persuade the timid earl, William unleashed

one of the most powerful weapons in his political arsenal – he asked Elizabeth to intervene. The king relied on Elizabeth's counsel in virtually all areas of his life, habitually consulting her on political matters as well as engaging her services as a shrewd negotiator. The letter she wrote to convince Shrewsbury offers an insight into her powers of persuasion. Elizabeth built a compelling case for Shrewsbury to accept the job, deftly balancing veiled threats with intense flattery. 'I found the king in a temper I wish you could have seen', she said ominously, before laying out William's reasons for wanting Shrewsbury to accept the role. She then switched gear to address him on a more personal level: 'I said I believed you so sincere, that it could be no other but your not being convinced, that he wished you to serve with the esteem that the world has of you. He assured me that he valued anybody as he did you.' One of her main tactics was to express certainty that Shrewsbury would indeed take the role: 'I cannot think you can refuse him. I said I thought it was impossible . . .'; 'I have a great satisfaction with the expectation of your answer, for I am persuaded you cannot fail in your judgement of this.' On top of all these blandishments, she added a dose of emotional blackmail, explaining that if Shrewsbury did not accept the post, the king would never forgive her.[3]

Shrewsbury was deeply affected by Elizabeth's letter, confessing that 'there is a word or two in your letter that makes me tremble when I think of it.' In his initial refusal of the king's offer, the earl praised Elizabeth's 'sincere and generous proceeding in this business' and expressed his admiration for her skilfully woven arguments. 'When you Madame have attempted to persuade, and failed, you may conclude the thing is impossible for better arguments no lady can find nor use them to agreeable manner,' he wrote, 'but the main objection still remains which is my own temper.' In fact, his refusal was probably due to political differences with the king, but either these were resolved, or something in Elizabeth's letter struck a chord, because in March 1694 he accepted the seals of office for a second time.

William was obviously intensely grateful for this sort of assistance. In November 1695, a few months after he had provided her with a source of income, he took the final step to restoring his former mistress to respectability. A match was arranged with George, fifth son of the Scottish Duke and Duchess of Hamilton, soon to be ennobled with the Scottish title of Earl of Orkney. Ten years Elizabeth's junior, George was a serious-minded man of few words – a severe stammer in his youth left him with a lifelong taciturnity, or as Swift put it: 'by reason of hesitation in his speech, [he] wants expression.' Contemporary depictions show a dark-haired, well-built man with a strong, aquiline nose and eyes fixed with a steady gaze. 'He is a well shaped man; is brave,' wrote Swift.[4] As a child he had been placed under the tutelage of his uncle Lord Dunbarton, and by the age of 18 had attained a commission as captain in the Royal Scots, the army's premier infantry regiment. By the mid-1690s George had become a distinguished soldier – he had fought in the Battle of the Boyne, and had been promoted to brigadier general after suffering a wound at the Siege of Namur in 1695. But such bravery failed to make him much money and he was still dependent on his mother's generosity to supplement his income: his mother, Anne, was Duchess of Hamilton in her own right, and remained in possession of the family estates despite the death of her husband.

The marriage was a straightforward trade: Elizabeth could offer George financial stability, while George could provide her with respectability. It was a standard arrangement for a time when the absence of love was not a bar to marriage. Nevertheless, some members of the Hamilton family were appalled by George's decision to marry a woman with Elizabeth's scandalous biography; his sister and mother would never speak to his new wife. Others, such as Sarah Jennings, detected greed in George's decision. 'Lord Orkney is the most covetous wretch in nature,' she wrote to her friend Arthur Maynwaring. 'And I think there does not need to be a greater instance of it than for a man of quality, who has a good post, to marry that woman for mere money.'[5]

Despite the unromantic nature of the deal, Elizabeth did, in fact, find contentment with George. Her new husband was in some ways profoundly familiar. Like William, George was a man of few words, and was uncomfortable with courtly banter. He was more at ease on the Continental battlefield than in the whispering rooms of political power. It was natural, given this disposition and Elizabeth's own increasing discomfort with court society, that the couple would look for a home outside London.

Shortly after their marriage, the couple visited Cliveden. Legal papers show that the Dowager Duchess of Buckingham, Mary Fairfax, was still living at the house as late as the mid-1690s.[6] When the Orkneys came to visit in 1696, Mary was

58 years old and had been widowed for nearly a decade. Having defended the house against the Manfields' attempts to reclaim it after Buckingham's death, she now found that it was far too big for her, and too costly to maintain. It is not clear whether she actually met Elizabeth, but it is tempting to imagine that there was contact, if only for one afternoon, between two generations of the house's mistresses.

Like Buckingham and Anna Maria in their time, Elizabeth was entranced by the unrivalled views of the Thames Valley and the elegant stretch of water meandering towards Windsor Castle. On 28 October 1696, Lord Orkney acquired the deeds to the house and Elizabeth became the next mistress of Cliveden.[7] The house that had once been a monument to Anna Maria's affair, and the melancholy site of Mary's fractured marriage, was now to become Elizabeth Villiers's shelter. After almost 15 years as a 'royal whore', Elizabeth had been provided with a fresh start and a chance to forge a new destiny.

Chapter 4

REBUILDING

By 1700 the girls who had played together in Richmond had grown into powerful women with status and responsibility. Mary had been a much loved and revered monarch, whose death was deeply mourned by her husband as well as the nation; her sister Anne was next in line to the throne and would become queen after William's death. Meanwhile Sarah Jennings had married John Churchill, a brilliant soldier whose later ennoblement would make her the Duchess of Marlborough. Elizabeth had been the closest confidante of the king and had saved herself from notoriety by retreating into a respectable marriage. In the years immediately after the marriage, she gave birth to three daughters – Anne, Frances and Henrietta – in quick succession. Left alone in England with these young children to care for while Orkney was at war, she hoped she might seek solace in the company of Sarah Jennings. Besides their childhood connection, the two women were in similar marital circumstances – from 1702 Orkney held the post of major-general under Churchill's command in Europe. But Elizabeth's warmth towards Sarah was not reciprocated.

On 21 February 1702, William's horse stumbled and the

king broke a collarbone in the fall. On 5 March a pulmonary fever took hold. William collapsed after walking in the gallery of Kensington House, weakened rapidly, and died three days later. In William's final hours, Archbishop Tenison – who had comforted the dying Mary – and William Bentinck remained by his side. Later that day, Anne was proclaimed queen.

Much of Anne's life had been spent on the sidelines, waiting to assume power. Repeated miscarriages and severe gout had taken a dramatic toll on her happiness, health and appearance. By 1704, an acute swelling in her foot left her in constant pain and unable to walk. At a meeting with Anne in Kensington in 1706, the Scottish politician Sir John Clerk 'had occasion to observe the Calamities which attend humane nature even to the greatest dignities of Life'. The queen's face was 'red and spotted' and 'rendered somewhat frightful by her negligent dress, and the foot affected was tied up with a pultis and some nasty bandages'.[1]

Anne was a woman who adored and despised with equal conviction, leaving no room for a middle ground. She particularly disliked Elizabeth on account of her 'insolent' affair with William; she was infatuated with Sarah, and was quick to grant the duchess three court offices, as well as privileges to stay at Windsor Lodge and an income of £6,000. Sarah also became the effective spokesperson of the Whig Party at court. It must have been difficult for Elizabeth to watch her haughty childhood friend prosper from a change in regime while she was left out in the cold.

One of the first Whig causes that Sarah promoted to Anne was the deployment of English troops on the Continent, against France. In 1700 King Carlos II of Spain died, leaving the throne to his nominated successor Philip, Duke of Anjou, grandson to the French king, Louis XIV. If Anjou acceded to the Spanish throne, France and Spain would eventually be united under a single crown, which would also command Spain's vast Mediterranean and South American empire. This was a terrifying prospect for England and Protestantism. As he had done in the 1690s, William once again joined forces with the Dutch Republic and Holy Roman Empire to forge a Grand Alliance, whose aim was to curtail French influence. In 1701 he pledged 40,000 troops to the cause, and, after his death, Sarah encouraged Anne to follow through with William's Whiggish, interventionist policy. On 15 May 1702 war was declared on France by London, Vienna and The Hague.

The protracted war was to have a profound impact on the lives of military wives like Elizabeth and Sarah. In the 18th century, wars were fought seasonally, in campaigns that usually began in spring and ended in late autumn. Soldiers of lower rank were billeted in villages and towns on the Continent, while generals such as Marlborough and Orkney had the opportunity to return to England for the winter. Most of the English campaigns in the War of the Spanish Succession were fought in the Netherlands, and men returning to England typically sailed from the Dutch Republic.

Orkney returned to England whenever he was granted leave but his morale was often low and his health fragile. 'I am strongly weary,' he complained to his brother. 'I am cut up with the scurvy, which breaks out upon my body in great blotches and with so violent aching that you can't believe how uneasy I am.'[2] To make matters worse, Orkney's financial demons, which he had hoped his marriage would exorcise, had returned to haunt him with a vengeance. Parliamentary discontent with the Irish land endowments had not gone away, and in April 1700 William begrudgingly gave his assent to a bill that appropriated for public purposes the Irish estates that he had divided between his favourite courtiers.[3] Elizabeth was summarily stripped of her £26,000 per year income. Orkney, who had married Elizabeth to alleviate his financial woes, now found himself encumbered with a large, dilapidated house and little money to renovate it.

Unlike Buckingham, who was governed by intense emotions, Orkney was an arch-pragmatist. He had planned his expenditure carefully against anticipated income from Ireland, and even then had still been worried about the scale of the works needed at Cliveden. 'I own I always thought it too great for me even when my purse could have sure tended to such a place,' he wrote to his brother after his finances had taken a turn for the worse.[4] Another practical consideration in his decision to buy Cliveden had been its proximity to Taplow Court, which he was also in the process of buying. But Taplow Court also needed renovation, and together the two houses had become a burden: 'now I may say I have got two old Houses upon my back,' Orkney wrote. In the same situation, the Duke of Buckingham would simply have borrowed money but Orkney, who was even more in need of the capital, hated 'the thought of paying Interest'.[5] What started off as a pleasurable project had been transformed by the confiscation of the Irish lands into an incredibly stressful undertaking.

Despite his financial constraints, Orkney continued to develop his architectural plans. The kind of house he imagined was a world away from the pleasure palace created by Buckingham. Orkney wanted to renovate Cliveden into a place that would help him escape from the 'hurry of life', and considered Winde's house, with its three tall storeys, red brick and steep roof, far too imposing. 'The rooms are so high that I don't like it, for there is 3 storeys they tell me 18 foot high besides Garretts,' he complained.[6] That the height of the house should be reduced was one of the few decisions Orkney made with any degree of certainty. Soon he was considering 'several projects' for Cliveden, and was being buffeted by conflicting advice from various architects. 'My head is turned with different opinions,' he wrote, 'for not two men agree, and I have heard the opinion of several of the chief men in England.'[7] Reading through Orkney's fraught correspondence on the subject of the house, it is hard not to concur with the verdict of the Whig writer and politician Arthur Maynwaring, that Orkney, despite having other redeeming qualities, was 'a very weak man' – in a domestic setting, at least.

One of the 'chief men' Orkney consulted was Thomas Archer. Archer matriculated at Trinity College, Oxford, in 1686; five years later, he travelled to Europe, where he became fascinated by baroque architecture. One of his first commissions in England was in 1704, when the Duke of Devonshire asked him to draw up plans for the north range of Chatsworth House. Coincidentally, at the time Orkney approached him, Archer was also in the process of designing Heythrop in Oxfordshire, for the Duke of Shrewsbury. At Cliveden, Archer supported Orkney's desire to reduce the height of the house and suggested building wings at either side of the main block, to be used as offices. Orkney was impressed by this vision but continued to panic about the costs. 'I am more embarrassed, for I find it will cost more than I expected considerably,' he wrote once again to his brother. 'I find what ever way one goes to work a great deal of money must be spent.' Betraying a lack of courage in his convictions, he begged his brother to advise him. 'I declare I don't understand it well,' he wrote.[8]

By the beginning of February 1706 work had finally started on Cliveden. The overall plan was still uncertain but Elizabeth was more than capable of managing the house while Orkney was absent; level-headed, clear-thinking, and supremely organised, she would establish herself as a self-sufficient mistress of Cliveden, able to instruct and rally the men around her far more effectively than her wavering husband.

Chapter 5

'THIS PLACE IS TOO ENGAGING'

Between spring and late autumn each year, Elizabeth was tasked with managing the finances of the building project and making decisions about the works. Sometimes legal or financial business required her to visit the capital, where she often attended Queen Anne. The queen was now constantly in the company of Sarah, Duchess of Marlborough. But Elizabeth was far more comfortable at Cliveden, where she could throw off the shackles of her court finery – with its constricting bodices, long trains and extravagant head dressings – and embrace the short skirts and loose cotton dresses of a country lady.

The Cliveden estate included arable land, a vineyard and a kitchen garden, so there were plenty of seasonal tasks to be completed in the grounds, and the early autumn, just before Orkney returned from the campaign season, was always a particularly busy time. While Orkney was away his younger brother Archibald Hamilton came to stay and wrote to another of the Hamilton brothers, Lord Selkirk, about his and Elizabeth's work overseeing the harvest in the searing heat of the autumn of 1707: 'We are now as busy here getting in our

Harvest . . . and in these parts most of the Corn is all in. Some time ago we had, I think, the hottest weather I ever saw in England.'[1]

Elizabeth sometimes consulted Archibald about plans for the house, and Archibald appears to have spent his time shooting and reading: 'I have already killed & taken above 20 brace of Partridges besides some Pheasants,' he wrote soon after his arrival. 'This dos not hinder me of leisure hours enough that I read in . . . notwithstanding all I can not but say I have a good many thoughtful hours.'[2] The only fault he could find in the place was that it was 'too engaging'. Elizabeth spent her 'leisure hours' playing cards and writing letters. She was a prolific correspondent, although sometimes, on account of her poor spelling and scrawling handwriting, she preferred to dictate. Her letters were warm, lively and peppered with her inimitable wit and self-deprecation. A postscript of a letter Elizabeth wrote to Jonathan Swift in 1712 read: 'When you read this I fancy you will think what does she write to me, I hate a letter as much as my lord Treasurer does a petition.'[3]

Even though there are many examples of Elizabeth's letters, parts of the jigsaw remain missing. Very little of Elizabeth's more personal correspondence, especially that concerning her children, survives. From everything we know about Elizabeth's warm and affectionate nature it seems highly improbable and out of character that she would not write about her children. It is more likely that such letters were destroyed by subsequent generations. There are many known instances of Victorian descendants who, in the course of archiving their grandparents' papers, employed a rigorous policy of sexual segregation: women's letters were discarded, unless they happened to shed light on 'male' spheres such as politics, meaning that a crucial tonality in the voices of women like Elizabeth have, to some extent, been silenced.

Elizabeth's surviving letters reveal that she took much interest in the health of her family and friends, and was well known for her home-made remedies. Writing to Lord Selkirk from Cliveden in July 1708, she passed on her prescription for alleviating his wife's rheumatism and headaches. 'In my opinion [the remedy] will help her if not cure her, if she takes it for weeks,' she wrote earnestly. 'Pray say how my lady Dutchess does.'[4] The previous summer, Archibald had had a fall at Cliveden, sprained his hip and been confined to the house for ten days. Elizabeth, in full maternal mode, nursed him back to health and 'was the only dr he had'. In a letter relaying the news to Archibald's brother, Elizabeth wrote that 'he had been very ill, as to extreme pain . . . he walks about the house, but easily,' reassuringly adding, 'but I don't doubt he will be well in a few days.'[5]

Accidents and illness aside, Elizabeth revelled in her days at Cliveden and dreaded her trips to London, which was no longer the city it had been before she left for the Dutch Republic. The capital's political and social life had been transformed by the events of 1688. Parliament now adhered to a strict timetable, and in order to access both Parliament and the court during the parliamentary season, members of the aristocracy began to reside in London for longer and more regular periods. This sudden influx of wealth and power prompted a flurry of building on the west of the city. Mass urbanisation wiped

out what was left of rural and suburban areas between Piccadilly and Chelsea; coffee houses – popular sites for political
discussion and commercial negotiation – proliferated. But the
squalor of the Restoration city had not been eliminated. In bad
weather even the newly built West End was 'foul with a dirty
puddle to the height of three or four inches', and vehicles and
buildings were encrusted with grime. Smog was an endemic
problem, often reducing visibility to only a few steps and leaving noxious deposits on buildings. One visitor remarked that
St Paul's Cathedral was so caked with soot that it looked like it
was 'built of coal'. Traffic jammed the streets and the vast
quantity of dung generated by all the coach horses elevated
pollution to intolerable levels.[6]

In July 1708, Elizabeth visited the city 'in order to finish the
purchase of Taplow [Court]' as well as to pay her respects to
Queen Anne, who 'honoured me most civilly', and the Duchess
of Marlborough who '[honoured me] wonderfully so'.[7] Despite
this unexpectedly warm reception, the sprawling metropolis
with its mephitic air and filthy streets came as quite a shock to
Elizabeth, who had grown accustomed to the serenity of country life. She 'could not bare' London, and rushed back to
Cliveden before even waiting to receive a letter from her husband in Europe.

The reception at court was perhaps not as genuine as Elizabeth had hoped. By the autumn of that year, she was already
confiding to Arthur Maynwaring that her childhood friend
was – once again – being venomous. Had Sarah decided to
settle her grievance, she could have benefited from Elizabeth's
experience in supervising and managing a large estate, for at

the same time as the Orkneys were working on their plans for Cliveden, Sarah and her husband had embarked on their own ambitious building project at the royal manor of Woodstock. In late January 1705, Queen Anne had announced to the Commons that she intended to give Marlborough both the manor, which encompassed 15,000 acres of land, and 'sufficient money to build a house of a scale commensurate with his triumph'. The triumph she was referring to was the momentous Allied victory of 1704 at the Battle of Blenheim, which would give the palace its name. The architect Sir John Vanbrugh was appointed to design Blenheim Palace, and had soon completed a scale model of his proposed building, an exuberant baroque masterpiece. Plans for the project occupied Marlborough during the 1705 campaign: in July he wrote to Sarah from Loos, giving her instructions for the display of the 'two suites of hangings that were made at Brussels', and suggesting that she use 'one of the marble blocks' for the room 'where you intend your buffet'.[8]

Marlborough clearly discussed the process of remodelling a house with Orkney, who recounted some of his friend's advice in a letter to Lord Selkirk: 'Duke Marlb, bid me get my whole design and do one part this year and so by degrees.' Given that Orkney was working from his own relatively meagre budget as opposed to a generous state fund, this would have been a sensible policy, but Orkney was impatient to start building. 'Truly as for what Housing [I] desire,' he wrote, 'I can't be without any of it immediately.'[9] His urgency is unusual: perhaps he was motivated by a spirit of competition with his military superior.

Elizabeth's diplomatic style was well suited to supervising a building project, but with her confrontational and waspish demeanour Sarah managed to alienate almost everyone working at Woodstock. She squabbled with artist Sir James Thornhill over the price of an allegorical painting he had done on the ceiling of the hall, and her relationship with Vanbrugh ended with her banning him from the grounds in order that he would never see his finished building.

Sarah was a mercurial character whose moods swung pendulously from elation to despair. She had the habit of brooding on her grievances, rather than taking them up with the offending party. Elizabeth had complained about this tendency in 1704, when she appealed to her friend not to 'condemn without leaving room to have exactly the truth known'.[10] Sarah did not modify her behaviour and four years later this trait still frustrated Elizabeth, who felt that Sarah was credulous of rumours and did not give her the opportunity to deny them. After he and Elizabeth had visited St Albans together, Arthur Maynwaring, who was a confidant of both women, reported to Sarah on Elizabeth's frustration, using a code in case anyone else read the letter ('240' was his code for the Duchess of Marlborough herself): 'She [Elizabeth] found 240 was mightily changed towards her of late; that some devil had told lies of her, which every body knew they might do safely, since 240 would never tell another, nor give people an opportunity of clearing themselves.' Elizabeth was convinced that Sarah's anger still, ultimately, stemmed from an old grudge over King William's dismissal of the Duke of Marlborough, which, given Elizabeth's relationship with William, Sarah felt she could have prevented: 'And she did run over a world of old histories even before 39 [Marlborough] was displaced by the king,' Maynwaring continued. 'And told me who did that, and how faithful a part she had always acted to him, however she had been misrepresented.'[11] Despite her perceived mistreatment, Elizabeth professed a serious and enduring affection for her childhood friend. Maynwaring reported that during his conversation with Elizabeth, she 'cried, and protested that she never had so much inclination to serve or oblige anyone in her life; and to convince me of it, she shewed me a letter which she had writ some time ago, with 240's answer; and said that, if every word of that was not true, she must be the greatest fiend on earth.'[12]

Whether Elizabeth's avowals of affection were sincere or driven by her desire to neutralise Sarah as an enemy is debatable. From her dealings with Shrewsbury, we do know that Elizabeth was capable of deploying emotions manipulatively. Maynwaring, for his part, did not appear to have been entirely convinced by Elizabeth's contrition. He couldn't resist adding, to the end of the story about Elizabeth's crying and showing him the letter, a feline little aside that pandered to Sarah's notion of her as promiscuous: 'I can't help telling that she mistook when she thought she had shewn me her letter to 240 [the Duchess of Marlborough], and gave me one she had writ to some man.'[13] A year later, Maynwaring again mentioned Lady Orkney in a way that implies he distrusted her ostensible affection for the duchess. In a passage praising Sarah's ability as a letter writer, he commented that 'Those who wish you the worst will all own that nobody ever had such a knack of letter writing, as they call it; and I never heard any one say more upon that subject than I remember my Lady Orkney did at St. Albans.'[14]

Sarah's grudge against Elizabeth only intensified with time. In her memoirs, she finally confirmed Elizabeth's suspicions about the origins of her rancour, writing that there were 'very good reasons to believe . . . Mrs Villiers did a great deal' to incite William's anger against Marlborough. 'Being a designing ill woman,' she continued, 'there was no doubt but she joined with everybody that were the duke of Marlborough's enemy, at that time, in order to remove him from his employment.' Though Sarah acknowledged that she had 'received Elizabeth with . . . coldness,' she put a wry, hard-headed spin on her conduct, arguing that she had only adopted this stance in order to save Elizabeth 'from giving herself or me any further trouble'. The only subsequent contact she entertained with Elizabeth, she claimed, was when she occasionally sent her an invitation to a party, though even that was 'much against my inclination'. She justified this insincere behaviour with a remarkable piece of misanthropy: 'The world was so very bad,' she wrote, 'that one must pass over such things unless one could have retired . . . out of it.'[15] For all Elizabeth's disagreements with the duchess, her correspondence of the early 1710s would be marked by a similar tone of cynical detachment.

In the middle of November 1709, Maynwaring's allegiance appeared to shift. In a letter to the duchess, he tentatively mooted Betty as a possible replacement as Whig spokesperson at court. 'What think you of resigning your place and interest to my Lady Orkney? Do you think she could be prevailed upon to take it?' he wrote, before protesting his own loyalty to Sarah a little too much. Maynwaring could also see what other Whigs could not – Sarah's aggressive lobbying for the Whigs at court risked alienating the queen. Later that month, Anne's instinctive sympathy for the Tories would be intensified by the decision of her Whig treasurer Godolphin to impeach a Tory clergyman, Henry Sacheverell, for preaching a sermon in which he questioned the right of a subject to resist tyranny – a key tenet of Whig political philosophy. Elizabeth was not only a more effective politician than Sarah, but she was also less tainted by association with the Whig 'Junto' and the Duke of Marlborough.

Maynwaring was not the only one trying to recruit Elizabeth. She had also been corresponding with Robert Harley, a Tory who looked likely to lead the charge on the Whig ministry. Being unassuming, frank and devoid of pretension, Harley exhibited many of the characteristics that most appealed to Elizabeth. In an age where manners were carefully scripted and ceremony strictly adhered to, he enjoyed receiving guests without pomp, and drinking a bottle of claret with them. He had previously held a number of influential posts, including that of Speaker in the Commons, but had been ousted from his positions by Marlborough in 1708, and had been plotting revenge against the Whig leadership ever since. The surge of public sympathy for the Tories following the prosecution of Sacheverell provided Harley with a platform to make his own play for power. He set about persuading Queen Anne to dismiss her most influential Whig ministers and replace them with ministers of his own choosing. A sense of crisis developed when the Bank of England warned that a ministry under the wrong leadership could cause financial collapse – 'all credit would be gone, stock fall, and the bank be ruined' – and the Dutch States General sent envoys opposed to a ministry with Harley at its head.[16] Harley's plans for a new ministry were consequently hatched beneath a veil of secrecy; the Duke of Somerset, a prospective candidate, was summoned to Harley's house in June 1710 in a sedan chair with the curtains drawn to conceal his identity.[17]

Elizabeth was corresponding with Harley throughout this crisis. It is not entirely clear what her role was, but she was certainly giving him advice and may have been involved more deeply, for instance in negotiating potential positions for her husband. With typical humility, she played down the possibility of her having any role at all in Harley's political plan: 'If 'tis known that you see me,' she wrote in July 1710, 'it will be made of more consequence than 'tis possible to be with me who am not of weight enough to give a pretense for our acquaintance.' In the carefully worded letter, Elizabeth maintained a fine balance between showing her support for Harley and protecting herself from scandal should his plan fail. 'I hope you will soon be at Windsor, and then I flatter myself I may have occasion to invite you to Cliveden; but to show you that fear never governs me, if you choose to come by daylight appoint your own hour and I shall be at home, but if I don't hear again in answer to this I shall expect you tomorrow as soon as it is dark with a great deal of satisfaction.'[18] Although there is no record of the ensuing meeting, it is evident from Elizabeth's excited tone how much she enjoyed the frisson of being caught up in political machinations.

Whatever advice Elizabeth gave Harley in their meetings, it appears to have been sound. During the spring and summer of 1710, successive members of the Whig Junto were removed from office by Anne. With Lord Godolphin's dismissal on 10 August, the rout was complete. There was no doubt in Godolphin's mind who was responsible for the fall: he thought Elizabeth was 'extreamly meddling' in affairs of state.[19] The new Tory ministry, with Harley as Chancellor of the Exchequer, immediately sought an end to the wars on the Continent.

Following Harley's appointment, the Duchess of Marlborough's relationship with Queen Anne went rapidly downhill, and when it finally combusted it did so with a vengefulness and intensity characteristic of the duchess. Having been told by the queen to vacate her Whitehall apartments, Sarah stripped the place of everything that wasn't screwed down, and some things that were: doorknobs and fireplaces joined the rest of the apartment's furniture and fittings in the back of a cart bound for the duchess's private residence.

The only significant obstacle to Harley's plan for peace with France was now the Duke of Marlborough himself. In order to topple the general, he would enlist the services of the brilliant Irish satirist Jonathan Swift who would, over the following years, become one of Elizabeth's closest friends.

The political and intellectual competition between Sarah and Elizabeth would have been unthinkable in the courtly environment experienced by Anna Maria, in which women were only able to exercise power informally, and most often through sexual relationships. The cultural change was rooted in the political debate surrounding the Glorious Revolution, which had resulted in the queen and king sharing power. It also had more practical causes: the perpetual state of war in the first 15 years of the 18th century took men out of the country for long periods of time, thrusting women into positions of unusual responsibility. This is exactly what had happened with Elizabeth and Sarah. It was a pattern that would be repeated 200 years later, during the carnage of the First World War, the ramifications of which would be even more profound, both for women in general, and for Cliveden's 20th-century mistress, Nancy Astor.

Chapter 6

'THE WISEST WOMAN
I EVER SAW'

H e has very particular eyes,' Alexander Pope wrote of
Jonathan Swift. 'They are quite azure as the heavens
and there's a very uncommon archness in them.'[1]
Swift had been born in Dublin but moved to England in early
1689, when Ireland stayed loyal to the banished Catholic king,
and the standing of Irish Protestants such as himself suddenly
looked precarious. After James was defeated by William in
Ireland, Swift was free to return to his home country; he
divided the rest of his life between London, where he made an
active contribution to politics, and Dublin, where he entered
the Church and was appointed Dean of St Patrick's Cathedral
in 1713.

By the time of his 1710–13 stay in England, Swift had already
published his first satire *Tale of a Tub* and was in high demand
as a political propagandist. Though he had started out writing
in support of the Whigs, in early 1710, during the Sacheverell
trial, he defected to the Tories. Soon he was attending Robert
Harley's exclusive dinner parties, which were effectively meetings of the cabinet-in-waiting, and in July that year, Harley
took him to Windsor for the first time. It was during one of

these visits that Swift became 'mightily acquainted' with Elizabeth, who, he wrote, 'lives at a fine place, five miles from hence, called Cliffden'.[2]

Swift's greatest contribution to the Tory cause would come a year later in the form of his anti-war pamphlet *The Conduct of the Allies*, in which he identified the true motive of the war as 'the aggrandising of a particular family' – namely the Marlboroughs. 'The duke was to command the army,' wrote Swift, 'and the duchess, by her employments, and the Favour she was possessed of, to be always near her majesty's person; by which the whole Power, at Home and Abroad would be devolved upon that Family.' The Whigs had been supported he said, by profiteers, 'whose Perpetual Harvest is War'. The idea that the war was being prolonged for the power and profit of a small clique became enormously influential. The pamphlet sold 10,000 copies, and on 30 December the Duke of Marlborough was unceremoniously dismissed from all his offices, to be replaced in the field by the Duke of Ormond.

Elizabeth was receptive to the ideas in Swift's pamphlet, but she was more than just an appreciative audience. Beginning in 1710 when the two were introduced through Harley, Elizabeth often hosted Swift at Cliveden. On 9 October 1712, Elizabeth spent from two in the afternoon until eleven at night engrossed in conversation about politics with Swift. He was enchanted by her quicksilver intelligence, describing her as 'the wisest woman I ever saw', 'a woman of quality, who had excellent good sense', and 'a person of as much good natural sense and judgement as I have known'.[3] Swift shared Elizabeth's sense of humour and was an intellectually worthy companion for her. The strength of their kinship lay in a united outlook. Since Queen Anne's accession, Elizabeth had become more circumspect about court life and was bored by its affectations. 'How vain is ambition if these are the ornaments of courts', she wrote of the louche figures who adorned Windsor. 'And upon serious consideration what is valuable but friendship maintained by true worth and how hard is that to be found uninterrupted by circumstances or malice.' Her relationship with her rival Sarah, Duchess of Marlborough, cannot have been far from her mind when she expressed these sentiments. When writing to younger women less jaded by experience, Elizabeth tried to rein in her cynicism. 'If I let myself run as far as my experience can lead me, I shall make you hate the world too early,' she wrote to Lady Harley, Robert's daughter-in-law.[4] Swift shared Elizabeth's suspicions about court life. On 26 April 1713, he noted in his journal, 'I was at court today, and a thousand people gave me joy; so I ran out. I dined with Lady Orkney.'[5]

One of Swift's favourite authors was the cynical French moralist La Rochefoucauld, who had a profoundly unromantic notion of love, arguing that while Venus, the goddess of love, may have presided over romance, real power lay in the hands of her son Cupid, a force of mischief and absurdity. Swift agreed with the importance of Cupid's role. He thought that love, especially men's love of women, could spring from all sorts of irrational feelings, including lust, and was particularly taken by one of Elizabeth's favourite aphorisms: 'in men, desire begets love, and in women, love begets desire'.[6] While there was no doubt a frisson in discussing these matters with Swift, infidelity no longer interested Elizabeth. Instead of seducing the writer, she mothered him, nursing him when he was ill, and insisting he take her remedies: 'Lady Orkney is my physician. It is hiera picra, two spoonfuls, devilish stuff!' he recorded.[7]

As the demand for Swift's company escalated, so did the rivalry between his female companions. Swift's closeness to the Duchess of Hamilton, wife of Orkney's spendthrift older brother, James, is particularly evident from his journal entries following the Duke of Hamilton's death in a duel. Hamilton fought Lord Mohun in Hyde Park on 15 November 1712. He stabbed Mohun first, but 'while the Duke was over him, Mohun, shortening his sword, stabbed him in at the shoulder to the heart.'[8] Hamilton collapsed on his way across the park, and died shortly after. As soon as he heard about the tragedy, Swift rushed to the duchess's side to comfort her: 'She has moved my very soul,' he wrote in his journal. The duel became a public sensation, inspiring prints and ballads and renewing old arguments about duelling, much as Shrewsbury and Buckingham's fight had done over 40 years before. The duchess openly despised Elizabeth and flew into a jealous rage when she learned that Swift was frequently dining with her. She 'could not have patience when people told her I went often to Lady Orkney's', Swift noted with amusement, adding, in case there was any doubt, that 'they hate each other'.[9]

The rivals also made and bought gifts for their mutual friend. In a bid to ingratiate herself, the duchess made Swift a pocketed belt with a special pouch for his snuff box, for him to wear in the summer when it was too hot for waistcoats. Not to be outmanoeuvred, Elizabeth announced that she was giving

Swift 'a writing table of her own contrivance [design], and bed nightgown'.[10] The gifts are indicative of the kind of interests Swift shared with each woman: the duchess's husband had given Swift a pound of snuff that was 'admirable good', and the writing table was a nod to Elizabeth's interest in Swift's work.[11] The nightgown that Betty promised never material-ised. 'Lady Orkney has just sent to invite me to dinner; she has not given me the bednightgown', Swift wrote in disappoint-ment on 12 December.[12] The following month, however, she presented Swift with a far more extravagant token of her affection – an original portrait by Sir Godfrey Kneller. Kneller was the most popular and highly sought-after painter at court, the Lely of his day, so this was more than just a gesture on Elizabeth's part. Swift thought the painting was 'very fine', but inevitably, writing to Stella, his 'perfect Friend' back in Dublin, he felt the need to deliver a backhanded compliment so the extravagant gift did not arouse suspicion: Kneller had 'favoured her squint admirably', he wrote.[13]

According to Swift the majority of men believed it the duty of women 'to be fools in every article except what is merely domestic', and the majority of women agreed, except for those who had 'as little regard for family business as for the improve-ment of their minds'. He vehemently disagreed with this myopic view and Swift often complained that Elizabeth did not do herself justice with her woeful spelling, telling a friend that 'a woman of quality, who had excellent good sense, was formerly my correspondent, but she scrawled and spelt like a Wapping wench.'[14] His criticisms, while caustic, were not intended to offend – they were his eccentric way of redressing the gender imbalance in the field of education. In an unfinished essay *Of the Education of Ladies* he criticised 'the modern way of training up both sexes in ignorance, idleness and vice'. He was committed to changing popular perception that the least valuable qualities in a woman were 'some taste of wit and humour . . . able to read and relish history, books of travels, moral or entertaining discourses'.[15]

Elizabeth's own interest in education is most apparent in her endowment of a school in Ireland. As part of the ongoing English effort to anglicise the Irish middle classes, there had been a tradition of royalty and aristocracy setting up schools in the colony. In 1690, when King William triumphed in the Battle of the Boyne, Mary implored him to uphold this tradition: 'I have been also desired to beg you not to be too quick parting with the confiscated estates,' she wrote, 'but consider whether you will not keep some for public schools to instruct the poor Irish.'[16] William ignored Mary's wishes, but as soon as she was granted the Irish lands five years later, Elizabeth took matters into her own hands by allocating a portion of her estates for the establishment of a school at Midleton, County Cork. The school survived the appropriation of her lands in 1698, and eventually opened its doors in 1717; the original 18th-century buildings are still in use by the school today.

Chapter 7

'I HAVE TIRED MYSELF
WITH FRIGHT'

On the morning of 23 May 1706 in the Flanders countryside, Orkney was preparing to lead his men in an
assault against French troops. The battlefield on
which the Allied and French armies were to engage was dotted
with rustic villages. Orkney was responsible for leading the
attack in the north of the field. In order to reach the French
lines, his men had to cross the marshy valley bottom, and a
stream called the Petite Ghee. As they crossed the stream they
would be vulnerable to attack from the skilled Walloon infantry, who had occupied cottages and made barricades on a ridge
overhead. It was a perilous mission. As soon as Orkney ordered
the advance, the sound of Walloon gunshots filled the air. The
English eventually 'got over with ten or twelve battalions', but
suffered a heavy death toll.[1] In desperation, the bodies and
body parts of dead and dying soldiers were used as 'foundations' to enable the soldiers to cross the marsh and stream.[2] It
was a horrifying spectacle, and the indignity and loss of life
was appalling.

Once the survivors had heaved themselves onto dry land,
Orkney led them in an audacious uphill sprint towards the

French lines. The ferocity of the English assault was such that Orkney's infantry could easily have taken the villages of Offus and Autre-Eglise, and broken through onto the plain beyond. However, concerned that the British cavalry would not be able to support the drastic advance, Marlborough sent orders for Orkney to retreat. Despite his quiet, hesitant nature, Orkney had a reputation for singlemindedness that some-times, amid the unconstrained brutality of battle, flared up into insubordination. Aware that the bloody advance would have left Orkney feeling belligerent, Marlborough dispatched not only ten aides-de-camp, but also his quartermaster, the Earl of Cadogan, to enforce his orders. Reluctantly Orkney withdrew and waited for the Allied forces to break through further south on the battlefield. When they did, he once again advanced, and the English dragoons 'made terrible slaughter of the enemy'.[3] The victory at Flanders was a turning point for the Alliance, which had experienced heavy losses that spring in northern Italy, in Alsace, and along the Rhine. By drawing the French army to the north of the field, Orkney had enabled Marlborough to break through further south. It was the moment that would consolidate Orkney's reputation as a fear-less general.

Two hundred miles away, Elizabeth waited anxiously at Cliveden for news of her husband. 'I have tired myself with fright,' she wrote. Elizabeth's letters on the subject of Orkney at war give a glimpse into the fear that military wives grapple with on a daily basis. Whatever her motivations for marrying Orkney, she had clearly grown to love him. Orkney, for his part, depended greatly on his wife. He admired her fortitude, resourcefulness and emotional resilience. They were a well-matched couple: Orkney, timid and reclusive as he was when not on the battlefield, showed no sign of turning his attentions to another woman, and Elizabeth made it her mission to create for him a nurturing home environment that was run with military precision. Orkney's letters to his brothers show that Elizabeth was constantly in his thoughts during his dangerous military exploits. He often apologised for not having time to write to his brothers, but would say that his wife could always be relied on to relay his news. 'The last letter I wrote to my wife giving her an account of the expedition of our little Army here,' he wrote to Lord Selkirk in August 1708. 'I had not time to write to you but bid her send you my letters which I doubt nothing but she has done.'[4]

Being on the Continent did not stop Orkney from obsessing over Cliveden. His angst about his own beloved property rendered him particularly sensitive to episodes of looting and pillaging – especially when they involved the destruction of beautiful houses. By August 1708, the Alliance had advanced through Flanders to the fortress of Lille, which had been fortified in the previous century by Sébastien Le Prestre de Vauban – the foremost military engineer of his age – and could only be taken with a protracted siege. During the siege of the city, Alliance soldiers made violent raids on the Lille suburbs, which lay outside the city's bastions and broad flooded ditches. In his letter of 1 August, written from a camp at Lens, about 30 miles to the southwest of Lille, Orkney wrote: 'We burnt the faubourgs [suburbs] and about twenty villages in Picardy and brought off some hostages but not of consequence . . .

They tell me they burnt a very fine house that was not yet finished and that the staircase was very fine this really vexes me to think such a thing can be done, I who am a-building.'[5]

The chaos wrought by looting also troubled Marlborough's conscience, although he seemed more concerned with its impact on people than on buildings. 'We sent this morning 3,000 horse to his [the Elector's] chief city of Munich, with orders to burn and destroy all the country around it,' he reported to his wife Sarah during the 1704 spoliation. 'This is so uneasy to my nature that nothing but an absolute necessity could have obliged me to consent to it, for these poor people only suffer for their master's ambition, there having been no war in this country for 60 years. Their towns and villages are so clean that you would be pleased with them.'[6] No doubt Orkney and Marlborough's humanitarian concerns were greater in retrospect than they were during the violent daily struggle of war. In an age where the phenomenon of traumatic combat disorders was not recognised, the burden of such experiences must have weighed heavily on military wives like Sarah and Elizabeth once their husbands returned.

Concerns over how to finance the redesign of Cliveden had already led Orkney to become involved in a number of dubious colonial ventures. Since 1698, he had been the absentee governor of Virginia, the most profitable and populous of England's American possessions. The colony had a lucrative tobacco-farming industry that was largely dependent on the labour of African slaves. Orkney, like most colonial governors, had money invested in his colony, and in 1707 attempted to recover a £1,000 return. However, as was often the case with transatlantic schemes, it was easy to invest, but fiendishly difficult to recover any profit. The same year, the new deputy governor of Virginia, who would have been responsible for tracking down Orkney's money, was captured by pirates on his way from England and was taken to France as a prisoner; it would be 1710 before a new deputy governor arrived in Virginia and it is not clear whether in the meantime Orkney received his thousand pounds.

Orkney had also invested in a much more speculative scheme to establish a Scottish colony in Central America in the region of modern-day Panama.[7] The venture, the Darien scheme, was conceived in the 1680s and aimed to produce a source of colonial wealth for Scotland in order that the country could stay independent from England. The first expedition set sail in 1698 with 1,200 settlers and arrived in October that year. The settler population was soon decimated by fever and food shortages. Before news of the disaster reached Scotland a second expedition had already set sail. The second wave of settlers suffered a similar fate, and the few survivors were forced to return home when a more powerful Spanish flotilla arrived to seize the territory. Investors in the Darien scheme were compensated under the terms of the 1707 Act of Union, which unified England and Scotland, but at most Orkney would have recovered his original investment – he certainly didn't make any money from the ill-fated scheme.[8]

With a meagre military salary and unpromising Atlantic investments, Orkney's last hope of raising money for Cliveden was the generosity of his mother, Anne, Duchess of Hamilton. It is clear from Orkney's correspondence that he received from the duchess an allowance, which he variously referred to as 'what my lady was pleased to give me' and 'my ... provision'.[9] Sound financial management was of particular significance in the Hamilton family, as the Duke and Duchess of Hamilton had gone to great lengths, in the late 17th century, to restore and protect the duchess's inheritance. Anne's father and uncle had contracted enormous debts during the Civil War, and the Hamilton estates had been broken up among Cromwellian commanders. The recovery took considerable effort and sacrifice: the couple only managed to repossess Hamilton Palace, where Orkney was brought up, by selling £7,000-worth of personal possessions. While Orkney was always grateful for whatever his mother sent him, he never asked for money. In part this was because he was loath to show any form of weakness, in part because he was intensely aware of his parents' struggles, and wanted to present himself as a prudent and financially secure successor.

The size and timing of his mother's financial gifts varied: in May 1710, after receiving £1,500 from her, Orkney wrote that 'this I think a blessing since I was not expecting it'.[10] He usually asked for the money to be sent directly to Elizabeth, so she could funnel it into the costly building works at Cliveden. On several occasions the money went straight towards paying off debts, which he had managed to rack up despite his aversion to paying interest: in October 1707 Orkney wrote that 'the chiefe work man was to have 12 hundred of it', and the £1,500 he received in May 1710 went towards a debt of £3,000 that he was obliged to pay by 10 June.[11]

By late 1712, Archer's modifications to Cliveden had been

completed. The hipped roof of Buckingham's house, which the diarist John Loveday described as 'monstrous', had been removed, endowing the new structure with more elegant proportions, and quadrant colonnades linked the main house to its newly built wings.[12] The result was a model of the fashionable neo-Palladian architectural style that took hold in England at the beginning of the 18th century. The classical simplicity of this style was a reaction to ornate baroque architecture, which its detractors associated with French decadence. Most of Archer's work was unmistakably baroque, and his redesign of Cliveden stands out as a rare example of neo-Palladianism within his corpus: maybe he decided that his usual high baroque mode would be inappropriate for a man who had made his name fighting the French. An illustration and description of the Orkneys' house appeared in the 1717 edition of Colen Campbell's *Vitruvius Britannicus*, an influential account of the neo-Palladian movement in England:

> Under the great Court in Front are arched Corridors that communicate from one side of the Offices to the other; a thing of great Use and Conveniency: Here is also a curious Grotto with a great Number of large and spacious Vaults and many other subterraneous Conveniences. The second and third Storeys contain many fine Apartments, magnificently furnished. The second Plate is the chief Front to the North, having the Offices joined to the House by Corridors of the *Ionic* Order, designed by Mr *Archer*. The third Plate is the South Front with the forenamed Terrace, which affords one of the most beautiful Prospects in the Kingdom.[13]

Inside the house, the rooms were panelled with Spanish oak and the landings on the staircase were inlaid with walnut-tree wood. The Orkneys were known for their good taste in art and furniture and visitors came to see the portraits and tapestries that adorned the walls. 'I know no tapestry that excels Lord Orkney's,' Loveday enthused.[14]

In the first decades of the 18th century, interior design became increasingly important. The boom in England's commercial trade, coupled with the declining price of food, meant that a larger chunk of aristocratic household budgets could now be allocated to decorating the inside of houses. Home-spun silks, available from the mercers in Cheapside, Covent Garden and Ludgate Hill, were used as curtains, wall hangings and bed coverings. A steady stream of exotic luxury imports – Chinese porcelain, silks, wallpaper and lacquerware furniture – made their way into stylish halls, closets and bedchambers. By the 1730s a 'Chinese room', decorated with imported paper and screens, porcelain vases on the mantelpiece and blue and white plate lining the walls, was an essential component of an elegant country house. Lightweight patterned Indian chintzes were liberally deployed as furnishing fabrics, providing a breezy contrast to the heavier silks and brocades of the previous century.

Queen Mary had been a great aficionado of what was generically known as 'china', which comprised many types of porcelain from the East, and the blue and white variety from Delft in Holland. This royal craze spawned its own microculture of competitive collecting – aristocratic women vied with each other over who could accumulate the most china, sometimes to comic effect. Daniel Defoe noted with amusement the 'strange degree' of china 'piled upon the Tops of Cabinets, Scrutons, and every chimney-piece'.[15] The Duchess of Somerset was famed for her pair of 'India Cabinets' surmounted by '22 pieces of China', and the 45 pieces of china displayed in her closet over the door and chimneypiece.[16] Elizabeth's time in the Dutch Republic had given her a head start in the craze for acquiring Delft imports, and her own collection of china, which was proudly displayed on the mantelpiece and in the corner cupboards of the great hall, became a popular talking point and inspired many people to journey to Cliveden just for a viewing.

In December 1712, the Orkneys spent Christmas at Cliveden. Previous Christmases had been overshadowed by Orkney's impending return to the European campaigns, but peace was now imminent. In January 1712, following the sensational popularity of Swift's pamphlet *The Conduct of the Allies*, the House of Commons had resolved by a margin of over 100 votes that the Duke of Marlborough's conduct had been 'unwarranted and illegal'. In the same month peace negotiations began in Utrecht, but Harley and Queen Anne had already held secret talks the previous year, leaving Marlborough's successor, the Duke of Ormond, with little power of his own. By August, a ceasefire had been agreed. Orkney would not have to return to the Continent in the spring of 1713.

Determined to make the most of the celebration, Elizabeth threw herself into planning every detail. She decked the entrance of the house with laurels, rosemary, ivy and any greenery that she deemed sufficiently ornamental. In the kitchen the family cooks prepared the traditional festive food – Christmas porridge, a rich broth of dried raisins, plums and spice, livened up by a generous slug of wine; seasonal pies stuffed with chopped meat, currants and beef suet; and plum pudding. On Christmas Day, the Orkney family attended church, then returned to Cliveden to feast on roast beef, with potatoes and turnips. After Christmas dinner, the family retired to the drawing room, drank tea and played cards. Elizabeth had arranged a puppet show to entertain the children. Gifts of rosemary, gingerbread, marzipan and wine were exchanged, while servants were given their annual 'Christmas box'. For Orkney, it was an idyllic end to a decade fraught with worry and warfare, and Elizabeth was relieved that her husband, unlike so many others, had survived the brutal battles in Europe.

The Marlboroughs' Christmas was not so carefree. In June 1712, Treasury payments for the construction project at Blenheim had been curtailed. Given the state of Marlborough's reputation, there was no way that the subsidy could continue. Privately, Queen Anne also linked the termination of funds to Sarah's behaviour on vacating her Whitehall apartments, reasoning that 'she would not build a house for one who had pulled down and gutted hers'.[17] Without the royal allowance, work could not continue. By the end of the year Blenheim was an enormous, abandoned building site, daubed with anti-Marlborough graffiti.[18] After the coronation of Anne's successor, George I, Marlborough would try to restart work on the house from his own purse, but he could not offer the same pay to his craftsmen, and many deserted the project. The duke's early field letters, with their excited talk about how to furnish the house – his Brussels hangings and Sarah's buffet – faded into the realms of fantasy. Meanwhile the Orkneys, within the constraints of their limited budget, nurtured Cliveden from strength to strength.

Chapter 8

THE GREEN REVOLUTION

I n the early 1700s, garden design was a male-dominated arena: aristocrats commissioned plans from landscape designers, or came up with their own designs in consultation with professionals; writers such as Alexander Pope toured their friends' estates, and wrote articles about the principles and aesthetics of gardening. Only flower gardens and kitchen gardens were thought of as female domains, due to their association with domesticity. Sarah, Duchess of Marlborough, considered flowers to be 'a very innocent pleasure' and took pride in her kitchen garden, which she used for vegetables and home remedies.[1] While Elizabeth enjoyed her own kitchen garden and certainly entertained herself by concocting various remedies, unusually she was also actively involved in the redesign of the gardens at Cliveden. As early as 1705, Elizabeth was supervising a workforce of '20 or 30' men at work at Cliveden, 'planting and other things doing'.[2]

It was always Lord Orkney's intention to remake the gardens at Cliveden once he returned from war. 'As for the Ground behind the House, I have a plan how I should turn it,' he wrote from the field in 1706.[3] The parterre, with terraces leading down to the river, had been part of Buckingham's garden, and Orkney wanted to enlarge and redesign the existing structure. The 'plan' he referred to in his letter was the parterre design drawn up for him in 1706 by Henry Wise, gardener to Queen Anne. The predominant style of garden design in early 18th-century England was French, although what was referred to as 'French' design was in fact a composite of French and Italian: from France came long straight avenues, *jets d'eau* and fanciful parterres; from Italy came the commanding position of the house at the centre of the garden, the cascading terraces, strict symmetry and elaborate statuary. All of these Continental design elements had been deployed by Buckingham in the gardens he built at Cliveden. While the outlines of their work were still highly formal, Wise and his partner George London added various Dutch fashions, such as the use of walls and hedges to compartmentalise gardens. However, soon after Orkney returned from his last campaign season, gardening fashion was transformed thanks to an article by Alexander Pope.

'We seem to make it our study to recede from nature,' Pope wrote in the *Guardian*, 'not only in the various tonsure of greens into the most regular and formal shapes, but even in monstrous attempts beyond the reach of the art itself: we run into sculpture, and are yet better pleased to have our trees in the most awkward figure of men and animals, than in the most regular of their own.'[4] The publication of Pope's essay in 1713 would later be seen as a seminal moment in the shift against the bombast and symmetry of French garden design, and a move towards a new homegrown style. With this tide change came the rise of the young Charles Bridgeman. He had worked under Henry Wise on the very formal designs for the gardens at Blenheim, but in the 1710s began to take on commissions of his own. His own designs were characterised by simplified components – less ornate parterres, plain grass lawns and, occasionally, plots of agricultural land – arranged in a way that was intended to mimic a natural landscape. The anti-French implications of this nascent new style of garden resounded with the Whigs, who had championed England's (and subsequently Britain's) involvement in the Continental wars: one of Bridgeman's first commissions was at Stowe in Buckinghamshire, the country seat of Viscount Cobham, a lieutenant general who had served with Orkney in the War of the Spanish Succession.

Orkney's options were suddenly thrown wide open and the political symbolism of his choice made more pronounced than it would have been a few years earlier. However, he did not show any immediate affinity with the new style of garden. The first designs he commissioned on his return to England were from Claude Desgots, chief garden designer to Louis XIV and very much part of the old French school. Desgots produced plans in exactly the formal, symmetrical style that the new school was reacting against: the parterre beds were to be planted in elaborate patterns; the colour scheme was to be based around the yellows and creams and purples of honeysuckle and syringa; and rows of oaks, elms and chestnuts were to be planted down the length of the platform. Orkney eventually discarded Desgots's extravagant and no doubt costly designs. When he remodelled the parterre ten years later, it wasn't according to the Frenchman's plans at all. Instead, his 'quaker parterre' – which he jokingly referred to as such because of its restraint and sobriety – was much more in keeping with the nascent 'English' style.[5] He replaced Desgots's ornate beds with a rectangular grass sward 1,000 feet in length; he forwent Desgots's oaks and chestnuts in favour of a simple border of elms alone; in place of Desgots's yellows and creams and purples, he opted for a muted palette inspired by the surrounding landscape. Equally, the subdivisions and enclosing walls of Wise's designs had been abandoned in order to create a bold view over the edge of the platform and across the valley.

It is tempting to see Orkney's final design as a result of his background: he had been brought up in a Scottish Protestant household, at a time when Protestantism north of the border had a reputation for being particularly severe; he had spent his working life in the austere surroundings of army camps and billets. In fact, his decision was, as ever, not precipitated by the courage of his own convictions, but by the advice of a stronger-minded friend: in this instance, Alexander Pope himself. Pope roamed his friends' country seats every summer, advising them on planting and design. 'I have above a month strolling about in Buckinghamshire and Oxfordshire, from garden to garden,' he recalled.[6] It was under the influence of Pope that Orkney's plans for the garden became simpler and more naturalistic.

Pope was very concerned with the utility of gardens, and satirised estates that were at the same time costly to maintain and unproductive. In his *Epistle to Burlington* he lamented the choices of his contemporaries who failed to make use of their land: 'Who then shall grace, or who improve the Soil / Who plants like Bathurst, or who builds like Boyle / 'Tis Use alone that sanctifies Expence / And Splendor borrows all her rays from Sense.' Pope must have approved of Cliveden's cultivated land and vineyard; as a further nod to practical usage, Orkney's final parterre featured a circle of turf where his horses could be exercised.[7] The friends continued discussing planting plans for years to come, as is seen in Pope's letter from his villa in Twickenham, itself a site for 18th-century horticultural pilgrimage, on 4 October 1736: 'I shall be a good part of ye Winter in London, & there I can have the pleasure of planning and drawing Schemes, as well as of seeing and consulting yours, ag[ain]st the next Planting Season. We may so far enjoy Cliveden, inspite of bad weather; and it may have some merit, in sacrificing to the place before I enjoy it.'[8]

At the same time as he was discussing the parterre with Pope, Orkney also commissioned Charles Bridgeman to build an amphitheatre, cut from the side of the cliff above the Thames. Amphitheatres of this sort were typical of Bridgeman's 'transitional' phase, between the formality of his apprentice work and the fully fledged naturalism of his later style. He had designed a similar one for Claremont. Orkney considered asking Bridgeman to design the whole garden, but once again financial constraints got in the way and the cost of the amphitheatre alone worried him: 'Bridgeman makes difficulties of nothing I told him if I thought it had been the one Half of what I see it will cost I believe I never had done it,' he wrote on 2 October 1723.[9]

In designing his own garden with expert advice rather than hiring a professional to do the whole thing, Orkney was participating in a growing Whig trend. All good Whigs liked to think of themselves as horticultural innovators, believing the garden of a country estate to be a sophisticated canvas upon which to write their own political manifesto – and the earl was no exception. Nor did the Orkneys think themselves above the physical labour of garden work: the family spent time together in the garden, digging and planting. One touching account of Orkney's time in the garden with his daughter Harriet survives. 'I have been with Harriet this fortnight at Cliveden struggling with rain and wind to get my trees planted that I may not lose a year,' Orkney wrote to his brother.[10] It is one of the few records of the Orkneys' interaction with their children.

Orkney also used the garden to celebrate his military achievements. One of his more whimsical plans was to commemorate the Battle of Blenheim by planting trees in a way that resembled the arrangement of armies in the field. The plan was never realised but the victory of 1704 was nevertheless memorialised in the construction of the Blenheim Pavilion. What happened at Cliveden was part of a wider phenomenon. Several other generals from the War of the Spanish Succession also built or developed their own country 'retreats' when they came back to England. While Blenheim Palace is the most famous example, a more revealing one in this instance is Viscount Cobham's house at Stowe, which like Cliveden was not funded by government money, and was a renovation rather than a new build. Two of the architects employed by Cobham, James Gibbs and Giacomo Leoni, were also employed by Orkney at Cliveden, and their designs exemplify the fashion among returning generals for commemorative architecture.

Leoni's design for Cliveden's Blenheim Pavilion, which was built around 1727, is similar to parts of Vanbrugh's stable courtyard at Blenheim Palace; military trophies are carved on the pavilion, and obelisks rest on cannon balls at either end of the parapet. Leoni also designed the Octagon Temple, which stands on the west side of the parterre. Four designs were produced, and Orkney characteristically chose the least ornate, dispensing with roundels, garlands, niches and busts.[11]

The houses built by returning military leaders can be seen as part of a larger aristocratic fashion for using country estates to commemorate one's travels. Many young aristocrats who took the Grand Tour in this period also built or remodelled stately homes on their return to England, and veterans of military and cultural tours alike used their homes to exhibit art and statuary acquired during their time away. Just as Orkney advertised his military achievements with a tapestry of the Battle of Blenheim in the main hall at Cliveden (it still hangs in the great hall at the house today), so Sir Francis Dashwood, remodelling West Wycombe Park, celebrated his own travels and education in the entrance hall, which he decorated 'as a Classical atrium, giving it a trompe l'œil ceiling . . . modelled on one in the southern adyton (unlit chamber) at the Temple of Bel (the Levantine god Ba'al) at Palmyra, Syria.'[12] Park buildings such as pavilions and temples offered opportunities to both sorts of builder: Orkney's Blenheim Pavilion and Octagon Temple had their equivalent, at West Wycombe, in various neo-antique features: a reconstruction of the Athenian Tower of the Winds, a Music Temple, and even a milestone copied from that in the Roman Forum.

In the century after Orkney remodelled the gardens at Cliveden, a distinctively 'English' style of gardens would arise out of the naturalistic austerity that marked Charles Bridgeman's transitional work. Under the guidance of Lancelot 'Capability' Brown, English gardens removed the corset that man had imposed on nature and allowed the countryside to sweep in. Whole artificial landscapes – including follies and carefully contrived 'wildernesses' – appeared across the grounds of country houses. The English garden would be exported internationally as *le jardin anglais, der englische Garten, il giardino inglese*. 'English' landscape gardens, and their political implications, would be imitated by German princes who wanted to state their independence from the Holy Roman Empire, and later became popular among Italians who wished to express their opposition to Napoleon's imperial ambitions.

By bringing together utility and ornament, the practical and the splendid, Orkney stamped his unique mark on Cliveden's grounds. A man of few words, he managed to express himself most eloquently – his need for solace in a rural setting, his appreciation of design and even his martial prowess – in the gardens of his country estate. Today the spirit of Elizabeth's husband is evoked by the unswerving terrace walks above the river, and the restrained elegance of the planting, set against the natural drama of the Thames.

Chapter 9

'IT WAS AS IF HIS MAJESTY HAD LIVED HERE'

In the summer of 1717, Elizabeth was expecting the most dignified of guests. Queen Anne had died on Sunday 1 August 1714 and at four o'clock that afternoon George Ludwig of Hanover had been proclaimed king as George I. There were many individuals who, in terms of blood, had a better right to the throne than George, but these potential heirs were Catholic and their claims had been pointedly overlooked in the Act of Settlement, which was passed by Parliament in 1701. As Anne's health went into inexorable decline, the army steeled itself for Catholic opposition to George's accession, and following the announcement of the queen's death, the nation held its breath. Emergency protocol was initiated; the Privy Council called out the militia, put a fleet on alert and placed the States General on standby to send military aid. Ports were closed and Catholics' weapons were confiscated. But such fears proved unfounded and George's accession went ahead without a glitch.

George I brought Elizabeth and Orkney further into the royal sanctum. The Whigs had been firm supporters of the Hanoverian accession and it was to be expected that they dominate his first ministry. As a newly appointed Gentleman of the Bedchamber, Orkney was in prime position to befriend the new king, whose insistence on loyalty and efficiency, which alienated other courtiers, endeared him to the former military commander. At the beginning of his reign, the king conducted a private lifestyle, dining alone and seldom participating in social events. This was made more noticeable by the lavish life-style of his son, George, Prince of Wales. From the summer of 1717, in an effort to make the king more popular and challenge the social prominence of the Prince of Wales, George I's min-isters advised him to up the ante on his social schedule. When the royal family went to Hampton Court for the summer in July 1717, George dined in public every day with 15 or more guests, chosen by Orkney.[1]

Soon Elizabeth was also involved in orchestrating the king's social crusade. In November 1718, a newsletter reported: 'The Lady Orkney did all the honours of the Court at Hampton Court, and now at St. James, preparing the tables, making the parties.'[2] Elizabeth became the quintessential court hostess, supervising a dizzying array of amusements. She planned nightly dinners for 50 or 60 guests, as well as drawing up guest lists for the twice-weekly balls. So much claret was spilt on the carpet at one such event that it was deemed necessary to pro-vide a protective cloth for future events, to prevent further damage.[3] The misanthropy of Elizabeth's earlier days had given way to a new-found enthusiasm for society. Towards the end of her life, Elizabeth was evidently coming to terms with the reality that political power and social influence went hand in hand.

In 1724 George stayed with the Orkneys at Cliveden. The visit had been planned for some time; Orkney had written of it six months previously. On 7 September the *London Gazette* recorded:

> The King dined at the Earl of Orkney's at Cliveden about seven miles from hence [Windsor], attended by divers of the Nobility and Gentry. At His return hither in the evening, this Town was all illuminated, and he was received here with loud acclamations of joy; as he had been in the several villages through which he passed.

Elizabeth was thrilled with the seamless execution of both royal visits, writing that she was 'told that things were in order, that it was as if his majesty had lived here'.[4]

The appeal of Cliveden and the Orkneys carried through to the next generation of royals. In 1727, George II succeeded his father, and on 30 July 1729, he came to stay with his wife Queen Caroline and their son Frederick, Prince of Wales. The *Gloucester Journal* for 5 August 1729 reported: 'Her majesty, the Prince of Wales, the Princess Royal and the Duke, were splendidly entertained at Dinner by the Earl of Orkney at his seat at Cliveden near Slough in Buckinghamshire.' Caroline was well-read, charming and witty, and her skill at playing cards matched Elizabeth's; she 'was never half an hour without saying something shocking to somebody and generally very improper discourse for a public room.'[5] In other words, she was very much Elizabeth's sort of woman.

When strolling around the gardens at Cliveden on a normal

day, Elizabeth wore a simple petticoat-style gown with a frontfastening bodice and white lace cuffs. She tied a white linen kerchief around her neck, and covered her head with a little straw hat. For such an important occasion as a royal visit, however, she was obliged to look the part. She dusted off her silk mantua, which she had bought for an inordinate sum, much to the consternation of her parsimonious husband. She was not at all comfortable in its constricting bodice and found the richly embroidered pagoda sleeves, with their voluminous pleated cuffs, cumbersome in the extreme. The ritual of heaving oneself into a formal gown was tedious, time-consuming and as far as Elizabeth was concerned, utterly pointless. Elizabeth's figure had continued to swell over the years and as a result cinching her waist into the buckled belt of the girdle was unmitigated torture. The presence of royalty also necessitated more sophisticated headgear, in the form of a cumbersome, ornamental hat festooned with feathers which obscured her vision. She longed for the comfort of her everyday uniform, in which she could actually breathe. Elizabeth may have become more sociable with age but her profound disdain for the frivolities of fashion had endured.

Unlike Anna Maria, who had performed her levee with sensual pleasure, Elizabeth eschewed the preposterous ceremony. The notion of starting each day by gossiping with a stream of visitors while wearing nothing but a negligee appalled and enervated her. She also had little patience for the intricacies of hairstyles.

Despite feeling suffocated in her formal attire, Elizabeth was determined to make Queen Caroline's visit a triumph. She

Anna Maria Talbot (née Brudenell), Countess of Shrewsbury,
painted by Sir Peter Lely.

George Villiers, 2nd Duke of Buckingham, whose appetite for pleasure was, according to the poet Samuel Butler, 'diseased and crazy'.

Buckingham's long-suffering wife, the 'spiritless but amiable' Mary Fairfax.

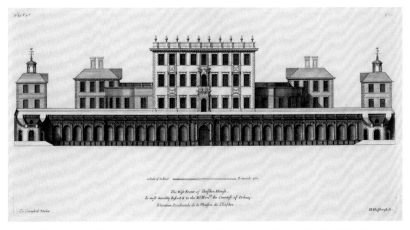

Designs for Cliveden, as they appeared in Colen Campbell's popular handbook of neo-Palladian architecture, *Vitruvius Britannicus*.

During his youth, the 2nd duke of Buckingham spent much time in Italy; guests later commented on the similarities between Cliveden's southern façade and the Villa Aldobrandini in Frascati, just east of Rome.

Elizabeth, Countess of Orkney, painted by Sir Godfrey Kneller.

William III, who conducted a 15-year affair with Elizabeth Villiers, before arranging a match that would restore her to respectability and lead her to Cliveden.

Queen Mary II's dying wish was that her husband terminate his long affair with Elizabeth Villiers.

Princess Augusta of Saxe-Gotha, painted by Jean-Baptiste van Loo.

Frederick's mother, the formidable Queen Caroline, born Caroline of Ansbach (1683–1737).

George II, who outlived his heir Frederick by several years, and was succeeded by his grandson George III.

Augusta, Princess of Wales, depicted with her children. Her husband Frederick, who was dead by the time the group portrait was painted, stands watch over his family from a frame on the wall.

had been planning the stay for weeks and had considered every detail. She had even laid out a special arrangement of stools for the royal family, because she knew that the princess royal (Anne, the king's eldest daughter) liked to sit as she would if she were playing the card game quadrille. This did not go down well with Lord Grantham, Chamberlain to the Queen, who ordered that the seating should be put away as there was to be no distinction between the ladies and the princesses. Grantham was also dissatisfied with the presentation of the table, and demanded it be layered with two thick tablecloths.[6] The food presented further problems. The second course of sweetbreads and egg fricassees was brought out prematurely and left by the fire, so by the time the queen was ready to eat, it did not look 'well dressed'.[7]

Elizabeth was mortified by this succession of faux pas and was convinced the stay had been an unmitigated disaster. But Caroline and George did not seem perturbed and greatly enjoyed the evening, returning home at four the next morning.[8] Elizabeth's letter to Mrs Howard, one of the queen's ladies-in-waiting, shows not only her changing attitude to royalty and royal ceremony, but her astute level of self-awareness regarding this transformation. Whereas previously she had 'turned my mind in a philosophical way of having done with the world', she could now see that she had 'deceived' herself, and felt involved with – and even sentimental about – court life. 'We all agreed her majesty must be admired; and, if I may use the term, it was impossible to see her and not to love her,' she enthused. 'For I am vexed and pleased with the honours I have received.'[9]

There were a number of factors that might have influenced Elizabeth's new-found sentimentality. It may have been that she had mellowed with age and was now acting with the self-assuredness of an older woman; it may have been that the Duchess of Marlborough's retreat from court life had given Elizabeth the confidence to move in court circles again; perhaps it was simply that she admired Queen Caroline on a personal level. Regardless, it could not have happened without her Thames-side estate. Cliveden had been the vehicle in which Elizabeth could manage her progress from royal whore, spurned and vilified by one queen, to society hostess, entertaining another.

Chapter 10

'THE SHOCK IS GREATER THAN I EVER HAD IN MY LIFE'

I n an era where the life expectancy for an aristocrat was around 60 years, Elizabeth remained robust and active well into her seventies.[1] Controversial to the last, she continued to provoke reverence and ridicule. Lady Mary Wortley watched Elizabeth heaving herself with considerable effort into the coronation of George II, and described a 'mixture of fat and wrinkles' with a 'considerable pair of bubbys a good deal withered, a great belly that preceded her'.[2] However, even in old age, Elizabeth retained her ability to communicate disdain in 'the inimitable roll of her eyes'. We can imagine her with 'grey hair, which by good fortune stood directly upright', sitting across from Wortley at Westminster Abbey as they listened to the first performance of *Zadok the Priest*, an anthem composed for the coronation by another Hanoverian immigrant, George Frederick Handel.

The twilight years of Elizabeth's life were marred by heartache. Five years after the coronation, her daughter Harriet, who had once planted trees with Orkney at Cliveden, died of a 'Mortification in her Bowels'. 'Our afflictions are great,' Elizabeth wrote to her bereaved son-in-law John Boyle, 5th Earl of

Cork, 'we mourn for ourselves, in this terrible loss.' She concluded, in an outpouring of grief and maternal pride, that 'though human she was so near perfection'.[3] Elizabeth was overwhelmed by the injustice of her daughter's untimely death and eloquently expressed the plight of a parent having to deal with the loss of a child. 'My age & youth made me hope I should not have had this great conflict between nature and reason,' she wrote.[4] Lord Orkney too was devastated by the loss. In a letter fraught with emotion, he described Harriet as 'so extraordinary a mother, valuable to all that knew her . . . this shock is greater than ever I had in my life.'[5]

Elizabeth's one consolation was her belief in a Christian heaven. 'We believe the immortality of the soul, then she is happy, and we mourn for ourselves, in this terrible loss we should consider that the delay of that bliss she is in, would have been a delay to the felicity that she now enjoys.'

Very little correspondence survives about Elizabeth as a mother or grandmother, but the letters surrounding the death of Harriet and the descriptions of contemporaries give the impression of a caring, nurturing mother, devoted to her family. Even Sarah, Duchess of Marlborough, temporarily abandoned her critical tone to declare that she 'has bred up her children very well'.[6] After Harriet's death, Orkney beseeched her widower to 'let somebody let us know from time to time how you are in your health [and] your little ones are all in perfect health'.[7] Elizabeth meanwhile stressed that she still considered John to be close family, beginning her letter with 'My Lord, and dear son, for I must ever call you by that tender name.'

Harriet's death took a serious toll on Elizabeth, and when

her health began to falter, she was taken to the Orkneys' London residence, located in Albemarle Street, which was so often blocked with carriages that it would later become the first one-way street in the capital. On 19 April 1733 Elizabeth Villiers, who hated the noise and filth of the metropolis, died in a house on its most congested thoroughfare. The 'wisest woman' Jonathan Swift ever met outlived her daughter by a painful seven months. Six days later, she was buried with minimal fuss at Taplow. It was an understated end to a remarkable life filled with scandal, political intrigue, romance and maternal love. Elizabeth had turned the rules of society on their head. She was not a beauty, but she captured the heart of a king; she was an abominable speller, yet captivated the foremost minds of her day; and she was a royal whore who had come to host royalty on her own terms.

Under Elizabeth's guidance, Cliveden had become a family home as much as an informal political salon. She brought a sophisticated and worldly touch to the house, setting the tone for centuries to come. The Earl of Orkney outlived his wife by four years. Three weeks before his death he was appointed England's first Field Marshal of 'all his majesties forces'. He was buried in the family vault in the grounds of Taplow Court in a simple funeral without pomp or ceremony.

PART III
AUGUSTA
1719-1772

Chapter 1

'RULE, BRITANNIA!'

CLIVEDEN, 1 AUGUST 1740

Augusta, Princess of Wales, the new chatelaine of Cliveden, made her way with languorous grace along a pathway through the garden. Two hundred pairs of eyes fixed on the 20-year-old princess and her husband, Frederick, Prince of Wales, as they took their place in the theatre that had been built for the evening's entertainments. As the sun went down, 100 lanterns were lit to illuminate the stage, and 50 uniformed boys, their heads covered with grenadier caps, appeared with large wax torches; the white candles were brilliant set against the cerulean blue of their costumes.[1] Most striking of all was the princess herself – her golden hair, tightly curled and swept away from her face, was adorned with a sculptural arrangement of white feathers; her pale primrose silk gown was decorated with whimsical floral embroidery.

The air was thick with the heady scent of roses, honeysuckle and jasmine, and an even more potent aura of anticipation. This evening was the premiere of *Alfred*, a masque with a score by the popular composer Thomas Arne and libretto by the Scottish dramatists David Mallet and James Thomson. The day of the performance had been chosen carefully: the first of

August was both the third birthday of the royal couple's eldest child, Augusta, and the anniversary of the accession of George I, Frederick's beloved grandfather.

The masque was not just an opportunity for the heir to the throne and his wife to showcase their Thames-side estate; it was an event freighted with political and social significance. Notably absent were the prince's parents, King George II and Queen Caroline, with whom Frederick had officially severed ties three years previously. The very public antipathy between the two generations of Hanoverians had spawned two rival courts; those in attendance at Cliveden had pledged their allegiance to Frederick. Around the royal couple was gathered a collection of the nation's most influential political figures: Sir Richard Temple, Viscount Cobham, the Grenville brothers and the future prime minister William Pitt, all swathed in their ceremonial finery.[2]

It is likely that the audience also included the writer and politician Henry St John, Viscount Bolingbroke, who was something of a political mentor to the Prince of Wales, and a leading theorist of the opposition parliamentary group with which the prince was deeply involved. Two years before, in 1738, Bolingbroke had published his polemic *The Idea of a Patriot King*, in which he envisioned a monarch who would end the tyranny and oppression that, according to the opposition, had taken hold during the reign of George II. He dedicated the work to Frederick. Bolingbroke had also written an accompanying history of medieval Britain, in which he portrayed the Anglo-Saxon King Alfred – the titular character of Arne's masque – as the embodiment of freedom and liberty.

Alfred, Bolingbroke claimed, was responsible for the creation of a strong navy, the defeat of the Vikings, and the establishment of trial by jury: as such, he was an icon for 'Free Britons'.

Frederick strongly identified with Alfred, or at least with Bolingbroke's version of him, and believed it was his mission as a king-in-waiting to become the 18th century's own 'Guardian of Liberty'. His rival court at Cliveden styled itself as a dynamic and patriotic counterpoint to the autocratic, old-fashioned style of George II. The king was a divisive character, quick to anger and obsessed with protocol. Though his reign saw both growing stability at home and the expansion of British interests abroad, George was widely regarded as neglectful of his people and little more than the puppet of his ministers.

Frederick, by contrast, expended a significant amount of energy portraying himself as a monarch who would rule as well as reign. *Alfred* was, in effect, his manifesto, an evocative mission statement for kingship, set to music. It was intended to reinforce his image as a custodian of English liberty.[3] The premiere of the masque at Frederick's Cliveden 'court' came at a crucial moment for the prince and his allies. The need for unity among the opposition was particularly pressing in August 1740 because of the deaths of two of their number, William Wyndham and the Earl of Marchmont.[4] With elections looming the following year, the performance of *Alfred* was the ideal opportunity to powerfully restate the opposition's core political tenets – a reduced army; a strong navy; a commitment to trade; and the preservation of English liberty, maintained by a balanced constitution of king, Lords and Commons.

The masque form, with its dazzling combination of poetry, music, dancing, acting, allegory and audience participation, was perfect for the prince's purposes in *Alfred*, which needed to be a spectacle befitting a king-in-waiting and his assembled court. The calibre of the entertainers, who were all brought in from the Drury Lane Theatre, reflected the importance of the occasion. William Milward, a popular actor on the London theatre scene, played Alfred, while the noted actress Kitty Clive took the part of the shepherdess Emma. The famed tenor Thomas Salway would have the onerous responsibility of singing the closing number, the soon-to-be-famous 'Rule, Britannia!'[5] For maximum impact Frederick had positioned the stage within Bridgeman's amphitheatre so that his guests could take full advantage of the views of the river while still remaining close to the comforts of the house. The Thames was the cradle of British naval strength and, as a backdrop to the masque, it became a shimmering prop in what Frederick hoped would be a public-relations coup.

At the time of the performance, Frederick and Augusta had been spending summers at Cliveden for nearly three years. The prince had first visited the property in 1729 as a guest of the Orkneys and was immediately struck by the splendour of the place.[6] His other residence at Kew was only a mile away from the royal palace at Richmond, but Cliveden perfectly suited Frederick's desire to live at a greater distance from his parents while remaining close to the centres of royal power. After the Earl of Orkney's death in January 1737, the house had passed to Elizabeth and Orkney's elder surviving daughter, Anne, whose husband, William O'Brien, 4th Earl of

Inchiquin, was an ardent supporter and close friend of Frederick's. It was quickly agreed that Anne and William would reside primarily at Taplow Court and lease Cliveden to the prince. Quarterly rent payments of £150 began in 1738 but, according to reports in the London press and household bills, the couple was already establishing their household at Cliveden in 1737.[7] For the next 14 years, they would use Cliveden as their summer residence.

It is easy to imagine the pride both Anna Maria and Elizabeth, those two former chatelaines, would have felt knowing that their country estate was finally in the hands of royalty. Given Elizabeth's disdain for courtly formality, she would not only have been impressed by the flamboyance of the production, but also highly amused by the more raucous elements of the evening: according to Jemima, Marchioness Grey, 'all the Common People were admitted, and were with most of the Performers made exceedingly Drunk.'[8]

Arne's masque followed King Alfred in his mighty conflict with nefarious foreign enemies. After losing a crucial battle, Alfred takes refuge on an island off the Somerset coast. During his exile, his resolve begins to falter, but his morale is roused by the spirits of three of his most glorious descendants, who are conjured up for him by a clairvoyant hermit. These royal phantoms – Edward, the Black Prince; Elizabeth I; and William III – rally Alfred and inspire him with a sense of his country's destiny. Re-energised and gripped by patriotic fervour, Alfred vows to protect his country from foreign oppressors. The narrative of the masque was absurdly fantastical but its message abundantly clear: England was in need of a new patriot king.

At the end of the drama, Salway took centre stage and performed the final song, climbing towards the now-famous chorus:

> When Britain first, at heaven's command,
> Arose from out the azure main,
> This was the charter of the land,
> And guardian angels sang this strain:
> 'Rule, Britannia! Britannia, rule the waves!
> Britons never will be slaves.'

'Rule Britannia!' was an instant hit and soon became popular as a song independent from the rest of the masque. It was performed as a stand-alone piece in theatrical entertainments and quoted by Handel in his 1746 *Occasional Oratorio*. Wagner would later claim that the first eight notes embodied the whole character of the British nation.[9] In the Victorian period, the lyric of the chorus came to be sung with an 's' on the end of 'rule', turning the song into a celebration of empire ('Britannia Rules the Waves!') rather than an exhortation to naval strength, as was intended by the original imperative, 'rule'.

In the context of the later success of 'Rule Britannia!' it is easy to forget that in 1740 the song had a very specific political relevance. In October 1739, Britain had declared war on Spain, in what became known as the War of Jenkins' Ear, named after the incident that triggered it – the captain of a Spanish patrol boat cutting off the ear of the British captain Robert Jenkins. The Country Party – as Frederick's loose opposition alliance of Tories and disaffected Whigs was commonly known, the name appropriated from the Duke of Bucking-ham's era as a claim to represent the interests of the whole nation and not just those of the metropolitan court – was in favour of declaring war on Spain in retaliation for this act of aggression. The defence of Britain by sea was a core policy of the opposition, who infinitely preferred a strong navy to George II's large standing army because the latter was so closely associated with repression and tyranny.

The war with Spain, which would be predominately a naval war fought in the colonies, sat well with this cause. It also provided yet another potent connection to King Alfred, who had become particularly associated with sea power, as he was thought, not without foundation, to have been the first native king to build a significant war fleet. At the end of the masque, after the famous finale, the oracular hermit both encourages and foresees British naval dominion:

> I see thy commerce, Britain, grasp the world,
> All nations serve thee, every foreign flood,
> Subjected, pays its tribute to the Thames . . .
> Britons proceed, the subject deep command,
> Awe with your navies every hostile land:
> In vain their threats, their armies all in vain,
> They rule the balanc'd world who rule the main.

The staging of *Alfred* at Frederick's Cliveden court thus made a powerful political statement. But the six hours of entertainment did not end there. Frederick had invited the noted Venetian ballerina Barbara Campanini (known by the theatre-going public as 'Barbarina' or 'Barbarini') to perform.[10] In 1739 she had made a great impression in Paris with an original, comic style of mime that drew on her Italian training. 'She jumps very high, has big legs, yet dances with precision. Although lanky, she does not lack grace . . . It is thought that her dance is inimitable,' observed the Marquis d'Argenson, who went to see her perform in Paris.[11] At Cliveden, seating was erected at the end of an illuminated path along which Barbarina cartwheeled, jumped and pirouetted with preternatural finesse; the Prince of Wales, Augusta, and their children sat on chairs at the front of the audience.[12]

The proceedings concluded with a spectacular display of fireworks, which were designed by the experimental scientist John Theophilus Desaguliers, and pronounced by the newspapers to be 'equal in their kind to the rest of the Performance'.[13] Desaguliers had long been a favourite in the royal household: he had been commissioned to perform several scientific demonstrations at Hampton Court by George I and had dedicated his book, *A Course of Experimental Philosophy* (1734), to Frederick, who also employed him as a chaplain.[14] That a scientist, who was at the cutting edge of 18th-century thinking, would be employed to design a fireworks display is testament to the expansiveness of contemporary scientific curiosity; the pyrotechnics were a visual manifestation of scientific knowledge and national pride.

Frederick and Augusta were so delighted that they requested that the whole entertainment be performed again the following night. This time, the weather was not so forgiving and, halfway through, the heavens opened. Undeterred, the couple insisted that the production be relocated to the house. The guests were ushered inside and Arne's band followed, taking up their trumpets, fiddles, oboes and brass, and trooping indoors with as much haste as possible. Though the audience was no longer able to enjoy the sweet-smelling theatre, they could still admire the view of the Thames, now shrouded in rain, from the back of the house. 'Rule, Britannia!' was sung once again and this time everybody joined in for the chorus.[15]

The newspapers greedily took the bait. 'The whole was conducted with the utmost Magnificence and Decorum,' raved the *General Evening Post* on 2 August; the *London Daily Post* and *London Evening Post* devoted many column inches to effusive descriptions of all the entertainments. *Alfred* had been an indisputable success. Frederick had showcased himself to glorious effect as a worthy future king, while Augusta had radiated the charm of a natural born queen. Cliveden had provided the perfect setting to consolidate the credentials of Britain's golden couple.

Chapter 2

RISE

Augusta's life had unfolded like an 18th-century version of the Cinderella story. She was born in 1719 to Magdalena Augusta of Anhalt-Zerbst and Friedrich II, ruler of the ducal court of Saxe-Gotha in Thuringia, Germany. Though the palace in which she grew up, the baroque Schloss Friedenstein, was undoubtedly grand, her father's court was of negligible importance in European politics, and as her parents' 13th child, her chances of marrying into a more powerful family were remote. Her eldest sister wed Johann Adolf, duke of the neighbouring Saxe-Weissenfels, and the best Augusta could have realistically hoped for was a similar match to a local ruler. In 1732, after the death of her father, she moved with her mother to a new suburban palace, where she lived a comfortable but unremarkable life.

Providence intervened in 1735 when George II, on a trip to his nearby electorate, Hanover, asked to meet with Augusta. He was looking for a suitable match for his wayward son, the heir to the British throne, Frederick, Prince of Wales. From their first encounter, the king was entranced by the 17-year-old German ingénue. Augusta's appearance was 'modest and good-natured', and George believed she had the potential to make a royal bride.[1] She had a fine head of fair hair, which the acerbic Queen Caroline harshly described as 'a sort of blond sheep's colour', luminous blue eyes, a slight figure, and a sweet, shy smile; not unusually for the time, her cheeks bore the scars of smallpox.[2] George was flattered by her deferential manner, impressed with her good sense and charmed by her innocence. In Augusta he had found an ideal partner for his son, someone who, he believed, would curb Frederick's appetite for the high life and keep him on the straight and narrow.[3] Augusta's mother and her brother, Friedrich III, eagerly approved the match, but failed to give her any practical advice in the weeks before her voyage to England. She did not even learn any of the language, having gathered the mistaken impression that following two decades of Hanoverian monarchs, most of the British court would speak German.[4]

Early in April 1736, Queen Caroline dispatched her courtier and friend Lady Irwin to The Hague to act as a chaperone for her son's bride-to-be. Lady Irwin carried advice from the queen, telling Augusta that she would be happier if she indulged her new husband's extramarital affairs: '[the queen] desired me in the strongest terms to recommend to the princess to avoid jealousy', Irwin recalled, 'and to be easy in regard to amours, which she said had been her conduct and had consequently procured her happy state she had enjoyed for many years.'[5]

On 25 April, Augusta arrived in her adopted country; the only companion she had from Saxe-Gotha was a jointed doll, the favourite plaything of her childhood.[6] She would be presented to her future husband the next day. Frederick, or 'Fretz' as he was known by his family, was 29 years old and a charming prince if not the archetypal Prince Charming. He had 'yellowish' hair, a 'face fair', and his eyes were 'grey like a cat'.[7] His legs, however, were weak and spindly as a result of suffering from rickets. Moreover, the unusual circumstances of his childhood had made an indelible mark on his character. On the coronation of George I in 1714, Frederick's mother and father had moved to England from Hanover, leaving the seven-year-old prince, alone and vulnerable, as the representative of the family in the government of Hanover. The queen, though initially reluctant to leave her eldest son, was eventually convinced to sacrifice maternal responsibility for royal duty. Believing he had been forsaken by his parents, Frederick came, unsurprisingly, to resent George and Caroline.

In the 14 years before he saw his parents again, Frederick developed a fondness for drinking, gambling, whoring and music. The flamboyant prince who moved to England on his father's orders in 1728 was in some people's eyes a charismatic bon vivant and in others', a self-indulgent, insincere spendthrift. His parents certainly fell into the latter camp. After coming to England, Caroline had given birth to a second son, William, the future Duke of Cumberland, whose arrival filled the emotional void created by her separation from Frederick. If her feelings towards her firstborn became indifferent during his time in Hanover, they turned to active dislike when Frederick reached England. Caroline was horrified by her son's transformation from an innocent seven-year-old into an 'avaricious and sordid' man.[8] Although some of Frederick's traits may have been disappointing to his mother, Caroline's vitriolic pronouncements on her son's worthlessness seem excessive. She declared him 'the greatest ass and the greatest beast in the whole world'.[9] One day, catching sight of the prince from her dressing-room window, she exclaimed to Lord Hervey, Vice-Chamberlain of the Household, 'Look, there he goes – that wretch! That villain! I wish the ground would open this moment and sink the monster to the lowest hole in hell.'[10]

Frederick's style had shades of some of the more colourful Restoration rakes and one can imagine him striking up a friendship with Charles II or the Duke of Buckingham. He was no stranger to London whorehouses; he played the cello well; he liked to think of himself as a poet; he fostered an interest in experimental science. Frederick thought Caroline and George mean-spirited, while his parents thought him profligate. Both sides probably had some legitimate grievances. At £50,000 a year, his allowance was half of what his father had received as Prince of Wales. On the other hand, there is plenty of evidence to suggest that Frederick was careless with money. Horace Walpole's *Memoirs of George II* offer an anecdote to illustrate how lightly the burden of repaying debts weighed on the prince: 'One day at Kensington that he had just borrowed five thousand pounds from Dodington . . . seeing him pass under his window, he said to Hedges, his secretary, "That man is reckoned one of the most sensible men in England, yet with all his parts, I have just nicked him out of five thousand pounds".'[11]

Among the things Frederick resented most about his parents was the role they had assumed for themselves as patrons of the arts and arbiters of musical taste. By the early 1730s, the London musical scene had been dragged into the intergenerational conflict. The king was a prominent supporter of George Frederick Handel, so despite appreciating Handel's operas himself, Frederick set up a rival opera at Lincoln's Inn Fields in 1733 under the management of Handel's rival, Bononcini. Once it became known that Frederick was chief patron of the new opera, the young and fashionable nobility deserted the King's Theatre in the Haymarket in favour of Lincoln's Inn Fields. The exodus from the Haymarket did not further endear Frederick to his parents. Royal visits to the opera were a spectacle scrutinised by the public, and poor attendance on a night when royalty were in their box was an embarrassment. As the crowds at the Haymarket dwindled, Caroline raged that her son's popularity 'makes me vomit'.[12]

Queen Caroline was correct when she warned Augusta of Frederick's penchant for women; the prince's little black book was brimming with names – on top of numerous courtesans in Hanover, there were, in England, Lady Archibald Hamilton, Anne Vane, Anne Vane's chambermaid, and many prostitutes besides.[13] Among the prince's paramours, Lady Hamilton, the wife of the Earl of Orkney's younger brother, Lord Archibald Hamilton, stood out for her maturity and intelligence. Though Jane had given birth to ten children and was not by any means an acknowledged beauty, she captivated Frederick. The pair were introduced by the Orkneys, but while it is tempting to imagine that they first met at Archibald's beloved Cliveden, it is more likely that Frederick and Jane's first encounter took place at the Hamiltons' house in the parish of

St Martin-in-the-Fields, in the fashionable West End of London. Soon after being introduced they were often seen walking together in St James's Park and in deep conversation at court drawing-room functions. The relationship was primarily, though not exclusively, cerebral, and contemporary accounts are divided over whether Archibald knew and approved of the affair, or whether the pair duped him into thinking they were just good friends.

Despite his romantic and sexual entanglements – and marriage would not bring an end to these affairs – Frederick was extremely eager to find a wife and start a family. A consort and legitimate children were essential for the prince to look like a convincing heir apparent and would, he thought, help him to acquire a larger and more secure income: as a bachelor, his £50,000 allowance was given at the grace of his father, but the finances of married heirs were generally established by parliamentary authority. In fact, parliamentary wrangling over the prince's allowance would continue until 1742, and would be one of the main issues around which Frederick's supporters in the Country Party could rally.

Augusta's situation echoed in reverse that of Queen Mary, who had left England 60 years earlier, similarly naive and unprepared, for a life in the alien Dutch Republic. Yet while Mary's husband William was aloof and disengaged, Frederick empathised with Augusta's plight and showed his 17-year-old bride affection and understanding. He was moved that she had been willing to give up her quiet existence in Germany for the very public, highly ceremonial life of a royal consort. According to Lady Irwin, on Frederick and Augusta's first meeting, 'he embraced her ten times when I was in the room'.[14] Frederick's protective stance towards Augusta enabled her to deal with the enormous public attention that their nuptials were to attract.

In the early 18th century a growing number of newspapers offered the reading public an unprecedented number of news stories, in greater detail than ever before. The first daily paper, the *Daily Courant*, appeared in 1702, and the first evening paper, the *Evening Post*, in 1706. By 1719, the *St. James's Weekly Journal* was reporting that 'both city, town and country, are over-flowed every day with an inundation of news-papers', and over the course of the century newspaper production would increase from 1 million to 14 million a year.[15] The ready availability of newspapers in coffee houses, which often identified themselves as either Whig or Tory in affiliation, and in taverns gave rise to a new urban cliché in the character of the *quidnunc* (literally a 'what-now'), a 'coffee-house politician' who devoted so much time to keeping up with current affairs that he neglected his own business.[16]

The rise in newspaper circulation was in no small part due to the birth of an opposition press. The most famous opposition journal, *The Craftsman*, was established in 1726 by Viscount Bolingbroke (whose *Patriot King* had so influenced Frederick), with the specific purpose of unseating the Whig prime minister Robert Walpole. Opposition papers published material that was critical of Walpole's government, carried editorials that employed slogans of the Country Party, and devoted many column inches to trumpeting their own influence.

In retaliation, ministerial papers ridiculed the opposition

output and Walpole's government made sporadic attempts to prosecute for libel and sedition. Opposition publications also had critics outside the ministry. In 1738 Lady Mary Wortley Montagu wrote that 'reams of publick papers have been filled with dissertations on the word Liberty, which has been wrested for a great variety of purposes, without one definition of the true significance.'[17] But despite such criticism, these papers continued to sell: many of them, especially those run by the renowned opposition editor Nathaniel Mist, were very profitable enterprises.

Most of the newspapers developed under the patronage of parliamentary groups and, in this sense, were closer in form to 17th- and 18th-century pamphlets than to the modern press. While opposition newspapers probably exaggerated the extent to which establishment papers were funded by the government, it is true that many journalists for the ministerial press received annual payments from the secret service. Ministerial newspapers – such as the *Daily Gazetteer*, the *Whitehall Post* and the *St James's Evening Post* – were distributed from the offices of the secretaries of state, and fanned out through a network of local officials, who could generally be relied on to help with distribution. Opposition publications had their own sources of support and sponsorship, Frederick among them. They even seem to have competed with the government over certain writers: James Ralph, for instance, spent the 1740s writing against the Walpole and Pelham ministries in opposition organs like *Common Sense*, *The Champion*, and *Old England*, before switching sides when he began receiving £300 per annum payments from the secret service in 1753.[18]

Historians have long associated the rise of the press in the 18th century with the emergence of a 'public sphere', a literate and influential community of civic, financial and commercial interests distinct from the court. However, a closer look at the British newspapers of the period reveals an ongoing preoccupation with the court, both as the source and the subject of news.[19] Events such as drawing-room functions were crucial opportunities for journalists to gather intelligence, and even international news was commonly prefaced with phrases such as 'it is whispered around the west end': clearly it was proximity to the court, rather than to the site of a newsworthy event, that made a report credible.[20] Scenes of aristocratic spectacle, such as levees and balls, were also the subject of lengthy articles, which gave exhaustive accounts of what people were wearing and who was there; the guest list of any given event revealed shifting political alliances, providing excellent fodder for discussion among *quidnuncs*. Before their marriage even took place, Frederick and Augusta benefited from this expanding coverage of royal events. Both ministerial and opposition papers carried excited reports of Augusta's arrival and the couple's first public appearances. The media-savvy Frederick realised that if he and Augusta presented themselves in the right way, they truly could become the object of a national obsession.

On Monday 26 April, Frederick set out 'between one and two in the afternoon' from St James's Palace, crossed the river at Whitehall, and then travelled to Greenwich on horseback.[21] There he dined with Augusta in one of the park-facing rooms of the palace, 'the windows being thrown open to oblige the curiosity of the people'.[22] After dinner, the couple appeared on the balcony whereupon they were cheered by 'not less than 10,000 persons'.[23] Augusta was an instant sensation. 'Her Highness had the Goodness to show herself for upwards of half an Hour from the gallery of the Palace, which drew the loudest acclamations,' the *London Evening Post* reported.[24] The prince had planned to throw £400-worth of shillings and sixpences into the crowd, but changed his mind when someone pointed out that 'ill consequences might attend such a distribution'.[25]

Following the balcony appearance there was more show-manship in the form of an extravagant river pageant. Accompanied by boatmen in gold-filigree costumes, Frederick and Augusta were rowed towards the city in the prince's rococo barge, which had been custom-made for him in 1732 to designs by William Kent. An entire floating string ensemble accompanied them upriver. The Thames was brimming with boats, all of which saluted the royal couple as they passed, hanging their streamers and flags in celebration. After the pageant, Frederick and Augusta returned to Greenwich, where the main gates of the park were left open late, so that the crowds could once again watch the couple dine together.[26]

This sort of spectacle struck a chord with many British subjects, who had been disappointed by the relative modesty of the first two Hanoverian kings and craved more theatricality from their monarchs. That Frederick and Augusta dined in public not once, but twice, on the day before their wedding was a powerful statement that they intended to go further than Frederick's father in embracing spectacle and ceremony.

The royal couple was evidently comfortable with grand, theatrical monarchy and capable of satisfying the public hunger for pomp and pageantry. When Frederick admitted to the Earl of Egmont that his barge was probably 'too fine', Egmont replied that 'fine sights please the people and that it was good natured to entertain them that way.'[27]

Chapter 3

'A PROFUSION OF FINERY'

The royal wedding took place on 27 April 1736. That morning Augusta was conveyed from Greenwich to the Chapel Royal in St James's Palace. She travelled to Lambeth in a coach drawn by six cream-coloured horses, was met 'with the loudest acclamations by several thousands of people', crossed to Whitehall in the king's barge, and then was carried to St James's in the king's chair. On her arrival, Frederick 'received her at the garden door, and upon her sinking on her knee to kiss his hand, he affectionately raised her up and twice saluted her'.[1]

When brought into the royal presence of George II, Augusta 'prostrated herself'.[2] The gesture was conventional, but nevertheless flattered the king who, according to Lord Hervey, 'set store by such marks of his status' and had been attracted to Augusta as a match for his son partly because of her obvious deference.[3] Whether or not her deference was genuine is debatable. Augusta's ostensive humility was something she would maintain throughout her marriage, while all the time working behind the scenes with Frederick's opposition group.

At half past eight in the evening, Augusta, enrobed in her

'nuptial habit of silver tissue, richly embroidered with the same and adorned with tassels and a fringe', processed from the Guard-Chamber to the Chapel Royal, accompanied by trumpeters and drummers. On her head rested a tiara glittering with diamonds; her robe was 'crimson velvet, turned back with several rows of ermine'. The princess's train was carried by four bridesmaids dressed in complementary silver gowns, and adorned with 'diamonds not less in value than from 20 to 30,000l [pounds] each'. The ceremony was conducted by the Bishop of London and Augusta was given away by the king. The chapel was finely adorned with tapestry, velvet and gold lace, and pews had been taken down to make way for raked seating, which could accommodate a greater number of spectators. A gallery was built over the altar, in front of the organ, for the musicians. The setting was magnificent, but the day did not go flawlessly – Augusta's poor English meant that Queen Caroline was obliged to translate the ceremony for her, and the anthem Handel had composed for the occasion, 'Sing unto God, ye kingdoms of the earth', was, in the Earl of Egmont's opinion, 'wretchedly sung'.[4]

After the ceremony, the bride and groom received George and Caroline in the drawing room at St James's, and at half past ten they had supper. The first course consisted of 15 cold and 15 hot dishes, the second of 30 hot dishes.[5] Reports abounded about the magnificence of the wedding feast. The *London Evening Post* reported:

[The dessert] form'd a fine Garden rising to a Terras, the Ascent to which was adorn'd with the Resemblance of Fountains, Grottos, Groves, Flowers &c. In the Middle was the Temple of Hymen, the Dome of which was supported on transparent Columns three Foot High. As the Meats were the most exquisite and rare that could be procur'd, so the Desert contained a Profusion of the finest Fruits, among which were Cherries in great Perfection, Apricots, PineApples &c.[6]

The final event was the bedding-in ceremony. The bride was undressed and helped into her gown by the princesses and escorted to the marital bed, where Frederick joined her in a 'night gown of silver stuff and a cap of the finest lace'.[7] The bride and groom were admired 'sitting up in bed, surrounded by all the Royal family'. The queen's favourite, Lord Hervey, a maven of gossip and assiduous chronicler of the Georgian court, tartly remarked that the prince's absurd nightcap was taller than any grenadier's hat, and that Augusta looked very refreshed the next morning, so must have slept soundly.[8]

Hervey and Frederick had been friends when the prince arrived in England but had irrevocably fallen out when Frederick started his relationship with Anne Vane, and Hervey's account of the Georgian court, as well as being consistently sympathetic towards Caroline, never misses an opportunity to mock the prince. The queen was Hervey's ideal partner-in-crime – apparently she too was 'amused' by Frederick's attire at the bedding-in ceremony. In a rare moment of sentimentality, she did, however, confess to Egmont that 'her son was exceedingly pleased with the Princess, and had told her that if he had been himself to look all Europe over, he should have pitched his choice on her.'[9] While Augusta and Frederick's affection for each other was undoubtedly genuine, their mutual contentment was an important building block of their public image, which offered Frederick as a welcome contrast to his father and grandfather. George I was already divorced when he came to the throne and arrived in England with his mistress, Ehrengard Melusine von der Schulenberg, and George II was notorious for his frequent trips back to Hanover to visit various women; the sex lives of both men were perceived as 'strange' by the British public. Frederick's marriage would be central to restyling the Hanoverian dynasty as domestically stable.

Frederick's commitment to Augusta didn't mean that Lady Archibald Hamilton was off the scene. She was made Lady of the Bedchamber, Privy Purse and Mistress of the Robes. Caroline protested that for a woman widely known to be her son's mistress to be given these appointments would cause a scandal, but Augusta had taken the queen's advice to heart – perhaps too much so. She insisted that she must have Lady Archibald. Subsequently, the two became close friends.[10]

There was just one request that Augusta made of her husband on her wedding day. She asked for her governess, who had educated her as a child, to be brought to live with her. The prince replied that 'there was nothing she desired but he would do', and sent for the governess, Madame Rixleiven, immediately.[11]

The day after the wedding, 'the greatest appearance of the nobility, Quality and gentry that has been known in the memory of man' converged at court to congratulate Frederick and Augusta.[12] Women attending court traditionally wore the

'Corps de Robe' (a stiff-bodied gown), though during the reign of George II it also became acceptable to wear a mantua, which, in the 17th century, had been considered formal but not appropriate for the royal presence – later in the 18th century, the garment would fall out of fashion completely and by the 1770s was only ever seen at court.

Another development in court fashion was the arrival, early in the 18th century, of the whalebone hoop. Jonathan Swift saw one in 1711 and was appalled by its sheer scale. 'I hate them,' he pronounced, writing to Stella and Rebecca. 'A woman may hide a moderate gallant under them.'[13] As the years went on, the hoops only got bigger and more cumbersome for the wearer. In 1786, Jane Austen's sister-in-law complained at having to stand from two o'clock until four o'clock in the afternoon 'loaded with a great hoop of considerable weight'.[14] It wasn't only their weight that made these gowns uncomfortable. The 'stomacher', a decorative cloth worn over the chest and stomach, was held in place by an array of pins, and women were obliged to stand rigidly upright to avoid getting spiked. But despite all these discomforts, women in the British court could at least consider themselves more fortunate than their French counterparts, who were expected to wear heavy make-up that contained red and white lead, even after concerns had been raised that its ingredients were poisonous and potentially fatal.

Many of the women who attended on the Prince and Princess of Wales the day after the wedding also donned elaborate headdresses, which around this time usually comprised sculpted lace worn over close-fitting stitched caps. Brussels lace became very popular in the court of George II, having previously been banned in order to protect British lace manu-facturers. The fineness of the thread made this sort of lacework elaborate but also extortionately expensive, as the process for spinning it defied mechanisation, which elsewhere pushed prices down. Others decorated their hair with feathers, jewels, ribbons or coloured powders, the most popular hues being blue, yellow and burnt orange. No fashionable court lady would be seen without the key accessory of the day – a fan. These were often painted with landscapes or scenes from clas-sical literature. The entire process of getting ready for court could take hours; on one occasion, the writer and courtier Fanny Burney attended on the queen from six o'clock in the morning, missing breakfast in order to prepare the consort for an afternoon function.[15]

A newspaper report from the day after the wedding speci-fied that 'most of the rich Clothes were the manufacture of England, And it must be acknowledged, in honour of our own Artists, that the few which were French did not come up to these in Richness, Goodness, or Fancy'.[16] Augusta immediately understood the importance of being seen to appreciate all things British, and the simplest way of accomplishing this, at a time when royal fashion was a national obsession from the lowest to the highest echelons of society, was through her dress. French clothing was then very fashionable among aristocrats, not only in England, but across Europe: every month, fashion dolls clothed in the most recent French dresses were sent from Paris to cities including London, St Petersburg, and Constan-tinople. But the preference for French designs had hurt native manufacturers, who, in England as elsewhere, frequently petitioned for protection against imports. Augusta cleverly eschewed the fanciful French designs favoured by Caroline and her court, and instead dressed exclusively in home-spun gowns. In the years following their wedding, Frederick and Augusta further reinforced their commitment to native industry by forbidding the wearing of 'French stuffs' in their presence, and by visiting textile workers – weavers in Spital-fields and wool-combers in Cirencester.[17]

While Augusta became a fresh and modern fashion icon, Queen Caroline's more traditional approach to dressing made her seem dated and out of touch with the nation. Their competing styles only served to widen the chasm between the two generations of royals. Where George II was austere, his son was munificent; where Caroline's preferences were foreign, Augusta's were quintessentially British; where the king and queen remained aloof from the crowd, Frederick and Augusta mingled with it. These tensions would soon reach a bitter climax, putting both Augusta and her unborn child in mortal danger.

Chapter 4

A HANOVERIAN
SOAP OPERA

It was not long before the celebratory atmosphere of the wedding disintegrated into something more awkward. In May 1736, Frederick claimed that he was going to be delayed in joining his mother outside London because Augusta had the measles. When he was unable to persuade a physician to verify this diagnosis, Frederick downgraded his wife's illness to a rash, and then to a cold. The queen 'having a mind to be satisfied of the truth of the case . . . pretended to believe her ill, and with great civility and maternal kindness, went with her two eldest daughters to London to see her'.[1] Upon her arrival, Caroline was unable to see much as Augusta's room had been kept dark – on purpose the queen suspected, in order to disguise the true state of her daughter-in-law's health. If it is unfair to blame Augusta for this first family dispute, in which she was clearly used as a pawn by Frederick, she was more directly responsible for the fracas that followed.

Augusta had been brought up a Lutheran. In the mid-18th century, religious conformity was still a matter of great political importance – the Hanoverian succession itself had been carefully engineered to protect the Anglican ascendancy. The

importance of piety in the role of the royal consort was represented in the coronation ceremony by the presentation of an
English Bible to the new queen. This moment was of great
significance and appeared on medals commemorating the coronation of 1727. When Augusta chose to take communion at a
Lutheran chapel instead of an Anglican church, it inevitably
raised eyebrows within aristocratic circles. Sir Robert Walpole
requested that the queen speak to the prince about his wife's
behaviour, warning her how badly the news would be received,
not only by the bishops and the clergy, but by the English
public in general. In fact, the matter was even graver than this
because, as Lord Hervey advised the queen, 'the Act of Succession enjoined the heirs to the crown, on no less a penalty than
the forfeiture of the crown, to receive the sacrament according
to the manner of the Church of England'.[2] Eventually, on these
grounds, Frederick convinced Augusta to, in Hervey's words,
'lull her conscience', and stop attending the Lutheran church.
The woman who was thought 'to have put this conscientious
nonsense into the princess' head' was Madame Rixleiven, the
same governess whom Augusta had requested from Saxe-
Gotha. After a few further heated conversations with Rixleiven,
the prince came to dislike her so much that he sent her back
'from whence she came'.[3]

On 5 July 1737, Frederick wrote to his mother informing
her that Augusta was pregnant. Caroline had openly broadcast her opinion that Frederick was impotent, so the news
came as a surprise and she was inclined to believe that her son
was lying. On Augusta's next visit to court, the queen interrogated her about when the baby was due. When the princess

repeatedly replied she did not know the exact date, Caroline was confirmed in her suspicion that Augusta was, in fact, not with child, and concluded that the fraudulent pregnancy was a plot to introduce a suppositious claimant into the line of royal descent. She wrote to Robert Walpole asking him to formally request that the Princess of Wales give birth at Hampton Court, in the presence of her parents-in-law. 'Sir Robert,' Caroline said to the prime minister, 'we shall be catched. At her labour I positively will be present, I will be sure it is her child.'[4] Walpole, ever cautious about exacerbating the family rift, never sent the letter, but Frederick was undoubtedly aware of his mother's suspicions and of her plans for the birth.

Meanwhile, the battle over Frederick's allowance had escalated. Furious that his funding had not been sufficiently increased after his marriage, Frederick was now canvassing for a parliamentary bill to grant him £100,000 a year, a sum he believed to be commensurate with his status. In order to achieve his goal, Frederick knew that he needed to build a parliamentary block that was large enough either to overturn Walpole's ministerial majority, or to threaten it sufficiently that his bargaining position was strengthened. It was during Frederick's attempt to form a parliamentary group in support of increasing his allowance that he began to patronise the opposition. But all his efforts came to nothing and the bill was defeated, by 30 votes in the Commons and 63 in the Lords.[5] Despite continuing to live under the same roof at Hampton Court and St James's Palace, Frederick and his parents ceased all communication.

Augusta's labour pains began on the evening of Sunday 31 July while the entire royal family was staying at Hampton Court. Frederick made an extraordinary, impulsive decision: he snatched his wife from Hampton Court and took her to St James's Palace. The principal surviving source for these events is the memoir of Lord Hervey, whose dislike of the Prince of Wales has already been noted. This prejudice notwithstanding, it is clear that Frederick behaved recklessly on the night of his daughter's birth.

Augusta's waters broke before Frederick could get her out of the house, leaving her in intense pain. With Monsieur Dunoyer, the dancing-master, on one arm, and Mr Bloodworth, one of the prince's equerries, on the other, Augusta was lugged downstairs and into the palace yard. At this point, the 18-year-old was writhing in pain, 'barely able to set one foot before the other, and was upon the rack when they moved her'. Lady Hamilton and Mrs Townshend, her ladies-in-waiting, warned against Frederick's imprudence, while Augusta herself screamed in agony, imploring her husband to reconsider. Frederick urged her to have 'courage'. Thereafter the party endured a wretched journey 'full-gallop to London', covering 15 miles on bumpy roads in little over an hour.[6]

By the time they had reached St James's, Augusta's skirts were soaked with 'the filthy inundations which attend these circumstances' and Frederick commanded the candles be snuffed out so that no one should see the unsightly manifestation of 'his folly and her distress'. Absolutely no preparations had been made for their arrival at the palace. The furniture was smothered in dust covers and the beds were stripped and damp. On Augusta's arrival there was a call for sheets. None could be found. The princess was laid on a bed between two tablecloths. A messenger was sent to find Mrs Cannons, the midwife. Lady Archibald frantically went in search of 'napkins, warming-pan, and all other necessary implements for this operation'.[7] At a quarter to eleven, within an hour of the party's arrival, the princess delivered a baby girl so tiny that Hervey described her as 'a little rat . . . about the bigness of a large gold toothpick case'.[8] It is likely that the child was premature, and nothing short of a miracle that mother and daughter survived the ordeal.

Back at Hampton Court, the king and queen were woken up and given the news. According to Hervey, 'the King flew into a violent passion', while 'the Queen said little, but got up, dressed as fast as she could.' Soon after 2 a.m. the queen and a group of courtiers left Hampton Court, and by four o'clock they had reached St James's. Upon their arrival Lady Archibald Hamilton presented the baby girl, wrapped in napkins. Caroline was horrified. 'God bless you, you poor little creature,' she cried, looking down at her wretched granddaughter, 'you have come into a disagreeable world.' The frailty of the 'little creature' did at least convince Caroline that the newborn was her son's.[9]

Disgusted by Frederick's behaviour, Caroline called a conference with Robert Walpole and the king. The assembled company freely referred to Frederick as a 'scoundrel and puppy, knave and fool, liar and coward' according to Hervey, who no doubt would have contributed a few slurs of his own given half the chance.[10] When the prince wrote to his parents at Hampton Court, it was made clear to him that he would not be admitted to their presence and, shortly afterwards, Walpole was persuaded that the prince and princess should also be evicted from St James's Palace as soon as Augusta was well enough to travel. The Duke of Grafton was instructed to keep watch at the doors of the palace and prevent Frederick from removing any furniture or fittings, as the Duchess of Marlborough had famously done when thrown out of her Whitehall apartment. Not relishing the prospect of having to confiscate furniture from the prince, Grafton suggested that the couple should at least be allowed to take functional items such as chests, as it would not be appropriate for the heir to the throne and his wife to transport their linen in baskets. 'Why not?' said George, 'a basket is good enough for them.'[11]

The shocking circumstances surrounding the birth of her first child did not leave Augusta unscathed and a less stoic woman would undoubtedly have been traumatised. But although the princess was visibly 'uneasy' in the ensuing weeks, she bore the turbulent events with maturity and equanimity far beyond her 18 years.[12] Horace Walpole would later commend her for her 'quiet good sense' and aver that the princess 'had never said a foolish thing nor done a disagreeable one since her arrival'.[13] Indeed, Augusta had become one of Frederick's principal assets. The shy, unassuming girl from Saxe-Gotha showed a remarkable ability to rise to every challenge. A fast learner, she had already mastered English by the time of her daughter's birth and was able to 'talk freely' with courtiers and subjects; many remarked that her command of English was far superior to that of any member of the royal family, even though she had been in the country for less than a year.

The couple's ongoing popularity, and their uniquely informal relationship with the public, is illustrated by the celebrations that attended the birth of their daughter, who had been named Augusta like her mother. On the Tuesday night after the birth, Frederick ordered that a large bonfire be set up in front of Carlton House and provided four barrels of strong beer for the revellers. Unfortunately, the local gentry were not impressed by the quality of the alcohol and 'threw great Part of it in one another's faces'.[14] A group of the prince's tradesmen, who had assembled in a nearby tavern with trumpets and kettledrums, quickly purchased several more barrels of ale to placate the crowd. The next day, rather than scolding the rioters, Frederick ordered that the whole celebration be repeated, this time with better beer. While the second round of festivities commenced in Pall Mall, the area around St James's was kept especially quiet for the benefit of Princess Augusta and her baby. Cleveland Row was closed to traffic and 40 bales of straw were put down in the surrounding streets to muffle any sound.

Following their banishment from the royal residences, the couple and their tiny daughter relocated to Kew. Letters from the prince himself were no longer being accepted at Hampton Court, but Augusta continued to communicate with George and Caroline.[15] Augusta's letters to her in-laws exemplify her ability to combine deference with determination. She began the correspondence by begging the king and queen to understand the actions of her husband, presenting herself as the 'innocent cause' of the breach and suggesting that Frederick had been misrepresented by others. She continued: 'I flatter my self if I had had leave to throw my self at your Majesty's Feet, I could have explained the Prince's Conduct in a Manner that would have softened your Majesty's Resentment', and signed off as 'Your Majesty's most humble and most obedient Daughter, Subject, and Servant, Augusta'.[16] The letter served its purpose. In his reply, George announced that despite his son's 'inexcusable conduct', Caroline was willing to act as baby Augusta's godmother.

Augusta immediately wrote to the queen thanking her 'most humbly for the honour you did me'.[17] Once again she tried to explain rather than excuse Frederick's actions, saying that both the doctors and midwife had advised her that the cramps she experienced at Hampton Court were not those of labour but in fact colic. The queen was sufficiently moved to respond: 'I am very glad, my Dear Princess, to hear you are perfectly recovered of your Lying in; you may assure your self, as you have never offended either the King or me, I shall never fail to give you every Mark of my Regard and Affection.'[18] However, she remained intransigent on the subject of her son. 'I think it would be unbecoming either of us to enter into a Discussion of the unhappy Division between the King and my Son,' she wrote. 'I hope Time and due Consideration will bring my Son to a just Sense of his Duty to his Father; which will be the only Means of procuring that happy Change, which you cannot more sincerely wish than I do.'

While Caroline and George expressed nothing but sympathy in public for their daughter-in-law, in private they thought she was not sufficiently grateful for their willingness to leave baby Augusta in her care. This they were by no means obliged to do. There was considerable precedent for the children of princes being removed from their parents' household at the instruction of the reigning monarch; it was one such event – the removal of James, Duke of York's children, Anne and Mary, to Richmond in the 1670s – that set Elizabeth Villiers on the path to her royal affair and eventually to Cliveden. George and Caroline also doubted that their daughter-in-law's submissiveness was entirely sincere, and their scepticism was, in part, justified. Though Augusta was young and familiar with the rituals of subservience, she knew that her future rested in the hands of her husband, and that a dutiful and supportive consort would strengthen his position as Prince of Wales and, ultimately, as ruler of Great Britain.

The final step in the family breach, and one that many courtiers were keen to avoid, was the full separation of the two courts. Some courtiers, in particular Robert Walpole, counselled against this, fearing that Frederick's popularity would increase in response to what would inevitably be perceived as an act of aggression, but the case for separation eventually won out. The king made it clear that he would not receive anyone who was also attending on his son. Aristocrats who had previously hedged their bets would now be forced to choose sides in the quarrel.

There were obvious attractions to the court of Frederick and Augusta over that of Frederick's parents. The main audience room at George and Caroline's court was the drawing room, which by the early 18th century had come to replace the

privy chamber as the main site of interaction between the king
and his trusted courtiers. During the 18th century the privy
chamber became a less exclusive domain and, in response to
this, the drawing room emerged as a new, more select space.
George and Caroline's drawing rooms were notoriously dull,
with the king's 'stiff and formal manner' inducing in attendees
'that restraint which they saw he was under himself'.[19] While
he was relatively at ease in the company of women, the king's
reticence and insistence on formal etiquette gave him an air of
haughtiness around men.

George and Caroline both had their own drawing rooms.
At a typical function the attendees would form a circle around
which the king or queen would move, sometimes engaging in
brief conversation with those they passed. These evenings
could be long and stiflingly tedious, made worse by the fact
that it was forbidden to sit down in the presence of the monarch. Those who were not in conversation with the host
generally indulged in small talk or, as Lord Chesterfield called
it, 'a court jargon, a chit chat, which turns upon trifles'.[20]
The ever-stoic Queen Caroline was even overheard complain-
ing of fatigue at one drawing room, sending a message 'to the
King to beg he would retire, for she was unable to stand any
longer'.[21]

Nevertheless, Walpole's fears about a mass desertion turned
out to be exaggerated. Despite the allure of Frederick's alternative court, people generally chose to remain with the reigning
monarch. Frederick found himself surrounded by an increasingly small opposition group that became ever more strident.
His appointment of the Tory politician George Lyttelton as his

secretary caused a good deal of unease among his dwindling moderate Whig supporters, as 'there was nobody more violent in the Opposition, nor anybody a more declared enemy to Sir Robert Walpole'.[22]

Though tales of the growing rift circulated widely in political circles, some effort was made to keep them away from the press: Sir Benjamin Keene, a British diplomat in Spain, was sent details of exchanges between George and Frederick along with the instruction not to share them with anyone else. Nevertheless, similar unedifying details somehow reached the editor of *The Gentleman's Magazine*, who could not resist publishing them. The same burgeoning press that had produced lavish coverage of Frederick and Augusta's wedding was also becoming confident enough to print stories that reflected less well on the royal family.

There were risks associated with printing this sort of contentious material. Despite the absence of any statutory prepublication censorship of the press, opposition papers did face serial prosecutions that gave editors reason to pause for thought before publishing. At the time, judicial action was not seen as an unduly censorious measure, but as an essential defence against factious or seditious comment. In cases where published material verged on the treasonous, sanctions were severe. After Nathaniel Mist's weekly journal published a pro-Jacobite satire in 1728, the Whig government ordered many presses to be destroyed, and both Mist and the satire's author, the Duke of Wharton, had to flee the country. Papers were also vulnerable to sudden and direct political interference to prevent their distribution, as happened on the eve of both the 1734 and the 1754 elections, when the government ordered the post office not to carry any copies of the *London Evening Post*. The extent of this interference was, however, tempered by ministerial fears that frequent trials would turn printers and newspapermen into martyrs. 'Liberty of the press' was already a familiar catch phrase, and failed prosecutions risked simply generating publicity for the opposition media.

Now that they were no longer able to stay at St James's or Hampton Court, Frederick and Augusta needed new residences both in London and in the country. For a London home, Frederick had long had his eyes on Southampton House, but despite 'having given unregarded hints to the Duke of Bedford', who owned the property, he wasn't invited to buy it.[23] The Duke and Duchess of Norfolk were more forthcoming with their residence, Norfolk House, though such was the fear of being caught on the wrong side of the Hanover rift that the duke was not willing to sell to the prince until the duchess had attended the queen and asked her whether the sale 'would be disagreeable to her and the king'.[24] The queen assured the duchess that it would not be disagreeable, and thanked her for her civility.

And then the country house: Cliveden's Thames-side location made it very attractive to Frederick, who loved the river, and although the proximity to his parents' residence at Windsor was not an unmitigated attraction, it was symbolic of his position as king-in-waiting. The house was modest compared to any of the royal palaces or the grand London residences, and this suited Frederick and Augusta well: according to Hervey, the couple's finances were in worse shape than ever before, and besides, they wanted somewhere on a more familial scale. Because their houses at Kew and Cliveden were directly on the river, a barge transported their possessions between the two.

The river was not just a functional thoroughfare for the prince and princess. Like his grandfather George I, who famously commissioned Handel's *Water Music* to be performed for him during trips along the river, Frederick formed an attachment to the Thames. He often cruised along the river to one of his favourite haunts, Spring Gardens at Vauxhall. In 1732 Jonathan Tyers, the new manager, redesigned the gardens, adding long gravel walks and a panoply of enticing features such as obelisks, grand ornamental arches, painted scenery on canvas, a hermit's cave, and a water mill with its own waterfall. Alongside these attractions, concerts, dances, masked balls, fireworks displays, ballets and horse shows were regularly on offer. Events at the gardens were incredibly popular: thousands attended a public rehearsal of Handel's fireworks music on 21 April 1749, and Thomas Arne's 'Rule, Britannia!' was a concert staple.

Beyond these entertainments, Spring Gardens also offered friends a place to gossip, lovers a setting in which to conduct illicit affairs, and poorer visitors the opportunity to spot famous beauties and minor politicians. The redesigned gardens proved extremely popular, drawing the crowds away from the pleasure gardens in St James's where Anna Maria had inspired the ardour of so many Restoration rakes. They also attracted hordes of commoners, much to the concern of the management, who in June 1736 introduced a ticketing system to prevent unde-sirables 'intermixing with those Persons of Quality'.[25] Frederick marked the opening of the gardens with a ceremonial entry via the Thames in his William Kent barge and, from 1738 onwards, Frederick and Augusta made many well-publicised journeys to Vauxhall.[26]

Chapter 5

THE QUEEN IS DEAD, LONG LIVE THE QUEEN

On 9 November 1737, while inspecting the new library at St James's Palace, which had been designed by William Kent, Queen Caroline was taken ill.[1] At first her ailment was thought to be a more severe recurrence of the gout that had afflicted her on several previous occasions. George, sensing that the situation was more serious than that, was distraught, and refused to leave her side; he even slept on the queen's bed in his nightgown.[2] Hervey was quick to prescribe a cocktail of patent medicines that he had found helpful in the past, including 'Daffy's Elixir' and 'Sir Walter Raleigh's cordial', but the queen's fever only worsened.[3] The royal physicians ordered the standard treatments of the time, bloodletting and induced vomiting. After Caroline had been in bed for several days, it transpired that her illness was, in fact, the result of a hernia, which had developed during one of her pregnancies.[4] Her condition was far worse than had initially been realised and could only be ameliorated by an operation that was in itself life-threatening.

Upon hearing news that his mother was dying, Frederick

rushed to London, but George would not even entertain the notion of receiving his son:

> 'If the puppy should, in one of his impertinent affected airs of duty and affection, dare to come to St James's, I order you to go to the scoundrel and tell him I wonder at his impudence for daring to come here; that he has my orders already, and knows my pleasure, and bid him go about his business; for his poor mother is not in a condition to see him act false, whining, cringing tricks now, nor am I in a humour to bear his impertinence; and bid him trouble me with no more messages, but get out of my house.'[5]

The queen, too, was unforgiving to the last. When George told his wife that he had refused their son entry to the palace and offered to reverse this decision if she so desired, Caroline replied: 'I am so far from desiring to see him, that nothing but your absolute command could make me assent to it.'[6]

The last few days of Caroline's life were tinged with macabre comedy. The king and queen's deathbed discussion about mistresses was a perfect travesty of William III and Mary's in 1694: when Caroline urged George to seek another wife, he responded amid tears 'Non – j'aurai des maîtresses' ('No – I shall have mistresses').[7] Sharp as ever, Caroline quipped: 'Dieu! Cela n'empêche pas' ('God! That needn't stop you'). She died on 20 November 1737, unreconciled with her son. Her death plunged George into profound grief that even Hervey, who was generally rather critical of the king, conceded showed 'a tenderness of which the world thought him utterly incapable'.[8] When Egmont attended the court in January 1738, he commented that George 'stayed not two minutes out, and had grief fixed on his face'.[9]

Caroline's death left Augusta in a uniquely influential position – she was now the only royal consort in the realm. Her enhanced role was reflected in portraiture: in 1739, Jean-Baptiste van Loo, who was known for his portraits of male political leaders, depicted Augusta sitting regally surrounded by her children and entourage. In a little over a year, the humble girl from Saxe-Gotha had risen to become, if not an actual queen, at least the undisputed first lady of the nation. At her 'courts' of Norfolk House, Kew and Cliveden, she and Frederick entertained relentlessly, receiving a wide cross-section of friends from the worlds of politics, literature and art. One of their guests was Sarah, Duchess of Marlborough, who was now 77, and had not become any less cantankerous with age: among her nicknames were 'Old Mount Aetna', the 'Beldam of Bedlam' and 'Her Graceless'. Augusta and the ageing duchess struck up an unlikely friendship: surprisingly, given her own behaviour, Sarah saw great value in Augusta's propriety. 'I think her conversation is much more proper to a drawing room than the wise Queen Caroline', she wrote to a friend, alluding to the late queen's well-known prurience.[10]

Frederick and Augusta did not even pretend to grieve for Caroline. This was particularly noticeable in a period when mourning was a very serious and prolonged process, with forms of grieving determined by the Chamberlain's Office and published for the public at large. The death of George I in

1727 set the pattern for 18th-century mourning, which in the case of a royal death passed through three 'degrees' over the course of at least a year. The first degree of mourning was the strictest and not only required that various black materials be used in clothes, shoes, hats, fans and gloves, but also that shiny surfaces such as buckles, buttons, or rivets in coaches, be covered. Mourning was so stringently observed that royal deaths generated huge demand for black material, in particular Norwich crepe, and seriously dented the income of those who manufactured colourful silks and ribbons. In 1709, during the two-year mourning for Queen Anne's husband, Prince George of Denmark, silk manufacturers protested to Parliament that if mourning was declared for a fourth fashion season their industry would not recover.[11] Perhaps the most succinct expression of Frederick and Augusta's disregard for mourning convention was the design of the new barge they commissioned in the spring of 1738, less than six months after the queen's death. The inside of the barge was not black, nor even dark, but bright green.[12]

By late 1737, Cliveden was being prepared for its royal occupants. In October, Augusta appointed the married couple Mr and Mrs Sallier as porter and housekeeper respectively and, in January of the following year, it was reported in the press that the house was 'getting ready for his Royal Highness the Prince of Wales' Residence next summer'.[13] Although Cliveden would principally serve as a summer residence, the Wales family also visited the property at other times of year. In March 1738 their entourage arrived 'in a Coach and Six, attended by another Coach and Six, with the Ladies of the

Bedchamber in Waiting, and Sir William Irby Bart, her Royal Highness's Vice Chamberlain, and six Servants on Horseback', and they returned again at the end of April for a month-long visit.[14]

On 4 June 1738, at Norfolk House in London, Augusta gave birth to her second child, the future George III. Not long afterwards a 'machine chair' was made for the baby prince and his older sister, so that they could take the air in the Cliveden gardens. The chair, which was said to exhibit the 'most exquisite Workmanship', was based on one 'belonging to the Children of France' and was 'sent from Mr. Bassnet's' shop in Piccadilly.[15] On 1 August, two years before the momentous premiere of *Alfred*, the little Princess Augusta's first birthday was also celebrated at Cliveden, with a 'grand entertainment to several persons of distinction'.[16] It was a happy time for the family. With Augusta's help, Frederick was able to overcome the vicissitudes of his upbringing to become a communicative, affectionate father. 'My dear children,' he wrote to them, 'you have given me too much joy today.'[17]

While Frederick and Augusta doted on their own heirs, the prince had also facilitated a limited reconciliation with his father. In the general election of 1741, Frederick achieved a parliamentary group of 25 and his members contributed to Walpole's downfall the following year. After this, Frederick formed a partnership with William Pulteney, who succeeded in negotiating the long-sought rise in the prince's allowance to £100,000 per year. But as soon as the question of finances was solved, Frederick abandoned his role in opposition politics, much to the chagrin of his former allies, who had been committed to the patriotic political agenda of the Country Party movement. Frederick's willingness to make peace with his father in return for an increased allowance damaged the reputation of the opposition. After campaigning so vocally against the venality of the court, they now looked like any other political faction, whose support could be purchased for the right price. Meanwhile, in a show of goodwill to George, Frederick appeared at a levee at St James's Palace, where his father politely inquired about the health of Augusta. The short and stilted conversation marked a temporary thaw in the Hanoverian cold war.

Meanwhile, the Wales's own family was growing: Edward was born in March 1739; Elizabeth, physically deformed but much-loved, in January 1741; and William Henry in November 1743. In pride of place in the nursery at Cliveden was Prince George's cradle, which had a crown carved in its head, and a quilt of yellow silk damask, to match the room's curtains.[18] George Wickes, a well-known silversmith based in Threadneedle Street in London, was commissioned to make not only silver toys for the children, but also tiny silver spoons and forks, mugs and porringers for use on formal occasions. Later, Augusta's English teacher, the Swiss pastor and scholar Caspar Wettstein, acquired maps of Europe for the infant George, to teach him the geography of Europe.[19]

Preparing a king for his rule at a time when infant mortality was still high involved making decisions about his health to ensure he reached his majority. Indeed Augusta was preoccupied with the health of all of her children and, in particular, with the question of how to protect them from smallpox. The previous two decades had seen the tentative adoption of inoculation, a process popularised in England by Lady Mary Wortley Montagu. In 1717 Lady Montagu, whose husband was the British ambassador to Turkey, had come across the method in Constantinople, and wrote of it enthusiastically to her friend in London, Sarah Chiswell. 'There is a set of old women, who make it their business to perform the operation, every autumn in the month of September, when the great heat is abated,' she wrote. 'People send to one another to know if any of their family has a mind to have the smallpox: they make parties for the purpose, and when they are met (commonly 15 or 16 together), the old woman comes with a nutshell full of the matter of the best sort of smallpox, and asks what vein you please to have opened.' Montagu continued: 'She immediately rips open that you offer her, with a large needle (which gives you no more pain than a common scratch) and puts into the vein, as much matter as can lie upon the head of her needle.'[20]

Inoculation had been introduced into Constantinople around 1672. From 1706 onwards, Continental physicians were becoming aware of the technique, but were slow to adopt it; British doctors were slower still. Lady Montagu, who had been left without eyelashes and with a badly pockmarked face following an attack of smallpox, became the procedure's greatest advocate. In March 1718 she had her five-year-old son inoculated by Charles Maitland, the embassy surgeon in Constantinople, and after returning to London in April 1721, she asked Maitland to inoculate her four-year-old daughter. This was to be the first professional inoculation in England. Members of the royal family began to take an interest in the method, influenced by Queen Caroline's near loss of a daughter from smallpox, and also by Sir Hans Sloane, president of the Royal Society, who had observed Lady Montagu's daughter after her inoculation and voiced his support of the procedure.[21] Though Frederick and his sisters had been inoculated in childhood, Augusta was fearful about the side effects and agonised over whether to subject her own children to the relatively new procedure. Despite her trepidation, she decided that the potential benefits outweighed the risks.

Frederick and Augusta's family life was not just a private matter – it was also used in propaganda in the form of portraits by popular artists such as van Loo and Allan Ramsay, to make the Prince and Princess of Wales look like secure heirs to the throne. While these portraits were commissioned for display on the walls of great aristocratic houses, they were also accessible to a broader audience: painters' studios were adept at producing copies, and mezzotints of popular images circulated both nationally and internationally. Contemporary portraits of Augusta surrounded by her children cast her as doting mother and supportive wife – a striking contrast to the popular portrayal of George II, who was seen as cold, unloving and, worst of all, more German than English. The couple's blissful family life at Cliveden, complete with strolls, picnics in the garden and children's birthday parties, formed the bedrock of this public-relations strategy. One notable 1746 portrait of the six eldest Wales children, painted by Barthélemy du Pan, is set in a landscape of romantic woodland, cultivated land, and landscaped 'English garden', which was by now widely associated with patriotism and liberty. The off-centre focus of the portrait is Prince George, who appears to have just won an archery contest, and is depicted as a wholesome, pastoral and freedom-loving heir.

But Frederick was not the only prince styling himself and his heirs as suitable kings-in-waiting. George II had long considered his younger son, William, Duke of Cumberland, as another possible successor, and it was rumoured that he intended to divide up his territories, sending Frederick back to Hanover as protector so as to clear the path for William to inherit the British throne. Moreover, William's recent military successes had given him the opportunity to style himself as an alternative, far more martial heir. In July 1745, Bonnie Prince Charlie, the eldest grandson of James II, landed in Scotland with an army, intending to reclaim the British throne for the Stuarts. In mid-September he took Edinburgh and his father was proclaimed King James VIII of Scotland. William was recalled from service in Flanders and sent north to meet the rebels. His troops came head to head with the Jacobite forces on 16 April at Culloden, a small village near Inverness. In the fighting that ensued, the majority of Charles's 5,000 men were slaughtered. William marched back into London triumphant and ready to capitalise on the status of national hero that the victory had afforded him.

Frederick's only contribution to the campaign was ordering the christening cake of his youngest son, Henry, to be made in the shape of Carlisle Castle, which the Jacobites had captured on their march south. Guests were invited to bombard the cake with sugarplums; in late December, his brother would besiege the real castle, take it back for the Crown, and send those within for execution.[22] Frederick's decision to counter Jacobite force with farce was a rare misstep; he risked being seen as the frivolous prince in comparison to his brother's soldier king. To reinforce his credentials as a worthy successor, Frederick would have to play his cards with greater care, and it was his family life with Augusta that remained his trump.

Chapter 6

THE CHARMS OF SYLVIA

During their summers, Frederick and Augusta revelled in the domestic felicity that they so heavily publicised in their propaganda. In his poem *The Charms of Sylvia*, Frederick celebrated Augusta's sensual allure, 'those breasts that swell to meet my loves', 'that easy sloping waist, that form divine', before concluding, as was conventional, by glorifying her character, proclaiming it was her 'gentleness of mind', 'that grace with which you speak and move', that most ignited his passion and 'set my soul on fire'.[1] Despite their evident passion for each other, the couple lived relatively independent lives – as was customary at the time. They breakfasted in their own rooms, where they were brought coffee or hot chocolate with bread, butter and muffins. Augusta's favourite drink was not served in the morning, but after dinner, either in the drawing room, where she invariably brewed it herself in a silver kettle, or in the Octagonal Temple, which she had converted into a tea room.[2] The use of space in country houses had changed during the early 18th century: the drawing room was becoming a more important place for socialising, and many owners now kept specialised 'dining rooms' as distinct from the great hall, which could be configured for many different purposes. Frederick and Augusta hosted many glittering soirées at Cliveden. The gradual improvement of highways meant that the travel time from London was decreasing, making it easier for friends to come for an evening. Better roads enabled Frederick and Augusta to lunch in London or dine at Cliveden whenever they wanted; in the next century the advent of train travel would further shrink the distance between the city and its surrounding country houses.

When Frederick and Augusta were not entertaining guests, they dined together, probably in Frederick's apartment. Their catering was run by James Douglas and Charles Hamilton, brother of Jane Hamilton, whom Frederick continued to keep as a mistress. Eschewing the aristocratic fashion for employing a French chef, Frederick retained two German 'yeomen cooks' to cater for Augusta's tastes. The couple's wine was bought by a man called Jephson, and Rhenish wine was a particular favourite of Augusta's.[3] When not hosting a formal dinner, Augusta liked nothing better than dining in the open air, or brewing tea on the terrace or the lawn under one of the large yellow canvas umbrellas George Cure, who managed the household, had erected to provide shade from the afternoon sun.

Augusta and Frederick shared the Orkneys' love of the garden at Cliveden, playing rounders and ninepin with their children as well as cricket, which Frederick famously enjoyed and also helped popularise.[4] Music was another daily feature of their life together, and when the weather permitted, performances took place outside. Frederick even kept a special barge moored on the Thames to act as a floating stage for orchestras during garden parties. Theatrical productions also took place in the gardens, both in the grass amphitheatre that Bridgeman had designed for Orkney, and on custom-built stages. *Alfred* was not exceptional among the performances that took place at Cliveden in its use of professional actors: Frederick often called upon his connections in the management of the London theatres to provide actors, set designers and singers for his garden shows. The ready availability of professional talent did not exclude those of the couple's children who were old enough from taking part.

These amateur dramatics were not simply for the idle amusement of the children. After the 1747 general election, Frederick returned to active political opposition, heading a party that was led in the Commons by William Pitt the Elder and Francis Ayscough. The election, like many early 18th-century contests before it, should have returned a Tory majority given the significant rural support commanded by the party. But the uneven distribution of votes and seats, as well as the limited nature of the franchise, rendered the Tories permanently in a position of minority opposition, sometimes, as on the issue of Frederick's finances, allied with disaffected Whigs. On his 1747 return to politics, Frederick would once again seek to forge an opposition group around his own personal concerns, though his current cause – that the crown not be diverted to his younger brother – had larger political ramifications than his previous campaign for a bigger allowance.

In 1749, Frederick returned to theatre as a vehicle to promote his patriotism and royal right when he had his children put on a production of Joseph Addison's *Cato*. Frederick had a clear vision of the dynastic roles his children should perform, and neatly expressed these in the parts he had them play. By having his eldest son, George, play Cato's eldest son, Portius, Frederick implied a parallel between himself and the titular statesman, whom the play shows resisting the tyranny and corruption of Julius Caesar. In case the parallel was not clear enough, in the prologue to the play Prince George announced himself as 'A boy in England born – in England bred . . . where freedom well becomes the earlier state. For there the love of liberty's innate'. Princess Augusta would later be married to the heir of the duchy of Brunswick-Wolfenbüttel, a fate expressed by her character in the play, who accepted that she must 'wed a foreigner, and cross the sea – God knows where'. Edward's future role as Elector of Hanover was reflected in his part of Juba, Prince of Numidia. The destiny of Frederick's younger son Henry, however, defied neat allegory: he would live in America as the head of a new seaboard colony, and be ennobled as Duke of Virginia.[5]

Frederick and Augusta also had to maintain estates befitting a king-in-waiting. They had always expected to invest heavily in the gardens at Cliveden: the Orkneys made it clear, when the prince took the lease, that they expected at least £300 per year to be spent on the development and upkeep of their beloved grounds. This was not an exceptional commitment for the royal couple, who devoted much time and attention to the gardens of all their estates. Work on the 9-acre garden of Carlton House (acquired by Frederick in 1732) started in 1735, and the nurserymen's lists show the immense variety of the planting there. Overall, some 14,100 products were supplied: 1,500 elms of various sorts, 400 cherries, 1,400 hornbeams, 1,000 chestnuts, 500 yews, 150 firs and the same number of hollies and oaks, several tulip trees, walnuts, mulberries, and large quantities of laurels, lilacs, laburnums, roses, honeysuckles, jasmines, laurustinus and bulbs.[6] At Kew, Augusta and her friend the Earl of Bute established what would later become the Royal Botanic Gardens.[7]

Although the alterations that Augusta and Frederick carried out at Cliveden were not on the same scale as those at Carlton House, they did stamp their mark on the estate, adding a coffee room adjoining an existing thatched house in the grounds, a stable block to accommodate five more horses, and several sheds and barns that evidence the ongoing cultivation of the estate grounds.[8] Perhaps the most unusual additions were two aviaries and a flower garden; at Kew and Carlton house, Augusta had attempted to combine her interests in bird-keeping and floriculture by selecting for her garden birds and flowers whose appearance, song and scent would complement each other. In the late 1730s she purchased indigenous and exotic birds including magpies, Virginia nightingales, parakeets, bullfinches and goldfinches, as well as bird cages and nets. Augusta's purchases for Cliveden are not as well documented as those for Carlton and Kew, but we can presume that the aviaries and flower garden at Cliveden were similarly ambitious, marrying the mating chorus with spring scents.

The couple also had plans for the interior of the house. In 1738, Sarah, Duchess of Marlborough, wrote that Augusta had incurred 'a good deal of expense at Cliveden in building and furniture'.[9] Frederick's bedroom was decorated with elaborate

Chinese wallpaper painted in a design of green poppies on a white background, with green and white borders. Linen was hung in some of the rooms, and new furnishings – such as a carved gilt frame for a glass in Augusta's dressing room – were installed with the help of George Cure.[10] Benjamin Goodison, the prince's cabinetmaker, made furniture for Cliveden, including a 'dressing glass' with an elaborately sculpted frame.[11]

Because Frederick expected his kingship to begin imminently, the couple did not make structural changes to the house. However, we do know that painters were employed to do maintenance work on the outside of the building, because in 1743, one of them fell to his death from some scaffolding. The story attracted interest from the newspapers and in May that year, the *London Evening Post* reported that the prince had arranged for the family of the workman to be provided for.[12] Frederick's actions in this instance fitted neatly into the role he had been given by the press, of a paternalistic people's prince. On 16 September 1740, the same newspaper had reported how 'his Royal Highness the Prince of Wales . . . out of his great Goodness and Generosity' had given an annual pension of 20 pounds to the widow of his head gamekeeper, Mr Shooman;[13] in November 1743, the papers carried stories about the prince's generosity towards a sailor, Thomas Adkens, who had been blinded in a fight with a Spanish privateer, and turned up at the gates of Cliveden asking for help. 'With that humanity and generosity so peculiar to his Royal Highness', Frederick promised to provide Adkens with both medical and financial assistance.[14]

Outside of these well-publicised acts of kindness, Frederick and Augusta developed a reputation for showing consistent care and generosity towards their staff. The Wales's footmen received £41 per annum and their coachmen £45, both generous salaries for the time, and humble employees such as grooms were provided with expensive medical treatment.[15] Moreover, during his stays at Cliveden and Kew, Frederick made time to visit the local cottages, sitting down and talking to the villagers about their lives. This became common practice among the Victorian aristocracy, but in Frederick's day it was unprecedented for a prince.

At Cliveden, Frederick was not above taking a mug of ale at the local public house, often accompanied by Bloodworth, the equerry who had assisted Augusta's night-time escape from Hampton Court in 1737.[16] There is more than a touch of a previous Prince of Wales, the Prince Hal of Shakespeare's *Henry IV*, in the idea of Frederick, banished from his father's presence, drinking in company that must have included commoners. It was not only in the pub that Frederick encountered ordinary Britons. He and Augusta pioneered the royal walkabout, visiting everything from workshops to fairground booths, and talking with the people who worked there. In this, as in their campaign for British clothing, they showed concern for the welfare of the up-and-coming middle classes, the 'trading' part of the nation. Subsequently, in a fitting tribute to its most famous patron, Cliveden's local pub was renamed The Three Feathers after the emblem of the Prince of Wales. Two hundred years later, Nancy Astor, a famous opponent of excessive alcohol consumption, would try to shut the pub down.

By the 1740s, George II had reached his mid-sixties and

Frederick was increasingly sure that his own kingship was imminent. George Bubb Dodington, the prince's staunch supporter, recorded dining with Frederick at Carlton House to discuss 'the immediate steps to be taken upon the demise of the King', and Frederick redoubled his efforts to promote his kingly qualities to the public.[17] In the summer of 1750, he made two tours of the south and west of England, highlights of which were reported in the *Remembrancer*, a relatively new newspaper sponsored by the prince. Frederick's confidence was palpable and his belief in his right of succession unshakeable. The prince's regal image had also eclipsed that of his brother, William, whose reputation as a soldier had transfigured into one of bloodlust and violence. In 1747, George II finally issued an official declaration citing Frederick as his successor, albeit with the bitter warning that King Frederick would 'live long enough to ruin us all'.[18] By the turn of the new decade, Frederick seemed poised to take the crown.

But despite all this preparation, Augusta and Frederick's long-awaited coronation was never to occur. In March 1751, Frederick was taken ill at Kew, 'after staying all day in the garden till night, in the damp rain and hail to look at his workmen'.[19] For two weeks, the prince suffered from 'a violent pain in his side', accompanied by fever and fainting fits. Augusta, distraught and pregnant with the couple's ninth and last child, maintained a bedside vigil throughout his brief and painful illness. Frederick died on 20 March, aged only 44. A rumour went round that he had died from a cricket ball hitting his head, but in reality the prince died as a result of a blood clot in his lungs. 'Je sens la mort,' he cried out, wrestling with death in vain, until he eventually succumbed, a little after nine o'clock.[20]

Ironically, George II, whose death had seemed imminent in the 1740s, outlived his son by nine years. For his part, George exhibited some hitherto buried emotion in the weeks following Frederick's death. In public George maintained an emotionally cold appearance but in private, with his son's wife and children, he showed more sympathy. He was said to have told his grandsons that 'they must be brave boys'; he embraced Augusta and 'wept with her'.[21]

Frederick was buried in Henry VII's chapel, Westminster Abbey, on 13 April 1751. Some members of his household, particularly George Bubb Dodington, felt that the arrangements failed to honour him sufficiently, as no music was commissioned for the occasion and Frederick's family, including George II, were predictably absent.[22] Nevertheless, the funeral was conducted with the same level of extravagance with which Frederick lived his life – it cost nearly £2,400, almost as much as would later be spent on the funeral of his father.[23] Frederick's death was a cataclysmic blow for Augusta; aged just 31 she had lost the man who had been her companion since her teens, and with him, her long-held expectation of becoming queen consort. Augusta's world had fallen apart.

Chapter 7

FALL

Following Frederick's death, Augusta allowed herself four hours to grieve, sitting in silent meditation by the body of her husband. At six o'clock in the morning she retired to her bedroom, only to reappear two hours later.[1] 'Mastering her shock', Augusta summoned Lord Egmont and Dr George Lee. She gave Egmont keys for Carlton House and instructed him to retrieve the contents of 'three solid trunks' full of sensitive papers. In order that he could remove the papers to Leicester House discreetly, 'she pulled off the silk covers of the pillow of a couch in the Prince's dressing room' and gave them to Egmont to use as bags. Some hours later Egmont returned in his sedan chair, bringing the papers through the back entrance into the prince's dressing room, where Dr Lee burnt them in the fireplace.[2] Augusta had for some time been privately involved with the Prince of Wales's opposition party; now she was destroying the evidence.

Historians have long been divided over the motives for Augusta's bold actions on that day. Because none of the princess's personal letters or diaries survive, we will never have the story in her own words, and so any account of why she did

what she did is necessarily provisional. But given the circumstances of her decision, some things can be said with certainty.
Augusta was undoubtedly an astute woman who had a firm
grasp on the political realities of her time. She knew that her
collusion in the activities of the opposition would alienate
George II. She also knew that without the backing of Frederick, she lacked any political clout of her own, and needed to
find another royal patron in order to prevent herself and her
son being sidelined; this might either have happened by statute
before George II died, or by force afterwards. She was particularly worried that if arrangements for her son George's regency
were not fully established by the time George II died, the
Duke of Cumberland would attempt a military coup. Clearly
the only person who could provide the security that Augusta
needed was George II himself. By incinerating all the evidence
of her involvement with the opposition, Augusta recognised
that her allegiance was now with the reigning monarch. In the
months that followed, many other opposition politicians would
follow her lead in returning to George's court.

The fact that Augusta was compelled to destroy the evidence of her political life in order to secure her future and
that of her son has had an incalculable influence on her portrayal by historians, who have seen her as a less politically
active figure than she was in reality. Though it is important
to acknowledge this misrepresentation, there is little of
detail that can be said against it, because the precise nature of
this involvement was, of course, lost in the flames. Once again,
the historically subordinate position of women – in this case,
Augusta's inability to continue to wield political influence

without a strong male patron – has brought about a lacuna in the manuscript record.

At her audience with George, Augusta conducted herself adroitly, 'flinging herself entirely into his hands'.[3] She assumed the demeanour of the credulous girl with whom he had been so enamoured 15 years earlier.[4] When her baby was born in July, Augusta named the new princess Caroline Matilda after her grandmother, Queen Caroline. Ostensibly, the king was won over by Augusta's protestations of loyalty and servility, and he 'embraced the Princess', declaring that 'nobody might come between him and her, and he would do everything for her'.[5] He assured Augusta that he supported her custody of the young George as well as the prince's eventual succession, and promised that he would not appoint Frederick's brother, William, as his next in line. He even agreed that in the event of him dying before George came of age, Augusta herself should be regent. This was a remarkable concession for him to make and a significant achievement for Augusta. To cement this victory, Augusta commissioned George Knapton to paint her family. In the portrait Augusta is surrounded by her children. In the background to her right is a portrait of Frederick gesturing down at his progeny, while to her left a statue of Britannia stands guard. It was a powerful statement that despite Frederick's death, the Hanoverian dynasty remained secure.

When George's promise materialised in legislation, it transpired that her powers as regent would be heavily circumscribed. The Regency Act of 1751 established an advisory council, which, in the event of the death of George II, would have to approve any major decisions made by Augusta. The king and his prime minister, Henry Pelham, a Whig, refused to give Augusta any influence over the appointment of young George's counsellors, among whom was the Duke of Cumberland. Not a single political ally of Frederick's had been appointed. Augusta was left powerless, engaged in a battle for survival as a woman in a political world controlled by men.

From 1751 until Prince George came of age in 1756, Augusta's mission was to groom her son for his future role. In order to protect George from William's controlling tendencies, Augusta isolated her son as much as possible from court society. She also had moral reasons for doing this. In spite of Augusta's formal conversion to Anglicanism, the outlook of her childhood religion appears to have stayed with her throughout her life and, in the wake of Frederick's death, she came to judge the court with Lutheran severity, as a place of vice and licentiousness. While Augusta was keen to insulate her son from this corrosive influence, she did not think it prudent to isolate him entirely from the centres of political power, and increasingly they were based in London; two weeks after Frederick's funeral, Augusta gave up the lease of Cliveden and had the furniture moved to Leicester House.[6] Her excessive privacy gave the impression that she was using her influence to indoctrinate the future king with her own political agenda, and public opinion, which had previously been so sympathetic towards Augusta, now began to turn against her.

Augusta was aware that she lacked the experience to induct the young George into the intensely masculine world of kingship and politics, and that her son would require tuition from a male aristocrat. The man she chose for this role was, rather surprisingly, John Stuart, 3rd Earl of Bute, an obscure Scottish lord who had become close friends with Frederick after the pair met by chance in the early 1740s over a game of whist at the Egham races. Bute was married to a daughter of Lady Mary Wortley Montagu and was reputed to have the best legs in London – knee-breeches were currently fashionable, so male calves were constantly on display. Though maverick, Augusta's choice turned out to be wise – Bute instantly won the young George's confidence and became his trusted mentor.

Rumours soon began to circulate that Augusta's interest in Bute was more than merely professional. Horace Walpole commented on the 'swimmingness in her eyes', the 'mellowing in her German accent' and her visible blushing when she was with Bute.[7] Given Augusta's circumspection about Bute's tuition of George – she instructed him to enter Leicester House by the back stairs – the rumours appeared credible and, when the prince dropped the political bombshell that he intended to appoint Bute as his Groom of the Stole, speculation was granted the status of fact. Politicians, newspaper reporters and caricaturists came up with all sorts of inventive ways to imply that Bute owed his meteoric ascent to sleeping with Augusta – the writer George Selwyn acerbically observed that the political alliance based at Leicester House, which included Bute and also the powerful jurist the Earl of Mansfield, was not a faction so much as a 'fuction'.[8] In all likelihood Augusta did not have an affair with Bute; it seems uncharacteristic that she would have indulged in such risqué conduct. Bute, for his part, was a conscientious and happily married man.

The perceived affair, along with other accusations of

political scheming and Machiavellian manoeuvring, exacerbated the shift in the popular perception of Augusta. She became an object of hatred, tormented by the public and vilified by the press, in particular by the *Oxford Magazine*, which declared: 'her name is tyranny'. The relationship between Bute and Augusta was a gift to the new generation of mid-18th-century satirists: a 1771 print, entitled 'Vice Triumphant Over Virtue, or Britannia Hard Rode', showed Augusta, whip in hand, riding a prostrate Britannia, who is suffering exquisite torture at the hands of a gang led by Mansfield and Bute.[9] Another, called 'The Excursion to Cain Wood', depicts her as a witch, riding a broom with the Earl of Mansfield towards his country house, while in the background London – and, by association, its traditional liberties – is engulfed by flames. 'Liberty to me is a joke', says Mansfield; 'My Lord is my sure counsellor', Augusta replies, 'what he dictates shall be a law'.[10]

Augusta's few public appearances were marred by heckling and attacks from the crowds who had once championed her, and, once Prince George came of age in 1756, she ceased these outings altogether. So anxious was Augusta about her public profile that she started to make her charitable donations anonymously, lest they be refused.[11] The accession of her son as George III to the throne in October 1760 did not do anything to restore her image in popular estimations, though it must have been a comfort to her that George finally acceded, and that the long-feared rebellion from William, Duke of Cumberland had not come to pass.

Augusta lived out the remainder of her life in a state of relative seclusion, away from the hostility of the public gaze. She occupied herself with projects at Kew, where she collaborated with the architect William Chambers to produce countless structures in the grounds. Some of these were whimsical and soon fell into disrepair, but others remained popular despite changing fashion. The pagoda she commissioned still stands today, although it is now painted in vermilion, rather than in the original green and white.

By the autumn of 1771 Augusta was terminally ill with throat cancer. On being informed that her death was imminent, George III reasoned that, given his mother's condition, 'it is almost cruel to wish to see her long continue'.[12] She fought off death for several months and by her last week she could not eat or speak, and was wracked with severe pain. None of this diminished her unremitting sense of propriety, which had done so much to impress George II upon their first meeting in 1735 and catapulted her out of obscurity and into the glamorous and fast-paced life of the British royal court. But in the last moments of her life, this decorum was directed towards not her father-in-law, but her son. Sensing that the end was near, Augusta signalled that she should be formally dressed and seated in a chair, so that she could receive the king properly for the last time. This was to be her final request – on the morning of 8 February 1772, aged 52, she was found dead in her chamber by an attendant.

Augusta's funeral was marred by widespread theft and disorder. The theft was opportunistic, as the Henry VII chapel was dark and the purses of wealthy mourners were easy pickings for thieves. The disorder, however, was targeted and personal – the crowd tore the black bunting from the scaffolding and the bier. The rage was in part directed at Augusta herself and in part at George III, who had imposed traditional mourning sanctions, to the detriment of the London textile trade, which depended on the sale of colourful clothes and fabrics. In her prime, Augusta had been the beloved champion of British manufacturers, but in death she had become a symbol of their discontent.

Despite her funeral being an occasion for protest rather than an outpouring of grief, she was remembered in some quarters for the good she had done as Princess of Wales. The *Daily Advertiser* of Tuesday 11 February 1772 printed a mournful poem that reminded the public of her kindness and compassion, and berated 'misted Britons' for maligning a 'virtuous' woman in the last years of her life. The poet appealed to the reputation Augusta shared with Frederick, of being comfortable in all sorts of company regardless of rank or class – 'When the Mechanic or the Peer was seen, She met them equally with Brow serene' – as well as recalling the couple's generous patronage – 'Where should the artist or the Tradesman now, Who never left her but with cheerful brow, Real patronage or kind protection find?'[13]

But this defence of the once-popular princess stood out against a widely held opinion that Augusta had been devious and controlling. In the 20 years since Frederick died, she had gone from darling of the media to arch-villain. Her precipitous fall from public affection, played out in a booming national press, serves as an early cautionary tale of just how fleeting the favour of the media can be. There is something peculiarly modern about the cycle of elevation and demotion, approbation and condemnation to which Augusta fell victim. A portrait of her and Frederick still hangs at Cliveden today, overlooking the great hall. Their expressions have been rendered with great warmth, showing something of the compassion and kindness that characterised their marriage. It is a constant reminder of the king and queen Britain was promised and then denied.

Chapter 8

'A SITE OF RUIN'

After Augusta moved out of Cliveden, Elizabeth Villiers's daughter, Anne, 2nd Countess of Orkney, and her husband, William, regained possession of the house, although the earl spent much of his time in Ireland, where he owned land. The couple had inherited the money woes of Anne's parents and were unable to carry out essential maintenance work on the house. As a result, in the decades after Frederick and Augusta's residence, Cliveden entered a period of neglect and deterioration. On 18 April 1762, the historian Edward Gibbon – a keen student of declining grandeur – recorded its lamentable state. While acknowledging the 'glorious prospect' and 'elegance' of the site, he declared that the place was 'very ill kept'.[1]

Nevertheless, the royal tenure at Cliveden had bestowed nationwide recognition on the house. Prints of the estate were advertised for sale and became highly sought-after collectors' items;[2] when two views of 'Cliveden House and Gardens' were part of a collection stolen from a house in Wandsworth in October 1765, a reward of five guineas was offered for the stolen goods.[3] In the 1760s, rumours bubbled that a 'great personage' was about to purchase the house.[4] It soon became clear that this 'personage' was Frederick and Augusta's son, George III: the *London Evening Post* of 21 February 1778 reported that 'the King is on the point of purchasing Cliefden House, near Maidenhead, for a summer residence'.[5] George's first ten years as monarch had been particularly turbulent, and although matters had stabilised in the 1770s under the ministry of Lord North, he had become disenchanted with his childhood mentor Lord Bute and suspicious of most other politicians. It is not surprising that he should have sought a summer retreat where he could escape the vagaries of court life. By 1778, the king had 12 children of his own and may also have wished to recreate for them elements of his own childhood summers by the Thames.

By this time, the house was in possession of Mary O'Brien, 3rd Countess of Orkney, who had succeeded her mother Anne in 1756. Anne's four sons had predeceased her. It seems that Mary clung to her childhood memories of Cliveden just as ferociously as George, because she refused to sell, even to a reigning monarch. News reports that George was on the verge of buying the house continued, but Mary stood firm. The *British Evening Post* of 16 May 1778 declared that 'the Proprietor of Cliefden ... refused to sell that seat'.[6] In 1780 another report confirmed that the rumours of the king's intentions to purchase the house were 'not true; the present noble proprietor of that charming spot, "the bower of wanton Shrewsbury and love", as Pope calls it, having lately laid out several thousand pounds in the further improvement of it'.[7] It is telling that Elizabeth's granddaughter maintained such an emotional attachment to the house.

Mary, like her four brothers, was born deaf and dumb. In a signed ceremony in 1753, she married her first cousin, Murrough O'Brien, 5th Earl of Inchiquin. Not much is known about Mary's life, although one story has survived. On one occasion her nurse saw her approaching the cradle of her newborn baby, holding a large stone. She dropped it to the ground and the child immediately woke up, startled by the sound. Fearful that her firstborn child had inherited her disability, Mary had been conducting a simple experiment; her child's tears allayed her concerns.[8] She also appeared fleetingly in the newspapers of her day, which reported that she was fitting out a ship 'entirely at her own expense' with 28 guns and 150 men, and naming it the *Royal Charlotte*, in honour of the queen.[9]

The 3rd Countess of Orkney died in 1790 and her daughter, also called Mary, succeeded her. This Mary was married to Thomas Fitzmaurice, whose brother, the 2nd Earl of Shelburne, had served a brief term as prime minister in 1782–3, and was in large part responsible for the negotiations that ended the American War of Independence. Mary and Thomas's marriage, although initially happy, was beset by money problems and threatened by Thomas's alcoholism and depression. From 1792, the couple were living separately, and a year later Thomas died.[10]

Mary's tragic circumstances culminated in 1795, when, five years after she moved into the house, Cliveden burned to the ground. In three hours, the magnificent building conceived by the Duke of Buckingham and developed by the Orkneys was destroyed – only the outer walls and one wing were left standing. The cause of the fire was not certain, but according to newspaper reports, it was believed that 'one of the chambermaids, turning down the beds in the evening, left a candle burning in one of the middle apartments, which set fire to the curtains'.[11] The flames erupted at nine o'clock at night, and were so voracious that all the furniture was consumed and much of the artwork ruined. 'So sudden and violent were the flames, that nothing was saved,' the papers reported.[12] Because of the elevated situation of the house, the blaze, which was 'exceedingly tremendous and awful', was seen 'many miles round'.[13] Mary lost all her jewellery, silver and clothes in the fire – one paper reported that 'not so much of wearing-apparel was saved as to furnish a change of any article to the family for the next day' – but fortunately there were no human casualties.[14]

Cliveden had been reduced to a charred ruin. Following the fire, Mary lived alone, a tragic figure, residing in the dilapidated wing that had escaped the flames. The remains of the house, along with their lone inhabitant, became a source of morbid fascination to the public. Her fallen situation and the ruins in which she lived fitted well with the late 18th-century trend for Gothic sites. In the latter part of the century, under the influence of writers such as Horace Walpole and William Sotheby, 'picturesque' and 'melancholy' settings began to attract artists, writers, and, as the fashion for the Gothic took hold, crowds of tourists. People visited ruins in order to gaze upon the collapsed grandeur of past ages, and in the hope of experiencing a profound sympathy for the previous inhabitants. For the melancholy, Gothic settings were also a reminder of the ephemerality of their own civilisation. Religious ruins were particularly popular: George Keate's 1764 poem 'The

Ruins of Netley Abbey' would spark an enduring public obsession with his subject, a dissolved abbey near Southampton. But
a house like Cliveden with its romantic history and its
pathos-evoking decline was also a natural site for pilgrimage.

Mrs Lybbe Powys visited the ruins of Cliveden on 29 July
1795. She recorded climbing up the 'very steep hill' and seeing
'a scene of ruin' – 'the flight of stone steps all fallen in pieces . . .
the hall, which had fell in, and was a mass of stone pillars and
bricks all in pieces'. In the middle of the scene, a pair of doors
remained standing, eerily untouched by the fire. Powys went
on to record a story about a mystery will, lost to the flames: 'It
seems she [Mary] was much affected by a will that was deposited in a place where the flames were too fierce for anyone to
venture, tho' she tried herself, and a man offer'd to venture too.
The contents were not known.'[15] Whether the will was real or
another Gothic prop borne out of rumour and local imagination, we will never know.

In 1805 Mary commissioned for the house a design that has
since been attributed to John Nash and George Stanley Repton,
but the cost was prohibitive.[16] Instead she continued living
alone among the ruins. In the autumn of 1811, the writer
Charles Knight visited the house to 'make a catalogue of a
large collection of books that had been long neglected', and
that must have weathered the fire in the surviving wing. Like
many 18th-century visitors, Knight approached the house
with Alexander Pope's description in mind. Although the
'principal front' had been burnt down, he wrote, the 'flame' of
the house 'was imperishable, as the "Cliefden's proud alcove"
of Pope'.[17] Knight enjoyed his time at Cliveden, rambling in

the woods and boating on the Thames, and was moved by Mary's stoicism and 'unaffected courtesy', which he saw as 'the memorial of a stately but genial aristocracy that was passing away'.[18] Whether or not the old aristocracy had been genial, its decline – or transformation – would become increasingly evident over the course of the century as it played out, sometimes to disastrous effect, in the lives of the house's subsequent mistresses.

Although unable to finance the rebuilding of the main house, Mary commissioned Peter Nicholson to design a riverside summer house, which would later be altered by George Devey and named Spring Cottage, on the site of a natural spring that been used as a spa by the Orkneys. In the 20th century, the hideaway was to become infamous as the retreat of society osteopath Stephen Ward, who achieved celebrity during the Profumo Affair.

Then, on 10 July 1821, Mary sold Cliveden in an auction at Garraway's Coffee House in Cornhill, London. The sale marked the end of the Orkneys' ownership of the estate, which had lasted over a century. Thanks to the relatively high standing of women in Scottish inheritance rights, the earldom of Orkney had been able to pass down the female line, and for three generations up to 1821, Cliveden had been owned by women. But at the start of the 19th century the house was in a bleak state of neglect. It was only under the nurturing care of the next chatelaine, Harriet, Duchess of Sutherland, that Cliveden would be raised up from the ashes.

PART IV

HARRIET

1806-1868

Chapter 1

'GOODBYE, CASTLE HOWARD!'

A portrait of Harriet, Duchess of Sutherland, still presides over the dining room at Cliveden. The artist, German court painter Franz Xaver Winterhalter, has immortalised Harriet as a classic Victorian beauty: a garland of leaves adorns her auburn hair; her eyes are warm and smiling, her cheeks plump and her complexion milky white. Winterhalter has succeeded in capturing the majesty of Harriet's public demeanour, as well as the warmth and maternal instinct that sustained her long, happy marriage. Majesty came easily to Harriet. Unlike her predecessors, she did not have to toil to reach Cliveden.

Harriet was the fifth of twelve children, her parents' third daughter, and the progeny of 'Grand Whiggery' – an elite tribe of grandee families who were arbiters of taste, champions of statecraft, patrons of the arts and connoisseurs of refined pleasure. Harriet's grandmother was the fashion icon, Whig activist and noted political hostess Georgiana, Duchess of Devonshire. In marriage, Harriet augmented her great political inheritance with a great industrial one. Her husband George Leveson-Gower was heir to a fortune unrivalled among the aristocracy of the early 19th century: his father had transformed a phenomenal portfolio of canal investments – inherited from his uncle the Duke of Bridgewater – into an even bigger fortune based in railways, and was known as a 'leviathan of wealth'. His mother, a countess in her own right, held Sutherland, an isolated million-acre territory in Highland Scotland. The family also owned vast swathes of property in England, including Trentham Hall, their main seat in Staffordshire. Between them, Harriet's ancestry and the family she married into represented two great aristocratic traditions: high politics and capital.

It was clear from the beginning that Harriet had inherited a balance of her mother's determination and her father's gentle nature. Her formative years were spent at the seat of her paternal grandparents, Castle Howard in Yorkshire. Built on the site of the ruined Henderskelfe Castle, it had come into the family in 1571. In 1699, the architect Sir John Vanbrugh – also the architect of Blenheim Palace, the building that had done so much to inspire the Orkneys' vision of Cliveden – had been charged with the redesign and had produced a baroque palace comprising two symmetrical wings and a central dome. Later, a further wing in the Palladian style was added. 'I have seen gigantic palaces before, but never a sublime one,' enthused the historian and purveyor of all things Gothic, Horace Walpole. The Whig writer and politician Macaulay declared it 'the most perfect specimen of the most vicious style'.[1] It was within this spectacular setting that Harriet was educated alongside her elder sisters, Caroline and Georgiana.

Even as a toddler, Harriet eclipsed her siblings both in

character and talent. 'Remarkably intelligent, talking more than her year-older brother, Harriet already, so their nurse puts it, "masters them all",' wrote her aunt.[2] Like Elizabeth Villiers more than a century earlier, Harriet learned French and was taught to draw, but Harriet's education also included history and literature. She wrote, 'I like Oreste [the Oresteia, Aeschylus's tragic trilogy]; like Athalie [Racine's masterpiece], it has shown me that a play can be interesting without love', while her history lessons allowed her to reflect on the nature of female power. In December 1820 she recorded a conversation with her grandfather where they discussed Queen Elizabeth, Lady Jane Grey and Marie Antoinette. Harriet's precocious intellect clearly engaged her grandfather, who was 'in good spirits and particularly kind'. Prolific and self-conscious letter writers, the sisters hoped their correspondence would be read by subsequent generations. With this in mind, after her sisters' deaths, Caroline spent years copying their letters into a series of books, a challenging task given Harriet's seismographic scrawl.

As the Howard sisters reached their mid-teens, their thoughts inevitably turned to marriage. In 1821, Harriet's eldest sister, Georgiana, became engaged to George Agar Ellis, the only son of Lord Clifden, a wealthy Irish peer. The match was thought by some to be rather 'business like', but it seems to have pleased Georgiana, who, after the wedding on 7 March 1822, wrote to Caroline saying that she was 'perfectly happy, so very much so . . . it is delightful thought to think of passing the whole of one's life with a person whom one adores'.[3] Georgiana's new husband was a serious-minded young man who occupied himself with historical literature and became some-thing of a connoisseur in art, as well as an author and a politician.[4] From oblique references in letters, it appears that Ellis, although devoted, 'was rather a difficult husband'. But Georgiana admired his attainments and aspirations, and 'upheld him against adverse criticism, if and when she came across it'.[5]

A year later, in April 1823, aged 16, Harriet journeyed from Castle Howard to make her society debut in London. More than ready to be unleashed from the schoolroom and start her adventure, as the carriage pulled away from her childhood home, she cried: 'Goodbye, Castle Howard! You will never see me Harriet Howard again.' At her inaugural ball she caught the eye of 'one of the most eligible bachelors of the day', her cousin George Granville Leveson-Gower, then Earl Gower and heir to his father's marquessate of Stafford. George was entranced by Harriet, and only a week later, the couple became engaged. The pocket diary of Harriet's mother records the breathless pace of events: Friday, April 25: 'My brother's Ball for Harriet.' Tuesday, April 29: 'Hope of Lord Gower.' Thurs-day, May 1: 'Lord Gower's note. Esterhazy's Ball.' Friday, May 2: 'Lord Gower proposed and was accepted.' Harriet's family was thrilled with the match.[6]

Aged 36 at the time of the engagement, George was nearly 20 years older than Harriet and, unlike his future bride, he had led a cosmopolitan life. George was educated first at Harrow and later at Christ Church, Oxford, but his passion was for travel. When he left Oxford in 1806 he was unable to take the Grand Tour, beloved of so many young aristocratic men in this period, as France and Italy were under the control of

Napoleon Bonaparte and Germany was well within the emperor's sights, blocking the route across Europe. George's hopes were not completely dashed, however. His cousin had been ordered to the Prussian court, which was desperately seeking allies against an advancing Napoleon. Resourceful George managed to persuade his cousin to allow him to join the mission as a dispatch carrier.[7] The political mission failed, but George was able to use the opportunity to travel to Hamburg, then Copenhagen, and finally on to Prussia.[8]

While at the Prussian court, George became infatuated with King William Frederick III's 'amiable, charming' wife, Queen Louise. On 7 February 1807 he wrote to his mother saying 'you would like her so very much'.[9] But while Louise clearly enjoyed George's company, she remained happily married. After a period serving his uncle, Lord Granville Leveson-Gower, British ambassador in St Petersburg, George returned to England in 1808. He was not to venture abroad again until December 1813, by which time Louise had succumbed to a mysterious illness and died – in her husband's arms.

During the next six years, George showed little inclination to marry; he twice visited Italy, and in 1812, was among the founder members of the Roxburghe Club, an elite association of bibliophiles. More than a decade after his friendship with Queen Louise, he eventually showed a brief interest in Lord Clanwilliam's sister during a visit to Vienna in 1821, but his advances came to nothing. Later that year, George made his first visit to Castle Howard. 'He is *bouché* [silent] completely on the subject of the [Howard] girls,' Harriet's aunt Lady Granville (who was married to George's uncle) wrote to her sister, 'and I dare not ask questions'.[10] But some months later, he admitted to Lady Granville that he liked Harriet and her elder sister, Georgiana, so much that 'were it not for youth he would think of one of them'.[11]

On Wednesday 28 May 1823, a month after their first dance, Harriet and George were married. At 16 years old, Harriet was the same age Anna Maria had been on the day of her wedding to the Earl of Shrewsbury, who was also, like George, 20 years the senior of his bride. Yet unlike Anna Maria, Harriet was no young girl leaping into the unknown. Despite her tender age, she displayed a sense of serene self-assurance that would shape her life and future relationships.

The wedding was received with the enthusiasm usually reserved for a royal wedding. The *Caledonian Mercury* of Saturday 14 June 1823 reported that 'the nuptials of the heir of the noble family of Trentham is an event which has excited, during the past week, the liveliest feelings of gratulation, attachment, and respect, throughout an extensive district in this county, and in that of Stafford'. The ceremony itself took place in the green drawing room at Devonshire House and was conducted by the Archbishop of York. Harriet was radiant in a 'magnificent robe of Valenciennes lace, with a veil of the same material, extending to the feet from the head'.[12] George's 'lovely bride' was thought to be 'highly endowed with mental attainments, and very beautiful'.[13]

The celebrations were conducted on a grand scale befitting the union of two such noble Whig households. An elaborate Gothic arch was constructed for the occasion, its turrets draped with garlands of ivy and oak. It was emblazoned with the motto 'Happiness and perpetuity to the House of Trentham'; on one side a banner was hung that bore the legend 'Gower' in gold lettering on a crimson background, and on the other, one that bore the name 'Howard'. The *Caledonian Mercury* reported that between two and three hundred guests had been invited to attend a 'splendid ball' to celebrate the wedding, and that they were provided with 'every refreshment'.[14] Provision was also made for the estate workers and their families to enjoy the festivities, which were as much an act of charity as a display of wealth. There was dancing and feasting, bonfires and the sounding of cannon, and a maypole was erected for the local children. 'Upwards of 200 persons partook of tea in a spacious booth erected for the purpose' and two roasted sheep, as well as 'plenty of bread, potatoes, and plumb pudding', were supplied for the cottagers on the estate.[15]

After the ceremony, George and Harriet set off in a 'beautiful chariot and four horses' for the family retreat in Richmond, where they were to spend their honeymoon.[16] As a wedding present from George's father, the couple received estates to the value of £20,000. It was a significant endowment, though tiny compared to what they stood to inherit on his death. Moreover, it had been bequeathed at a time of widespread popular protest, much of which was directed at extremes of wealth and the exclusiveness of political power. It was this protest, as much as the endowment itself, that would shape Harriet and George's first decade together.

Chapter 2

REFORM AND REVOLUTION

here is something so beautiful, so interesting and so
lovable in this place, that I feel every day more fond of
it,' Harriet wrote effusively to her mother-in-law, Elizabeth, of her first stay at the family's Sutherland seat, Dunrobin
Castle. By September 1823, Harriet had settled happily into
married life. In the months following the wedding she com-
municated regularly with Elizabeth. Her letters are warm,
lively, full of anecdotes and peppered with literary allusions
and French phrases. The couple had visited Trentham Hall in
August, which Harriet thought 'the most palace like thing I
have ever seen', and later that month Chatsworth House. 'I
have been delighted with all I have seen, and much interested
with all that has been and is still doing,' she enthused.

Harriet's self-assuredness was palpable; in January 1824 her
maternal aunt Lady Granville came to stay and 'found her a
very handsome, blooming, somewhat matronly woman, whom
I should have pronounced to be about twenty-five'. Harriet
was in fact only 17. George also thrived in the relationship. 'As
to his happiness, I never saw anything like it,' Lady Granville
commented, observing that 'his mind and manner have

expanded under her influence.' Harriet also inspired the ardour of her mother-in-law, who 'quite worships her ... [and] says she has not the shadow of a fault'.[1] The sheltered teenager who had barely ventured beyond the walls of Castle Howard had proved herself to be more than capable of rising to the demands of her new role. This must have come as a relief to the Howard family, who continued to be haunted by the spectre of Georgiana, Duchess of Devonshire's unhappy marriage; despite being charming, stylish and intelligent, Harriet's maternal grandmother had famously struggled with the pressures of being a duchess. Harriet could not have been more different. She flourished, so much so that she incurred the jealousy of some society women who felt that her head seemed 'nearly turned by the splendour and independence of her new situation'.[2]

One aspect of her new life that perplexed the young bride was other people's cynicism about her marriage. She confided to Lady Granville about her 'danger in society', and asked why it was that 'just married and passionately fond of her husband, flirting with her should occur to others; and that, unlike other brides, everybody was speculating whether she would flirt or no'. Lady Granville replied that although she knew Harriet was sincerely in love with George, 'nobody believes it'. In a society where marriage was considered to be more of a transactional arrangement than a matter of the heart, Harriet's devotion to her husband was unusual, especially given the wide age gap. Writing to Lady Morpeth, Lady Granville explained how Harriet's strong moral compass, her innate sense of right from wrong, was the bedrock of her character. 'With such excellence, such freedom from all wrong, her conduct can never err,' she wrote, adding that her niece was not of the disposition 'to be amused by the mere mechanical apparatus of society, dress, light, crowd, small talk'. But as the gossip died down, even the harshest social critics were charmed by the vivacious and amiable Howard daughter. Madame de Lieven declared that 'il est impossible d'avoir des manières plus distinguées [it is impossible to have more distinguished manners]' while Lady Granville herself concluded that her niece simply 'wins all hearts'.[3]

Lady Granville's assertion in January 1824 that Harriet was 'blooming' was truer than she realised. Harriet was pregnant. 'I am going to make you a very premature disclosure of my hopes,' she wrote to her mother-in-law in November 1823. 'I cannot resist communicating the expectations of that, which it gives me such pleasure to tell and that I know will be very pleasant and welcome intelligence to you dear [Elizabeth].' The contrast between Harriet's warm and open relationship with her mother-in-law and Princess Augusta's stiff, contrived and infrequent communications with Queen Caroline could not be more stark. Harriet's first child, named Elizabeth after her paternal grandmother, was born in May 1824.

Motherhood did not prevent Harriet from venturing abroad. At the beginning of March 1825, the Gowers set sail for Paris and Harriet, who was already pregnant again, made the difficult decision to leave her baby daughter behind in England. 'The parting with one's child is most dreadful,' she lamented to her sister Caroline. 'You have no idea of the treasure her little likeness is to us; we have it out and look at it constantly when by ourselves.' In the same letter Harriet also recounts her crossing. Her stress-free and relatively short trip across the Channel was an entirely different experience from that of Anna Maria 200 years earlier. The first mistress of Cliveden had endured a wretched crossing to France, lasting more than eight hours; Harriet embarked at Dover and reached '*le beau pays de France* in the space of four hours and a half'. When she arrived on the French mainland she was greeted with the charming sight of French ladies 'in white caps and long gold earrings'. She headed straight to 'a very good inn, l'Hotel de Bains', where she rested and 'had some broth'. Afterwards, she took a gentle stroll around the ramparts of the town and was amused by the locals, who reminded her of 'an exaggerated French play'.[4]

For ten years now, Britain and France had enjoyed peace, even if relations were still a little strained. After Napoleon Bonaparte's final defeat at the Battle of Waterloo on 18 June 1815, Louis XVIII of the Bourbon monarchy returned to the French throne. During this time, the French were more concerned with the shape of their own constitution than with antagonising their old rivals, and the British had no reason to resume hostilities since Louis had been their preferred candidate to rule France. Jokes and insults were tossed back and forth over the Channel, but Britain and France would never again be at war with each other. France quickly became a popular destination for English holidaymakers intrigued to discover more about the sights and culture of their erstwhile foe.

Paris proved to be a social merry-go-round of parties, balls and plays. Harriet enjoyed the theatre, which she attended 'beautifully *coiffée* in heron's plumes'. However, she was not impressed with the Parisian balls, which she found crowded, and neither was she particularly taken with French fashion: 'their dress is nothing remarkable here,' she wrote to Caroline. She also remarked on the dubious dancing skills of her hostess the Duchesse de Berri, whose steps were 'entirely composed of an ungainly sort of jump, given with the look of a country girl', acerbically adding that 'her manner is most like Miss [Maria] Foote's in that play where she tries to disgust her love, only that our Duchesse is uncommonly aided by nature to produce that end'.[5] Despite extensive commentary on her social escapades, family was never far from Harriet's mind: she concluded one of her letters from Paris by asking if Caroline had yet weaned her 'little man'.

At the time of Harriet's visit, Paris was ablaze with opulent celebrations surrounding the coronation of Charles X, brother of Louis XVIII, who had died without an heir in the autumn of 1824. On Monday 6 June 1825, Harriet watched from an oculist's balcony as the new king made his ceremonial entry into Paris. 'The prettiest part almost was seeing all the ambassadors defile on their way to Notre Dame,' she wrote. Despite the music and 'the gayest looking crowd', and the firing of guns at the Tuileries, Harriet observed that Charles X was 'evidently not popular'. The ultra-royalist principles of the king did not sit well with a public who remembered the vicious battle for popular sovereignty that was the first French Revolution of 1789. After several more weeks of entertainment, including a trip to Versailles 'to see the grand *eaux* play for the ambassadors extraordinary', the Gowers left Paris at the end of June.[6]

High child-mortality rates and the importance of producing a steady succession of heirs meant that serial pregnancies were desirable among women of Harriet's class and generation. Just over a month after their return to England, on 8 August, Harriet gave birth to another daughter, Evelyn, and two years later had a third girl, who was christened Caroline. 'I was called this morning with the delightful news of dearest Harriet's safe confinement,' recorded the baby's namesake, Harriet's sister. 'We went up to town [from Roehampton] immediately after breakfast, and found her and the little girl (not quite so welcome this time) going on as well as possible . . . It is the finest child she has had, but it ought to have been a boy.' Caroline's acknowledgment that a boy would have been 'more welcome' highlights the pressure on aristocratic women to provide their husbands with a son. Thankfully, George was less exacting than the husband of Harriet's grandmother Georgiana, who had been notoriously impatient and unforgiving about her inability to produce a male heir. Harriet adored her girls and was amused by Lady Granville's dictum: 'All boys and men are odious'.[7] Nevertheless, she finally fulfilled her dynastic duty when, on 19 December 1828, she gave birth to her first son, George, Viscount Trentham.

During this period of intensive childbearing, Harriet and George were based at Lilleshall, a Shropshire estate that Lord Stafford had given to his son at the time of his marriage. Harriet's days at Lilleshall were full of nursery and household management, on which subjects she frequently wrote to

Caroline. Maternal pride shone throughout her correspondence. Of their eldest daughter, Elizabeth, Harriet wrote that she 'grows a young woman; feeds herself and has a great spirit of order and neatness', and also, a few days later, that she 'becomes very accomplished; digs, plants, waters, and nods to the [village] children'. Although content, Harriet at times found her daily routine banal and repetitive. 'The only part of this life I do not approve is that it gives one nothing to tell, as one day is strictly like another,' she wrote, adding that she did not disapprove of this in reality, 'because the one day is pleasant'.[8] In the ensuing years of emotional upheaval, Harriet would yearn for these days of simple domesticity.

Harriet's letters at this time also give an insight into the elements that Lilleshall lacked, and what she might have been looking for in Cliveden. She warned Caroline, who was about to visit Lilleshall, that 'you are not to expect this place the most enjoyable or loveable, naturally and instinctively . . . you know that we are in a manufacturing district and we must see smoke. Still love and enjoy it I will; tho' the dove perhaps would not have rested here after the deluge.' At the time, however, what Harriet truly desired was not a new country home, but a grand house in London. When Lord Stafford purchased the lease to York House for £72,000 in 1827, she must have had high hopes that her father-in-law would give them the property as a London residence. But he kept it for himself and, worse, decorated it not in Harriet's preferred modern style, but with a selection of his many pictures. Under Lord Stafford's ownership, the house became known as Stafford House. In letters to Caroline, Harriet wrote with aching restraint on the subject of her deprivation: 'I must be all candour with you; I do not feel the not having [Stafford House] a welcome respite, tho' I hope you will believe in the same candour, that I am not discontented.'[9]

On 24 June 1830, Harriet delivered her fifth child, another daughter, Blanche. She was confined at Hamilton Place in Mayfair, and had a succession of visitors, including her parents-in-law, Lord and Lady Stafford. But this happy event was soon to be overshadowed by worrying developments in national politics. Two days after Blanche's birth, King George IV died without an heir and his younger brother, William IV, ascended the throne. Not strong enough to leave the house, Harriet watched the celebrations from her window, wistfully observing to Caroline that 'the dense crowd, the waving of *les panaches blancs* [white feathers], the applause and the troops made a beautiful sight.'[10]

At the time, the death of a monarch necessitated a general election, and this took place during July and August 1830. Although the Tories had dominated government for the last 18 years, the election came at a bad time for the Duke of Wellington and his party. The Tories were divided over policy, and the pressures of industrialisation and a post-war economic downturn had created tensions that were now reaching boiling point. In southern England, from Dorset to East Anglia and Lincolnshire, agricultural disturbances and distress were rife: arson had broken out in April 1830 as furious labourers on starvation wages burned hayricks and smashed threshing machines.[11] Many among the aristocracy recognised that – for their own protection as much as anything – something had to change. The electoral franchise was already severely restricted, and rising populations in urban areas coupled with the depopulation of some rural constituencies had made Parliament even more unrepresentative of the country than it had been in the previous century. Though Wellington was able to cling on to his position as prime minister, there was a significant shift in the balance of power, with his party losing 30 seats to the Whigs and to a new parliamentary group, the Radicals.

Harriet watched the world around her being stripped of its old certainties with a mix of alarm and incredulity. In London, the establishment of the 'New Police', instituted by Sir Robert Peel, then Home Secretary, was 'intensely resented' by many people, including many Whigs. In a letter of 30 October, however, Harriet made it clear that she was a supporter of the new police force, whom she imagined as a bulwark against the mob. She showed little sympathy for traditional Whig views that the police were a threat to liberty; the main influence upon her politics was raw, undiluted fear. 'I think there is no danger that restraining our liberties can be attempted in days like these, and I think all is to be feared from the people,' she wrote. Popular resistance to Peel's method of law enforcement was, in her opinion, 'blood-boiling and odious'.[12]

Harriet viewed advances in technology with a similar sense of foreboding; change of any sort frightened rather than excited her. In September 1830, just a week before the inauguration of the Liverpool and Manchester Railway, Britain's first ticketed railway line, Harriet hosted a dinner at Trentham Hall for William Huskisson, MP for Liverpool, and his wife, Emily. The Sutherlands were heavily involved in the Liverpool–Manchester railway: Lord Stafford was an early investor, having purchased a fifth of the railway's shares in December 1825. George, his younger brother Francis, and Huskisson were among the dignitaries invited on the maiden journey between Liverpool and Manchester. Their train, pulled by the *Northumbrian*, would be one of a number running in the 'gala' day. 'The drive on the railway has an alarming sound,' Harriet wrote, adding that Huskisson's wife 'seems to dread Liverpool'.[13] Their apprehension proved prophetic.

On 15 September the line was officially opened by the Duke of Wellington and the celebratory journey from Liverpool Crown Street to Manchester Liverpool Road was soon underway. The *Northumbrian* had to stop at Parkside, halfway to Manchester, in order to take on more water. Ignoring safety advice, 'twelve or fourteen of the party', Huskisson among them, got out onto the tracks to view the water-supplying apparatus and to visit the Duke of Wellington in his carriage at the front of the train.[14] Then disaster struck. Another train, pulled by Robert Stephenson's *Rocket*, was coming in the opposite direction. Most of the men on the track rushed to a position of safety, either away from the trains or between the tracks, which were far enough apart to leave a safe gap between passing trains. But Huskisson panicked and grabbed the door of a carriage being pulled by the *Northumbrian*. The door swung open and he was hit by the oncoming train. He was thrown forward onto the track where the *Rocket* crushed his legs, leaving them 'weltering in blood'.[15] He was taken to Eccles for medical treatment in a train driven by Stephenson himself. Huskisson was given a large dose of laudanum, but died soon afterwards, becoming the first railway fatality in history.

For Harriet, Huskisson's demise became symbolic of the high price of progress in a brave new world. As the railways were expanding across England, connecting communities up and down the country, Harriet's own world of aristocratic privilege and entitlement seemed to be unravelling. For the first time, she feared the future.

Chapter 3

FEAR in a TIME of CHOLERA

Harriet anxiously followed the violent clashes that raged between London crowds and the newly created police force, viewing the whole episode as a struggle to defend aristocratic power and values. She was particularly upset by the use of knives – as distinct from swords, which were only carried by the higher orders – as weapons: 'The anti-police cry is most barbarous against these unfortunate unarmed people; one was said to have been struck with many knives the other night, and this use of the knife, if it becomes habitual, is frightful.'[1] The threat of disorder and dispossession continued to dominate Harriet's correspondence and many other aristocrats echoed her fears: on 29 November her sister-in-law Lady Carlisle wrote of an acquaintance who 'is altogether in a most desponding state since his expedition into Hampshire [where there had been riots] . . . he talks as if it was all over with the landed property'.[2]

One way to avoid such a dramatic outcome, political pragmatists of the day argued, was parliamentary reform. The electorate in 1830 was three per cent smaller than it had been in 1640, despite a threefold rise in the population. The smallest and most underpopulated constituencies were known as 'rotten boroughs'; with an electorate consisting of just seven people, Old Sarum in Salisbury still returned two MPs to every Parliament. Given the depth of these problems, it seemed to many at the top of society, as well as those further down the social hierarchy, that change needed to be made. But addressing the House of Lords, Wellington declared that the parliamentary system could not be improved upon, and absolutely ruled out any reform bill, even one of a moderate character.[3] In the aftermath, according to Harriet, the town was 'full of reports' that Wellington was 'going out' of power; 'after that unaccountable speech on reform, I do not see how he can stay in,' she wrote.[4]

Harriet was right: Wellington could not sustain his government and, on 16 November 1830, he resigned his premiership. The new prime minister was Charles Grey, 2nd Earl Grey, who as a young man had an infamous affair with Harriet's grandmother. In February 1831, as the campaign for reform was gaining momentum, Harriet dined with Grey and his wife, Mary. She also attended many dinners at which Grey's new government was the main topic of conversation. 'I wish you had been in town for this most interesting of all times,' Harriet wrote to Caroline, commenting on the debates surrounding the first reform bill, introduced to the Commons by Lord John Russell on behalf of the Whig administration in March 1831.[5] The bill was more radical than both the Tory opposition and some Whig ministers expected.

Harriet was undecided as to whether she supported the bill. Though she sympathised with the Whig idea of reform and still referred to the parliamentary opposition as 'the enemy', she did not think that it was safe to give 'the people' any more of a voice than they had already – which was, of course, no voice at all. 'I admire the plan more than I can express,' she wrote, but continued, 'I fear the results and certainly do not think these are times in which the voice of the people ought to be more heard.' Harriet's ambivalence towards electoral reform highlights her cautious politics and desire to preserve the status quo. She must, then, have been somewhat relieved when progress proved difficult: the bill eventually passed by one vote in the House of Commons, but failed in the House of Lords.

Undeterred, the Whigs continued to push for reform, aided by ever-increasing public support and their Commons majority. In September 1831, the second reform bill passed through the Commons, and in October it was debated in the Lords. Harriet went to watch the debates; it was the first time she had visited the Lords and, despite the gravity of the topics under discussion, her letters recall a somewhat frivolous enjoyment of the occasion. 'I went at ½ past 3 with George and Morpeth to the House of Lords, the 1st time I had ever done it, and staid till 11,' she wrote, 'I never was more entertained; there was a great deal of lively talk upon petitions.' With the same unforgiving wit she had brought to bear on Parisian high society, she mocked the oratorical style of the key parliamentary players: 'Lord Grey's manner is very fine, but over haughty, and I think I see his great vanity constantly piercing. Lord Holland was very violent – gesticulation, that must make it immense physical labour, and Lord Goderich is the same in this respect; it would be dreadful to come within the *rioché* of his strong arm.' Her own father's efforts she treated with a dutiful kindness that bordered on damning with faint praise: 'Papa said a few words very well, and hardly gave one time to be nervous.'[6]

Harriet was not the only aristocratic woman attending the Lords to support members of her family. 'I was pretty well placed next to [Lady] Clanricarde; we had a wall to lean against and saw very well when standing up, but . . . it made me very ill indeed, and it is melancholy and humiliating not to be able to do these things without impunity.' Evidently struggling with the long parliamentary sittings, Harriet and a group of ladies retired briefly to drink tea. But here too, politics seems to have dominated their discussion, rather to Harriet's discomfort. She complained of feeling 'very out of my water' in the group of 40 women, 'a terrible number', and all Tories. Despite her reservations about the bill, in a group of opposition wives, she felt her political identity strongly. Party-political affiliations were not the only factor which determined the women's opinions on reform. Over tea, Lady Clanricarde, 'a very clever person with *un esprit très mâle*', came out in support of the bill, not because of its content, but because she took a 'liking [to] the Ministers'.[7]

It is unlikely that many, if any of the women present, had thoughts of lobbying for the extension of the franchise to women. That task was left to a few radical critics, such as Henry 'Orator' Hunt, who presented to the House of Commons a petition from a wealthy Yorkshire woman, Miss Mary Smith, proposing that unmarried women who met the bill's property requirements should be given the vote. Smith and Hunt saw this as an attempt to recover old rights, as during the Tudor and early Stuart monarchies, women freeholders and burgesses had been entitled to vote in parliamentary elections. In response to the attempted amendment, MPs in the Commons had the wording changed so that it referred to 'male persons' instead of simply 'persons'. Like most women of her acquaintance, Harriet identified primarily with her class, rather than her sex. If she had reservations about extending the franchise to the upper middle class, she would have been even less ready to support its extension to women. In this respect, she conformed to the 19th-century prejudice that held politics to be a 'male' domain.

Harriet's fears about reform were well represented in the Lords, where the second bill was also defeated, this time by 41 votes, prompting widespread rioting and disorder across the country. The spectre of 'mob rule' hung over Britain as rioters set fire to Nottingham Castle and another group gained control of Bristol for three days. In London, stones were thrown at Apsley House, the residence of the Duke of Wellington, who had been a symbol of resistance to reform since his ministry collapsed. George found a stone in his carriage and Harriet's mother was jeered at, which made Harriet fear that 'we should all go about in omnibuses soon, without livery servants, and one's coronet in one's heart.'[8] On 16 October, Harriet saw Wellington at a party thrown by Madame de Lieven, and felt deeply sorry for him, 'since I heard the groans and hooting that accompanied the crash of his broken panes; 2 stones struck Lady Lyndhurst's picture in the throat'.[9] Against threats like these, the old divide between Whigs and Tories seemed insignificant. The world they shared was under attack.

The violence took on an even more frightening edge when viewed alongside recent events in France. On 29 July 1830, shortly before the battle for reform had begun in Britain, revolution had broken out in Paris. The absolutist tendencies of Charles X's monarchy had finally become too much for the French people, who rose up after the king issued *ordonnances* that dissolved the Chamber of Deputies and muzzled the press. Paving stones were pulled up and thrown at soldiers, barricades sprang up around the city, and on 2 August, Charles was forced to abdicate. Harriet wrote sympathetically, 'What a journey the unfortunate King of France's must be, and the Duchess of Berri's, and the empty titles! . . . I dread the cold blooded executions as much as other horrors.'[10] Events in France intensified fears that the contagion of revolution would spread to England. Convinced that reform was the only antidote, the Whigs pressed on with their mission; in the spring of 1832, they made a third attempt at passing a reform bill. They had, however, learnt from their previous experience. Knowing that the bill would fail in the Lords, the Whigs tried to persuade William IV to create a raft of new Whig peers with a view to establishing a pro-reform majority in the upper house. The king was uneasy about making such a bold move. Against the advice of his entire cabinet, he refused to create the necessary peers. At this news, Grey resigned and Wellington was invited to form a new government. Public anger at these developments led to a violent ten-day period of rioting known as the 'Days of May', with some protesters advocating the non-payment of taxes, and others encouraging a run on the banks.

Amid all the chaos and despite promising moderate parliamentary reforms, Wellington found himself unable to form a government. William had no choice but to recall Grey, assent to the creation of new Whig peers, and write to the Tory peers, pleading them to cease their opposition to the reform bill. In the end, enough Tories abstained from the vote for the bill to pass through both houses. The Representation of the People Act – also known as the Great Reform Act – became law on 7 June 1832, irrevocably changing the character of British politics. Seats were redistributed to better represent the populations of constituencies, and the worst of the rotten boroughs were abolished. Some in the upper middle classes found themselves newly enfranchised. Debate about parliamentary reform was far from over, but Harriet's apocalyptic fears had been allayed; reform had stopped revolution in its tracks.

Harriet was too preoccupied with the drama of her own life to observe the passage of the third bill. By November 1832 she was back at Lilleshall, fraught and anxious about illness, chiefly cholera. Her letters are written in an entirely different key from those first heady years of marriage. However, it was not cholera but a common virus that was to be the cause of Harriet's greatest misery yet. In December 1831, shortly after the failure of the second reform bill, she wrote that baby Blanche had developed a fever and was steadily deteriorating. 'I have found my baby hardly better, if at all,' Harriet wrote, 'her nature is excessively altered, she is so quiet and melancholy.' It seems that six-month-old Blanche was not strong enough to withstand the regular 'fits of hot and cold fever'; she was, said Harriet, 'so fractious that it makes it difficult for the doctors to judge [her condition], as she will seldom allow herself to be touched'.[11] For a time there was some improvement and Harriet wrote optimistically that her 'little woman' was getting better, but this hope proved misplaced. Blanche died in February 1832 and was buried at Trentham Hall on 19 March.

Events both on the national stage and within Harriet's own family were conspiring to force the intelligent young girl from Castle Howard to grow up. With this would come both maturity and a new pessimism. 'I no longer possess the zest and freshness, and to say the truth, the happiness of former days,' she wrote. In the space of a decade, the light-heartedness of her honeymoon days had evaporated, to be replaced with a persistent 'melancholy', a word that would recur in so many of her letters over the next ten years: Harriet was suffering from what would now be diagnosed as depression.

Chapter 4

NORTH AND SOUTH

Hopeful that a change of scene would alleviate their anguish, the bereaved Gower family headed to Scotland for the summer. But Harriet was more afraid than ever of cholera, which continued to claim victims among her circle of friends and acquaintances. She began a July letter to Caroline with a reference to Mrs Robert Smith, whose sudden death from cholera sent shock waves throughout London society: 'Mrs Smith's death had given one to see in the most striking way the melancholy liability of all.'[1] Her depression cannot have been helped by a visit to Holyrood Palace in Edinburgh, where the deposed king of France, Charles X, and his family were spending their exile. Scotland seemed a safe place to Charles, who had lived at Holyrood between 1796 and 1803, but he and his wife were vastly changed from the resplendent figures whose ceremonial entry into Paris Harriet had witnessed in 1825. In particular, Harriet was shocked by the degeneration of the dauphine, who 'had a great deal of grey hair about her face' and whose 'abord is graceless, her voice and manner rough'.[2] To Harriet, the exiled monarch was the living incarnation of the carnage wrought by revolution.

At the end of July Harriet, her family and their trusted maid Mrs Penson travelled to Uppat, a village near Dunrobin. Two decades later this journey would be transformed by the construction of the Highland Railway, in which the Sutherlands invested heavily. But in 1832, the entire trip still had to be undertaken by road. After a few days Harriet, already in a despondent mood, became claustrophobic. 'A great deal is very dreary,' she wrote to her sister, ' . . . it inclined one to feel melancholy . . . One might fancy that the mountains would close about one and not allow one to return.' In the same letter, Harriet reports the news that cholera had appeared in Sutherland. It would be the late 1840s before John Snow deduced that cholera was transmitted through the drinking of contaminated water and was not, as presumed in the early 1830s, a 'miasmic' disease.[3] The paucity of medical knowledge about the disease rendered it particularly terrifying to Harriet, who wrote that 'I feel very low at the first news of it'.

The Highland landscape that stretched before Harriet had undergone traumatic changes in the last century. In the wake of the failed Jacobite uprising of 1745, whole communities of crofters and farmers had been forced off their land by new landlords who had been installed by the Hanoverian Crown and wished to make their estates more profitable. In the process of this brutal agricultural revolution, much of the clan culture was obliterated and all feudal obligations swept aside, in favour of a capitalist system that focused on the 'improvement' of land to yield greater profit. These 'improvements' were not solely directed at estate revenues, but also at the Highlanders themselves, who were thought to be ill-bred and uncivilised.[4]

George's father, the 1st Duke of Sutherland, had invested heavily in the Highland clearances, but Harriet had been familiar with this displacement scheme long before her marriage. Her childhood letters make several references to Samuel Johnson and James Boswell, whose accounts of travelling around the Highlands in 1773 brought attention to the subject of the transformation of that region. Johnson's opinion on the new Highland landlordism was ambivalent. While he endorsed the 'improving' cause, he was moved by the remnants of the older feudal society and was concerned that increasing rents were depopulating the Highlands. Overall, his analysis of the 'Highland problem' (as it was commonly referred to at the time) championed gradual improvement, while objecting to the severe measures of some landlords in pursuit of profit.[5]

In reality, change was anything but gradual or moderate. The Sutherland clearances were the most extreme of all the so-called 'improvements' in the early 19th century. In the immediate aftermath of the Battle of Culloden in 1746, the Sutherland estates had forgone drastic change due to the relative poverty of the Sutherland dynasty. In 1785, George, Harriet's father-in-law, married Elizabeth Gordon, Countess of Sutherland in her own right, but it was not until 1803, when George inherited his father's fortune, that the process of 'improvement' began. It was Elizabeth and not her husband, as has been traditionally thought, who masterminded the Sutherland campaign. Influenced by the work of agricultural theorists George Dempster and Sir John Sinclair, Elizabeth became confident that a radical redistribution of farmers would transform the productivity of the region. She hoped that sheep farmers, who were willing to pay vastly increased rents, would settle in the mountains and glens, while the displaced tenant population could be used to advance the fishing and manufacturing industries in coastal areas. Elizabeth's vision of modernisation involved not just the resettlement of a large number of tenants and the reassignment of land to more profitable consolidated sheep farms, but also the creation of new industrial centres populated by displaced crofters. She was certain that the industrial success of Lancashire and Lanarkshire could be replicated in faraway Sutherland and the West Highlands.

Such confidence turned out to be misguided. The Sutherlands failed to convince existing tenants that resettlement plans would provide them with a better life and, after some relatively peaceful early clearances, crofters began to resist eviction. Opposition only served to further convince Elizabeth that her tenantry was backward and ignorant. 'Our efforts are being rejected', she fulminated, 'and as the people resist by force, no one can complain if they are bought to reason by the same means.'[6] Elizabeth forced through the clearances at a frantic pace. Between 1813 and 1816 several thousand people were cleared, their pastures burnt and their villages razed. Despite public controversy over the way in which the clearances had been conducted, efforts were renewed in 1817 and there were further waves of clearances in 1818, 1819 and 1820. Some starved or froze to death in the ruins where their houses had once been, or in the new coastal resettlement areas which were bedevilled by famine, unemployment and disease.

By 1821, most of the clearances were complete. The final 'improvements' occurred amid growing public condemnation and widespread allegations of cruelty and violence. Wounds from the clearances are still felt to this day: in the 1990s a campaign was launched to have a statue of Harriet's father-in-law, which stands on top of Ben Bhraggie, a peak near Dunrobin, destroyed, 'preferably by dynamite'. The campaign failed but the statue is perennially defaced, and there are frequent vigilante attempts to bring it down.

It was an inheritance that one might expect to have been thought-provoking to the liberal-minded, compassionate Harriet. Yet none of her correspondence appears to question the Sutherlands' cavalier disregard for their tenants. During her 1825 trip to Paris, she 'could not help quarrelling' with her dinner companion Lord Glenlyon, on account of his 'advocating the cause of ignorance, and declaring himself against all the improvements in Scotland'.[7] Whether she was demonstrating her loyalty to her family, simply ignorant of the scale of the human suffering wrought by the Highland clearances, or truly thought this suffering was justified by the increased rent yield, it is difficult to reconcile Harriet's casual acceptance of the 'improvements' with her empathetic character and her later humanitarian views on the abolition of slavery.

Perhaps it is too much to expect Harriet to have addressed these issues by the time of her trip to Scotland; in 1832, she was an anxious and recently bereaved young mother, and still in her early twenties. While staying at Uppat House, her little boy, George, was taken ill. Initially there were fears that he had contracted cholera, but it turned out to be a mild complaint, and George made a full recovery. Nevertheless, the episode deeply affected Harriet, who wrote often of her anxiety during her son's illness. Perhaps the most telling sign of her honesty here is that her prose became refreshingly straightforward and her various affectations, in particular her use of French phrases, were abandoned. 'I shall be ashamed,' she wrote, 'at least if he gets well I shall be so, to think how terribly nervous I have been, and to feel how unfitted I am now for the care of my sick children.'[8] When she turned to other subjects, such as her children's lessons, the 16th-century house at Uppat and dinners at Dunrobin, she reverted to her customary, more florid style. 'I find that the children's lessons take the day entirely *d'un bout a l'autra* [from one end to the other]. I wonder how people manage who take no governess.' Harriet took great pleasure in watching her children play, but like so many other things around this time, the sight led her to darker thoughts. Of a fishing trip in September she wrote that 'the children enjoyed themselves extremely and it is twice the enjoyment having them, particularly after the flower of one's own zest has left one, I should think, forever.'[9] As time passed in the Highlands, Harriet showed signs of recovering her appetite for food as well as life, attending dinners where she was served 'four different sorts of fish, red deer and excellent common fruits'. Glimmers of Harriet's *joie de vivre* were beginning to shine through the bleakness of the previous months. 'I think the country with a few of those loved ones would be perfect, and *je me porte sourven en idee* [I often have thoughts] to the being here with you,' she wrote warmly to Caroline.[10]

Later in September, the Gowers set off on their journey back to the south. On the way they made several visits that would inform Harriet's architectural and artistic taste and shape her vision for Cliveden. She admired the neoclassical style of Lord and Lady Grey's Northumberland residence, Howick Hall, which she described as 'a most comfortable, liveable modern house'. In the gardens, Harriet appreciated 'the good trees down to the sea and quantities of flowers about it': later, she would enjoy a similar effect in the wooded Thames-side slopes of Cliveden. At Alnwick, the seat of the Duke of Northumberland, Harriet was greatly impressed by the reception they received: 'Crowds of footmen await one at the door and lead one to the Duke and Duchess who are models of good humour and cordiality.' She also liked her bedroom, which was 'beautifully furnished and had means of being well lighted, having 16 candles', but otherwise disapproved of the castle's Gothic interior, which she thought 'ill decorated'.[11]

In late October, Harriet received news that her maternal uncle the Duke of Devonshire, known affectionately as 'Uncle D', had organised a series of 'sumptuous entertainments' for the young Princess Victoria at Chatsworth House. At the time of her birth in 1819, Victoria had not been particularly high in the line of succession. She was the daughter of Prince Edward, Duke of Kent and Strathearn, who was the fourth son of George III (George himself was, of course, the son of a former mistress of Cliveden, Augusta). Edward was preceded in the succession by his elder brothers, George, Frederick, and William. Victoria languished fifth in line to the throne, with little expectation of acceding, and it was only through a series of young deaths and childless marriages that she became heir apparent. At the time of the Duke's 'entertainments', Harriet was heavily pregnant with her sixth child and so was unable to attend the party to meet the princess. It would be another year before Harriet and Victoria met, and formed an intense friendship that became central to both their lives.

At the start of 1833, after the difficult birth of her second son, Frederick, Harriet and her family went to the fashionable spa resort of Brighton, where they were joined by her sister Georgiana and her husband, Lord Dover. Brighton had long been a popular seaside resort, and in the 19th century George IV's fondness for the town had cemented its reputation as an aristocratic holiday destination. George's ambitious building projects in the town culminated in John Nash's Indo-Saracenic Royal Pavilion: a bold, fantastical building renowned for the opulence of its decor, which included a pendulous dragon chandelier in the dining room, and for the exotic entertainments hosted there. After George's death, William IV continued to stage events at the Pavilion. While inveterate guests derided William's dinners as puritanical compared to the orgiastic entertainments of his elder brother, the Brighton season remained an early-year fixture in the aristocratic calendar.[12]

It was during Harriet's stay in Brighton that her father-in-law was made a duke. News of the ennoblement spread rapidly. Her sister Georgiana was the first to know – Lady Grey whispered the news 'with great glee' during a dinner at the Pavilion. Georgiana immediately rushed to inform Harriet, 'who knew nothing about it'. In the gossipy atmosphere of Brighton, the news soon became 'a secret, which is no longer one'.[13] On hearing the news from Georgiana, Harriet hastily wrote to Caroline, with the expectation that gossip had preceded her letter. 'You will have heard I fear before *mon announce*, as I should like to be the first to tell you anything that concerns us, that Stafford is to be a duke.'[14] Stafford chose the title Duke of Sutherland, in honour of his wife's heritage. The news put Harriet in the spotlight at Brighton, and her attendance was much anticipated at the Pavilion. Her debut was on Tuesday 29 January and her second appearance on Friday 1 February; Georgiana wrote to Caroline that Harriet 'was looking very well both nights'. She cut a fine figure, wearing on the first night a gown of 'pink velvet and pointe lace' and a 'rose in her hair', and on the second, a dress in 'black satin, embroidered with coloured flowers' and a pale lace headdress.

Stafford's ennoblement was life-changing for Harriet and George, firstly because the dukedom would pass to George on his father's death, and secondly because it meant that they inherited the marquisate of Stafford. Little George, Viscount Trentham, became Earl Gower in his father's place. Georgiana wrote proudly to Caroline about the rearrangement of names: 'the Staffords . . . how difficult it will ever be to call them so! They had at first settled to remain as they are but the King called him Lord Stafford and told him it was so, which decided the case differently.' She also added an endearing aside about little George, who 'is very amusing about his new name [Earl Gower] . . . and thinks himself ready to become "Papa"'.[15]

The newly made Staffords returned to London on 2 February and Harriet began preparing to move from Hamilton Place to Bridgewater House, which overlooked St James's Park. 'I have been in a state of hurry and interruption, not knowing what to pack and how to pack,' she wrote.[16] But

Harriet was not able to luxuriate in her new title for long. Shortly after her return to London, the health of her sister Georgiana's husband, which had never been robust, relapsed. Harriet stayed by her sister's side during his painful illness; George Agar Ellis died aged just 36. Devastated, Georgiana retreated to the Isle of Wight and, with the exception of seeing her children, lived in complete seclusion until her death.

Ten days after Ellis's death on 19 July, Harriet's father-in-law, the Duke of Sutherland, died at Dunrobin. Harriet was unable to attend the funeral, and George, the ever-attentive husband, sent her a long account of the lavish event, suitable for 'the richest individual who ever died'.[17]

Overnight, Harriet had become the richest wife in England. George wrote to her from Dunrobin expressing his desire that they use their fortune wisely, 'In short, my dearest love,' he ended, 'I hope you will have a great deal of enjoyment, and of the purest sort.'[18]

Chapter 5

'A LEVIATHAN OF WEALTH'

As the new duchess of Sutherland, the world lay at Harriet's feet. She had at her disposal Stafford House, one of the grandest residences in London, as well as the smaller house Westhill in Wandsworth. Outside the capital, there were Lilleshall and Trentham Hall, the most imposing mansions in the Midlands, not to mention Uppat and Dunrobin in Sutherland, her vast Scottish territory. The Sutherlands also possessed boundless capital to invest in their properties. With her strong opinions on design, it was inevitable that when the couple embarked on extensive renovations, Harriet took the lead. The most ambitious of her early building schemes was the transformation of Stafford House, on the north side of St James's Park in London. Harriet's father-in-law had been making improvements to the property since he purchased it in 1827, but the house was still not finished when Harriet and George inherited it in 1833. Harriet immediately set to work, developing an elaborate plan for the house in consultation with Charles Barry, who would later work on Trentham Hall, and Cliveden.

Harriet's vision for Stafford House involved the addition of another storey.[1] The subsequent flurry of building work caused considerable grief to nearby residents, resulting in a number of complaints, including those from William IV and his wife, Queen Adelaide. Though Buckingham Palace would not become the principal royal residence until the accession of Queen Victoria, it had come into increasing use during the early 19th century, especially after a fire destroyed much of St James's Palace in 1809. Under the guidance of George IV and then William IV, Buckingham House had been transformed into the John Nash palace that survives today. The Sutherlands had taken the proximity of the Palace into account when planning their renovation and were mortified to discover that their builders were disturbing the royals. The king and queen, Harriet anxiously reported, 'had been woke at 5'. Worse, the queen already had a headache, 'which the noise did not mend'. Harriet, who was prone to momentary outbursts of rage, or 'explosions'[2] as Lord Melbourne, the Home Secretary, called them, immediately ordered 'to have the early work stopped'.[3]

The project also ran into trouble at the other end of the social spectrum, due to struggles over unionisation. Since the late 18th century, the Combinations Acts had made it illegal for workers to combine into trade unions, but between 1825 and 1826 these laws were repealed, effectively decriminalising unions. Despite this legislative shift, attempts to unionise had been vigorously countered by employers and the judiciary. During 1834, the masters of various trades attempted to force their workers to sign pledges that they would not unionise. In response, a number of different trades planned strikes. Harriet was very aware of this unrest, as she had been of the agitation surrounding reform: 'The last time we went over the upper part [of Stafford House] we were struck with the less agreeable looks of some of the men, and we hear that there is to be a general strike on Friday,' she wrote in August 1834. She had little sympathy for workers' rights: 'they must be beat', she wrote emphatically.[4] The strike eventually took place on Monday 18 August.[5] It was followed, on Thursday, by a public meeting of working builders at the Black Horse pub, on Curtain Street in Shoreditch; those present passed a motion that described the anti-union declaration as 'forging chains for their own necks'.

Despite these problems, Stafford House, a neoclassical landmark, was complete by 1835. The great hall measured 120 feet from floor to ceiling, and the stone and marble staircase was 'matchless'. The state drawing room and the music room, which served also as a dining room, were lavishly decorated in the style of Louis XV. The great gallery housed George's magnificent art collection, which included works by Raphael, Tintoretto, Titian, Velázquez, Rubens, Van Dyck, Watteau and Murillo, a reflection of the passion for art that led to George's appointment as a trustee of the National Gallery that same year and later, in 1841, as a trustee of the British Museum. The house itself, however, received mixed reviews from contemporaries. The poet Rogers likened it to a 'fairy palace' with Harriet as its 'good fairy', but others were affronted by its sheer scale and sumptuousness.[6] 'Was it *really* true that the Sutherlands are *obliged* to add a story to Stafford House?' Baron Wharncliffe jibed.[7] The Sutherlands, however, were immune to such criticism. Stafford House quickly became a centre of artistic patronage. Queen Victoria famously quipped, 'I have come from my house to your palace' and when she visited in the 1840s, she found a scene almost absurdly full of creative activity: while Franz Xaver Winterhalter painted his famous portrait of the duchess, 'a clever French artist' was sketching the grand staircase, and Stanislas David, a French 'littérateur', was reciting poems for the guests.

It was at Stafford House that Harriet established herself as the leading society hostess of her day. Harriet's previous London residences, and to some extent her pre-inheritance finances, had prevented her from hosting anything on a particularly large scale. Her inaugural event at Stafford House on 6 June 1835 featured a piece of theatre and a concert, with performances from baritone Antonio Tamburini, soprano Giulia Grisi, and Spanish mezzo-soprano Maria Malibran, a trio of the most celebrated opera singers of the time. Guests including the Duchess of Cambridge, Earl Grey and the Duke of Wellington stayed until four in the morning, enjoying the 'cold suppers' and 'luxuriant desserts', as well as a guided tour of the house. In a detailed description of the festivities, George wrote to his mother that 'the music was excellent and said to do better than at the opera.' The staircase, he said, had been ingeniously illuminated by gas lights and mirrors to spectacular effect. But George's warmest praise was reserved for his wife who 'looked very well, and was thought to do the honours in a distinguished manner'.[8]

The glittering soirées of Harriet's early years at Stafford House were famed for their opulence but lacked the intimacy and purpose which later characterised her parties. But even as she began to use her social position to make powerful statements – as she did with her high-profile support of Caroline Norton – she viewed her actions as belonging to a personal and domestic rather than a political domain. Caroline Norton was a witty and beautiful poet married to George Chapple Norton, a man with a quick temper and strong jealous streak. These character traits often translated into violent rages, especially where Caroline's flock of male admirers was concerned. Among her devotees was the brilliant and raffish Whig Lord Melbourne, who had become prime minister for the second time in April 1835, and with whom Caroline maintained a close but probably platonic relationship. Caroline and George Norton's relationship became increasingly strained and by 1835, Norton had denied his wife access to the family home and to her children. In June 1836, he began divorce proceedings by bringing a legal case of 'criminal conversation' (adultery) against his wife and Melbourne, suing the latter for £10,000 in damages. The case went to court but the trial, a sanitised alternative to duelling which had finally been outlawed in 1815, was over within hours, the jury being unwilling to condemn Melbourne – who was after all the prime minister – on sketchy evidence and the testimony of unreliable witnesses.

This would have been little comfort, however, to Caroline, who remained trapped in an abusive marriage. De facto separation from Norton meant that Caroline, like Anna Maria 200 years before her, was barred from any contact with her three sons, in addition to the loss of all income and financial support. While Anna Maria was able to seek support from the Duke of Buckingham after her husband's death, Caroline was left with no male patron. Melbourne offered financial support but, fearful of his reputation as prime minister, withdrew from the friendship. Norton made a plangent case to Queen Victoria, protesting the 'grotesque anomaly, which ordains that women shall be non-existent in a country governed by a female Sovereign'. Victoria responded ferociously to what she saw as 'this mad and wicked Folly of Women's Rights'. 'God created men and women differently,' she wrote. 'Let them remain each in their own position.'[9]

Victoria was wrong to detect feminism in Norton's protest, as the poet herself made very clear: in 1838 she wrote to *The Times* that 'the natural position of women is inferiority to man . . . I never pretended to the wild and ridiculous doctrine of equality.'[10] Likewise, we should not misconstrue Harriet's support for Norton as a consciously feminist gesture, but rather as a means of addressing what she considered a grievous wrong. The duchess could not bear to watch her friend be so ill-treated by the men around her. In a bid to ease Caroline's path back into respectable company, Harriet took her driving through the streets of London – a very public and highly visible gesture of support. Caroline was so moved by the expression of solidarity that she dedicated her *The Dream, and Other Poems* (1840) to the duchess. In 11 stanzas, Caroline committed her gratitude to paper. 'So Thou, with queenly grace and gentle pride / Along the world's dark waves in purity dost glide,' she wrote of Harriet's kindness. '*Thou* didst not shrink – of bitter tongues afraid / Who hunt in packs the object of their blame.'[11] Harriet continued to support her friend, making sure she was a regular fixture at Stafford House festivities. On one occasion, the writer Charles Dickens scandalised guests at Stafford House when he was asked whom he thought was more beautiful, the Duchess of Sutherland or Mrs Norton, and replied: 'Mrs Norton is perhaps the most beautiful, but the duchess to my mind, is the more kissable person.'[12]

Early on the morning of 20 June 1837, William IV died at Windsor, aged 71, and Victoria, who had only recently turned 18, found herself acceding the throne. Victoria and Harriet had finally been introduced at a dinner held at Kensington Palace on 24 April 1833, when Victoria was 14 years old and Harriet was 27. By the spring of 1835, Harriet had begun to receive comment in Victoria's journals, singled out for her beauty, elegance and grace. On 28 May, Victoria described Harriet as one of 'the handsomest people' present at a royal drawing room attended by 2,200 guests; soon after, Harriet appeared on a list of 'the prettiest persons' at a dinner hosted by Queen Adelaide. On 1 July 1836, Harriet was described in the diary as 'handsome'; on 9 July as 'very handsome'; and in November as 'handsomer in figure, and altogether handsomer' than Lady Barham, who herself was 'very handsome'. In April 1837, she topped the list of the 'handsomest' people at another drawing room.[13] Victoria was clearly entranced by her new friend, even if her praise was rather monotonous. Despite Harriet's sharp intellect and reputation for diverting conversation, her appearance remained, to Victoria, one of the most remarkable things about her. Victoria, who was notoriously insecure about her diminutive stature and unremarkable appearance, was dazzled by Harriet's beauty.

Upon her accession, one of Victoria's first acts was to

appoint the 31-year-old duchess as Mistress of the Robes. 'I am delighted to have [Harriet] as my Mistress of the Robes,' Victoria wrote of the appointment, adding in her usual style that the duchess 'was looking so handsome and nice'.[14] Thus Harriet became a royal official as well as a friend to the queen. Far from being a titular appointee, the Mistress of the Robes was expected to perform many well-defined duties – more so than most other female roles at court, and on a par with offices of state held by men. Harriet was head of the office of robes, putting her in charge of a team of four: the Groom of the Robes, the Clerk of the Robes, a messenger, and a furrier. She purchased Victoria's robes of state, settled the queen's personal clothing bills, provided salaries for the queen's dressers, hairdresser and wardrobe maids, and issued warrants for the appointment of tradespeople. The Mistress of the Robes was also the first person to whom the queen would turn with enquiries about potential courtiers for official appointments. She was responsible for drawing up rotas of maids and ladies-in-waiting, and for developing contingency plans should a lady-in-waiting not be able to attend the queen for reasons such as pregnancy or illness.[15] The Mistress of the Robes herself attended the queen at levees and drawing rooms and on important state occasions. The most momentous of these was 28 June 1838, when the trembling 19-year-old Victoria was crowned at Westminster Abbey. Harriet spent the hours before the coronation dressing the queen and attending to her every need. No record survives of the conversation that occurred between the two friends on that day, but we can speculate that Harriet calmed Victoria's nerves with a mixture of maternal reassurance and inane chit-chat.

Harriet was a sensation at Victoria's court. Admirers marvelled at how the statuesque duchess 'moves like a goddess . . . and looks like a queen'.[16] Such adulation may have posed a challenge to her friendship with the tiny monarch, only 4 feet 11 inches in stature. Yet for the first months of her reign, Victoria retained her girlish admiration for Harriet. The queen's diaries indicate that she spoke of the duchess almost as often as she spoke with her – and she spoke with her a lot. Between 1837 and 1840 Victoria recorded frequent instances of them visiting the opera, travelling together in the state coach, and sitting next to each other at dinner. They spent hours in conversation while Harriet dressed Victoria, discussing politics, horse riding and everything in between. No one was more emotionally intimate with the queen, or so consistently close to her person. Indeed, when Harriet accompanied Victoria on her first official visit to the Continent, the Mistress of the Robes was mistaken for the queen herself. Harriet's aunt Lady Granville jokingly referred to 'that other Queen, Harriet the First'.[17]

Another figure who had an inordinate influence on Victoria during her early reign was her first prime minister, Lord Melbourne. Victoria adored Melbourne and sought his advice on every matter under her consideration. 'He is so sensible and so reasonable upon every point and has such right feelings about everything,' Victoria wrote in her journal in December 1837.[18] Melbourne was one of the few people to appear in its pages as often as Harriet. A conservative Whig with a profound distrust of social change, Melbourne had a deep influence on the political outlook of the young queen. He educated her in statecraft, constitutional practicalities and government, while offering her the emotional guidance and adoration she craved. At 58, Melbourne assumed the role of Victoria's surrogate father, guardian and mentor. But their mutual devotion teetered on romantic infatuation. Victoria was entranced by his animated grey-blue eyes and often remarked on his appearance, especially when wearing the 'Windsor uniform' of dark blue and red, or when his hair became dishevelled in the wind. She was fiercely possessive of her beguiling prime minister.

Lord Melbourne was also a vocal admirer of Harriet, to Victoria's occasional irritation. Victoria's journals from the late 1830s recount a number of episodes that illuminate the various jealousies, suspicions and loyalties of this three-way relationship. 'I never liked letting the Duchess of Sutherland sit near him (which she happened to do),' the queen noted one evening in August 1839, 'as she always took him quite away, by talking to him . . . Lord M. said it was not her fault, and laughed.'[19] In spite of her occasional jealousy, Victoria usually stood up to Harriet, even if it meant disagreeing with Melbourne: in December 1839, the queen rebuked Melbourne for accusing Harriet of flirting with the Duke of Richmond.[20] These were minor episodes of tension in the otherwise solid friendship between the queen and her Mistress of the Robes. Soon, however, the women's friendship would come under the national spotlight in the first political crisis of Victoria's reign.

Chapter 6

CRISIS IN THE
BEDCHAMBER

A ll my happiness gone!' Victoria mourned in her
journal. 'That happy peaceful life destroyed!'[1] In the
spring of 1839, the young queen faced the biggest
crisis of her reign. Events had unfolded at an alarming pace.
On 7 May, her beloved Lord Melbourne was forced to resign
due to insufficient parliamentary support. The next day, Victoria reluctantly summoned Robert Peel to form a new ministry.
Under Peel's leadership, the Tory Party had taken steps away
from the reactionary politics of the Duke of Wellington and
was increasingly referred to as the Conservative Party. But
their disagreements with the Whigs were still significant and
Peel was only willing to form a ministry on the condition that
Victoria dismiss her ladies of the bedchamber, in particular her
Mistress of the Robes. If Victoria acquiesced, she would lose
Harriet, her dearest and most loyal ally. If she refused, she
would appear truculent and spoilt at best, at worst autocratic
and absolutist. Overwhelmed with a mixture of fear and fury,
the 20-year-old queen agonised over the decision. 'I felt too
wretched; the change; the awful, incomprehensible change
that had taken place, drove me really to distraction,' she noted

in her journal, 'and with the exception of walking up and down the room . . . I could do nothing.'[2]

Peel had made a convincing case for Victoria to dismiss her ladies. It would be impossible, he argued, to head a new Tory ministry without the complete support of the queen. Although a monarch was expected to keep a dignified distance from political partisanship, it was widely known that Victoria had Whig sympathies. *The Times* of 15 May 1839 highlighted this by listing each Lady of the Queen's Bedchamber and their political allegiance: Victoria was demonstrably surrounded entirely by Whig appointees. Aware of the Whig dominance in the royal household, Peel insisted that Victoria replace her Whig attendants with the wives of Tory politicians – or at least make a couple of changes.

At the core of Peel and Victoria's disagreement lay a constitutional question concerning the role of the bedchamber.[3] It had been over a century since there was last a queen regnant, Queen Anne, so the precedent for who controlled appointments to the queen's bedchamber was unclear. While Peel viewed the bedchamber patriarchally as an extension of the political sphere, and therefore the rightful domain of the current prime minister, Victoria saw it as a domestic space. 'Was Sir Robert so weak,' she taunted him, 'that *even* ladies must be of his opinion?'[4] She even argued, rather tenuously, that they never discussed politics – only 'music and horses'. The public responded sceptically to these claims, and Victoria's protestations of neutrality were widely perceived as a ploy by Melbourne to maintain influence over the queen during Peel's ministry. In one cartoon a satirical parallel was drawn between the Bedchamber Crisis and the taking of Zhoushan, in what is now known as the First Opium War (1839–42). It was reported in *The Times* that when British troops took the port of Zhoushan, they found the place deserted, except for one old man holding a sign that read: 'Spare us for the sake of our wives and children'. In the cartoon, Melbourne is represented as a Chinese man, holding a similar sign, as a last-ditch attempt to keep possession of the government against the advancing Tories.[5]

There was also a moral dimension to Peel's argument. Shortly before the bedchamber debacle, a political scandal had erupted over Lady Flora Hastings, a lady-in-waiting to the Duchess of Kent, Victoria's mother.[6] Lady Flora was from a Tory family and was known to hold Tory sympathies. In early 1839, Victoria had noticed a swelling in Flora's abdomen and became convinced that she was pregnant with the child of John Conroy, the favourite of the Duchess of Kent. The queen was furious and insisted Flora be summarily dismissed from court. A subsequent medical examination, however, revealed that Lady Flora was not pregnant, but gravely ill. When she died in July 1839, the Tory political press made much of this scandal, portraying Flora as the innocent victim of a callous monarch presiding over a depraved Whig court.[7] The Flora Hastings affair became, for many detractors of the queen, a symbol of Victoria's abuse of power. Seen in this context, Peel's attempt to remove Victoria's existing Whig ladies of the bedchamber was an effort to solve the queen's public image problem. However, by acquiescing to his demands, Victoria would be conceding that her Whig ladies were a malign influence.[8]

After three more days of pacing, hysteria and self-imposed starvation, Victoria came to a decision. Incandescent that political exigencies had stripped her of Melbourne, she adamantly refused to sacrifice her ladies, especially Harriet. Faced with losing her dearest friend or maintaining the stability of her government, Victoria chose the former. On 9 May she informed Peel that the ladies of the bedchamber were of no concern to him. Enraged by Victoria's intransigence, and without a political majority in the House of Commons, Peel declined to form a new ministry. Lord Melbourne was reinstated. The unyielding, headstrong queen had got her way.

On the morning of 16 May 1838, Harriet had given birth to her eighth child, a daughter named Victoria. The christening had taken place at Stafford House and Victoria recorded the duchess looking 'lovely' in an off-white dress. On her wrist she wore a gift from Victoria – an enamel bracelet decorated with the queen's likeness. On 19 June 1839, only weeks after the Bedchamber Crisis, baby Victoria suffered a seizure and died. The queen lamented that she was 'so very sorry' about little Victoria's death, 'particularly as she was my godchild'.[9] Although deeply affected by the loss, remaining 'pale, sad and low' for some weeks, Harriet did not succumb to the depression she had suffered after Blanche's death. This was in no small part due to Victoria's unswerving support. The queen corresponded with Harriet on a daily basis, sometimes writing to her twice in one day. She frequently dined with her, visited her at home, spent time with her children and accompanied her to church. In August, Harriet showed her appreciation for Victoria's support by throwing a banquet in her honour. The queen recorded the evening in her journal, marvelling at the splendour of Stafford House. 'The Duchess showed us all the pretty rooms downstairs, and then took us up to see her beautiful bathroom, bedroom, dressing room, and sitting room,' Victoria noted. 'We then went upstairs, and the hall and staircase, lit up, with a band in it, was really the handsomest thing I ever saw.'[10] Victoria finished the evening as she had ended so many others, by sitting next to Harriet on the sofa in an intimate tête-à-tête.

In October 1839 Prince Albert of Saxe-Coburg, Victoria's cousin, visited Windsor Castle. Victoria was impressed by his good looks and youthful zeal. 'Such beautiful blue eyes, an exquisite nose and such a pretty mouth,' she noted in her journal, 'a beautiful figure, broad in the shoulders and fine waist.'[11] Protocol dictated that as Queen of England, Victoria had to propose to her future husband. The wedding took place on the rainy day of 10 February 1840; Victoria wore a white satin dress trimmed with English Honiton lace, and a simple wreath of orange blossom on her head. Harriet accompanied her in the carriage from the palace to the Chapel Royal at St James's.

Meanwhile, the consequences of Victoria's intransigence continued to be felt in Parliament. Victoria's refusal to capitulate to Peel had consigned Lord Melbourne to two more years of ineffective minority government. By early May 1841, his position had once again become untenable. The prospect of another governmental collapse resurrected the controversy over appointment to the bedchamber. On this occasion, however, the topic was handled differently, to a large extent due to the stabilising influence of Victoria's new husband.

The political negotiations of 1841 were led by Albert's secretary, George Anson, who represented a far more conciliatory queen than Peel had encountered two years earlier. It was thus agreed that, if the government resigned, the queen would draw up a list of acceptable replacements as ladies of the bedchamber; Peel would choose his appointees from this shortlist. The government in fact decided not to resign but to request the dissolution of Parliament. The ensuing general election of 1841 provided the Tories with a parliamentary majority and a new ministry was formed in August. In the following days, the three main Whig ladies at court – the Duchess of Bedford, Lady Normanby, and Harriet – tendered their resignation. They realised that Peel's vision of a politically subservient bedchamber had, with time and marriage, won out over Victoria's opposing view.

Victoria, although saddened by the loss of Harriet, was more sanguine this time. 'I saw the Duchess of Sutherland and said how grieved I was to lose her,' she noted on 28 August 1841, 'but that I only consider it temporary and should always consider her as belonging to me.'[12] The hiatus in Harriet's official role was to last five years. In 1846, a new Whig government under Lord John Russell was formed and, in keeping with the precedent of 1841, Whig ladies were once again invited into the bedchamber. Harriet was reinstated as Mistress of the Robes. 'The Duchess of Sutherland will accept, & I had a very kind letter from her about it,' Victoria wrote in relief.[13] This pattern of appointment and resignation as governments rose and fell was to continue for the next 20 years of Harriet's life.

During the 1840s, Harriet's family continued to grow. In 1843, she gave birth to Albert, for whom Victoria's husband stood as godfather; baby Ronald followed two years later. In 1848, at the age of 43, Harriet gave birth to her last child. Victoria was appointed godmother to the 'lovely' Aline, whose name was a shortening of Alexandrina, the given first name of the queen.

The exuberance of Aline's christening celebrations belied the aristocracy's apprehension at the resurgence of political unrest in Britain and throughout Europe. In 1848, the Continent was struck by a series of revolutionary upheavals that were, and are, without parallel in European history. The first significant revolt occurred in Sicily in January, though this was little commented upon at the time. In February, revolution in France led to the overthrow of Louis-Philippe's constitutional monarchy, and the establishment of the French Second Republic. During the spring, there were revolutions and attempted revolutions in Germany, Denmark, Poland, Ireland, across the Habsburg Empire, and in several Latin American countries. In Britain, meanwhile, the pacifying effect of the 1832 Reform Act had worn off. Protests for parliamentary reform erupted across the country once again: this time the demand was for full male enfranchisement.

On 10 April, 150,000 people marched to Westminster to present to Parliament the 'People's Charter', an immense petition demanding drastic reforms such as universal male suffrage, annual elections to Parliament and the secret ballot. The Charter was signed by five million people, making it so large that it would have to be taken to Parliament on a farm wagon pulled by four horses. Its delivery was preceded by a 'monster rally' on Kennington Common, an event that remains the biggest political rally in British history, and was captured in one of the earliest political photographs. Royals and aristocrats held their breath. Was this to be a peaceful call for reform or a presage to bloody revolution? Harriet and Victoria would have been well aware that a 'Charter' had marked the beginning of the demise of the regime of Charles X in 1830. In anticipation of the People's Charter, 85,000 men were recruited to supplement the 4,000-strong police force of Sir Robert Peel, and 8,000 troops were summoned to the capital. Volumes of *Hansard* were used to barricade the doors of government offices against the crowd, and Victoria was advised to take refuge on the Isle of Wight.

In the final analysis, fears of a British revolution proved to be overstated and the 'Chartists' protested peacefully. But the scare highlighted how easily a government might be toppled under the weight of popular protest. Victoria noted many occasions on which she was booed and hissed at as she travelled through London. On 19 May the following year an attempt was made on the queen's life by Irishman William Hamilton, who fired a pistol at her carriage as it crossed Constitution Hill. As it turned out, the pistol contained powder but no bullet, but it was enough to shatter the already frayed nerves of the court. Despite claiming she was unruffled, in the immediate aftermath of the incident Victoria sought comfort in the reassuring company of Harriet. 'Saw the Dss of Sutherland with my godchild who is a real beauty,' she wrote the day after the shooting, 'with such blue eyes & a very small mouth.'[14]

Harriet also craved refuge from the tumultuous events of the time. She needed respite, a base away from the seething metropolis of London, but sufficiently close to her beloved queen. It was vital for Harriet to maintain what she would later refer to as 'that privilege of place and intimacy'. She found her answer in Cliveden.

Chapter 7

A MARRIAGE, A DEATH
AND A BLAZE

Harriet first viewed Cliveden in early 1849. In terms of scale and grandeur, Cliveden could not compete with Stafford House, but Harriet was drawn to its charm and potential as a domestic retreat. It was the view from the back of the house, what her son Ronald would remember as 'Cliveden's secret landscape', that most appealed to her. Because of the legal doctrine of coverture, under which all of a married woman's rights and obligations were subsumed by her husband, it was necessary for George to buy the house and then sign a conveyance that gave Harriet effective ownership of the property by permitting her to 'hold, occupy and enjoy the said hereditaments [Cliveden] for her life and during her coverture as her separate estate and freed in all respect from the interference of the said George Granville Duke and Earl of Sutherland his heirs or assigns.'[1] The property had come on the market due to the death of its previous owner, the politician Sir George Warrender, who had bought the house from the Orkneys in 1824, and commissioned the architect William Burn to replace the main block, which by that time had been burnt out for some 30 years. From the outset, the Sutherlands had decided that Cliveden would be Harriet's house. It was a perfect family home and later an ideal setting in which to entertain her political circle. For the next 20 years, Cliveden would become Harriet's most rewarding project, her calm retreat and enduring legacy.

On 27 June 1849, before the conveyance had even been processed, Harriet hosted her first event at Cliveden, the wedding of her eldest son George, now 20, to Anne Hay Mackenzie. Due to the failing health of Anne's father, Harriet had volunteered to oversee every aspect of the nuptials. The silk weavers of Spitalfields, whom Augusta had championed a century earlier, were commissioned to create gowns for the bridal party. Harriet's own dress was a white silk and lace affair, while Anne chose a more modest white lace dress to reflect her bridal innocence; she carried a wreath of orange blossoms and myrtle, a homage to Queen Victoria's wedding bouquet.

Decades later Harriet's son Ronald recalled the bustling activity of the wedding day.[2] Scores of servants scurried around the grounds placing large vases brimming over with Harriet's favourite white camellias; vast platters of meats garnished with rare chutneys and spices from India were arranged on an immense banqueting table, to be followed by sherbets and ice creams, and platters of ripe and jellied fruits. Wax candles in ornamental gold candelabras decorated the spread. George and Anne's wedding cake towered over this decadent feast. It was a rich, dark fruitcake, with white royal icing and decorated with sprigs of flowers. As had been the fashion since Queen Victoria's wedding in 1840, a model of the bride and groom surveyed the room from atop the cake. The rail link from London had opened during Warrender's ownership, and all morning a steady stream of carriages transported London's elite, from Taplow station, to the estate. At ten o'clock in the morning, Anne swept into the drawing room, which had been designated for the ceremony, and shortly after, the Dean of Lichfield pronounced the couple man and wife.

Later, as the party was in full flow, a maid summoned Harriet to Aline's room. The previous day Aline had been well enough to go out in the grounds and pick flowers for the wedding bouquets, but during the ceremony she had developed a fever. The child's condition had deteriorated precipitously in the course of the afternoon, and she now looked dangerously ill. In the absence of a doctor, Aline was tended to by the maids, who were unable to do anything more than cool her with wet towels. Just before dawn she stopped breathing. This was the third daughter Harriet had lost, and Aline's death was even more sudden and senseless than the previous two.

Harriet was inconsolable; the dark shadow of depression that had possessed her after the death of Blanche crept over her once again. In her grief she withdrew herself from society, rejecting even Victoria's company – between Aline's death in June and the following November, there are virtually no references to Harriet in the queen's journal. Cliveden, which just months before had represented an exciting future, was now a painful reminder of Aline. Harriet fled to the Highlands, where she and George retraced their melancholic steps of 1832 back to Dunrobin Castle. Her decision to spend time away from Cliveden would have catastrophic consequences.

It was on a Sunday, while the servants were at church, that the fire broke out. It started in the library, consuming bookshelves rich in fine, old editions of the French classics, and quickly spread throughout the house with devastating effect. The *Illustrated London News* of 24 November reported the details:

> [T]he accident seems to have originated in the library where some workmen had been employed until nearly ten o'clock on Thursday morning week. The flames were first observed through the front windows of the mansion, about one o'clock pm on that day by some persons near the spot, who hastened to the house and gave an alarm. Messengers were instantly dispatched to Maidenhead and in a very short period two engines arrived, but the fire had by that time attained so great a mastery that although an ample supply of water was at hand very little effect was produced upon the conflagration.

Queen Victoria saw the flames five miles away at Windsor and also dispatched fire engines, but to no avail. Harriet returned from Scotland to see the blackened walls of her house being pulled down.

When the house went up, so did its valuable contents. An inventory of March 1849, taken by 'Messrs Farebrother, Clarke and Lye' gives a snapshot of the opulent interiors immediately before they were consumed by fire. The fittings included Venetian and Brussels carpets; among the furniture were gilt bed canopies, mahogany bidets, antique oak tables and wardrobes, and tens of ebony tables and bookcases; there were globes, china jars, and a rosewood pianoforte built by Kirkman, one of the first English companies to make the instrument. The art in the house included sculptures in marble and bronze, a bust of the Duke of Wellington, and several paintings from George's prized collection, including works by Velázquez, Lely, and Kneller.[3]

Harriet retreated to Stafford House to evaluate her options. For some time she considered abandoning the Cliveden project entirely, fearing that she lacked the energy to embark on yet another demanding building scheme. But over the course of 1850, as the last ruins of the charred house were cleared, Harriet resolved to rebuild her life. Charles Barry, whom the Sutherlands had employed to complete Stafford House, was currently in the midst of overseeing the construction of the new Palace of Westminster: the old palace had, like Cliveden, been consumed by fire. Despite the bureaucratic wrangling and engineering challenges of the Westminster project Barry would find the time to produce designs for a new Cliveden. Harriet and Barry would collaborate to raise the house from the ashes.

Chapter 8

A RESURRECTION

Charles Barry was born in London, the fourth son of a prosperous Westminster stationer. He learnt the practical side of his profession during his time working for Middleton and Bailey, a firm of Lambeth surveyors, but the formative influence on his architectural imagination was the trip he took around Europe, the Mediterranean and North Africa between 1817 and 1820. He left England alone and travelled by himself through France and Italy, before joining the artist Charles Locke Eastlake to tour Greece and Turkey. Between 1819 and 1820, Barry was employed by the archaeologist David Baillie, to record in sketches the landscapes and buildings of Egypt and Syria.

The abiding influence Barry acquired from his Continental tour was Italian. His *palazzo* style was an appealing alternative to the predominant Greek and Gothic styles of the time. The Travellers' Club, his grand Italianate building in Pall Mall, appeared exactly when architectural critics were looking for an alternative to the tired fashion for Greek revival, and established him as the leading British practitioner of the Europe-wide Renaissance Revival. However, Barry was not an inflexible designer and some of his most iconic buildings were executed in very different fashion to his signature Italianate style. Most notable in this respect was his design for the Palace of Westminster, home to both Houses of Parliament. The palace had burnt to the ground in October 1834, after an oven being used to destroy the Exchequer's old tally sticks (wooden sticks used to calculate tax) overheated and set fire to the House of Lords. A Lords committee on the rebuilding of Parliament rejected the possibility of a neoclassical replacement on the grounds that the style was too closely associated with revolutionary republicanism. The committee resolved that submissions for the competition to design a new palace should be either Gothic or Elizabethan. Barry's winning building was Gothic in style, though his own classical predilections showed through in his proposal: the underlying proportions of the building were Palladian and he would rely on the pioneering Gothic architect Augustus Pugin to provide the detailing and the interior design.

By the time he was employed to work on Cliveden, Barry had received many commissions from the Sutherlands. In the 1830s he had transformed Trentham Hall from an unfashionable, 'supremely hideous' Georgian house into an impressive Italianate mansion. He had also worked on Dunrobin, for which he produced designs in a Scottish baronial style, a fusion of French and Scottish architecture introduced to Scotland in the days of Queen Mary.[1] Barry had a reputation for being rather doctrinaire about achieving consistency of style within a project. For instance, when converting Trentham into an Italian style, he wanted to alter not only the unfashionable

Georgian parts of the house, but also the old Norman church. 'When Barry was changing the exterior of plain old Georgian Trentham into the semblance of an Italian palace, he had the incredibly bad taste to suggest that the church, with its fine old Norman pillars, should be converted into a building more suitable to the Italian fashion of the hall,' Ronald Gower recorded in his memoirs. 'Luckily,' he continued, 'my parents had better taste than their architect.'[2] Budgeting was also not high on Barry's agenda, and his first design for Cliveden was put aside 'for economic reasons' – quite a feat given the size of the Sutherland fortune.

Barry's second attempt at a Cliveden proposal looked to the past, taking inspiration from the Orkneys' Cliveden as it appeared in the architectural manual *Vitruvius Britannicus*. He kept Winde's grand terrace, Archer's two wings, the colonnades joining the wings to the main house, and the roof hidden by a distinctive parapet lined with urns. Italianate architecture had also been very popular during the Restoration period, then partly due to the influence of Inigo Jones, who, like Barry, had travelled extensively in Italy, and was heavily influenced by the Renaissance architecture of Vincenzo Scamozzi and Andrea Palladio. Contemporaries of the Restoration era often likened Buckingham's first house to the Villa Aldobrandini. More than 200 years later, Barry's conception of Cliveden inspired comparisons to the same architectural canon. In the words of Ronald Gower: 'Anyone who has seen the Villa Albano near Rome, and compares it with Cliveden, will see the likeness between them.'[3]

Perhaps the most distinctively 19th-century feature of

Barry's new house was its use of cement cladding to disguise the brickwork underneath. Prior to the 19th century, many Italianate buildings had been executed in red brick, but in the late 18th and early 19th centuries, an inexpensive alternative to red brick became available. 'Roman Cement', which could be sculpted to look like stone, was invented in the 1780s by James Parker, a clergyman and manufacturer, and patented in 1796. The product was not in fact like anything used by the Romans, but the brand name is revealing of the contemporary fashion for neoclassical buildings, in which cement was often used as a cheaper alternative to real stone. The product really took off in the 1820s, when the patent expired and various manufacturers began selling their own improved version of the building material. In an age when brick was often associated with 'plain' institutional architecture, such as workhouses, schools, and asylums, cement cladding had a certain aspirational appeal. Indeed, an aversion to brick probably explains Ronald Gower's dislike of Orkney's Cliveden: 'To judge by last century prints of the place,' he wrote, referring to the images in Campbell's *Vitruvius Britannicus*, 'the old building was plain unto ugliness.'[4]

The rebuild began in earnest in 1850 and the majority of the work was completed in the following year. An insight into the course of the early building is given by a letter of June 1850, from Barry to Harriet. Barry's correspondence to the duchess generally exhibits a degree of affection, and a familiarity with her family. Their letters also show Harriet to have taken an active role in adapting Barry's designs to her own preferences. 'My dear Madam,' Barry began his letter of 12 June 1850,

'There will not be any difficulty in shifting the Breakfast Room for Cliefden to adjoin the Drawing Room, as you wish now, or getting a good entrance to it from the staircase, as well as an independent entrance to the Dining Room in a lobby adjoining the staircases which will amend the necessity of making the Breakfast Room a passage room to it.'[5] The new layout described in Barry's letter exists today.

Harriet not only had the task of overseeing the building and interior decoration of all her six homes – she was also responsible for managing them. A head servant was tasked with the practical day-to-day running of each Sutherland property, but Harriet was expected to oversee his work and ensure that the many departments within the household functioned efficiently. Mistress of the house was a two-pronged role that required correct management of servants as well as guests, and Harriet was the commander-in-chief of a vast workforce. At Stafford House, there was a minimum of 41 servants in attendance, including a tutor, governess, secretary, cook, eight housemaids, three kitchen maids, a butler, steward and housekeeper. At Cliveden, household staff numbered around 27 during the week, and increased to as many as 50 at weekends.[6] Each of the main rooms in the house was equipped with a cord that was attached, through a system of wires, to a corresponding bell in the basement. The master board of 27 bells, each one labelled according to its room, can still be seen in the basement.

The pay given to staff varied enormously between roles, and between different households. Generally, it seems that the wage scales of the large aristocratic households became more hierarchical in the course of the 19th century. The Sutherlands may have been ahead of their time in this respect, as by the 1840s they were already paying a wide range of salaries even within the same department. Their laundry maids were paid between £1 and £37. At the top end of that scale was Madame Rousseau, who worked alongside a lady's maid, a personal confectionery maid and a French needlewoman as one of Harriet's four body servants.[7] Just as Harriet's role as Mistress of the Robes to Victoria implied more than a mere service relationship, so the most intimate and demanding roles around the Sutherland house allowed for friendship and support that extended far beyond formal obligation, and could be reciprocal. One long-standing servant of whom Harriet was particularly fond was Mrs Penson. In a time when most servants lived in fairly sparse dormitory accommodation, the inventory for Mrs Penson's room at Cliveden is remarkable. In 1861, the contents of her room included a 'scroll frame Couch on mahogany bedstead and throw over chintz hangings', a 'rosewood frame lounging chair ... spring stuffed and covered in loose chintz canvas', a 'crimson baize cover table', a 'zebrawood centre table ... on pillar and carved claw', 'two japanned circular washstands', a 'handsome satinwood winged wardrobe', a 'foot Ottoman', and a 'time piece in Brass case and stand'.[8]

There was one area of domestic management from which Harriet was spared. George was responsible for controlling the expenditure of each household, a task he was not well suited to – contemplating finances made him 'deaf and stormy in the head'; he left most of the work to his estate manager James Loch, who was as frugal as George was extravagant.[9] Despite Loch's sharp sense of economy, the Sutherlands were, like

Frederick and Augusta, caring employers, often arranging entertainments for their household staff and local artisans. On one occasion, they 'granted access to the magnificent grounds of Cliveden' for a fete for the families of workmen who had contributed to the rebuilding of the house. All the shops in Maidenhead were closed that afternoon to enable shopworkers to attend, and Harriet and George laid on 'a variety of amusements' including pleasure boats to transport the partygoers along the Thames. Very much in the spirit of Frederick, Prince of Wales, the Maidenhead Musical Society and Coldstream Guards arrived by barge to entertain revellers with music. The 'conservatories and gardens of Cliveden were thrown open', so that visitors could inspect the flowers and shrubs or saunter through the shaded groves. Harriet was given 'three hearty cheers' twice, and dancing continued well into the evening – as well as on the boat home.[10]

The rebuilding of Cliveden and management of domestic life was not the only project that occupied Harriet in 1851. She had become actively involved in promoting and supporting plans for a 'Great Exhibition'. Since the French Industrial Exposition of 1844, there had been calls for an equivalent British exhibition, to celebrate and promote the nation's achievement in manufacturing, commerce and the arts. A small exhibition in December 1844, hosted by the Society for the Encouragement of Arts, Manufactures, and Commerce, was considered by its organisers to be a failure, having drawn only 150 people.[11] However, a slightly more effective repeat exhibition in January 1845 attracted the attention of Prince Albert, the president of the Society, who had a personal interest in the subject of design and manufacture. With the encouragement of Prince Albert, the Society began working on plans for a much larger event, the scope of which would be international, embracing foreign productions as well as British ones. In January 1850 Queen Victoria established a royal commission that would be responsible for the administration of the exhibition.

The success of the event depended on the support of the leading manufacturing and commercial players of the time, both for the exhibits and for subscriptions.[12] The Sutherlands, of course, with their unlimited capital and industrial might, were needed to champion the project. At 11 o'clock in the morning of 21 February 1850, Harriet attended a meeting of Westminster residents at Willis's Rooms in St James's to discuss the best means of promoting the exhibition. Bubbling with excitement, she dashed off a letter to Queen Victoria giving a 'very enthusiastic account' of the meeting and its 'beautiful & interesting speeches'.[13] One of these speeches was delivered by Harriet's brother Lord Carlisle, who set out the aims of the exhibition in the rather optimistic and grandiose style that had come into fashion among the aristocracy after the much-feared revolution of 1848 failed to materialise in Britain. It was 'but natural and becoming at the period of the world at which we [are] arrived, that industry, that skill, that enterprise, should in turn have their own ovation, their own triumph, their own high holiday,' he proclaimed.[14] Harriet's attendance at this and other local meetings to promote the Great Exhibition shows the extent of her influence on the event. But newspaper accounts name only the attendees who gave speeches, who were all men.

In fact, Harriet was so impressed by the meeting that she invited a number of friends to Stafford House to discuss the best means of women supporting the event. This informal 'Ladies' Committee' included Countess Granville, Lady John Russell, Lady Mary Stanley, and a number of other influential aristocrats. The committee collected subscriptions, and within a few weeks had raised a remarkable £975.[15] The *Illustrated London News* of 9 March carried a picture of the committee meeting in the grand hallway at Stafford House. Harriet had discovered a natural aptitude for rallying and organising those around her. Following the establishment of the Ladies' Committee, Harriet continued to attend other important events in support of the exhibition. Most notable among these was the Mansion House banquet of 21 March 1850, at which Prince Albert outlined his idealistic vision. 'We are living at a period of most wonderful transition,' he said, 'which tends rapidly to accomplish that great end – to which all history points – the realisation of the unity of mankind.' Harriet immediately wrote to the queen after the banquet, expressing zealous admiration for Albert's speech.[16]

In just over nine months a gleaming beacon of modernity, built from glass and cast iron, was erected in Hyde Park. At more than one-third of a mile long, the colossal Crystal Palace, designed by the engineer Joseph Paxton to be assembled from prefabricated parts, was the largest enclosed space in the world. Among its supporters, it became a symbol of the self-confidence and rightful optimism of the Victorian age. On 1 May 1851, a misty-eyed Queen Victoria and her prince consort opened the Great Exhibition. It was 'the greatest day in our history',

Victoria declared; she would return 13 times with her children before the exhibition closed. Winterhalter evoked the spirit of the Exhibition in his painting *The First of May* 1851, which depicted Crystal Palace bathed in celestial light.

Crystal Palace brimmed with more than 100,000 exhibits and 14,000 exhibitors. 'Every possible invention and appliance for the service of man found a place with its embracing limits; every realisation of human genius, every effort of human industry,' the exhibition guide stated.[17] There were sections devoted to raw materials, machinery and manufactures; there were model homes, electric telegraphs and adding machines; there were courts designed to resemble different times of history and different places on earth; there was a stuffed elephant, an 80-blade sportsman's knife and a steam hammer that could with the same degree of accuracy forge the main bearing of a steamship or gently crack an egg. Queen Victoria was particularly enamoured with a bed that automatically tipped its occupant into a bath in the morning. In five months, six million visitors – more than double the population of London at the time – paid their one-shilling admittance. Harriet was a frequent visitor and, on one occasion, took her six-year-old son Ronald to the exhibition. Thirty years later, Ronald was still mesmerised, rhapsodising with childish glee in his memoirs about 'the splendour and height of the roof; the sensation of being within an enchanted place'. He was especially taken with the 'Turkish court' where he was given dates to eat, and the 'German department', decorated with 'stuffed frogs and weasels', as well as some elms which had been adorned with 'crystal fountains and marble statues'.[18]

Even though the exhibition failed to usher in Prince Albert's lofty vision of an age of universal peace and prosperity, the experience of contributing to its organisation had bolstered Harriet's confidence and given her a new-found sense of purpose. Not only was she beginning once again to enjoy her place in society, but for the first time she realised she was in a position to take an active role. Harriet's Ladies' Committee was her first step towards becoming one of the most prolific political and social campaigners of her time. Aged 48, she had evolved from a young woman fearfully watching events at a distance to a formidable force ready to create her own agenda.

Chapter 9

'THOU HYPOCRITE'

O n Friday 26 November 1852, Harriet confidently claimed her place in history, though not without controversy. As dusk settled over London, a large party of women, including the Duchesses of Bedford and Argyll, the Countess of Shaftesbury, Lady Ruthven and many more, convened in the grand hallway at Stafford House. Silence descended as Harriet climbed to the top of the staircase to make her inaugural speech. 'Perhaps I may be allowed to state the object for which this meeting has been called together,' she began.

> But very few words will be required, as all, I am sure, assembled here must have heard and read much of the moral and physical suffering inflicted on the race of negroes and their descendants, by the system of slavery prevalent in many of the States of America. Founded on such information, a proposition appeared a short while ago in several of the newspapers, that the women of England should express to the women of America the strong feeling they entertained on the question, and earnestly request their aid to abolish, or at least to mitigate, so enormous an evil.[1]

It was an elegant, somewhat restrained battle cry, but Harriet had declared war on slavery. In doing so, she would cross swords with formidable foes, including the wife of a former US president and the author of *The Communist Manifesto*.

The 'proposition' that Harriet referred to in her speech was the cumbersomely titled *Affectionate and Christian Address of Many Thousands of the Women in England to their Sisters, the Women of the United States of America*. She went on to recite this in its entirety. In language redolent of Prince Albert's utopian vision – and strikingly similar to the rhetoric employed in the US constitution of 1789 – the address spoke of a new world of freedom, liberty and 'inalienable rights'. At its root, the address was a deeply religious document; it decreed that slavery was wrong because it contradicted the teachings of the Bible and the 'spirit of the Christian religion'. Drawing particular attention to the way in which the American system of slavery prevented lawful marriage between slaves and stopped the children of slaves from receiving a religious education, Harriet declared that it was the moral responsibility of women to speak out against slavery. In a passage that recalls Victoria's reasoning during the Bedchamber Crisis, Harriet argued that her cause related 'altogether to domestic, and in no respect to national feelings', and therefore fell into the female sphere of interest.[2] Having delivered her mission statement, Harriet mapped out her plan of action: a committee, with an office at 13 Clifford Street, off Bond Street, would be formed with the responsibility of collecting signatures for the petition and then of transporting it to the United States. 'There is every reason,' Harriet concluded, 'to hope that the matter should be terminated in a short space of time.'

Although sincerely committed to the cause, Harriet did not claim to have written the proposal herself. The author was, in fact, a man. Like Harriet, Anthony Ashley Cooper, 7th Earl of Shaftesbury, boasted an impeccable Whig pedigree. In 1852 Shaftesbury read Harriet Beecher Stowe's famous anti-slavery novel *Uncle Tom's Cabin* and was, as he wrote in his diary, 'touched to the very core'.[3] As an influential politician, his own ability to protest against American slavery was circumscribed by the recent history between England and America. The American War of Independence had ended only a generation previously and attempts by British politicians to foist policy onto their former territory were still likely to be rebuffed as colonial. The commonplace that women were not intellectually equipped to deal with politics provided Shaftesbury with an alternative and potentially very effective means of protest.

On 6 November 1852, Shaftesbury penned an 'Address from the Women of England to the Women of America' to 'try to stir their souls and sympathies'. The same day, he circulated his work to the newspapers.[4] It was only after writing the draft that Shaftesbury looked around for a woman who could front the operation. Harriet was the natural choice. She came from an illustrious liberal family, she had entertained leading American delegates during the World Anti-Slavery Conference in 1840 (with a few special exceptions, women were banned from attending the event as delegates, and generally found themselves acting as hostesses), and she was already sufficiently associated with the anti-slavery cause that she had been asked, in the 1840s, to subscribe to a 'Negro College at Bermuda'.[5]

In the following months, 571,325 British women signed the petition, making it the largest anti-slavery document ever drawn up.[6] In the spring of 1853, Harriet Beecher Stowe, the author of the novel that had first inspired Shaftesbury to write the address, came to England in order to collect the signatures. On 7 May, Beecher Stowe was received in magnificent style at Stafford House. She was particularly enamoured with her hostess, describing the duchess as 'the most beautiful woman in the world'.[7] Later that evening, Harriet presented Stowe with 'a gold bracelet formed like a slave's shackle, with the date of the abolition of slavery in the British colonies inscribed on one of the links'. Space had been left on another link, so that the date of American abolition could be inscribed when it came to pass.[8]

The reception for Beecher Stowe, and the array of establishment figures in attendance – William Gladstone, Lord and Lady Palmerston, Lord John Russell, and Harriet's brother Lord Carlisle to name just a few – did much to make the British abolitionist campaign respectable. Plans were even mooted for the writer to be received by Queen Victoria, but this was abandoned after the American Embassy intervened, arguing that such a reception would be interpreted as an official royal endorsement of the abolitionist cause.[9] Nevertheless, Beecher Stowe triumphantly returned to America where she presented the petition to an anti-slavery meeting. The signatures ran to 26 volumes and the address was 'splendidly illuminated on vellum'.[10]

The London response to the address was mixed. Several papers, including the *Standard*, ran supportive accounts of the event, but others were highly critical. A piece in the *Spectator*

rebutted the women's pretensions to being apolitical, counter-
ing that their argument was inescapably political, and therefore
that they, being women, were not qualified to make it. 'To
meddle with the internal institutions of a foreign country' was
'a doubtful step even for men; much more so for women
unversed in public affairs'.[11] Not all of the critical or misogy-
nistic responses came from men: in the letter pages of *The
Times*, a writer who simply signed herself 'An Englishwoman'
reasoned that because slavery was a subject for legislation, it
was not a subject for women. She expressed concern at the idea
that women might 'show so entire a misconception of their
own peculiar character as to force themselves into their exercise of functions for which their merits and their defects
especially disqualify them'.[12]

The Americans did not wait for the illuminated vellum
copy of the address before wading in on the debate. Within
two weeks of the Stafford House meeting, the complete text of
the address appeared in the *New York Times*, and was quickly
the subject of criticism in the United States.[13] Some replies
from America were printed in English newspapers, including
one that drew attention to the great social inequalities of England. Everything was listed, including the abundance of
starving, overworked needlewomen, the lack of public education facilities, the high rate of illegitimacy in rural areas, the
general state of immorality, and the scarcity of Bibles in some
parishes. In a parody of the address's hortatory style, one
American respondent urged English women to 'raise your
voices to your fellow-citizens and your prayers to God, for the
removal of England's shame from the Christian world'.[14]

Given that she had married into such extreme industrial wealth, and had done little until this point to address the lamentable conditions experienced by Victorian factory workers (women and children included), Harriet was particularly vulnerable to such objections.

Perhaps the single most interesting riposte to the address came from Julia Gardiner Tyler, the second wife of John Tyler, the tenth president (1841–5) of the United States. As 'Mrs Presidentress', the youthful Julia Tyler (at 24, she was 30 years younger than her husband) had a reputation for enjoying the high life, and after her husband's retirement to his James River plantation, on which he kept some 70 slaves, Mrs Tyler maintained her extravagant lifestyle. Tyler's response to Harriet first appeared in the *Richmond Enquirer* of 28 January 1853, and was soon reprinted in several publications on both sides of the Atlantic. Throughout the piece, she addressed Harriet personally and laconically, accusing her of hypocrisy of the highest order:

> Go, my good Duchess of Sutherland, on an embassy of mercy to the poor, the stricken, the hungry and the naked of your own land – cast in their laps the superflux of your enormous wealth; a single jewel from your hair, a single gem from your dress would relieve many a poor female of England, who is now cold, and shivering, and destitute ... Leave it to the women of the South to alleviate the sufferings of their dependents, while you take care of your own.[15]

Tyler's response was not alone in addressing Harriet by name. Personal hostility towards the duchess spilt over into popular culture and ballads, such as in the following song, which would have been sung to the tune of 'Oh Susanna':

> Oh, Lady Sutherland
> To comfort you I'll try.
> Mrs. Tyler gave you what was right
> But Duchess don't you cry.[16]

Unsurprisingly, it was only a short time before Harriet's association with the Highland clearances began to gather attention. In January 1853, the *Boston Post* gave an account of how, during the clearances, 15,000 crofters were evicted, to be replaced by 29 families and 100,000 sheep; a short time later, in the *Richmond Dispatch*, the number of evicted crofters appeared as 20,000. Even though she was a child of five years old at the time and not yet affiliated to the Sutherland family, the duchess was lambasted for 'standing idly by' while these abuses took place.[17] The more effective critics avoided overstating Harriet's personal responsibility for the clearances, and were content to point out that her current wealth arose in part from these historical abuses. Such was the argument of a polemic that appeared in the *New York Tribune* and the radical British publication, the *People's Paper*, written by Karl Marx. The bulk of Marx's tirade against the duchess was taken up by an account of the various 'usurpations' that culminated in the transformation of what was previously clan property into private property. His brief history climaxed in an emotive description of the clearances ordered by the Countess of Sutherland, Harriet's mother-in-law, whom Marx accused of 'systematic' expulsion and extermination. 'All their villages were demolished and burned down,' Marx wrote of the dispossessed Highlanders, '. . . An old woman refusing to quit her hut was burned in the flames of it.'

Given the explicitly Christian nature of Harriet's 'address', and the appeal within it to the 'spirit' of the Bible and the Christian religion, Marx's attack was pertinent. Looming large in the subtext of his criticism was the Christian interdiction on hypocrisy, as most famously expressed in Matthew 7:5: 'Thou hypocrite, first cast out the beam out of thine own eye; and then shalt thou see clearly to cast out the mote out of thy brother's eye.' It was this ethic, or some secularised version of it, that informed Marx's peroration: 'The enemy of British Wage-Slavery has a right to condemn Negro-Slavery; a Duchess of Sutherland, a Duke of Atholl, a Manchester Cotton-lord — never!' Harriet was not in the least perturbed by Marx's excoriating article. When Harriet Beecher Stowe arrived at Stafford House in May, she was greeted at the door by two Highlanders in full costume. The duchess would continue to present herself unabashedly as both an opponent of slavery, and a benefactor of the Highland culture from whose destruction she was accused of profiting.

In the course of Harriet's heated fight for abolition, Charles Barry completed most of his work on Cliveden. It was now in a fit state to receive guests and, on Tuesday 20 April 1854, Queen Victoria made her first visit to the house. 'The Duchess showed us all over the house, which is finished & being fast furnished,' Victoria recorded, 'it is quite beautiful, in strictly Italian style & the rooms so light & cheerful. They are arranged without actual splendour, but with all the Duchess's rare taste.' The rooms upstairs were also 'charming, such pretty wall papers & chintzes, all so well chosen'. The queen was equally delighted by 'the view of the valley of the Thames', which she thought 'very lovely'.[18] After the guided tour, Harriet and Victoria took the first of what would be many walks around the estate. The women's gentle meanders through the 'beautiful woods' along the river would become a motif of their friendship; they would both relish Cliveden's riverside landscape until the end of their lives.

In a neat historical irony, the original Italianate vision of the Duke of Buckingham, a man who heavily invested in slavery, was only realised by a mistress whose mission was to abolish this 'enormous evil'. By 1855, Barry's work at Cliveden was nearly at an end. The following year, Beecher Stowe returned to England, and this time visited Harriet at Dunrobin. Despite the very public controversy surrounding her participation in the anti-slavery movement, Harriet's devotion to the cause continued to grow. Abolition would become one of the most frequent subjects of debate at her famous Cliveden weekends of the early 1860s. Harriet had finally found her voice, her vocation, and her ideal home, but was about to lose her husband.

Chapter 10

'WHAT A HOLD A PLACE
HAS UPON ONE'

I n January 1855, Charles Barry presented the Duke of
Sutherland with a bill for his work at Cliveden. Outraged
by its contents, George dispatched a furious letter to his
financial controller James Loch: 'Sir C. Barry has taken me by
surprise,' he fulminated. 'Journeys and travelling expenses [to
Cliveden] £105.6.o!!! ... Arrangement of Statues! ... what
statues he has had to place I do not know . . . the choice of place
seems more expensive than the cost of the statue – if the charges
were not so provoking they would be ridiculous.'[1] George paid
the bill, but fired Barry.

At the time of the Sutherlands' falling-out with Barry, there
were still further works the couple wanted done in the house
and grounds, and two years later they approached new architects, George Devey and Henry Clutton, with a view to
completing the project. The former was known for his vernacular cottages, and was commissioned to design several new
buildings for the grounds of the house; the latter would work
on completing structures left unfinished by Barry, including
the offices, the kitchens, and the stables. Clutton's greatest task
at Cliveden was, however, one that Harriet did not foresee: the

erection of a water tower. There is an irony in Barry being dismissed before the construction of a tower became necessary, because he was famous for adding towers to everything he touched. A joke on the subject by Lord Melbourne even made its way into Victoria's diary. In an entry in August 1839, the queen recalled Harriet's visit to Walton House, which had been altered by Barry. 'Talked of the duchess of Sutherland's having been to Walton, and it's being such a fine house, though rather too large for the place,' she wrote. ' "Mr Barry always builds a tower", said Lord M. "It's exactly like the Houses of Parliament in small"; which made us laugh very much.'[2]

The joke was ultimately on Harriet. Although Barry's initial designs for Cliveden did not include a single tower, the changes made by Clutton increased the need for a better system of water storage and supply. In the late 1850s, Clutton mocked up images for a water tower, to be situated adjacent to the kitchens and stables. The design for the tower was based on Barry's 1840 clock tower at Trentham: it would be 100 feet tall, with a head large enough to create room for 15,000 gallons of water.

Meanwhile, Devey was adapting Spring Cottage, and designing a number of new outhouses, including a dairy and a boathouse. The construction of vernacular outhouses was becoming increasingly fashionable in this period – they were the mid-19th-century equivalent of the rather grander, often commemorative pavilions that were popular in Elizabeth and Orkney's time. Aristocratic gardens such as Kew were, by the end of the century, littered with cottages and faux-rustic dwellings. While the British landscape was changed beyond recognition by the 'dark satanic mills' of urban manufacturing and industrialised agriculture, the aristocracy commissioned follies that evoked an idealised, pre-industrial past.

On a windy afternoon in April 1858, Victoria visited Cliveden for the first time in three years to inspect the finishing touches that had been added to the mansion. Harriet's penchant for French phrases is echoed in the queen's diary entry for the day. Victoria admired the '*objects d'art*, china and glass' and pronounced the house a '*bijou* of taste'. Harriet's '*boudoir*' had been transformed (at a cost of £900, the equivalent of £54,000 today) into an 'enchanting' haven with hand-painted plasterwork of flowers, foliage and trellises.[3]

The reception rooms had also been finished to the most exacting standards. Central to the great hall with its floor of Minton tiles stood a life-size bronze of Joan of Arc by Princesse Marie-Christine d'Orléans, third daughter of the French king and a celebrated artist and sculptor. Harriet had a special devotion to the French martyr, whom she considered the embodiment of 'all that is good and beautiful'.[4] The statue can still be seen in the gardens of Cliveden. The ceiling of the staircase (all that remains of Harriet's interior design today) was painted with her children depicted as the Four Seasons. In the sitting room overlooking the garden her children were depicted again, this time as cupids, and two pictures by Sir Joshua Reynolds portrayed her grandfather Lord Carlisle and her grandmother Georgiana, Duchess of Devonshire. A copy of Titian's *Assumption* was on display in the dining room, while a portrait of the Duke of Buckingham hung on the wall overlooking the staircase. The library opened into a magnificent drawing room decorated, Versailles-like, with a row of mirrors, which reflected the view of the Thames to stunning effect.[5] In the gardens, Harriet had planted a succession of 'stately flower beds', which included an arrangement of 4,000 geraniums known as the 'scarlet ribbon'. The scent of the flowers hung seductively in the spring air – a smell Victoria would always associate with Cliveden. To conclude the royal visit, Harriet once again accompanied Victoria on a long walk 'above the river', passing along 'the most splendid yew trees, 400 years old'.[6]

Among the finishing touches put to the outside of the house during this period was a frieze, inscribed in Latin along the entablature, and painted gold. The frieze was made up of four panels, starting on the north side of the house and ending on the west:

> Constructed upon foundations laid long before by George Villiers Duke of Buckingham in Charles the Second's reign.

> Completed in the year of Our Lord 1851 when Victoria had been Queen by God's grace for fourteen years.

> Restored by George Duke of Sutherland and Harriet his wife on the site where two houses had previously been burnt down.

> Built by the skill, devotion and design of the architect Charles Barry in 1851.[7]

The Latin words for the frieze were contributed by Harriet's friend, William Gladstone. The pair had known each other for some time but it was in September 1853 when Gladstone was staying at Dunrobin that their acquaintanceship evolved into something significant. During the stay, he was struck down by erysipelas, a bacterial skin infection which induces fevers, shaking and vomiting, and Harriet read to him 'full of the utmost kindness and simplicity' during his unexpected month-long confinement.[8] The period of proximity and care was the beginning of an affectionate bond that would sustain Harriet for the rest of her life.

Gladstone was a brilliant yet troubled man grappling with many irreconcilable traits. The son of a Liverpool merchant who had transformed a modest family inheritance into a great fortune, he had been educated at Eton and then Oxford, and took a seat in Parliament at the age of 23 as the Tory MP for Newark. An evangelical Christian and deeply contemplative man, Gladstone was brought up to believe in the redemptive power of perpetual self-examination, which at its most intense resulted in a periodic fascination with sexual temptation. Gladstone's twin preoccupations of sex and religion propelled him, in the mid-1840s, to embark on a mission of 'rescue work' with prostitutes. This involved walking the streets of London at night to reclaim women from a life of vice. Although his work fell firmly within the bounds of Christian charity, it raised eyebrows in political circles as well as provoking a personal crisis of conscience within Gladstone himself. He regularly confessed in his diary to committing 'adultery of the heart', 'enjoying thinking of evil without the intention of action', and being 'out at all hours' to put himself 'in the way of contact with exciting causes' and 'the path of danger'.[9] The path induced in him 'uneasy' thoughts, which led to excruciating bouts of guilt and shame. In his diaries a curious black mark often appears after encounters with prostitutes or evenings with illicit books: this mark was his symbol for a small whip known as a scourge. Gladstone appears to have gone through periods in which he whipped himself as punishment for sinful thoughts.

Among the salacious books that periodically tempted Gladstone were several volumes of the *Fabliaux et contes des poètes français du XI–XV siècles* [Fables and tales of the French poets of the 11th–15th centuries], which he first came across in May 1848. Of his first session with the *Fabliaux*, Gladstone wrote: 'I began to read it, and found in some parts of it impure passages, concealed beneath the veil of a quite foreign idiom: so I drank the poison, sinfully, because understanding was thus hidden by a cloud – I have stained my memory and my soul.'[10] He set down a black mark against the day. A few months later, he punished himself after stumbling across 'two vile poems' by the Earl of Rochester (the Duke of Buckingham's friend), and in February 1849 he succumbed once again to the temptations of the *Fabliaux*.[11] Such was Harriet's soothing influence on Gladstone that during his years of intense friendship with her, the ominous black mark ceased to appear in his diary entries. It is just one striking expression of the significance of their relationship.

Following his time with the duchess at Dunrobin, Gladstone became a regular guest at Cliveden. In July 1854 he visited the house and 'sculled on the river, the first time in many years'; he made at least two weekend visits in 1857, and several more during the summer of 1859.[12] He went for trips in the carriage and in boats on the Thames, and during a visit in August, 'read Tennyson, Tennyson, Tennyson'.[13] Throughout their friendship, the pair maintained a regular and lively correspondence. The letters Harriet wrote to Gladstone are bound together in six volumes in the British Library and amount to 2,000 folios of correspondence. It was a mutually beneficial relationship; while Gladstone gave Harriet the confidence to take an active interest in politics, the duchess's wealth and social connections gave him status and credibility to pursue his political agenda.

The British party-political landscape in the 1850s was undergoing seismic change. The two-party system of the Tories – who had traditionally represented the cause of the High Church and landed wealth, and had been resistant to social and political change – and the Whigs – who had typically been more receptive of reformist and commercial causes – had begun to fracture during the 1840s. In 1846, old allegiances were shattered by Robert Peel's decision to repeal the Corn Laws. These were tariffs on foreign cereal imports that had existed since the end of the Napoleonic Wars, when they were introduced in order to protect British cereal manufacturers from foreign competition. Critics of the laws claimed that they artificially inflated food prices and stymied economic growth; opponents of the laws included manufacturers and merchants, as well as workers who were suffering from the high cost of bread at a time when factory owners were cutting wages.

Commercial middle-class opposition to the laws reached its

apotheosis in William Cobden and John Bright's Anti-Corn
Law League, which was established in 1838 to agitate peacefully for reform. Many in the Tory Party were fierce supporters
of the laws, and feared that repeal would undermine the status
of landlords economically and politically, thus endangering
Britain's traditional 'territorial constitution'.[14] Peel's conversion to free trade made him a traitor in the eyes of many Tories,
and the Corn Law vote caused a split from which the party
would never recover. The economically liberal Peelites had a
lot more in common with free trade Whigs and Radicals –
themselves an offshoot of the Whig Party – than they had
with the traditional 'territorial constitutional' rump of their
own party. An alliance of Peelites, Whigs and Radicals was
attempted under the Peelite prime minister Lord Aberdeen in
the early 1850s, but it was only in 1859 that a lasting alliance
would be formed.

On 6 June 1859, in the surroundings of Willis's Rooms,
where the Westminster meeting on the subject of the Great
Exhibition had taken place almost ten years previously, the
new Liberal Party was formally established with the assent of
274 Peelite, Whig and Radical MPs.[15] The alliance would
allow Lord Palmerston, who had begun his political career as
a Tory but now favoured the new Liberal politics, to form an
effective ministry, and on 12 June, the queen asked him to
become prime minister. Though he would not be prime minister for another decade, Gladstone's work as chancellor in
Lord Palmerston's government set the tone for the new liberal
economics that came to dominate the latter half of the 19th
century. His budget of 1860 included a tariff-reducing treaty

with France, and a controversial plan to abolish the duty on paper, which was known as a 'tax on knowledge' because of the way it inflated the price of newspapers.

During his stint as chancellor under Palmerston, Gladstone saw the Sutherlands frequently. While he often saw the duke and duchess together, it was with the latter that he had a more natural bond. During the summer of 1861, he spent five separate 'weekends' at Cliveden. In the mid-19th century, the term 'weekend' did not exist, and in many lines of work, politics included, Saturday was treated as a workday. Practice varied between different prime ministers, but Palmerston used Saturday as a cabinet day, with business running from one o'clock in the afternoon to around half past four. Gladstone consequently invented his own 'weekends' around this schedule, heading straight to Cliveden after Saturday cabinet meetings. In the Restoration era, travel from the capital to the estate involved much time and planning; by the 1860s, the short train journey did not take significantly longer than it does today. Cliveden could be accessed from London within an hour. The expansion of the railways allowed Gladstone and Harriet to pioneer that quintessentially English phenomenon: the country-house weekend.

As well as serving the house, the Great Western Railway transformed the Thames Valley landscape in which Cliveden stood. The new topography of the river at Maidenhead was given a particular significance by J. M. W. Turner's painting *Rain, Steam and Speed*, which was first exhibited in 1846. The work depicts a passenger train thundering over Maidenhead bridge and, in the bottom corner, a fleeing hare. Behind the hare and the approaching train, the scene is half-formed; even the foreground scene looks at risk of being submerged in the turbid landscape. Turner's image captured the conflict between old and new, and expressed both excitement and doubt at the way in which a settled past was being devoured by technology and speed. This must have struck a chord with Harriet, who had expressed similar trepidation about steam travel as early as 1830. The river, which in Georgian Britain had so often been a site of pomp and pageantry, was now being carved up by new and unprecedented thoroughfares.

Gladstone did not merely view Cliveden as a leisure retreat, but also as a base from which to conduct and reflect on his political affairs. Throughout 1860 and 1861, these affairs were fraught. The embryonic Liberal Party had not yet established a clear identity. Lord Palmerston was less economically liberal than Gladstone, and less concerned about economic retrenchment (the administration had inherited a public debt of nearly five million pounds from the previous government). The prime minister's expenditure on costly projects such as fortifying the south coast horrified Gladstone, who believed that in a time of peace nothing but dire necessity should induce a government to borrow. The two also disagreed over foreign policy, Gladstone being an opponent (for both economic and ethical reasons) of Palmerston's strident interventionism. On several occasions during 1861, these tensions brought Gladstone to the brink of resignation. During a weekend at Cliveden in June that year, he wrote: 'My resignation all but settled.'[16] But despite several such claims, he remained chancellor until 1866.

At the end of 1860, Harriet wrote ecstatically to Gladstone

about the election of Abraham Lincoln, a well-known abolitionist, as president of the United States. The election, she
believed, with rather naive optimism, was an unmitigated victory for her cause and one of several events that had made
1860 'a year of grace'.[17] The path to abolition would, in fact,
prove to be a long and bloody one.

In the bitterly cold January of 1861, George suffered an
attack of paralysis. 'I wish you to hear from me first that my
dear Duke has been . . . ill this morning,' she informed Gladstone on 8 January.[18] Later that month, as the gravity of the
duke's condition became clear, Harriet wrote to Victoria,
resigning her position as Mistress of the Robes, but the queen
refused to accept, displaying her own great need of her friend
and, perhaps, stubborn optimism that George might still
recover. In February, the duke's condition deteriorated further. 'The poor dear Duke of Sutherland is I am afraid dying,'
Victoria recorded in her journal. 'He will be such a loss.'[19]

By the end of the month, Harriet's husband of nearly
40 years was dead. At Cliveden, George's study – perhaps the
only room to truly reflect his simple but refined tastes – stood
empty. Harriet was haunted by her loss. 'Even then I felt as if I
could not see Him Die, or if I did that I should lose my mind – &
yet I have witnessed I have heard the last breath,' she wrote to
Gladstone in her misery. 'I am often composed. I have cried
enough. I have slept. In my last letter I feel as I had seemed
satisfied – alas you know that this is *not* so . . . The Bible has no
allusion to *this* Parting . . . I wish there had been – There is
much to soothe.'[20] A few months later, she reflected on her
bitter-sweet memories of George at Cliveden. 'I have rested in

the place at Cliveden where our children were married – & grandchildren baptised,' she wrote to Gladstone. 'What a hold [a] Place has upon one.'[21]

George's death had serious financial as well as emotional ramifications for Harriet. The Sutherland estate passed immediately to Harriet's eldest son. Unlike Augusta, however, who was entirely at the mercy of her male patrons, George had made ample provision for his much-loved wife. The house had been conveyed to Harriet in 1849 partly in the expectation that George, 20 years her senior, would die before she did. There was, however, the problem of ongoing works on the house, the largest of which was the construction of the water tower, still incomplete when the duke died in 1861. Thankfully Harriet's son, George, who was now the 3rd Duke of Sutherland, arranged 'to gratify his mother by executing the work for her, as would have been the case had his father lived'.[22] The new duke's concern for his mother is a touching demonstration of the strong bonds that existed between the Sutherland family. The water tower was finished later the same year, having cost £3,000 in total. An elaborate structure with an ornate blue clock-face, it became a monument to the second duke, with his name and dates inscribed on the pediments.

The queen, who during George's illness had so resisted Harriet's attempts to resign, now felt obliged to accept the grieving Harriet's decision. In April, 'full of Grace and Sorrow', she released her from her duties as Mistress of the Robes. This time, Harriet would not return to the role. In her place, Victoria appointed the Duchess of Wellington, as she reported in her diary on 6 May: 'Saw the dear Dss of Wellington, who is now my Mistress of the Robes, the poor dear Dss of Sutherland having resigned.'[23] But the Duchess of Wellington would never occupy such a position of influence and intimacy with the queen as Harriet had done. Later that year, when Victoria suffered her own life-changing bereavement, it was Harriet she relied on for support – this time in no official capacity, but simply as her best friend.

Chapter 11

AN INDEPENDENT WIDOW

I n the months following George's death, Harriet became increasingly dependent on Gladstone for emotional support. Gladstone too sought comfort in Harriet's friendship. On 16 April 1861, Harriet wrote to Gladstone suggesting he visit her alone at Cliveden; it was the first time they had seen each other since the duke's death. 'Would you come for a visit & would Mrs Gladstone let it be the first time alone,' she appealed. 'It must be sad & solemn.'[1] Gladstone followed her wishes: the guest book for Tuesday 23 April records only Harriet and Gladstone as having been in residence at the house.[2] Harriet was alert to the possibility that Gladstone's wife Catherine would feel marginalised, or even betrayed by the closeness of their friendship. At the start of May, she invited Gladstone and Catherine to visit for a weekend, and on two further occasions (in May, and then in June) suggested that the couple visit for a meal, or to spend the night. The invitation she extended to both of the Gladstones in early May is especially attentive to Catherine – she mentions wanting to see them both, and in a postscript emphasises: 'Pray tell Mrs Gladstone that I shall much like to see her.'[3]

After civil war broke out in America in mid-April, Harriet had a particularly prolonged correspondence with Gladstone on the subject of the war and slavery. Harriet viewed the war in providential terms, as both the inevitable consequence of slavery, and a God-given opportunity to end it forever. She believed that the vicissitudes of war were worth enduring, if they stamped out a greater evil. 'The curse of war will sweep away a curse quicker still,' she wrote with almost religious fervour.[4] Gladstone, on the other hand, saw the war as a conflict over the constitutional rights of the southern states to secede from the Union, and considered slavery to be an unrelated matter. At the time, there was much truth in his view, for while Abraham Lincoln was an opponent of slavery, he had promised not to interfere with the southern system of slave-holding; indeed, until 1862, officers in the Unionist army were still obliged to return runaway slaves to the belligerent South.

In early summer, Harriet was staying in London at Stafford House. Although the residence now belonged to her son George, she still had rooms there. On 8 July she wrote to Gladstone asking him to accompany her to the British Institution in Pall Mall to see their annual exhibition of Old Masters, which included Sir Joshua Reynolds's painting of her grandmother. The exhibition was a key event in the social calendar of the nobility, who dominated the membership, and the summer exhibition at the Institution was a highly visible event for a chancellor and a dowager duchess to attend together. Harriet's desire for company did not blind her to the possibility of gossip: at the end of her letter, she wondered if the engagement would be 'too public'.[5] In her first year of widowhood, Harriet's emotional state was fragile. This was her first London social season without George, and everywhere she went, she was reminded of previous visits with her husband. Likewise the summer exhibition at the Royal Academy of Arts reminded her that she had visited the exhibition with George 'after I had told him I would be his wife – an old but so fresh a recollection'.[6]

In mid-July Harriet, cutting a far more corpulent figure than she had in her youth, travelled to Paris to get treatment for her cataracts, which had worsened to the point where it made reading and writing difficult. No less than London, the city was haunted by memories of the early days of her marriage. 'The Louvre is full of pleasant memories of having first seen & enjoyed it with my dearest Husband,' she wrote on 20 July.[7] Her intense neediness brought on by grief and ill-health was causing some strain on her relationship with Gladstone. After waiting more than a month for him to reply to a letter, Harriet sent another, testier note to her friend: 'Is it unreasonable to think I should perhaps hear from you . . .' the letter began.[8]

Harriet did not have long to dwell on her disappointment with Gladstone, because she was soon forced to set her own emotions aside in order to take care of her other great friend. In December 1861, Queen Victoria's husband Albert contracted typhoid and, later that month, aged just 42, he died. Victoria recorded his last moments in her journal: 'Two or three long but perfectly gentle breaths were drawn, the hand clasping mine and . . . all, all, was over,' she wrote. 'I stood up, kissed his dear heavenly forehead and called out in bitter and agonising cry, "Oh! my dear Darling!"'[9] Victoria's despair was extreme. She shut herself away with her family, seeing her cabinet ministers as rarely as she could, and eschewing her duties as queen and the ceremonial functions of monarchy. Entirely self-conscious about her solitude, she referred to it in her journals as 'my seclusion'. There was only one person she wished to see – Harriet.

Within days of Albert's death, the queen called Harriet to her side. Harriet rushed to Windsor and found Victoria sitting alone in her room. The tormented queen embraced her, then looked deep into Harriet's eyes, repeating the phrase 'you loved him', before leading her into the room in which Albert's lifeless body lay. The queen knelt before the couch in quiet contemplation and 'extended her arms' to Albert, speaking 'every word of endearment as if he had lived'. Muttering incoherently about the 'beauty of the face' which even death had not impaired, Victoria tenderly stroked Albert's forehead. All the while, Harriet stood by her side in shocked silence. Finally, as if slipping into a grief-induced trance, Victoria raised her eyes to the heavens and left the room. Harriet spent the ensuing days comforting the distraught queen. At times Victoria felt she was 'going mad with grief'. She confessed to Harriet that she was utterly lost without her husband and felt unable to continue. Who, she asked, could she confess her 'every thought . . . anxiety or worry to' now that her husband had died? Victoria interspersed these outpourings of misery with graphic 'almost hour by hour' accounts of Albert's illness. Harriet, now shouldering the burden of Victoria's loss as well as her own, sought some solace in Gladstone, to whom she wrote of her 'very harrowing' experiences caring for the queen.[10]

In January, while still making regular trips to Windsor to look after the queen, Harriet was going through a particularly difficult period in her own grieving, for the month marked the first anniversary of George's death. 'I live in the thick blows of last year,' she wrote to Gladstone in February.[11] She was touched – and maybe, given the self-involved nature of the queen's mourning thus far, surprised – to receive a letter from Victoria expressing sympathy on the anniversary. 'I like to tell you of the Queen,' she wrote to Gladstone. 'Is it not most kind & considerate of her to recollect the Day of my bereavement.' She quoted Victoria, who had written: 'I have not forgotten what to day is – I think of *you* – of what you lost with my poor bleeding heart & again I can feel for you.' Victoria also took the opportunity to express her own ongoing agony. Harriet informed Gladstone that 'she tells me that she feels very weak & continues getting thinner & thinner' and reported her saying 'how terrible life is all is black & for ever here – he was the light, & the life of my existence – I have now only the reflection of it'.[12]

When Harriet returned to Cliveden in the spring of 1862, she could feel the fog of her grief lifting. She had endured a wretched first year of mourning, but was beginning to yearn for company and conversation and, once again, began to invite people to her country estate. Perhaps unconsciously, she was redefining herself as an independent widow, a role she inhabited with even greater ease than that of a society hostess. Unlike Augusta, Harriet was able to forge a rewarding, new life for herself after George, surrounding herself with a group of nurturing and intellectually stimulating friends.

At Harriet's Cliveden weekends of the 1860s, members of the clergy, including Samuel Wilberforce, the Bishop of Oxford, and architects such as the Crystal Palace visionary Sir Joseph Paxton, dined with politicians, sculptors, artists and poets. Despite her relatively diminished financial resources, Harriet continued to entertain in style, keeping an average of 45 servants at her disposal on any given weekend. In May 1862, Alfred, Lord Tennyson, the poet laureate, paid Harriet a visit. Tennyson was averse to large gatherings, so on the occasions he visited Cliveden, Harriet tried to keep the guest list as short as possible. Predictably, this meant occasionally asking Gladstone to stay without Catherine. Gladstone and Tennyson had known each other when they were younger and had both been obsessed by the English poet Arthur Hallam, whose death at the age of 22 prompted Tennyson to write *In Memoriam*. Their weekends together at Cliveden were an opportunity to renew their old acquaintance. 'Conversation with T[ennyson] & the Duchess,' recorded Gladstone, one Monday evening after a weekend at Cliveden. 'At 11 am ended this most interesting visit: & I really feel I have got nearer to this great simple man.'[13]

On several visits during the spring, Tennyson read drafts of new works to Harriet, Gladstone and a few other select guests. During one weekend visit in May, he read from *Pericles* on the Friday and *Guinevere* (from the larger cycle *Idylls of the King*) on the Sunday.[14] Harriet was struggling with her cataracts, and had recently been told by an eye doctor in Paris that she should stop trying to read so much, so the experience of the poet laureate reciting his works for her in his 'growling voice' was extremely gratifying. There were further writerly endeavours going on in the wings: during the evenings, as well as drafting speeches and reading biographies and works of political economy, Gladstone was working hard on his own trochaic translation of Homer's *Odyssey*, or, as it appears in his diary entries, 'the Trochaic Version'.[15] As in the days of Elizabeth Villiers and Jonathan Swift, Cliveden had again become a hive of literary conversation.

Harriet's enjoyable weekends at Cliveden were punctuated by regular trips to Windsor to care for the grief-stricken queen. Despite being emotionally drained by Victoria's depression, Harriet remained attentive as ever towards her friend's needs. 'I am exhausted as I always am after seeing the Queen,' she wrote to Gladstone in April, 'but I am anxious to tell you that I thought her much better today. She showed me [Albert's] rooms in great detail but calm. She took me again into the room of Death where in the bed was a crop of white Camelia.'[16] The following month, Harriet reported to Gladstone that Victoria was 'still more depressed'.[17]

As the second anniversary of Albert's death approached, Gladstone became increasingly frustrated by Victoria's grief-induced paralysis; the queen was still neglecting her official duties. She remained at Windsor, swathed in her famous black shrouds, wedded to the past and uninterested in the future. As the projected cost of a planned memorial to Albert escalated, Gladstone wrote darkly about public discontent in tones reminiscent of Harriet's fearful politics of the 1830s. 'If the sense of exaggeration once even suggests itself,' he wrote to Harriet regarding the queen's grief, 'it will grow: and when it gains ground it will have a chilling effect.'[18] Then, during a conversation with Victoria at Holyrood Palace in Edinburgh, he made the fatal miscalculation of speaking his mind. 'I told her that she would not give way . . . that duty would sustain her,' he recorded in his diary. Appalled at the perceived upbraiding, Victoria 'hustled' Gladstone out of her presence.[19]

The handsome and charismatic Tory politician Benjamin Disraeli understood that the route to the queen's favour was to appeal not to her sense of duty, but her vanity. He coaxed and caressed her ego, fawned over and flattered her, and delivered effusive speeches in Parliament that deified Albert's legacy. There were shades of Lord Melbourne in the alluring, witty and sophisticated politician; undoubtedly he reminded the queen of her more carefree past and, within months, Disraeli became Victoria's acknowledged favourite. Thus, in a neat twist of fate, during their respective widowhoods Victoria and Harriet fell in love with the two men who were to become the fiercest political rivals of their time. And yet it was not Gladstone or Disraeli, but another more exotic leader, who threatened to drive a wedge between Harriet and the queen.

Chapter 12

GARIBALDI-MANIA

Have you heard that Garibaldi is likely to be here soon?' Harriet enthused to Gladstone in April 1864.[1] Possessed by a quasi-religious zeal, she began organising a series of luncheons and dinners at Stafford House and at Cliveden, where Garibaldi could meet with senior English politicians and the stars of high society.

The exploits of the Italian nationalist General Giuseppe Garibaldi had a cult-like following in 1860s Britain. In his youth, Garibaldi had embraced republican nationalism and had dedicated his life to liberating Italy from the shackles of the tyrannical Bourbon monarchy – the same dynasty that had produced the ousted Charles X of France. Garibaldi had won international fame during the 1848–9 revolutions in Italy, where he had heroically organised a doomed insurrection against the French. In attracting some limited support from British aristocratic liberals, the insurrection was exceptional among the many that occurred during those years. He had then spent the early 1850s in exile before re-emerging in 1860 to head the 'Expedition of the Thousand', which sailed across the Mediterranean to bolster the revolution that had broken out in

Sicily. His intervention led to the collapse of the Bourbon monarchy of the Two Sicilies, and the overthrow of papal power in central Italy, and presaged the creation of an Italian nation state. Following the success of the Expedition, Harriet wrote to Gladstone celebrating 'the liberation of ten or twelve millions of Italians from oppressive misrule'.[2]

Italian nationalism had been a hobby horse of both Harriet and Gladstone for the last decade. In the summer of 1851, after a visit to Naples, Gladstone published two *Letters to Lord Aberdeen*, expressing his outrage at the politically repressive rule of the Bourbon monarch Ferdinand II. The *Letters* triggered an international uproar against the treatment of Italian prisoners, and in particular of Carlo Poerio, a poet and political activist whom Gladstone had visited in jail.[3] Despite the Europe-wide mobilisation of liberal opinion against the inhumane conditions in which Poerio and his contemporaries were forced to reside, it was 1858 before Poerio was finally released from prison. On his release, he and other prisoners were loaded onto a ship bound across the Atlantic, but the vessel was forced to land in Cork after one of the crew led a rebellion against the captain. From Ireland, Poerio made his way to London, where he soon became a sought-after dinner guest in progressive circles. In a letter to Gladstone of 6 April 1859, Harriet wrote: 'I would much like . . . to make the acquaintance I have so long desired – Poerio's.'[4]

A few weeks later, having met Poerio once in London, she wrote to Gladstone from Cliveden, saying 'I would much like to have Poerio for a day here.'[5] By this time, Gladstone, who had initially approached the 'Italian Question' as a reformist rather than a nationalist, had become convinced of the more radical case for unification. Harriet had also arrived at a similar conclusion, but for different reasons: her enthusiasm for the Italian revolution and subsequently for Garibaldi arose from her religious, not ideological beliefs. A committed Anglican, Harriet saw the Italian cause as a symbolic defeat for 'popery', the spectre of Catholic threat that had antagonised British Protestants for centuries.

Though Garibaldi had collaborated with the Sardinian monarchy of Victor Emmanuel II in order to ensure the birth of an Italian nation in 1861, his career in Italy and previously in South America, as well as his skill in rallying popular support, meant that he was still seen as a figurehead of radical nationalism. Many of Harriet's contemporaries feared, with good reason, that a Garibaldi-esque revolution in Britain would mean not only the end of the monarchy, but the end of the aristocracy too. Harriet's ardour for the revolutionary republican seems incongruous, not only with her proximity to the queen, but also with her aristocratic inheritance and, most strikingly, with her own long-running fear of revolution and 'mob rule' at home. Repeatedly her inclination towards liberal politics strained against the identity and status she had inherited from her ancestry and parents-in-law. When she campaigned for abolition she was held to account for the oligarchic abuses of a previous generation of Sutherlands, and now, in the 1860s, some of the friendships she had forged as the daughter of 'Grand Whiggery' did not sit easily with her admiration for Garibaldi. Most at risk was her friendship with Victoria who, unsurprisingly, detested revolutionaries, Italian or otherwise.

In the spring of 1864 Garibaldi finally reached England. His visit was an ideal opportunity to court the British public and lobby the British government to support the young Italian nation.[6] On his arrival he showed himself eager to reassure the nervous establishment when he issued a press release calling for calm: 'Dear Friends, I do not want any political demonstrations. PS. – Above all, don't incite riots.'[7] But his supporters could not contain themselves and Garibaldi-mania swept Britain. A swarm of 500,000 journalists, fans, politicians and socialites, many of them provocatively wearing the Italian national colours, turned out to greet him.

On Tuesday 12 April, Garibaldi's first full day in London, he attended a luncheon hosted by Harriet. The Earl and Countess Russell, the Earl and Countess of Clarendon, Viscountess Palmerston, the Earl and Countess of Shaftesbury, and Mr and Mrs Gladstone all congregated to pay their respects.[8] The following evening, Harriet held a glittering reception for the general at Stafford House; she even provoked a frisson of scandal by inviting him into her 'boudoir' to smoke a cigar. This caused 'great astonishment and amusement', according to the Earl of Malmesbury, because Harriet's boudoir, 'which is fitted up most magnificently with hangings of velvet and everything that is most costly', was 'considered such a sacred spot that few favoured mortals have ever been admitted into its precincts; and to allow someone to smoke in it is most astonishing to all who know the Duchess'.[9] In addition to all the events at Stafford House, Garibaldi also escorted Harriet to a banquet at the Fishmongers Hall, wearing a red shirt, the distinctive uniform of his nationalist troops; all the other guests were in full evening dress.

It was even suggested that Harriet, now aged 58, ought to marry Garibaldi. In fact the general had a wife back in Italy, but this only gave rise to a further witticism that linked the Harriet–Giuseppe frisson to the legendary oratorical skills of William Gladstone. According to *The Economist* 'it was objected that the General had a wife living. "Oh, that does not matter," was the reply, "Gladstone is here, and we could easily get him to explain her away." '[10]

On Friday 22 April, Garibaldi left Stafford House for Cliveden 'in an open carriage, drawn by four beautiful greys'.[11] Newspapers across the country carried exhaustive accounts of his stay. 'Garibaldi, true to his island custom, was up at an early hour, strolling in the grounds of Cliveden', the *Leeds Mercury* noted. Garibaldi's morning constitutional was followed by a trip to 'inspect the model farm at Windsor', accompanied by Harriet and the Duchess of Argyll; for lunch the three returned to Cliveden, where yet another party – this time with 30 guests – was held in the general's honour. Later that afternoon Garibaldi and a 'party of gentlemen' went out in boats on the Thames. According to the report, Garibaldi was 'delighted with the surrounding scenery and especially with the picturesque appearance Cliveden presented from the river'.[12] The view of the Thames from the back of the house was said to remind him of river prospects in South America, where he had cut his teeth as a revolutionary.

Harriet was utterly mesmerised. After Garibaldi's departure from Cliveden, she wistfully wrote of the 'void' he had left. 'Come back, dear General,' she implored, 'I think so often about your sad words on life! How I would like to bring it some consolation! Can you give me the friendship of your beautiful spirit?' Like a love-struck teenager, she continued: 'do you remember the day you took my finger and placed it on the deep scar of your wound. Dear General, how you have suffered in your noble life, and I worry so, and often, that I did not express all the sympathy that I felt and will always feel.' Henceforth, Harriet kept a portrait of her idol at her bedside: 'It is next to me and looks at me with great indulgence.'[13] Harriet was one of a number of women who formed obsessive attachments to Garibaldi during his visit. Her daughter-in-law Anne wrote to him amorously that 'I so wanted to kiss you when saying goodbye.'[14] Mary Seeley, who with her husband entertained Garibaldi on the Isle of Wight, treasured a lock of his hair and one of his old cigar ends, and sent him a lump of Stilton cheese after he left.

Victoria was not in the least amused by these antics. 'The folly about Garibaldi continues, & my good Dss of Sutherland & her daughters are behaving in a most foolish & undignified manner,' she wrote disapprovingly in her journal, adding in another entry that 'the people in England have gone really quite mad' about Garibaldi. The Reading firm Huntley and Palmer had even named a biscuit after him. Though she conceded that the general was 'Honest, disinterested & brave', he was in her final analysis 'a revolutionist leader!', a status which, she believed, could not be excused.[15]

With an optimism typical of her late politics, Harriet put the queen's dislike of Garibaldi down to misinformation. Instead of being concerned by the damage that her own Garibaldi-mania could cause to her friendship with Victoria, she was worried that the queen did not share her infatuation. In early June, she wrote to Gladstone with dismay about Victoria's attitude. 'I am distressed at hearing from Argyll that the Queen has the falsest ideas on the subject of Garibaldi,' she complained. It upset Harriet that Victoria thought the general was 'a man who shot deserters with his own hands', a 'poison' she thought had been spread by Victoria's uncle Leopold II as 'a way of accounting for the extraordinary love [Garibaldi] inspires'.[16] She even visited the queen with the purpose of changing her mind. On Sunday 10 July, the queen recorded a 'long visit from the good Dss of Sutherland who got quite excited & over-enthusiastic in speaking of Garibaldi, & of his divine Compassion, his head being so like Our Saviours . . . I am so sorry for her having such *exalté* & to me foolish views about him'.[17] Victoria later acknowledged that she found Garibaldi's visit 'humiliating', and it is testament to the depth and sincerity of her feelings for Harriet that the episode did not drive a permanent wedge between the friends.[18]

Perhaps Victoria, who was after all 13 years her friend's junior, put Harriet's behaviour in part down to the eccentricity of old age. Throughout the 1860s, Harriet's health had been going into steady decline. In July 1863, she had succumbed to a severe bout of flu, which never completely cleared up. From that point on, she was often wracked with 'intense pain' and weakness, which rendered her bedridden for weeks at a time. Harriet's physicians recommended opium, a frequently prescribed remedy in the period, to dull her body aches. In the 19th century, doctors thought of opium as one of the most effective medications. There were numerous opium-based preparations stocked by chemists' shops – pills, lozenges, opium powder, vinegar of opium, wine of opium, and the famous tincture of opium (essentially opium dissolved in alcohol) known as laudanum. There were even special opium-based preparations for children, including Godfrey's Cordial and Dalby's Carminative.[19] The drug enjoyed a startling popularity, achieving something of a cult 'cure-all' status. Gladstone was famous for taking laudanum in a cup of coffee to steady his nerves before his speeches in the Commons.[20] Her increasing dependence on the drug became a source of great frustration to the fiercely independent Harriet. 'I am distressed at not finding myself able to leave off opium which is a sort of slavery,' she wrote to Catherine Gladstone.[21]

At the start of December 1864, Lord Carlisle, Harriet's brother, died after a long illness. Harriet, now intensely aware of her own mortality, described his demise to Gladstone: 'It has been in many ways a sudden death with prolonged existence,' she wrote. 'We can now say that we could not wish for life with such conditions of existence – I had not known that such could be.'[22] It was a poignant moment for Harriet, who had lost not only a brother but also an ally in her political and philanthropic causes. Like his sister, Carlisle had been a committed supporter of abolition. 'He, at least, was never scared by the possible greatness of America, when purged of her great crime,' Harriet's son Ronald wrote of his uncle. 'He, at least, was incapable of swerving from that hostility to African slavery which he had professed from his youth up.'[23]

At the end of July, accompanied by Ronald, Harriet travelled to Vichy in France to take the waters. They stayed in an elegantly appointed, spacious chalet on the banks of the river, spending their days walking in Vichy's 'pretty park' beneath the chestnut trees. However, the trip was cut short when Harriet's maid, Mrs Penson, who had served her for over 40 years, was taken ill and died shortly after. 'We have lost the truest, kindest, and best of friends, good and faithful Penson,' Harriet sadly announced to her family. She returned to England and buried her loyal friend and servant near Trentham.[24]

Throughout all of this, Harriet's own health continued to blight her daily life. 'I cannot get rid of pain, of exhaustion, of a constant anxiety,' she lamented to Gladstone.[25] Only in the grounds of Cliveden was she momentarily able to forget her woes. 'Life is still accompanied with pain & weakness,' she philosophised, 'but when it is life in the Country in a place one loves – after worse pain & at home one must not complain & I do not.'[26]

Chapter 13

THE PUSHING STICK

I n May 1866, Windsor was bustling with 'the noise and turmoil of Ascot' and Victoria needed a 'change of air'.[1] In the two years since the Garibaldi episode, relations between Harriet and Victoria had thawed sufficiently for the queen to ask Harriet a favour. Accompanied by an entourage of 90, including four of her nine children, two governesses, eight policemen, two doctors and five footmen, the queen made the short journey to Cliveden. She would stay there for ten days from 26 May. 'Her Majesty will occupy the central portion of the mansion, the drawing room, library, dining-room, and boudoir, which are on a level with the south terrace,' reported the *Western Daily Press*. 'The east and west wings will be placed at the disposal of the Royal Household and domestics.'[2] Victoria spent her time at Cliveden enjoying long walks by the Thames and sitting on the terrace, reading or sketching. She breakfasted at half past nine in the morning, had lunch at two o'clock, enjoyed tea in the garden beneath the trees at five and dinner at eight. Victoria slept in Harriet's bedroom, keeping a photograph of Albert at the head of her bed. It was a perfect respite. On her departure, the queen wrote that 'we passed a nice peaceful time'.[3]

While Victoria reposed at Cliveden, Harriet remained in London solicitously following the progress of the reform bill. In April 1866, Gladstone, as Leader of the House, had introduced a new bill to the Commons on behalf of the Liberal Party. It was a cautious piece of legislation, which would have enfranchised a proportion of working-class men (those who earned an income of more than 26 shillings a week), eliminated most of the remaining very small boroughs, and increased the number of country and large borough seats. When it came to the vote, however, the bill was defeated by a coalition of Tories, led by Benjamin Disraeli, and reactionary 'Addullamites', who did not identify with the new Liberal Party to which many of their old colleagues had defected. The Liberal government crumbled.

On 26 June 1866, a new minority Tory administration, with Lord Derby as Prime Minister and Victoria's favourite, Disraeli, as Chancellor of the Exchequer, was formed. Derby could not ignore the popular protests sweeping the country, and was forced to introduce a reform bill of his own. The Liberal Party was still divided over the question of franchise reform and the Derby/Disraeli Bill was partly intended to split the party and undermine Gladstone's leadership. In this it nearly succeeded, for Gladstone failed to carry significant amendments against the bill and as a result once again considered resignation. Thankfully, he kept his position: the new franchise brought about by the 1867 Representation of the People Act, or the Second Reform Act, would play a large part in his future electoral success, and he went on to become prime minister four times, finally resigning in 1894 at the age of 84.

Harriet's health had gone into further decline and, confined to her bed, she relied on members of her family for updates on the latest debates in the Commons. 'Between 4 & 5 a heavy step made gentle came into my room, & told me of the little member & the finest speech Stafford thought you had ever made,' she wrote to Gladstone, 'how much these words fill my heart, & I found there was a very unconscious tear when he left me which I did not feel weak tho others followed.'[4] As a young woman, Harriet had been present during the passage of the First Reform Act, yet had lacked the confidence and interest to act as an advocate for the bill. Now, in her sixties, she was desperate to play a part, but was thwarted by her frail body. 'How I would like to be a clever clerk and work,' she wrote wistfully, 'and to listen to every word you say.'[5] But in the final decade of her life, Harriet was forced finally to acknowledge the limitations imposed on her by her gender as well as by her failing health.

Nevertheless, Harriet was far from isolated and retained her love of good company. From August to the end of November 1867, she received a small selection of guests at Cliveden, including the queen. 'Drove off directly after luncheon with Lenchen [Victoria's daughter Helena] to Cliveden, where I had the pleasure of seeing my dear friend the Dss of Sutherland,' Victoria recorded in her journal. 'Found her really wonderfully well, though she has again been very suffering. She was so kind & affectionate & was in very good spirits.'[6] The queen visited Harriet on two further occasions that year. Though frustrated by her ailing body, Harriet was determined to continue the tradition of walking the grounds at Cliveden with Victoria. A device known as 'the pushing stick' was therefore designed to help the duchess climb uphill from the river. The wooden stick, which is on display in the west wing of the house today, had a curved section at one end for support: it was held by a servant who walked behind Harriet as she painstakingly put one foot in front of the other. Once the two women had arrived on the banks of the Thames, they would often spend the rest of the afternoon bathing at Devey's Spring Cottage. As sun set, they would make their way back, the house appearing in Harriet's fading vision as a glorious blur of colours.

When Harriet became too weak to walk, she was pushed around the gardens in a chair. In her fragile condition, horticulture had become increasingly soothing for her. 'I cannot say what the flowers & the verdure are to me,' she wrote to Gladstone.[7] The recent work of Harriet's gardener John Fleming had become famous, and the Cliveden gardens were much admired and copied throughout the country. Fleming had described his planting schemes in the *Journal of Horticulture*, and they were published in book form in 1864 as *Spring and Winter Flower Gardening Containing the System of Floral Decoration as Practised at Cliveden*. He dedicated it to Harriet, describing her as a 'great patron' and 'noble employer'.

In 1868, Fleming designed a bed of brightly coloured plants laid out in the shape of Harriet's initials, 'HS'. Each bed measured over 240 feet in length and was filled with more than 2,000 plants, including between 600 and 800 tulips. At the centre of each bed was a vibrant explosion of rhododendrons and azaleas. Connecting the two enormous beds was 'an immense circle with a grassy centre' encompassed with yet more flowers in blue, red, white and yellow hues. Fleming also set to work planting spring flowers in the surrounding woods of Cliveden and bluebells on the banks of the river. Maintenance of the 250 acres required a workforce of 21 men, whose responsibilities included mowing 16 acres of grass.[8] Fleming's ambitious, geometric scheme not only sparked an international gardening trend in the 1890s, but also stood the test of time: the parterre design he laid out for Harriet was preserved by the Astor family and remains intact today. Ronald Gower recalled his 'childish grief' at the 'great waste of lawn' being changed 'from a huge field of grass and wild flowers' into its current state.[9]

By October 1868, Harriet's health had reached crisis point. She was transported in an 'invalid chair' to Stafford House in London for urgent medical attention and her family was summoned to her bedside. Every day she lost more strength and suffered increasing pain, inching closer and closer to death. On 27 October, the *Morning Post* reported that 'the Duchess Dowager of Sutherland is so seriously ill that no hopes are entertained of her recovery'. Her son Ronald stayed by her side, cradling his mother's head in his hands. In their last conversation, Harriet asked for her 'maids and nurses to be remembered'. Her final words to her family show that she was resigned to death: 'I think I shall sleep now; I am so tired.'[10]

Just after one o'clock that day, Harriet's pain was, at last, over. She was 62.

'The loss is that of a very kind, devoted friend, whom I loved dearly, as she did me,' Victoria recorded in her journal. Showing emotion previously reserved for her beloved Prince Albert, she described Harriet as 'such a true friend', a woman 'adored by her whole family & a large circle of friends'. She was, the queen wrote, 'so loveable, so noble, in body & mind, so handsome & so full of zest in everything in life'. Victoria also recorded her personal debt to the duchess: 'for 31 years she had been my friend . . . She was with me from my accession in all the eventful moments of my life!'[11]

Gladstone opened the 'black bordered letter' that announced Harriet's death with equal heartache. 'I have lost in her from view the warmest and dearest friend, surely, that ever man had,' he lamented. 'Why this noble and tender spirit should have had such bounty for me, and should have so freshened my advancing years, my absorbed and clouded mind, I cannot tell.' His grief, he wrote, had reduced him to a childlike state: 'I feel, strange as it might sound, ten years old for her death.' He concluded that 'none will fill her place for me'.[12]

Harriet was buried on Tuesday 3 November 1868 in the family vault at Trentham, in Staffordshire. Her coffin was covered by a rich black velvet pall edged with white satin. As it was lowered into the ground, Victoria's eldest son, Bertie, the Prince of Wales and future King Edward VII, placed a wreath of camellias and lilies upon it. Gladstone was one of six pall-bearers. 'Peace and light be hers ever more and more,' he wrote in his journal, 'until the end cometh, and God is all in all.'[13]

Shortly after Harriet's death, her sons sold Cliveden to Hugh Lupus Grosvenor, Earl Grosvenor, later Duke of Westminster. With the sale, the house did not entirely lose its connection to Harriet: Grosvenor had married the Sutherlands' fifth daughter Constance in 1852, and the couple had spent their honeymoon at the estate. Queen Victoria was pleased that 'dear Constance' had succeeded her mother as the new chatelaine of Cliveden, and she continued to visit the house, even taking her customary strolls around the grounds, although these must have been lonely occasions without the company of her beloved friend.

Grosvenor was a philanthropist and a keen horseman. In the course of his charitable work he chaired a July 1894 meeting at which a draft constitution for the 'National Trust for places of historic interest and natural beauty' was approved. In 1942 Cliveden would be donated to the National Trust, as the organisation became known. The earl was also a political ally of Gladstone, sitting as a Liberal in the House of Commons and later in the House of Lords. On 17 February 1874, at the end of his first term as prime minister, Gladstone wrote to Grosvenor informing his friend that he had 'received authority from the Queen to place a Dukedom at your disposal'.[14] Cliveden once again became home to a duke and duchess. Like her mother, Constance was a skilled hostess. Invitations to her annual parties for Royal Ascot each June were highly sought after among the social elite. Constance was also a doting mother, who gave birth to eleven children, eight of whom survived infancy. During her time at Cliveden, the house remained a family home as much as a social and political hub. Constance was also keen to preserve the essence of Harriet's house and made very few changes to its structure and interiors. Her only major addition was the construction of a stable block to accommodate the duke's many racehorses. For this, she turned, as her mother had done, to the architect Henry Clutton.

However, at the end of 1879 domestic harmony was shattered when Constance was diagnosed with Bright's disease, a fatal condition. Just nine months later she died from kidney failure, aged only 45. Two years after her death, the duke married his second wife, Katherine Cavendish. Thirty-two years his junior, Katherine was younger than some of the duke's children with Constance, but somehow she won over the entire family. The duke and his children enjoyed playing games in the woods and riding ponies on the estate. Among the guests who spent a summer at Cliveden were the teenage Winston Churchill and his brother Jack, who went rowing on the Thames; in the evening the precocious brothers took the Cliveden boatman to Maidenhead and bought him dinner and a cigar. By 1893, the burden of supporting 15 children, in addition to honouring a vast array of charitable commitments, was putting increasing strain on the duke's finances. Consequently, he made the difficult decision to sell Cliveden.

On 15 August 1893, the house passed, for the first time in its 300-year history, not only from British to American hands, but also from aristocratic to plutocratic ownership. The buyer, William Waldorf Astor, was the great-grandson of John Jacob Astor I, an illiterate German immigrant who had made his fortune in the New York fur trade and had gone on to become

America's first millionaire. 'It is grievous to think of it falling into these hands!' Queen Victoria thundered. But she was out of touch with the new contours of wealth and influence that had emerged by the end of the 19th century: in the following decades many further aristocratic residences would 'fall' into wealthy American hands.

PART V

NANCY

1879—1964

Chapter 1

THE CHRONICLES OF CLIVEDEN

Beneath the starched cotton sheets of the newly installed hospital beds at Cliveden lay soldiers from the battlefields of Mons and Ypres. Some had mutilated limbs, others were paralysed from shrapnel wounds, and many had been blinded by poison gas. They were the first of 24,000 wounded to arrive at the house straight from the muddy killing fields of Europe.[1]

By 1915 Cliveden had been transformed by war. The manicured gardens where Harriet and Victoria had passed many tranquil afternoons and 'Rule Britannia!' had been performed were stripped of their foliage, ploughed and sown. Uniformed aides and nurses scurried around the grounds unloading men and medical supplies from convoys of thundering trucks. The glamour of the house was, for now, overlaid by the grit of modern war, the ornamental replaced by the functional.

Cliveden had been a gift from William Astor to his son, Waldorf, and the Virginian divorcee Nancy Langhorne, on the occasion of their marriage. When war broke out, Waldorf Astor volunteered for the army, but was rejected on medical grounds. Four days after the fighting started, he offered

Cliveden for use as a hospital. Refused by the British War Office, Waldorf turned to the Canadians, and upon inspection, the chief commissioner of the Canadian Red Cross accepted. Although the main house was deemed unsuitable for conversion to a hospital, facilities could be built about a mile away on the covered tennis court and bowling alley. Construction began in September 1914, funded by the Astors themselves.[2]

The first casualties arrived at Taplow station in April.[3] They had endured a bleak journey from the trenches. When there was no space on the ambulance trains, any available transport – coaches, vans, trucks – was used. Where possible, railway carriages were cleaned and disinfected, but the volume of maimed men was so overwhelming that many arrived from the front in dirty freight trains, with only a covering of straw on the floor.[4] Compared with the transport, the new Duchess of Connaught's Canadian Red Cross Hospital was state-of-the-art. It was 'thoroughly up to date, complete and convenient', equipped with X-ray apparatus, 'a laboratory for pathological investigation, a dispensary', 'a Thresh Steam Disinfector', 'a perfect system of electric light' and operating theatres.[5] The architect, Charles Skipper, had designed wards with tall south-facing windows so that they received as much sunlight as possible. Prevailing medical wisdom dictated that wards be kept cold and well-aired. In his First Eastern Military Hospital at Cambridge, Skipper had designed wards that were entirely open to the south, but the canvas sun-blinds rattled noisily and let in rain, so at Cliveden, he reverted to a more conventional design by stretching gauze across the window frames.[6] The wounded were also well nourished: 'great sides of the best

English beef' and 'rows of plump chickens' hung in the hospital's larder, along with dozens of eggs, home-made jams and Canadian biscuits.[7] Parts of the main house were used as a convalescent wing. 'I warn you we shall be broke & may not be able to live here for some time,' Nancy Astor wrote to her sister of the cost. 'It will be so expensive, but who cares?'[8] The hospital could accommodate 110 patients; this would increase sixfold over the course of the war.[9]

The new chatelaine of Cliveden, a five-foot-two dynamo with a deceptively delicate frame, fine fair hair and piercing blue eyes, was in charge of running the hospital. It provided an ideal stage for her boundless energy as she bustled from one bed to the next, a frenetic Florence Nightingale, rallying the wounded, forbidding any self-pity, goading them to defy death. The characteristics that had made Nancy a celebrity in pre-war society – her comic timing, her disarming candour, her effervescence – were now deployed to lift the spirits of the stricken men and pull them back from oblivion. At times, she sat up all night with terminal patients, reading to them in their final hours. On other occasions, she resorted to plain insults to bring her men back to life. 'No wonder you don't want to live, if you come from Yorkshire!' she once berated a dying sailor, fixing him with a steely gaze. The patient raised himself on one elbow, and declared that Yorkshire 'was the finest place in the world'. He was, he vowed, going to defy death and return to Yorkshire.[10] Several months later, in no small part thanks to Nancy's harsh invective, he did. Bribery too was part of her arsenal. To a Canadian soldier, she bet her Cartier watch that he would be dead the following day, because he had 'no guts'.

The soldier rallied: he attributed his survival to Nancy's tough love and kept the watch for the rest of his life.[11]

When war was declared, Nancy was a 35-year-old mother of four. She had a son, Bobbie Shaw, from a disastrous first marriage, and three further children, William, David and Wissie, from her marriage to Waldorf Astor in 1906. Nancy was born in 1879 in Danville, Virginia. Her father, Chiswell Dabney Langhorne, or 'Chillie', as he was known, was a volatile, heavy-drinking bully, capable of intermittent flourishes of charm and charisma. Nancy's mother, Nanaire, was his saintly counterpart – softly spoken, genteel and altruistic. Chillie had suffered financial ruin in the American Civil War, after which the family had endured years of privation. When Nancy was eleven, Chillie won a big railroad contract and the family's fortunes soared. The Langhornes moved to Mirador, a picturesque Virginian country house framed by cedar trees. It was in this romantic setting that Nancy spent the rest of her childhood, although the memory of that poverty-stricken youth stayed with her throughout her life. She grew into a confident, self-possessed young woman, with a tomboyish beauty and contagious vitality. Like Harriet, Duchess of Sutherland, Nancy admired Joan of Arc and Mary Queen of Scots – though an equally important heroine was the American frontier markswoman Annie Oakley.[12] Forthright and fierce, with an acerbic wit, Nancy was to become one of the most powerful and compelling women of her era.

Religion was central to Nancy's life. Her greatest desire in childhood was to become a saint so that 'everyone can feel my influence when I walk into a room'. At the age of 14, Nancy formed a deep bond with her parish priest, the Oxford-educated Venerable Archdeacon Frederick Neve. She was inspired by his missionary work and his compassion for the old, sick and poor: in her early teens, she accompanied him on a mission through the poverty-stricken Blue Ridge mountains that overlooked Mirador. Neve imbued in Nancy the sense that she must guide others in the way of righteousness – an ethos she retained throughout her life. It was this strong sense of religious vocation that eventually led her away from the Protestantism of Neve and towards the new and controversial religion of Christian Science. Devised in the late 19th century by Mary Baker Eddy, 'CS' was a sect that held illness to be a trick of the mind, a mere illusion that could be overcome by prayer. 'I deny disease as a truth,' wrote Baker Eddy. 'But I admit it as a deception.'[13] Drugs and medicine, which conspired in the 'materialistic' illusion of illness, were strictly forbidden to practitioners of the faith. Even though Nancy's attempts to compel soldiers to survive by sheer force of will were in line with the self-healing doctrine of her adopted religion, the conventional medical treatments administered at her own hospital at Cliveden were affirmatively not.

Nancy was one of five sisters: Lizzie, the eldest, who was stern and matronly; Irene, renowned for her beauty and elegance; the soulful, empathetic Phyllis; and fun, frivolous and flighty Nora. It was her relationship with Phyllis, 18 months her junior, that dominated Nancy's life. Even as children, the two were deeply enmeshed. Although very different in temperament – Phyllis was more passive and contemplative than Nancy – they suffered similar difficulties as a result of catastrophic first marriages. Nancy loved Phyllis fiercely and unconditionally. 'She and I were always inseparable,' Nancy recalled in her autobiography. 'We were really devoted to one another.'[14] In the summer of 1914 Phyllis came to England, ostensibly to help Nancy with the arrangements for the hospital, but mainly because it was the only place where she could meet Henry Douglas Pennant, known to the sisters as 'the Captain'. Phyllis and the Captain had fallen in love in 1910, but were forced to keep their relationship secret because Phyllis was married, albeit unhappily, to Reggie Brooks. The Captain was a welcome relief from Phyllis's heavy-drinking, polo-playing dilettante husband: after leaving the army Pennant had taken up the dangerous and exciting pursuit of hunting game, collecting specimens for the Natural History Museum in South Kensington. During his absences, postcards arrived from remote and exotic locations, and on his return to England there were always stories of perilous treks and near-fatal encounters with wildlife. In the Rift Valley, he was mauled by a leopard, sustaining gaping wounds that exposed his vertebrae. Despite extreme pain, he managed to travel 130 miles on an improvised litter, swimming across flooded rivers, until he reached the nearest village. So extensive were his injuries that he spent a month in a Nairobi hospital; his wounds took a year to heal.[15]

The Captain was determined to marry Phyllis and begged her to obtain a divorce. Nancy, who was wildly possessive of her sister, resented the hold this charismatic adventurer exerted over Phyllis. She described him as a 'half-wit' and snobbishly wrote to Phyllis: 'My goodness, don't you want a superior? . . .

No Phyl that aff. will never have my blessings I warn you so don't expect it.'[16] Nancy and the Captain fell out decisively in October 1914, when they were seeing Phyllis onto the boat-train to America. As the train pulled away from the platform, the Captain jumped aboard; this grand romantic gesture enraged Nancy and she began shouting at him, running alongside the train and waving her arms frantically.[17] Later, angered not only by the train incident but also by the fact that Phyllis had sent a goodbye telegram to him but not her, Nancy demanded a meeting. He refused. She sent various letters to Phyllis criticising him; he wrote to Phyllis that her sister was 'veritably crazy'.[18]

In mid-November 1914, the Captain joined the war. Before sailing for France, he left a strikingly insightful letter for Nancy. 'I am off today,' he wrote. 'I should not like to go away without making one or two things plain. Heaven forbid that you should think I dislike you . . . I know you are at times very jealous of my having intervened between yr affections and Phyllis. But its no use being like that, you will only lose over it and give Phyllis no happiness. Whether you like it or not she will love me alive or dead better than anything else, it is natural for woman to love man more intensely than for woman to love woman. Not even you can prevent that.'[19] Nancy forwarded the letter to Phyllis in astonishment, writing: 'You see he really thinks that I am personally jealous of him and thinks I am so small as to stand . . . in the way of your happiness.'[20] Her reply to the Captain reassured him that she was not in fact 'so small', and that it was merely his 'lack of understanding' that made him so certain of Phyllis's happiness. At the end of February, the Captain warned Phyllis that he was being moved to a more dangerous part of the line, but in March, reprieve came in the form of an offer of a senior staff job in the Welsh Guards, a new regiment. This would allow the Captain to leave the trenches immediately, but meant he would have to continue his military career for at least ten years. Instead of expressing relief that her love had been spared the perils of trench warfare, Phyllis was disapproving: 'I must confess I never dreamt that this, for years to come would be soldiering!'[21] She later tempered her initial reaction to the prospect of the Captain's future in the Welsh Guards, writing in a further letter: 'Don't think me a timid, weak-kneed sort of person when I write you that I wd like to see you safely back with the W. Gds. I shd. of course like it but not if it meant you came because you thought it safe. Thank heavens you are not built that way. It is one of the many things I like about you my old darling.'[22]

Tragically, due to postal delays, the Captain only received her first, disapproving message. On 10 March, in what was to be his final letter, he apologised with heart-rending earnestness for having suggested a career in soldiering, realising that such a future was 'distasteful' to Phyllis. After reading her letter, he had immediately cabled the general to decline the job. 'I know you well enough . . . that you do not like my soldiering project. So the show is off. It was not quite fair of me to give you such a fright and I'm sorry my darling I did so! . . . So you can look at life under a pleasanter aspect than as a Major's wife.'[23] The Captain was killed on the morning of 11 March. His death came three weeks before the first wounded soldiers arrived at Cliveden. Distraught and guilt-ridden, Phyllis attempted to assuage her grief by helping the wounded. For the first time, she was able to witness the horror of the Captain's existence at the front and grasp the devastating effect of war.

Once the hospital was fully operational, Nancy swung into action. With electrifying pace and efficiency, she set about organising weekly events and activities for the patients. In May 1915, Winston Churchill, then First Lord of the Admiralty, visited the hospital, and a few months later the prime minister of Canada arrived, followed by George V and his wife Mary. At Christmas there was a fancy-dress ball; one boy in a wheel-chair was dressed as a baby and given a bottle, and, according to Nancy, 'he was delighted with himself, and kept bawling in a most realistic manner at intervals.'[24] Soldiers were able to borrow books from the Astor library: Corporal Bell wrote to Nancy from his bed in the Queen Alexandra Ward of the hos-pital to thank her for the loan of *The Influence of Sea Power Upon History* and *Animal Heroes*.[25] The patients even formed their own magazine, *Chronicles of Cliveden*, to create 'a perma-nent record of our life at Cliveden'. It contained poetry, short stories, and a column called 'Ward Notes', which recorded hospital news and gossip. Amusing anecdotes included tales of one patient who could 'eat nine porridges in any morning', and another who 'took a fancy to Sister Miller's soap one bright morning, and incidentally took possession of it at the same time?'[26]

Although Nancy tried to maintain a semblance of normal-ity at Cliveden in the summer of 1914, the outbreak of war had an immediate impact on the running of the house. One of the servants, a part-time special constable, took on the role of recruiting men from the estate, and by the middle of August 1914, Nancy reported to Phyllis that 'Every one of our men from here have gone & all of the footmen, odd men, school room Samuel & the lot all but Edward who is here & George but they may go this week, I am really v proud of them.'[27] As the men of Cliveden went off to fight, female members of staff were expected to take over their duties. Housekeepers set about planting potatoes and cabbages, which had replaced the flowers in the gardens, while maids tended to the sheep and poultry now on the lawns, assisted by members of the Women's Land Army.[28]

Nancy wrote regularly to friends and members of the Cliveden staff who had joined up. The postal system that distributed letters to the front was known as the 'Field Service', and letters reached the trenches from Cliveden within two or three days. Nancy often sent out copies of Mary Baker Eddy's work to accompany her letters, which were received variably: Julian Grenfell, the son of Nancy's neighbour Lady Desborough, resisted Nancy's efforts to discuss 'the soul'.[29] Viscount Cranborne began reading Eddy, and was 'really much more impressed than I expected', but wished that she had 'a superior education in the English language'. For a 'prophetess', he thought, 'her style is deplorable'.[30] He soon gave up and 'relapsed into the trashiest novels'.[31] Waldorf's pheasants, dispatched to the front weekly from Cliveden, were altogether better appreciated.

Nancy's youngest sister Nora was also at Cliveden during the war. Like Phyllis, she was unhappily married, though to an Englishman, the architect Paul Phipps. The pair had been living in Canada with their two children. In August 1914, Nora left Phipps for the famous American football player, 'Lefty' Flynn, with whom she set out across the States, performing in music halls to earn money. She was quickly sought out by her father and sisters and ordered back to England. Phipps, who had returned to England after Nora's desertion, met her off the boat and immediately forgave her. His indifference to the affair enraged Nora. At Cliveden, Nancy put her sister to work at the hospital. Phipps had been declared unfit for military duty and took a part-time job at the Admiralty in London. Nora took advantage of her husband's absence, spending time with the Guards officers who came and went from Cliveden. 'Nora went through the Guards like a knife through butter,' her niece Nancy Lancaster recalled. Nancy, characteristically, took a harsher line. 'She is too free and easy with everyone and I've warned her,' she noted. 'I shall try to send her away for a week or so. I believe it would do great good but she really has v few friends. She has let people down so dreadfully . . . I'm trying to hold the right thought. It is the only thing that can help.'[32]

Nancy's work in the hospital, her access to the Astor fortune and her avowals of 'ardent feminism' inevitably attracted the attention of the suffragette movement.[33] 'Everyone knows that you are in a position to do extremely valuable war work and are doing it splendidly,' Emmeline Pankhurst wrote to Nancy in July 1915.[34] Pankhurst sent Nancy editions of the revived *Suffragette* magazine, wrote to her with news about meetings with Lloyd George, and expressed surprise to her at the *Observer*'s lack of coverage of the need for women's work.[35] The Astors owned the *Observer* and the *Pall Mall Gazette*, so Pankhurst undoubtedly brought up this omission in the hope that Nancy would intercede. Despite her interest in Pankhurst's cause, Nancy disapproved of the violent tactics – arson and looting – employed by the more extreme suffragettes. Nancy's religious dogma and sexual prudishness also left her with limited sympathy for the plight of unmarried mothers, another subject on which she and Pankhurst disagreed. In May 1915, Pankhurst wrote of the bad conditions in which illegitimate children were often raised, and although Nancy's response does not survive, it must have been negative: in her follow-up letter Pankhurst protested that 'you . . . seem to misunderstand what I am trying to do. You say if I saw the things you have seen! I have been seeing them and sorrowing over them for 30 years and because I have seen them I seldom blame either young men or young women for being what bad education and false ideas of the relationship of the sexes have made them. It is because I realise that to alter these bad conditions you must begin at the beginning that I want to do something for illegitimate children.'[36] In spite of their different perspectives, Nancy admired Pankhurst on a personal and ideological level. As well as attending a march during the First World War to agitate in favour of women working in munitions factories, Nancy invited Pankhurst to Cliveden, and encouraged Waldorf to donate money to cover hiring halls for suffragette meetings.[37]

In January 1916, Waldorf was informed that the title Baron Astor of Hever had been conferred on his father William (in 1917, it was upgraded to Viscount). It was an honour William Astor had been pursuing for years: during the Boer War he had funded an artillery regiment, and in the following decade he had donated vast sums to the Conservative Party and then the Conservative–Unionist government. His contributions to the war effort – including $125,000 to the Prince of Wales's war fund and $200,000 to the Red Cross – amounted to around £10 million in today's money.[38] Like many wealthy Americans of the late 19th century, William saw in the British aristocracy an opportunity to varnish his wealth with the patina of age and respectability. He had previously attempted the same thing genealogically, commissioning a family tree that traced his blood line back to the crusader Count Pedro D'Astorga of Castille, who was killed in AD 1000 by the Saracen King of Morocco.[39]

Unfortunately for William Astor, his son and daughter-in-law were not so prone to lavish historical fantasies. While Harriet and George Sutherland had been elated by the family's ennoblement, Nancy and Waldorf were crestfallen. A barony, Waldorf feared, would sound the death knell for his political career. On his father's demise, he would automatically inherit the title, and consequently be forced to relinquish his seat as Member of Parliament for Plymouth. Peers were ineligible for election to the Commons and were, by law, unable to disclaim their title. Not only was Waldorf averse to leaving the Commons, he resented the idea of joining the Lords: the Parliament Act of 1911 had emasculated the upper house by effectively abolishing its right to reject legislation. If William Astor viewed the aristocracy in the nostalgic glow of a bygone age, his son saw it in the harsh light of the age to come: he could tell that the old landed constitution was disintegrating, and that power was shifting from the Lords to the Commons. William could not understand his son's objections, and retaliated by changing his will: much of the Astor wealth would now skip a generation and go directly to his grandsons. The ensuing enmity between father and son lasted a lifetime. Nancy expressed equal distaste at the elevation, although as fate would conspire, Waldorf's enforced resignation as MP would later present her with the greatest opportunity of her life.

Despite his disappointment about his father's elevation to the peerage, Waldorf continued to pursue a political career. In December 1916 the first wartime governing coalition collapsed; Asquith resigned as prime minister and Lloyd George took his place. Waldorf, a long-time supporter of the new premier, was appointed Lloyd George's private secretary. His post necessitated spending more time in Westminster, leaving Nancy to represent him at meetings in his Plymouth constituency. In May 1917, the new president of the Board of Education, H. A. L. Fisher, came on an official visit to Plymouth. Nancy was tasked with introducing him to an audience. Standing on the podium she declared, 'I am very keen about education because I suffer from a lack of it, and if you want an ignorant woman to take the chair at an educational meeting, you could not have found a better if you had searched Europe.'[40] This talent for comic, candid and effective oratory would serve her well in her own political career over the following years.

On 11 November 1918, the epic and brutal conflict that was the First World War ended. Nancy insisted on creating a cemetery within the grounds for those servicemen who had died at the Cliveden hospital. She chose a peaceful spot in a sunken garden on the west side of the house; 42 inscribed stones marked the graves of her fallen soldiers. Presiding over the cemetery was a bronze statue of a woman, her arms outstretched, her face bearing more than a passing resemblance to Nancy's. In fact, Nancy had commissioned the Australian sculptor Bertram Mackennal to execute a symbolic figure representing Canada to stand in the cemetery. He had agreed, on the condition she sit for him as the head. As the finishing touches to the memorial were completed, the hospital at Cliveden was being demolished. Nancy wrote wistfully to a former patient, Jimmy Boyden: 'The hospital is being pulled down and it is exactly like seeing your home go.'[41]

Chapter 2

THE THRILL OF THE CHASE

N ancy had grown up in the shadow of her beautiful sister Irene, six years her senior, and known as 'Queen Bee' in the Langhorne household. Irene was an instant sensation when in 1890 she entered the southern 'marriage market'. She was invited as guest of honour to events across the country, from the cotillions and masked balls at White Sulphur Springs, the most fashionable spa resort in the south, to the Patriarchs' Ball in New York, which was hosted by Mrs Caroline Webster Schermerhorn Astor, the high-priestess of fashionable society. She is 'tall and fair', the *New York Times* wrote of Irene. 'Her carriage is queenly and her complexion perfect.'[1] A succession of suitors from the north made the pilgrimage to Mirador, hoping to ensnare Irene. Nancy, competitive by nature, kept tabs on all her sister's proposals. By 1894, when Irene met Charles Dana Gibson at a dinner in New York, the count had reached 62. Gibson was a talented graphic artist employed by *Life* magazine. He had made his name by sketching the Gibson Girl – a strong, sexy and athletic young woman who represented a new model of female beauty. *Life* rewarded Gibson by paying him $100,000 for

Portrait of Harriet Howard, Duchess of Sutherland, painted by Franz Xavier Winterhalter.

Harriet's husband, the cultured George Granville, 2nd Duke of Sutherland.

The Duchess of Sutherland's assembly at Stafford House, in honour of Garibaldi.
The exploits of the Italian nationalist General Guiseppe Garibaldi had a cult-like following in
1860s Britain. Excited about his visit to England in the spring of 1864, Harriet organised
a series of luncheons and dinners in his honour.

Harriet's close friend William Gladstone.

Nancy Astor painted by John Singer Sargent.

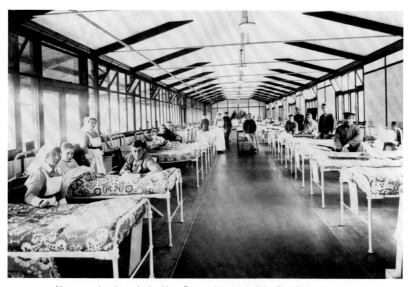

Nurses and patients in the New Brunswick ward of the Red Cross Hospital, which was built over the estate's tennis courts.

During WWI, hospital patients formed their own magazine, *Chronicles of Cliveden*, to create 'a permanent record of our life at Cliveden'. It contained poetry, short stories, and a column called 'Ward Notes', which recorded hospital news and gossip.

An example of the Astors' eclectic entertaining: Nancy with George Bernard Shaw (right), Amy Johnson (left) and Charlie Chaplin (second left). During their trip to Russia in 1931, Nancy was charged by Shaw's wife with keeping his beard in order.

Nancy on a motorbike in front of Cliveden. On more than one occasion she rode pillion to her friend T. E. Lawrence, who later died in a motorbike crash.

Lord William Waldorf Astor visiting with his wife, Lady Nancy Astor,
in her study at their Cliveden estate.

Cliveden from the parterre, courtesy of Cliveden House Hotel.

his invention – the highest annual contract on record. The day after their first encounter, Irene visited Charles at his studio. They fell in love and were married in Richmond the following November. Henceforth, Irene and the Gibson Girl became inextricably entwined in the public mind. Nancy, who was bridesmaid at the wedding, pretty in a French taffeta gown and long white gloves, was now the next Langhorne in line to be married.

The business of courtship was more of a chore than a pleasure for Irene's prudish younger sister. Uncomfortable with flirting, she tended to befriend or even compete with her beaux, rather than beguile them. Unlike Phyllis, who felt comfortable with the rituals of seduction, Nancy showed a profound disdain, bordering on physical revulsion, for gestures of romantic love. Letters or poems from admirers rendered her 'nauseous'.[2] Nancy's diffidence made her, in her mother's opinion, too unpredictable to take part in her debutante season. Instead, Nancy was dispatched to Miss Brown's Academy for Young Ladies, a finishing school in New York. It was an experience she despised, and when Nanaire and Chillie came to visit her, she pleaded to be released. They acquiesced and by the summer of 1895 Nancy was back at Mirador, running and riding, thrilled to have turned her back on 'that ghastly finishing school'.[3]

When she returned to New York the following spring to visit Irene and Dana, she came not as one of Miss Brown's young ladies, but as a self-styled Virginian, 'petite, freshly turned out, sparkling with life' – though to the newspapers she was still 'the Gibson Girls' younger sister'.[4] That summer,

Nancy was introduced to Robert Gould Shaw. The son of a distinguished Boston family, extremely rich, and a spectacular polo player, Shaw was a thrilling prospect. As soon as he saw her, he knew he would marry her. Nancy was 17, Robert in his mid-twenties. Although Nancy had not been officially launched onto the marriage market, rumours of an impending engagement began to swirl. Delighted to be the centre of attention, Nancy persuaded herself that she was in love with Bob. 'I suppose I was flattered and pleased to have made this spectacular conquest,' she later confessed. 'It was pleasant to be the centre of the picture all of a sudden. But in my heart I was never sure.'[5] At one point, she called off the engagement to the idle, indulged Shaw, but ultimately she yielded to enormous pressure from both families.

The wedding took place in October 1897, with a reception at Mirador that was memorable only for its 'gloom'. Nancy had spent the previous night lying awake 'praying the church would burn down'.[6] After the ceremony, the couple travelled to the Homestead Hotel, Hot Springs, in the Appalachian mountains. Although the details of their honeymoon remain opaque, Nancy, now aged 18, appears to have been deeply shocked by her first experience of physical intimacy. After three torturous nights, during which she resorted to sleeping on her stomach to avoid contact with her new husband, she begged to return to Mirador. Whether Nancy's distaste for sex was the result of an unpleasant initiation on her honeymoon, or something more deeply ingrained in her psyche, we will never know, but the nights at the Homestead Hotel must have played a role. Later, she would pronounce sex to be a base and shameful pursuit, and quip that her children were conceived 'without pleasure'.[7]

Chillie persuaded Nancy to go back to Boston, but it was clear that the marriage was doomed. Bob Shaw resumed an old affair and started drinking heavily again, a habit he had briefly curtailed in order to persuade Nancy to go through with the union. Nancy ran away from the Shaw home several times, yet surprisingly, three months after the marriage, she was pregnant. She later claimed that she had no recollection of the conception, besides waking up one night to find Bob in the bedroom clutching a chloroform-filled sponge. When she finally left Shaw, her rationale was that she simply could not 'risk having any more children by him'.[8] The baby, a son christened Bobbie, was born in 1898. Nancy refused the advice of her family and friends to get a divorce, and instead signed a deed of separation in 1901, which prevented her from marrying again. Aged 22, 'unwanted, unsought, and part widowed for life', she returned to Mirador with Bobbie.[9] Shaw, however, seemed to misunderstand the meaning of a separation, and married his mistress, Mary Converse, opening himself up to charges of bigamy, a crime punishable by imprisonment.[10] The Shaw family begged Nancy to agree to a divorce. After much bargaining, she consented on the grounds of adultery. The marriage was officially dissolved in a Charlottesville courtroom in 1903.

Nancy may have gained her freedom from marriage, but she felt trapped and listless at Mirador. The death of her beloved mother Nanaire in October 1903 plunged her into grief and depression. 'The light went out of my life,' she later recalled. 'I was ill for months, in a wretched, nameless fashion ... The anguish of it never seemed to grow any less.'[11] Despite her fiercely independent streak, it was a loss from which Nancy never truly recovered. Chillie was concerned about his daughter's emotional state and suggested a change of scene. He could see that it was unhealthy for someone so young to remain at home, absorbed in misery. Nancy's future, he insisted, was not hopeless. At the end of 1904, at her father's instigation, Nancy left for England, accompanied by Phyllis and their children.

'I had always loved England,' Nancy wrote. 'It always gave me a peculiar feeling of having come home, rather than visiting a strange land.'[12] Her feelings towards the old world had a touch of William Astor about them, but they also had a progenitor closer to home: Chillie's own research had speculatively traced the Langhorne line back to Wales and the West Country. Nancy and Phyllis rented a small house in Market Harborough, Leicestershire, with the intention of partaking in their first English hunting season. This was an audacious move for two American outsiders; fox hunting was a serious sport governed by a set of rigorous rules and conventions, which immediately separated the experienced riders from the amateurs. Although Phyllis was soon summoned home by her husband, Nancy was more than up for the challenge. In her autobiography, she recounted a number of tales from her hunting trip. 'I hired the biggest horse I had ever ridden. It must have been 16 hands,' she recalled. On her first day out, her horse stumbled on a branch, throwing Nancy into a ditch. A man came galloping up. 'Can you mount from the ground?' he asked. 'If not I will get down and help you.' Nancy looked up at him in bemusement and retorted, 'Do you think I would be such an ass as to come out hunting if I could not mount from the ground!' Another anecdote involves her interactions with English women, one of whom, Edith Cunard, wife of the industrialist Sir Gordon Cunard, asked whether she had come over to England to take her husband. 'If you knew the trouble I had in getting rid of mine,' Nancy told her, 'you would know I don't want yours.' Edith was suitably amused and the two became firm friends.[13]

The stratified world of fox hunting was intrigued by this straight-talking, teetotal, God-fearing Virginian divorcee. 'I often wonder now what they really thought of me in those days,' Nancy mused in her autobiography. 'I had a sharp tongue, and I was quick off the trigger. Things just popped out . . . ! Many people were afraid of me, but I don't think I made any enemies, except amongst those I could do very well without.'[14] Nancy's quick wit and crisp beauty made her a much sought-after guest at dinner parties and soon she was juggling a handful of suitors. In the late 17th century, a cold caught during a fox hunt had ended the life of Cliveden's creator, the Duke of Buckingham; over 200 years later, a reputation made while fox hunting would launch a new life for the house's last mistress.

It was during her heady first season in England that Nancy fell deeply in love. The object of her affection was John Baring, Lord Revelstoke, chairman of the merchant bank Baring Brothers and 16 years her senior. Since 1891, he had been having an on-off affair with Ettie Grenfell, later Lady Desborough, and Nancy's future neighbour at Cliveden. Nancy was drawn to Revelstoke, both physically and emotionally. Revelstoke, although attracted to Nancy, was in no rush to commit. Nancy had grown up in the quintessentially southern courting culture, which dictated that beaux should propose immediately, and thus interpreted Revelstoke's delay in suggesting marriage as a sign of reticence or, worse, rejection. Humiliated, she immediately went on the offensive and lost her temper, accusing him of snobbery, selfishness and coldness. The romance inevitably broke down. 'I have been & am still going through tortures – you can't realise it – I never did before – All is off between John & me,' she lamented to Phyllis. 'There are many reasons – which I can't write I can only explain – but I have decided its best never to see him again . . . I can't eat sleep or think & weep as I am spoken to! A nice state of affairs.'[15] Heartbroken, Nancy resolved to return to Virginia. As she was departing on a train to Liverpool, another suitor, Sidney Herbert, the 16th Baron Elphinstone, jumped aboard and asked her to marry him.

Nancy did not stay in Virginia for long, and when she returned to England in December 1905 with her father, Elphinstone assumed she would be his wife. He planned to meet her at the Liverpool dock, but he arrived to find that he had a rival: Nancy had met Waldorf Astor on the boat. Waldorf was modest, distinguished, faultlessly polite, quietly clever, and also, coincidentally, the same age to the day. He had heard all about the gregarious Langhorne girl, and arranged to travel on the same steamship so he could meet her. At first, Nancy, who was suffering from seasickness, declined Waldorf's invitation to dine with him. Unperturbed, he spent the subsequent days charming Chillie and making his intentions to marry his daughter abundantly clear.

Nancy now had two extremely viable marriage options and she agonised over her choice between Astor and Elphinstone. 'I sit and think here by the hour but I can't decide . . . one has one thing I like best & the other has another,' she wrote to Phyllis. 'As soon as I have selected the unfortunate young man I will wire you! . . . Waldorf sends flowers fruits vegetables potted food and everything imaginable and Ld E the same!'[16] A strong clue as to the 'thing' of Waldorf's that Nancy 'liked best' came later in the letter, when she informed Phyllis that her Astor admirer was in line to become the 'fourth richest man in the world'. She later wrote, 'The gig's up and I am engaged to Waldorf – & better still I am *v v* happy & I know you will love him.'[17] The marriage took place on 3 May 1906 at All Souls' Church, Langham Place, under a blanket of secrecy. They were both 27 years old. 'The Astor diamonds are wonderful,' Nancy wrote to her father. Unusually for Nancy, this was an understatement: the 55-carat, pear-shaped Sancy diamond given to her as her wedding present had previously belonged to James II and Louis XIV. Nancy and Waldorf spent their honeymoon in Cortina, in the Swiss Tyrol, then crossed the Atlantic to visit the Langhorne family, before starting their new life back in England.

Chapter 3

THERE'S NO PLACE
LIKE HOME

The historical obsessions of Waldorf's father had not stopped at fanciful genealogies and a veneration of the British aristocracy. Cliveden itself had become a canvas for his fantasies. A vast 16th-century fireplace from a French castle was the centrepiece of the grand reception hall, while wild tamarind wood panelling from South Africa had been installed in the library. Perhaps most impressive was the Louis Quinze rococo panelling from the Château d'Asnières, the hunting lodge near Paris once occupied by Madame de Pompadour, a mistress of Louis XV.[1] In a nod to Cliveden's past, William Astor and his Gothic Revival designer John Loughborough Pearson had built an imposing staircase featuring carved statues of some of the most important figures in the story of the house – Anna Maria, the Duke of Buckingham and Elizabeth Villiers. William had also sourced surviving 18th- and 19th-century architectural drawings, garden designs, engravings and manuscripts relating to Cliveden and bound them together in a large album for posterity.[2] For the garden, he had procured the balustrade of the Villa Borghese in Rome, along with an assortment of sarcophagi, which he had set within the yew hedges. A pagoda that had stood in the Paris Exhibition of 1867 had been reassembled in the grounds, and, as an additional flourish, a skating pond built around it. At the head of the driveway to the house was the 'Fountain of Love', a vast marble cockleshell surrounded by cavorting nymphs and cherubs, created by the Anglo-American sculptor Waldo Story.

In 1906, Nancy and Waldorf spent their first Christmas at Cliveden as a married couple, and began discussing alterations to the house. 'I was horrified at the size of it,' Nancy wrote. 'It is magnificent and beautiful but it did not look to me like a place anyone could turn into a home.'[3] A month later, 120 workmen began transforming Cliveden according to Nancy's instructions. In the space of two months, most of the appurtenances of William Waldorf's solitary and fantastical existence – the mosaics, the urns, the dark historic furnishings – were removed in favour of more modern decor. Lighter, brighter colours arrived in the form of chintz curtains, furniture throws and large bowls of mixed flowers, an import from Nancy's Virginian childhood. Nancy placed a voluptuous red sofa in the hall, to soften the impact of her father-in-law's austere 16th-century stone fireplace. In her autobiography, Nancy neatly explained the shift in style between William Waldorf's Cliveden and her own take on the house. 'I set about making a good many changes. The key-note of the place when I took over, was splendid gloom,' she wrote. 'Tapestries and ancient leather furniture filled most of the rooms. The place looked better when I had put in books and chintz curtains and covers, and flowers.'[4] Harriet Sutherland, whose wallpaper, throws and chintzes Queen

Victoria had praised for being 'so light and cheerful', would have undoubtedly approved of Nancy's taste in interior design. However, the Minton tiles laid by the duchess in tribute to her family's Staffordshire loyalties were unfairly grouped with the rest of William's gloomy styling, and torn up.

Nancy and Waldorf moved into the house before the works had been fully completed, sleeping on the third floor and eating either in the schoolroom or library. 'The Hall is much improved in fact the whole house is,' Nancy wrote to Phyllis in April 1907. 'I think it will be *so* lovely some day – my room is a dream *but* an unfinished one.'[5] Her bedroom, which she painted yellow, was the brightest room in the house and had a long balcony. Nancy did not erase every aspect of her father-in-law's house. She retained Waldo's bombastic 'Fountain of Love' and the balustrade – though whether because she liked them or simply because they were too enormous to move is unclear. The octagonal temple, which William had turned into a chapel, was remodelled for the same purpose, rather than being turned back to its previous use as a tea room. However, a large proportion of the other antiquities were dispensed with, the Roman relics removed from the grounds and William's skating pond redesigned as a modish oriental water garden. The Astors certainly changed enough that they were grateful for a May 1907 letter from William in which he expressed his desire 'not to see what you have done and to content myself with my modest and humble arrangements as I remember them'.[6] When William did eventually visit Cliveden from Hever Castle, in the grounds of which he had constructed an elaborate 'Tudor village', it caused Nancy such anxiety that she ran upstairs and took to her bed. Her panic proved unnecessary – whatever William really thought of the transformation, he had enough grace to compliment Nancy's taste, describing her bedroom as 'beautiful' and the hallway and drawing room as 'much more liveable'.[7]

Although she felt deep affection for Waldorf, Nancy still struggled with physical intimacy; she resented having to share a bed with her new husband and supposedly developed a habit of biting into an apple to distract her from the distasteful business of sex. She was also quick-tempered and prone to giving verbal lashings, a liability she readily acknowledged. 'My greatest battle is with my tongue,' she said. 'It's far too sharp and inaccurate.'[8] To make matters worse, she was constantly in poor health – typical diary entries in the first year of her marriage read 'bed all day', or 'dog tired' – and she was pining dreadfully for her 'soul companion' Phyllis.[9] 'Not another thing I have to say except my eternal longing for you . . . if you were here all would be well. I love you more every day,' she signed off one letter. In another intense declaration of love, she wrote: 'You stand alone in my affections. I can only say that I love you like mother, father, child, husband all in one and every night I thank God for giving me such a perfectly understanding sister.'[10] Nancy was unequivocal about the order in which her affections were ranked – it was Phyllis, her son Bobbie and then Waldorf. 'I think if anything happened to you, Bobbie or my family I should feel inclined to jump off the house top,'[11] she wrote, somewhat melodramatically. Her revulsion for sex notwithstanding, Nancy became pregnant in early 1907, and on 13 August she gave birth to the couple's first child, a son christened William Waldorf Jr. Yet Nancy was not filled with maternal love: when Bill was just five days old, she wrote to Phyllis comparing him unfavourably to nine-year-old Bobbie. 'He's not so nice as Bobbie was,' she said bluntly. It was a sentiment that she would retain throughout her life: 'We can never love any children like one's first borns, can we?'[12]

Nancy's love for Bobbie brought problems of its own. After leaving him at boarding school for the first time, she retreated to a hotel in St Leonard's-on-Sea and wrote a distraught letter to Phyllis. 'I have wept my eyes nearly out and must now pour out my sorrow to you . . . there were two other new boys and when I left the lone figure of my darling in the school room, you cant conceive of the over-whelming feeling of loneliness that came over me.'[13] For Bobbie himself, the difficulty of separation from his mother was compounded by having to leave Cliveden, and he struggled to stay afloat academically and socially in his first months at school.

Around the time of Bobbie's departure, Nancy was sitting for the painter John Singer Sargent. Sargent, who was a cousin of her first husband Robert Shaw, met Nancy in 1907 and was interested in her as a subject partly, he said, because of her resemblance to Ophelia, by which he presumably meant the art-historical Ophelia, the Ophelia of Millais, though Nancy took the comparison rather more straightforwardly: 'in other words, "bats"', she wrote.[14] Though he was an American, Sargent had become the most celebrated society portraitist in Edwardian England. Since the death of Queen Victoria, whose snobbery towards America was succinctly captured in her reaction to the Astor purchase of

Cliveden, British haughtiness towards Americans had relented slightly. Edward VII was far more comfortable in transatlantic company, and his court gave Americans opportunities for social and professional status that had hitherto been far harder to attain. In 1910, after being exhibited at the Royal Academy, Sargent's portrait of Nancy was hung in the hall at Cliveden, where it joined a selection of pictures – including some by Gainsborough and Reynolds – collected by Waldorf's father. The work remains a focal point of the hall today.

King Edward was sufficiently comfortable with the house's new owners that, in 1908, he asked to visit. The visit was brokered by Lady 'Ettie' Desborough, chatelaine of the neighbouring Taplow Court, which in the 18th century had been owned by the Orkneys. At Taplow Court, Desborough presided over an intellectual and literary clique known as 'the Souls'. Also among the Souls were Arthur Balfour and Lord Curzon – both of whom would later play significant roles in the social life of Cliveden. Though it would be a few years before Nancy began to host political soirées in a way that would set her up as a rival to Ettie, the pair had other reasons to be wary of each other. Nancy had recently learned not only that Lord Revelstoke was infatuated with Ettie, but also that his infatuation had overlapped with their own brief and unsuccessful courtship. The visit of Edward VII – with his mistress, Mrs Keppel, in tow – was one of the earliest occasions on which the Taplow Court group attended Cliveden en masse, and if Ettie did not make any mistakes it would be necessary to invent some. 'Lady Desborough telephoned Waldorf that the king wished to come over so he came followed by 16 courtiers for tea and stopped for two hours and went over the house and garden and seemed v pleased with it all,' Nancy wrote to Phyllis after the event. 'I don't think the Desboroughs enjoyed the visit but behaved "nicely" – though I think it slightly strong to bring 16 people. It made us 40 for tea.'[15] Forty guests was a negligible number compared to many of the parties hosted by the Astors around this time. Nancy thought nothing of throwing night balls of major proportions, sometimes for a thousand people, at 4 St James's Square, her London residence.

The most well-known and enduring social fixture inaugurated by Nancy around this time was the annual Ascot party hosted at Cliveden. Harriet, Duchess of Sutherland, had also made use of the house's proximity to Ascot by throwing grand parties in the early summer to coincide with the races. For the Astors the event had an even greater importance because of Waldorf's personal obsession with horses: in 1900 he bought his first thoroughbred mare, Conjure, for £100, and over the following decade invested more and more seriously in his stable, until 1911 when he spent 4,500 guineas on Maid of the Mist, a thousand of which he was able to recover immediately by selling on the horse's unborn foal.[16] His undergraduate hobby had become a serious business. Conjure, Maid of the Mist and Popinjay were the foundation of the Cliveden stud, whose successes would attain eminence for Waldorf in the racing world. In 1907, 26 people were invited to the first of Nancy's Cliveden Ascot parties. After this initial success, the number of guests increased dramatically, to the point where the parties received specific mention in the resignation letters of household staff who found themselves overworked.[17]

On her arrival at Cliveden, Nancy had been struck by the sheer number of household staff, and the diversity of their roles. 'At Market Harborough I had had one butler, single-handed – a dreadful cook and a faint-hearted housemaid. Here at Cliveden I found the household consisted of: 1 Butler, 1 Groom, 3 footmen, 1 Valet, 4 in the kitchen, including a Chef, 2 in the Stillroom, 1 Housekeeper, 5 Housemaids, 1 Odd-man, 1 House Carpenter, 1 Electrician,' she recorded in her memoir. 'It took me some time to grasp what the duties of all these people were. The odd-man especially was a new one on me. As far as I could make out, his main work was running round after the others and picking up what they had dropped.'[18] Nancy would soon find that this 20-plus army of staff was barely sufficient to keep the house running.

To some extent, Nancy and Waldorf's remodelling of the house had modernised its infrastructure – for instance by introducing telephone lines and electricity. But for the most part, the machinery of the house was no different in the 1910s from how it had been in Harriet's or even Anna Maria's time. There was no central heating, and the plumbing was so rudimentary that most guests chose to be doused by their valets in front of their bedroom fire, rather than queue in the corridor for the use of one of the bathrooms. In the absence of central heating, fires had to be made to keep the house habitable, and, in the absence of lifts, coals had to be carried upstairs in scuttles. All of the 100 tons of coal that were burnt each year had to be pushed to the house in carts along a light railway that ran from the coal store under the west wing to the main basement, and then lugged up to the rooms by hand. The coal store, railway and subterranean storage formed a 'working underground' that sat alongside the 'leisure underground' of Buckingham's sounding room.

The Cliveden payroll shows the Astors to have gone through several butlers in quick succession as they attempted to find someone personable who could cope with the demands of the role. First, there was T. Southwood, who was paid £120 per annum. He lasted from October 1906 to June 1907, when he was dismissed under the note 'Honest, but bad manager'. They had also been employing an 'H. Bartly' on £130 per annum, but dismissed him in March on the grounds that he was 'capable', but had 'too big an idea of his position' – perhaps it was the extra £10. The most persistent source of butler trouble, however, was also the most time-honoured. In January 1908 Arthur Webb was dismissed under the payroll note 'Drink', and on 21 June 1909 his replacement, a W. Dennison, was 'dismissed for drinking'. Dennison was succeeded by Mr William Parr, who had been kept on at Cliveden from William Waldorf's time. In Parr the Astors found – for the time being, at least – a less bibulous butler. He stayed in his position until the early 1920s.[19]

As his superiors fell prey to their vices, Mr Edwin Lee, the last of five children from a Shropshire farming family, rose through the ranks of what Nancy referred to as the 'sort of aristocracy among the servants'.[20] Lee's most important promotion would come in 1920, when the long-serving Mr Parr was sacked by Nancy. As well as succumbing to the drinks cabinet, Parr had become frustrated with the excessive demands of his role, and his rows with 'her ladyship' were constant. After dismissing Parr, Nancy 'didn't actually offer me [Lee] the job so much as tell me I was going to do it'.[21] Lee would go on to become one of the finest butlers in the world, later providing the model for Stevens, the repressed and precise Englishman who serves the wealthy American Mr Farraday in Kazuo Ishiguro's novel *The Remains of the Day*.

As if the management of domestic staff was not enough to occupy her time, Nancy's new house soon became a sort of HQ for controlling the movements, spending habits and romantic liaisons of her sisters, two of whom visited Cliveden in 1908. First came Nancy's eldest sister Lizzie, en route to Paris. Before the Langhorne fortunes were transformed by Chillie's railroad investments, Lizzie had made an impecunious marriage to the Virginian Moncure Perkins. She was the only one of the Langhorne daughters to remain in Virginia, and became resentful of her sisters' glittering lifestyles. By the time of Lizzie's visit to Cliveden, Moncure was drinking himself to death in Richmond. He had given her $300 dollars for the trip to Europe, to which Nancy added $200 as a birthday present. Soon the money had run out and Lizzie was forced to ask Nancy for more funds. By the end of her European folly, Lizzie had spent close to $45,000 on furs, jewellery and clothes, much to the annoyance of Nancy and her father.[22]

Attempts to prevent Nora from repeating Lizzie's marital errors would only lead to further discord within the Langhorne sorority. For two years now, Nancy had been trying to persuade Chillie that he should send Nora to England, where Nancy would find her an appropriate husband. Then, at the age of 19, Nora fell passionately in love with Baldwin Myers, a

Virginian with no breeding and no prospects. After all the trouble she had recently gone through with Lizzie, Nancy refused to sanction her younger sister marrying another Moncure Perkins in the making. In October 1908, she insisted that Nora come to England. Nora did, writing home to her father with a mixture of sadness, masochism, and apprehension about what life would be like at Cliveden under the iron rule of her elder sister. Whatever she anticipated, Nora was not prepared for the tirade of criticism and the controlling regime to which Nancy subjected her. She wrote home describing Cliveden as 'the lonesomest place in the world'.[23]

At Christmas Phyllis was back at Cliveden, with Reggie, to join Nancy in exhorting Nora to marry an Englishman. For a while the most eligible candidate appeared to be Lord Elphinstone, whom Nancy had rejected in favour of Astor, but Nora could not take him seriously, least of all when he proposed to her among the potted plants in the conservatory at Cliveden. In the spring of 1909, there emerged a new favourite. Paul Phipps, a charming architect whose reputation as a dancer (the best in London) far outstripped his reputation in his chosen profession, had been attending Cliveden weekends throughout the winter, watching the Elphinstone debacle from afar. Now that Elphinstone was no longer a contender, the Langhorne conclave, Nora included, swung behind Phipps. Somehow the sisters' letters and cables to their father failed to make the situation clear, and Chillie was furious when, in early March 1909, he discovered that he had given permission for his daughter to marry not a Scottish baron, but a dandyish professional who had a collection of bow ties and a slight rhotacism. In the end,

Nora and Paul had to travel to Virginia and win Chillie over in person. He allowed himself to be won, but vented his frustration by passing on to Nora all the letters Nancy had sent him in the course of the marriage negotiations, replete with lines like 'The tragedy is his!'[24]

By 1909, Nancy and Waldorf's parties had evolved into rather more serious and more political events than they had been two years previously. Nancy enjoyed her early experience of gilded London functions, and her 1907 letters to Phyllis have a sort of youthful gossipiness to them: at one 'very pretty and great fun' ball, she encountered the queen – who 'looked lovely'.[25] However, it wasn't long before Nancy wrote to her sister declaring that 'I am getting too old for balls' and announcing her preference for 'political parties'. Increasingly, Nancy's Cliveden weekends were noted for their conversation just as much as their glamour, although guests were waited on by liveried footmen, who still, on occasion, powdered their hair using flour and water. Nancy was fastidious about choosing the right guests. Many of the literary visitors came via William Waldorf's *Pall Mall Gazette* – H. G. Wells, J. M. Barrie, and Kipling were all frequent guests who had their careers launched by the paper. The French writer Hilaire Belloc was another regular visitor – at least until he and Nancy fell out and broke off all communication. It has been suggested that the root of their quarrel was Belloc's rabid anti-Semitism, though given Nancy's own hostility towards Jews, this sounds improbable: when the Zionist pioneer Chaim Weizmann was invited to an Astor dinner party, Nancy introduced him as 'the only decent Jew I have ever met'.[26]

Churchill came to Nancy's Cliveden, and Chaplin, the Asquiths and Arthur Balfour. The eclectic but increasingly political atmosphere of the 1909 weekends is conveyed in an account by the wealthy German heiress Daisy, Princess of Pless. 'The house is full of people, amongst these being Sophy Torby and the Grand Duke Michael, and Winston Churchill, who sat next to me at dinner,' she wrote on 24 July 1909. 'I am awfully sorry for him; he is like a racehorse wanting to start at once – even on the wrong race track; he has so much impetuousness that he cannot hold himself back, and he is too clever and has too much personal magnetism . . . He is not happy if he is not always before the public, and he may some day be Prime Minister – and why not, he has energy and brains.'[27] To the newspaper-reading public, the Princess of Pless was known for her pearl necklaces and family scandals, but over dinner at Cliveden, she, like everyone else, was talking politics.

The political drift of the Astor parties was no coincidence, for around this time Waldorf was embarking on a career in the Conservative Party. In January 1910 he stood for election as MP for Plymouth. He was defeated by his Liberal rival, but the campaign afforded Nancy her first taste of electioneering, and she found herself to be a natural. 'Addressed a collection of workmen,' she wrote in her diary. 'I am becoming a mob orator. A female Lloyd George – God forbid.'[28] Actually, the campaigning concerns of the Liberal chancellor – whose radical 'People's Budget' of 1909 proposed a brace of new taxes on the rich in order to fund social services, pensions, transport, agriculture, research and rearmament – were not too far off Waldorf's own priorities, though for her part, Nancy instinctively disliked the idea of an interventionist state, and preferred that wealthy and conscientious individuals should make their own choice to undertake good works. In this respect her politics were already to the right of her husband's, a gulf that would increase with time. Waldorf was inspired by the reforming politics of Lord Shaftesbury – who had penned Harriet's anti-slavery manifesto – and diverged from his Conservative Party colleagues in his support for the People's Budget. It was one of several points in which he would have been quite at home in the Liberal Party, and his decision to join the Conservatives may have been more to do with a sense of propriety than with a real ideological affinity: Lloyd George's party was seen by many in the upper classes as threatening and populist, and even if this view was not held by Waldorf, it was certainly held by his father, and by Nancy.

The January 1910 defeat wasn't enough to deter Waldorf and Nancy from poaching their seat. If the mood of the constituency was for the Liberals, they would work to find a new mood, rather than a new constituency. The feud between the Commons and the Lords over the attempt of the latter to block the passage of Lloyd George's budget meant that there was a second election in December of that year, and this one they intended to win. For Nancy, the Plymouth constituency had already taken on a sort of spiritual-historic significance. Not only had the Pilgrim Fathers set sail from there, but there were apparently more personal connections too. 'It was not like a new place to me. I felt that here was where I belonged. I remember sitting down and writing to father and telling him all this,' she reminisced. 'He wrote back saying there was nothing strange about it. One of the Langhornes was Member of Parliament in St Just – a Cornish town – in 1697.'[29]

Waldorf and Nancy bought a large town house at 3 Elliot Terrace on the Hoe, from where Francis Drake had set out to defeat the Spanish Armada, and began devising a campaign strategy. Unlike Waldorf, who was a stern but unassuming figure, Nancy commanded attention. Mastering her debilitating fear of cats – which, in the narrow, dilapidated streets and alleys of the poverty-stricken Barbican district, were numberless – she marched from tenement to tenement, dressed in her fur and jewels, knocking on every door, and delivering the same line: 'I am Mrs Astor. My husband is standing for Parliament. Will you vote for him?'[30] In December, thanks in part to Nancy's energy, Waldorf won the election.[31]

Chapter 4

LIFE AMONG THE RUINS

For all the growing serious-mindedness of Nancy's parties in her first decade at Cliveden, her guest lists would never calcify into a single clique along the lines of Lady Desborough's Souls at Taplow Court. The closest she came to presiding over such a group was not, as the popular press of the time presented it, in the thirties, when she was lampooned as the hostess to an influential pro-Nazi cabal – for this 'Cliveden Set', as it became known, was largely a work of fiction. Rather, it was in the 1910s, with a lesser-known group of very young and very bright diplomats known as the Round Table group.

The key members of the Round Table group had met working for the high commissioner for South Africa, Lord Milner. Between 1899 and 1902, the British Cape Colony fought a war with the two Boer Republics, the Transvaal and the Orange Free State. The latter years of the Boer War were a brutal guerrilla conflict in which the British adopted a scorched-earth policy, attempting to deprive the guerrillas of sustenance by burning houses, destroying crops, poisoning wells and interning the Boer population in 'concentration camps' – a term that came into general usage in this period. Even in 1900, before the tide of the war had turned in favour of the British, Lord Milner was devising plans for a future Union of South Africa in which the former Boer Republics would be given a degree of self-government within a context of overall British control. Before this ambitious plan for the colony could be realised, there was an enormous amount of more fundamental post-war reconstruction that had to take place. Anxious to avoid a conventional administrative system, Milner recruited in a personal and haphazard way, largely through an Oxford old-boys network that drew in recent graduates from Balliol, New College, and All Souls. The youth and inexperience of the recruits earned them the nickname 'Lord Milner's kindergarten'.[1] Two of the *kinder*, Bob Brand and Philip Kerr, would have a particularly profound impact on Nancy's life.

Brand was the seventh child of Viscount Hampden of Glynde, but had the air of a very middle-class intellectual, and Nancy was shocked when, years into their friendship, she discovered him to be 'an Honourable'. Philip Kerr came from a devoutly Catholic family and later succeeded his cousin as Marques of Lothian. He was serious and academic-minded like Brand, but far more impressionable. In South Africa, when they were not visiting mining camps, trekking across the Veld, or otherwise administering the vast and foreign territory into which they had been dropped, Brand, Kerr and Milner's other young men held 'bachelor parties' at their shared house and talked long into the night. On their return to England, many of the *kinder* were drawn into another Milner-inspired project, the Round Table group, which aimed to advance the project of a federal British empire, united in a central Imperial Parliament. But the precocity of the young men's political experience had come at a personal cost. Milner's protégés were highly neurotic young men – serious about ideas, but emotionally immature and overwrought about sex. In short, they were perfect playmates for Nancy.

Bob Brand first came to Cliveden in 1912, for a weekend with J. L. Garvin, the editor of the *Observer*. While Nancy's frankness and energy surprised and excited the young men, she also shared their seriousness about religion, and her prudishness outflanked even the most awkward of the *kinder*. One afternoon Bob and Nancy were sitting in the garden at Cliveden and saw two pigeons flying overhead. 'You know, Bob,' Nancy said to him, 'I can't even see two mating birds without wanting to separate them.'[2] Nancy first met Philip Kerr during a trip to Hatfield in 1910, and the following summer Kerr appeared in the Cliveden guest book for the first time. 'There was an affinity between Philip and my mother, love on his side, and something deeper than friendship and less passionate than love on hers,' Nancy's son Michael would later observe.[3] But it was their near simultaneous conversion to Christian Science that allowed their companionship to mature into the very affectionate, quasi-romantic bond that they shared for many years. He appeared in her letters to the others as a saint, priest and prophet and they shared a secret, exclusive language of election, as evident in a note written by Nancy in the flyleaf of a book she gave to Philip:

You and I have found the secret way
None shall hinder us not say us nay.
All the world may stare and never know
You and I are twined together so.[4]

At other times, it simply came down to deflecting physical desire with orisons. In a rare admission of having experienced any sexual feeling, Nancy would later inform her niece that on one occasion, when she and Philip found themselves overcome with desire for each other, they solved the problem by dropping to their knees in prayer. As one of her sons put it: 'There isn't any question that they were in love, and also that it was never consummated in any way.'[5] Waldorf appears to have been tolerant of the relationship, and responded to Philip with warmth: 'I must say Philip comes closer to making Waldorf talk than anyone I have known,' wrote Nancy to Phyllis. 'That is a Godsend.'[6] Waldorf knew that Nancy and Philip had a peculiar, ecstatic connection in which he couldn't share, even if he converted to the religion himself – this he would do, in his own more diffident way, in 1924. Though he sometimes 'found it a bore having Philip Kerr round the house the whole time', he approached the unusual friendship with tact, tolerance and a remarkable lack of jealousy.

In 1912 Nancy gave Bob Brand a letter of introduction to Phyllis. Phyllis was in New York seeing lawyers about her separation proceedings from Reggie, and the two first met at a dinner given by Irene at her house on East 73rd Street, a fashionable road of old carriage houses. Bob was 'knocked over' by Phyllis, and managed to wangle an invitation to the family home at Mirador. He travelled down from Washington, where he had been on business, wearing his 'Wall Street Suit'. The rest of his luggage was mistakenly shipped to Florida, and so the Wall Street Suit became his uniform for the trip. He ate dinner with Phyllis in his Wall Street Suit, went horse riding in his Wall Street Suit, fell from the horse in his Wall Street Suit, and bled from his nose all over his Wall Street Suit. The only time he wore anything else was in bed, when he wore Phyllis's pink silk nightgown.[7] By the time he left, he'd fallen in love. Barred by etiquette from attempting to start a correspondence, Bob bade his time. Eventually, Phyllis wrote. She was 'so glad that you did come to Mirador' and thought it was 'most awfully good of you to have taken so much trouble for those very few hours'.[8]

Much to Nancy's irritation, Bob did not displace the Captain in Phyllis's affections. Bob was, Phyllis wrote to Nancy, 'the most liveable sort of creature, like a cosy liveable room and as you say a clever being . . . but of course not so clever or farseeing as the C!!!'[9] Upon the Captain's death, Bob maintained a respectful distance before resuming correspondence. There followed two years of tumultuous friendship, in which proposals from Bob were followed by fraught silences from Phyllis and then attempts to resume their relationship on platonic terms. Eventually, in 1917, after much patience on Bob's part, Phyllis summoned him to her room at Cliveden, and announced that she would marry him if he still wanted. They were married in June 1917 at the Savoy Chapel, London. The Brands had intended to spend their honeymoon in America, but in April 1917 America had entered the war, and passenger ships departing from Liverpool were now used as vessels of combat, with a brief to shoot at German submarines. The few brave civilians who dared to embark on these treacherous voyages were issued with waterproof suits and helmets in case of attack. Phyllis and Bob delayed their crossing, spending their first week of marriage in the Adelphi Hotel in Liverpool, awaiting clearance. When they finally did board a ship, rough weather and fear of German submarines did not make for a romantic crossing.

When fighting finally ceased, both Bob Brand and Philip Kerr went on to play a central part in the negotiations to remake Europe. The Paris Peace Conference, which began on 18 January 1919, was a meeting of the victorious allied powers, called in order to agree the peace terms that would be imposed on Germany following the armistices of late 1918. Brand and Kerr were both members of the British delegation, Kerr as Lloyd George's private secretary, Brand on loan from his job at the bank Lazards to advise Lord Robert Cecil, a government minister and chairman of the Supreme Economic Council of the Allies. In Paris, the Round Table kinship between Bob and Philip would be forever fractured as the two became embroiled in the violent disagreements over the treatment of Germany. In the bitter aftermath of war, Europe's economy was falling apart – inflation was soaring, food was scarce, and an aggressive strain of nationalism was rearing its head. Both the trauma of the recent conflict and relief at it having ended were visible all over the city. While a few of the conference delegates found their way out to the Folies Bergère or to the city's nightclubs where couples danced foxtrots and tangos, many more saw the boarded-up windows and the crater in the middle of the Tuileries rose garden, and none could avoid the crowds of scarred and limbless soldiers who begged in the streets.

Paris was an emotive choice of location for the conference: of all the powers present, it was France who most wanted to make Germany pay for wreaking this global havoc. Kerr was broadly in favour of a treaty that imposed substantial reparation payments on Germany, but Brand advocated a more moderate line. The German economy, he argued, was just as shattered as her European counterparts and she simply could not afford to pay the 'wild figures' the Allies were demanding. Instead he supported a scheme of debt cancellation and much smaller reparations put forward by the economist John Maynard Keynes, head of the British Treasury delegation. Ultimately, however, it was the harsh line supported by Kerr that was adopted, a decision that would have catastrophic consequences for Europe and the rest of the world in the following two decades. Kerr was personally involved in the final peace terms, having drafted some of the most controversial passages, including the infamous 'war guilt clause', which forced Germany to admit full responsibility for the carnage of the conflict. On 4 May, when Keynes saw for the first time an outline of the proposed peace settlement, he reacted with horror. The reparations clauses were 'unworkable' and showed 'a high degree of unwisdom in almost every direction'. To a friend he wrote that 'the Peace is outrageous and unworkable and can bring nothing but misfortune . . . with such a Peace as the basis I see no hope anywhere.'[10]

Nancy arrived in Paris on 6 April 1919, excited to witness

this flurry of diplomatic activity. She asked Philip Kerr to secure accommodation and the services of a chauffeur, an unenviable task in a city heaving with delegates from across the world. Kerr, who was wretchedly overworked attending meetings from early morning until midnight, was concerned he would have little energy left for Nancy, but his letters immediately after her visit suggest that they did spend time together, often among the city's Christian Science community. The CS scene in Paris comprised 'all sorts of races, French, American, Canadian, British', who testified together at the Christian Science church and met at the CS Reading Rooms where Kerr often worked. On 23 April, Kerr wrote to Nancy: 'I was glad to hear that you had got back safely. But you never told me what you had seen. Did you get to Ypres and Passchendaele?' He concluded: 'I enjoyed your visit very much. In fact I don't think I ever had a better time in my life than that whole trip.'[11]

Later that year, a death in the Astor family would turn Nancy from a spectator of politics into an actor of seminal importance. Events unfolded at a precipitous pace. On the morning of 19 October 1919, Waldorf received a phone call informing him that his father William had died the previous night. Discreet to the last, William had eaten a dinner of mutton and macaroni, withdrawn to the toilet, and died there of a heart attack. Waldorf had little time to digest the news: he now became Viscount Astor and his political career in the House of Commons was over. A new member for his constituency, renamed the Sutton division of Plymouth following boundary changes that carved the city into three separate districts, would have to be found within a few weeks, and a by-election fought. On 23 October, Waldorf appealed to Lord Stamfordham, the king's private secretary, for permission to renounce his peerage. He reasoned that he could do more good in the Commons than in the Lords, and that natural aptitude, dedication and hard work were of far greater consequence to him than a meaningless title. But it was to no avail – Stamfordham rejected Waldorf's case. Given that the Astor name was well known within Plymouth, local party officials were keen to find a replacement from within the family. Their first inclination was to approach Waldorf's younger brother John, and the constituency chairman, Frank Hawker, was dispatched to London to persuade him to stand. When John declined the invitation, the party evaluated their options. It was only a matter of time before they looked to Nancy.

By 1919, women were able to stand for Parliament. The monumental Representation of the People Act of February 1918 had extended the vote to women, though only to those aged over 30, and even then with property qualifications. Nine months later, the Qualification of Women Act allowed women to stand for Parliament and to sit and vote as members of the House of Commons. In December 1918 seventeen women candidates stood in the election, and one – Constance Markiewicz – was successful. Markiewicz was an Irish radical who had fought for the Irish Citizens' Army during the Easter Rising of 1916, as second-in-command of the St Stephen's Green area of Dublin. Like other successful Sinn Fein candidates, after being elected in December 1918 she refused to take her seat. If Nancy was selected and returned as MP for

Plymouth Sutton in the November 1919 by-election, she would be the first woman to sit in Parliament.

The prospect of Nancy's selection divided the local party association. The main objection of this group was, obviously, that Nancy was a woman. In a statement they decreed: 'Though we admit that nobody could have done more benevolent work than Lord and Lady Astor, we say that neither a kind heart nor a coronet fits a woman to take her place in Parliament.'[12] There were other objections too: her straight-talking manner was seen by many as 'abrasive', and her behaviour in debates as 'bolshie' – though in a man, these attributes would surely have been described differently, and not seen as impediments to a political career.

After much dispute and manoeuvring, the local Conservatives eventually resolved their differences, and on 22 October Nancy received a telegram inviting her to stand. Fully cognisant of the implications of the offer, she agonised over the decision. Although Nancy's experience of campaigning with Waldorf had given her a taste for electioneering, she had never considered an independent career in politics. If she did agree to stand, she reasoned, it would only be a temporary measure, carried out to support her husband, and in the hope that Waldorf would succeed in his latest bid to reclaim his seat, this time by obtaining an Act of Parliament. 'It seemed that it was best to keep it in the family,' she later said.[13] Hopefully, she would not be taking her husband's seat, only keeping it warm until his return. Eventually, at a loss, her 'moods changing hourly', Nancy called for her butler Mr Lee. 'Oh Lee,' she said, 'I've talked to so many people about Plymouth, what do you think

I should do?' 'I should go for it my lady,' he replied. In his memoirs, Lee recounted the rest of the story: 'Now I'm not so big headed as to think that my opinion swayed her in any way but a couple of days later she again sent for me. "Lee, I've decided to take your advice. I'm going to 'go for it', as you said." '[14] Nancy wired Hawker and the Unionist Association of Plymouth: 'Fully conscious of great honour and grave responsibility, I accept the invitation to stand for Plymouth.'[15]

Chapter 5

'A LADY FOR PARLIAMENT'

Nancy's selection sparked a transatlantic media furore. Sensing that something remarkable was about to occur, newspapers across Britain and America headlined the story. The reaction of her friends was mixed. The Marquess of Salisbury's stance was perhaps typical of most of Nancy's circle, who were supportive of her personally, but unsure of the political implications should she be elected. 'I am as usual lost in admiration of your energy and public spirit. Of course it is a new idea to me and you know I am a hopeless mass of prejudice,' he wrote. 'I am torn by conflicting emotions – on the one side friendship and on the other purblind fossilized Toryism!'[1] Others were less self-aware. The author J. M. Barrie, who had often been a guest at Cliveden, dashed off a furious note. 'I hear of your presumptuous ambitions at Plymouth. How any woman can dare to stand up against a man I don't understand. What can you know about politics?' he thundered. 'These things require a man's brains, a man's knowledge, a man's fairness, a man's eloquence. Women's true sphere in life is to be a (respectful) helpmeet.'[2]

But tirades like Barrie's only spurred Nancy on. On

3 November 1919, she addressed the voters at Plymouth's Masonic Hall:

> If you want an M.P. who will be a repetition of the 600 other M.P.s don't vote for me. If you want a lawyer or a pacifist don't elect me. If you can't get a fighting man, take a fighting woman. If you want a party hack don't elect me. Surely we have outgrown party ties. I have. The war has taught us that there is a greater thing than parties, and that is the State.[3]

Canvassing began immediately. Nancy's campaign committee booked many of the local public rooms and scheduled a series of women's meetings for every weekday afternoon until polling day, which was fixed for Saturday 15 November.[4] She had a hard fight ahead of her. Sutton was an unpredictable constituency. Waldorf had done well in the 1918 general election, winning a majority of 11,757. But interest in the Labour Party was rising, and Sutton had a large working-class population – railwaymen, fishermen, servicemen and chemical workers – who mainly lived in the oldest part of town, known for its slums. Unemployment was soaring after 6,000 dockyard workers had been laid off at the end of the war. William Gay, the Labour candidate, looked to be in the ascendant.

Nancy began her campaign by appealing to the women of Plymouth. Posters targeted women directly, with slogans such as 'Sutton Women! Vote for Lady Astor', and 'If you vote against Astor you vote against Lloyd George who gave women maternity benefit' – Lloyd George was head of the coalition government supported by the Conservatives. She called women-only meetings, and created an instant sorority by repeating the phrase 'we women'. 'I think that women had better put a woman in the House of Commons,' she declared. 'Much as I love you, Gentlemen, you have made a terrible muddle of the world without us.'[5] Nancy claimed that unlike her opponents Isaac Foot, standing on the Liberal ticket, and William Gay, her sole priority was the interests of the voters, not partisan loyalty: 'You have not got much of a choice if you don't elect me,' she announced matter-of-factly at one such gathering. 'Mr Foot is pledged to Mr Asquith. I like Foot much better than his leader, but as for Mr Gay, my other opponent, he belongs to the most poisonous section of the Labour Party that ever existed on earth.'[6]

Nancy's claim that she was not a 'sex candidate' has some-times been interpreted as to suggest that her campaign was not feminist, but in the light of her connections with the suffra-gettes and her statements about the inadequacies of male politicians, it reads more like a declaration that she was not standing on her sex *alone* – that she was a serious politician, and not a novelty. Nancy was a self-identified 'ardent femi-nist'.[7] Women, she believed, were morally and cerebrally superior to men, and men needed to be kept 'in their place'.[8] She frequently cited her care for women and children and her knowledge of 'the working man' as qualifications for the job. The former was a much more plausible claim than the latter, and her approach to labour politics often boiled down to trite appeals to the Victorian distinction between deserving and non-deserving poor. In one meeting she accused Mr Gay of representing the 'shirking classes', whereas she represented the 'working classes'. Her concern for 'women's issues' was more authentic. In a speech to a gathering of women at Palace Street School she announced: 'Unless I cared tremendously about the things which affect the women and children of England I could not, I would not, want to go into the House of Commons. But I do care tremendously.' Men, she continued, were 'only grown-up boys. If men have failed us, it is our own fault. Women have a great parliamentary vision. And now they must go out and fight for it. Men think they have to help us; but it is a great mistake – it is really we who have to help them.'[9] She may not, she often acknowledged, be an expert on economic theory, but her 'practical knowledge', 'sound ideals', and experience of motherhood more than made up for it. Most importantly, she never failed to draw attention to what her election would mean for womankind. Slogans included: 'Make history and the first lady M. P.', and 'A woman for economy. A lady for Parliament. Astor for Plymouth.'

While this direct targeting of women was essential to Nancy's campaign, she was also keen to emphasise the continuity with Waldorf's term in Plymouth. One handbill carried that slogan 'Astor once again', while another quoted past election results, and predicted the future one: 'Astor first in 1910. Astor first in 1918. Astor first in 1919.' Nancy recognised the importance of the Astor name and made every effort to appear in public with Waldorf by her side. They braved the icy November weather to tour the constituency in a horse-drawn carriage, which was decorated with red, white and blue rosettes and driven by a local called Churchward. Decked out in her pearls, furs and white gloves, she blazed a trail through the bleakest parts of the city – the dockyards, gasworks, wharves and tenements. She visited wives, widows and children, stopped in at church bazaars, street gatherings and her opponents' rallies, and turned up uninvited at birthday parties.[10] Nancy's bold and unconventional campaigning style delighted the press, who were fixated by this 'peppy' American and her crusade. She was fearless on the hustings, and did not hesitate to wag her finger at irksome hecklers and deliver her favourite admonition: 'Now you just shut up!'

Though a natural performer who relied on instincts, wit, quick thinking and confidence to carry her through, Nancy was 'lamentably ignorant of everything she ought to know' about politics.[11] To disguise her lack of expertise, she became particularly adept at deflecting technical questions. The *Daily Herald* reported from one meeting that 'there was in the audience one of those learned men of a statistical turn of mind and an insinuating politeness, who launched one question after another on income taxes and super taxes and suchlike awkward things.' Nancy simply replied that she did not know. 'I am not a paid politician,' she cried, 'therefore I can afford to speak the truth and declare straightforwardly I don't know.'[12] Phyllis, who was on hand to support her sister through the campaign, captured Nancy's predicament. 'The campaign seems to be going well, always overflowing meetings, but the Liberal opponent has hit Nancy's weak spot when he asks her to state what she stands for, Tariff Reform, etc.' she wrote in a letter to Bob Brand. 'Last night Nannie . . . was not at her best, and there was a large gathering of middle-class serious-minded people out to hear facts, and facts are not her strong point.'[13] Nancy found these 'serious-minded', middle-class hustings far more arduous than her visits to Plymouth's working-class districts. At the gasworks, she mounted a lorry and addressed the employees during their lunch break; in the streets of the Barbican, she remonstrated with dissatisfied mothers and angry coal-heavers. 'A woman,' one constituent told her, 'should be at home looking after her children.' 'Well, I want to help you look after yours,' Nancy fired back.[14] On the final day of campaigning, she spent 12 hours canvassing throughout the city. Tokens of goodwill, from teddy bears to laurel wreaths, were tossed into her carriage. Later on, she held her final rally, at which the prime minister's wife, Margaret Lloyd George, spoke in her support.

The count took place on 28 November; Nancy received 51 per cent of the vote and was elected with a comfortable majority of 5,000.[15] Plymouth reacted rapturously, and Nancy was paraded through the streets in a hired carriage pulled by her supporters. Afterwards she stood on the balcony of the Guildhall, smiling and waving, though visibly moved. The priorities of the newspapermen present left something to be desired. 'They all wanted me to talk about what I was going to wear,' Nancy wrote in her diary. 'Especially in the matter of hats, but that was just newspaper foolishness.'[16] The first she saw of Cliveden, as she returned there the evening of her victory, was the glow of celebratory bonfires. At the Fountain of Love, Nancy and Waldorf stepped into a Victorian carriage, and were pulled up to the entrance of the house by cheering staff.

On 1 December 1919 Nancy Astor, aged 40 years old, arrived in London with Waldorf to make her debut in the Commons. In reply to the newspapermen, she wore a simple black skirt suit with a white satin blouse, and a three-cornered velvet hat; 'It is obvious that women MPs must dress in a business-like way,' she wrote. But the question of clothes was not so easily dismissed: when she visited the new room for lady members, she found it full of boxes sent by milliners who 'want me to accept a House of Commons hat from them'.[17] She sent them all back. Her skirt suit, blouse and hat were to be her uniform for the next 25 years. Just before four o'clock, the Speaker summoned the country's first female member, and Nancy, flanked by Arthur Balfour and the prime minister Lloyd George, bowed and stepped forward to take the oath of office. The chamber was filled to capacity. Phyllis and Nora looked on from the spectators' gallery: their father Chillie had died of 'paralysis' a few months previously, missing the moment his daughter walked into the annals of history. Even at this most portentous moment of her life, Nancy could not resist her impulse to chat. She and Balfour were so engrossed in conversation that they did not notice the Speaker's summons, and Lloyd George, who had inadvertently proceeded on his own, had to be pulled back. Later, in October 1943, Nancy described the event in a BBC documentary. 'I was introduced by Mr Balfour and Mr Lloyd George, men who had always been in favour of votes for women. But when I walked up the aisle of the House of Commons I felt that they were more nervous than I was, for I was deeply conscious of representing a Cause, whereas I think they were a little nervous of having let down the House of Commons by escorting the Cause into it.'[18] As Nancy sat down in her corner seat to watch her first debate, she did so not only as a Member of Parliament, but as a symbol of female power. Five hours later, when she left Charles Barry's Gothic Palace of Westminster for his neo-Renaissance villa at Cliveden, Nancy must have been struck by the splendid peculiarity of her position – mistress of one great house and pioneer in another.

Chapter 6

'A RATTLESNAKE IN THE HOUSE'

Nancy delivered her maiden speech in February 1920 on a subject close to her heart: the evils of alcohol. 'I know that it was very difficult for some hon. Members to receive the first lady MP into the House,' she began. 'It was almost as difficult for some of them as it was for the lady MP herself to come in. Members, however, should not be frightened of what Plymouth sends out into the world.'[1] She went on to argue that alcohol consumption posed a profound threat to the welfare of the community, and should be actively discouraged. Wartime alcohol regulation, Nancy explained, had brought 'moral gains': fewer convictions of drunkenness among women, fewer deaths from delirium tremens (a condition caused by withdrawal from alcohol), and fewer accidental deaths of children from smothering. 'I am thinking of the women and children,' she said. 'I am not so tremendously excited about what you call the freedom of the men. The men will get their freedom. I do not want to rob them of anything that is good. I only want to ask them to consider others.' She firmly believed that drink impaired not only the judgement of men, but also their ability to work productively. Thus, she argued, excess alcohol consumption and economic stagnation went hand in hand. She stopped short of advocating prohibition – 'I am far too intelligent for that,' she told the House. But she did 'hope very much from the bottom of my heart' that England would eventually become alcohol-free of its own accord, and predicted that it would. 'I do not want you to look on your lady Member as a fanatic or a lunatic,' she concluded. 'I am simply trying to speak for hundreds of women and children throughout the country who cannot speak for themselves. I want to tell you that I do know the working man, and I know that, if you do not try to fool him, if you tell him the truth about drink, he would be as willing as anybody else to put up with so-called vexatious restrictions.'

Drink was an emotive subject for Nancy. She had experienced, all too painfully, its effects on both her father and first husband. Though Nancy's prophesied prohibition never took place, the ban on under-18s buying alcohol did, and was one of her enduring legacies. Her 30-minute maiden speech, delivered in a studied English accent given away by only the occasional dropped G, was deemed a success. 'Quite a good performance. Style rather "street corner" but delivery good, and points made well,' was the reassuring verdict of the government whips. 'Very few members could have done so well.'[2]

Despite this positive reception, Nancy's first months as an MP were trying and humiliating. Even the services of her large army of privately paid staff, which included the prominent feminist writer and activist Ray Strachey as a part-time parliamentary secretary and adviser, could not shield her from the vicious onslaught of abuse from her colleagues.[3] Nancy was forced to confront the reality of being the only woman in a parliament of over 600 men, many of whom would have preferred a 'rattlesnake in the House' to a female member.[4] There was a tacit consensus among Tory MPs that Nancy had gone against the natural order of the establishment. Their aim was to marginalise, ostracise and discourage her, in the hope of deterring further candidates of her gender. Even politicians whom she had previously considered to be friends, her own brother-in-law John Astor included, turned their backs on her. Winston Churchill made it his personal mission to ritually insult Nancy, declaring that 'I find a woman's intrusion into the House of Commons as embarrassing as if she burst into my bathroom when I had nothing with which to defend myself, not even a sponge.'[5] Other members resorted to childish tactics to embarrass her, often huddling together in a row to block her from reaching her seat, and sniggering at her ungainly attempts to squeeze past them, or conversing loudly in lewd language whenever she was in earshot.[6]

Nancy's refusal or inability to grasp time-honoured rules of the House further incited her opponents. One of her earliest skirmishes occurred when she began sitting in the seat usually occupied by Sir William Joynson-Hicks, which was vacant due to his long trip to India. On his return, Hicks reclaimed his position, reserving it with his card, as was the custom. When Nancy arrived and found Joynson-Hicks's card already in place, she replaced it with a pink card with her own name on it. Outraged by the contravention of etiquette, Joynson-Hicks made a speech listing his complaints, and concluded by tearing up Nancy's card and throwing it to pieces on the floor.[7] Even for someone as resilient as Nancy, these bullying tactics caused 'unbearable strain' and she often returned home on the verge of tears. Her parliamentary uniform, chosen for its business-like quality, now came into its own. 'Often my knees were shaking so I was glad that women wore skirts,' she wrote.[8] Her only comfort in these bleak, solitary days was the milestone she had reached on behalf of her own sex. 'I had to do what the women wanted me to do,' she sighed. 'I just had to sit there.'[9] Important words of encouragement came from Milli-cent Fawcett, who had recently retired as the leader of the National Union of Women's Suffrage Societies. In July 1920, Nancy wrote to Fawcett asking her to 'please always tell me when you think I am doing wrong.' Fawcett replied that Nancy was doing exactly as she had hoped. Later, Nancy would look back on the day she received this reply as 'the proudest moment of my life'.[10]

In April 1920 Nancy faced her toughest challenge yet, fol-lowing her contribution to the debate on a new divorce bill. Lord Buckmaster, the former Lord Chancellor, had intro-duced a bill into the House of Lords proposing that additional factors, such as adultery, cruelty, habitual drunkenness, incur-able insanity and imprisonment for life, be considered as a valid grounds for divorce. After passing in the Lords, the bill was introduced into the Commons for its second reading. Nancy, apparently forgetting that she herself was a divorcee, strongly objected to the bill, citing the effects of divorce on children and its destructive impact on the family. Her speech was subjected to excoriating attacks from press and public alike. Outraged, Sir Arthur Conan Doyle, the president of the

Divorce Law Reform Union, declared: 'I have read Lady Astor's speech and I am shocked by it', and a Labour Party women's conference resolved that Nancy had no right to represent all women on this subject.[11] Lady Astor was on dangerous ground. Like the Duchess of Sutherland with her well-intentioned pronouncements on slavery, she had exposed herself to charges of hypocrisy.

While Harriet's nemesis arrived in the forbidding form of Karl Marx, Nancy's took the rather less memorable form of Horatio Bottomley, self-confessed misogynist and editor of the Westminster gossip rag *John Bull*. Ever since Nancy had spoken out against his pet project, the Victory Bonds scheme, Bottomley had been looking for an opportunity to torpedo her career. Now, investigating the circumstances of Nancy's first marriage, Bottomley found two incriminating items: first, a mistake in Waldorf's Debrett's entry, claiming that Nancy was the widow of Robert Gould Shaw; second, a report from the *New York Herald* of 1903, which suggested that Nancy and Robert Shaw had sanctioned illegal actions relating to their divorce.[12] Bottomley published his finds in *John Bull*, and advertised the story with street posters proclaiming 'Lady Astor's Divorce'. As in many times of personal hardship, Nancy sought solace in the Bible, reading her favourite passages time and again to soothe her shattered nerves.

Nancy gradually developed a thicker skin and toughened up to the daily barrage of abuse, developing her own coping strategies to counter the antagonism. Attack was the best form of defence. Nancy's style was that of a 'fighting woman', heckling her critics, muttering a voluble running commentary on speeches she did not agree with, interrupting continuously. A newspaper account of a typical day described how Nancy had interrupted fifteen speeches. She even fired off insults at other members when it was her turn to speak. Although her feisty stance was becoming, as she put it, 'a nuisance' to some members, and sometimes resulted in her making rash or ill-considered comments, it was a vital asset in confronting the misogyny of the House.[13] 'I really do believe it needed someone with just my qualities to be the first woman in parliament,' she reflected. 'It had to be someone who didn't give a damn what they thought or said; and strong, and all that vitality; and rich too, why it cost thousands.'[14]

Her belligerent manner was also extraordinarily effective for her causes, which she pursued with dogged determination. Nancy became the champion of women and children, demanding reforms in healthcare, housing, childcare and education, as well as agitating for greater opportunities for women in the workforce. 'I knew I had to represent women,' she later wrote. 'Men have ruled the world for 2,000 years, and why in heavens name they took upon them to think that the Christ's message was for men I do not know . . . As I told the Archbishop the other day, when you get to heaven God's not going to ask whether you put on skirts or pants.'[15] Nancy made it her mission to bring a plethora of concerns to the attention of the House: from the improved treatment of women in prison to the supply of milk to the poor; from the protection of the young from indecent assault to the need for nursery schools; from the abolition of the death penalty for pregnant women to the importance of slum clearance. She spoke out in favour of a government bill to introduce juvenile courts, and called for more female appointments to the Civil Service. Nancy's 'fight' in Parliament did much to bolster the women's movement, not only in terms of work and welfare, but also organisationally: in 1921, she established the Consultative Committee of Women's Organisations, an outreach organisation which linked MPs with women's organisations. By the end of 1921, there were more than 60 groups operating under the umbrella of the Committee.

On 22 September 1921, a second woman, Margaret Wintringham, was finally elected to the Commons. Like Nancy she became the representative of a parliamentary seat formerly occupied by her husband. Mr Wintringham, an Asquithian Liberal and MP for Louth, had died of a heart attack in the library of the House of Commons.[16] Although Wintringham's election marked a Conservative defeat, Nancy sent a telegram of congratulation, which was published in the press: 'Rejoicing over your victory. Shall welcome you in the House of Commons.'[17] This was typical of Nancy's attitude towards other women MPs: she saw them as allies, even if they were technically representing different parties. Following her election, Wintringham confided in Nancy her anxieties about embarking on a career in Parliament. 'Never has an MP taken up duties feeling so unsuitably equipped in every way as I do,' she wrote. 'It petrifies me to think what I'm in for, and it will be a tremendous thing if you will "stand by" me . . . I shall be proud to help you even in the smallest way in carrying out the reforms we both so much want.'[18]

Nancy kept on fighting through the 1920s, winning four

elections in the course of the decade. The fluctuations in her support mirrored nationwide trends: in the 1923 election that brought the first Labour government to power under Ramsay MacDonald, her majority fell to 2,500, a result that prompted her to lash out at Conservative intransigence on social reform: 'they are as stupid as owls,' she wrote.[19] In the 1924 Tory land-slide that followed the Labour government's collapse, her majority increased to 5,000, and in the Labour victory of 1929 she held onto her seat by only 200 votes. The same year, Nancy was joined by 14 women MPs, most of whom were Labour, and promptly invited them all to lunch to discuss the possibility of forming a 'women's party'. The bond that women shared, Nancy believed, was stronger and more enduring than any ideological divisions. In the light of the patent political dif-ferences between herself and many of the other female MPs, Nancy's hopes of a women's party looked somewhat naive. But it is possible that she saw strength in the variety of their opin-ions. She had, after all, spent a few lonely years in the House. 'As one woman,' she later wrote, 'it was hopeless to try and express what women thought on all the complex matters in public affairs, and I began to feel impatient for the arrival of women of every shade of political thought in the House of Commons.'[20]

Chapter 7

THE DOMESTIC DESPOT

The energy that Nancy poured into her parliamentary causes, among which children's welfare was foremost, was energy that she ultimately failed to devote to her own children. At the end of 1924, Bobbie Shaw was 26; Bill, 17; Wisse, 15; David, 12; Michael, 8; and Jakie, 6. Even if Nancy was not quite as 'saintly' as her own mother during her children's early years, she was a loving and committed parent, entertaining them with fantastical anecdotes, southern American songs and popular impressions of her more pompous friends. 'With children she was in her element,' wrote Michael Astor. 'Her idea was to make it laugh. She scored success after success . . . This was her age group: the very young and the wholly unselfconscious.'[1] In her most ebullient moods, Nancy behaved with her own brand of childish irreverence. She was certainly the first mistress of Cliveden who is on record as having performed cartwheels in the hall. But there was also Nancy the prude and proselyte, the mother who insisted on her children starting every day with a session of Bible reading, after which she immersed herself in an icy bath.

In her early years of marriage, her role as a hostess had,

when it was political at all, been auxiliary to Waldorf's job as an MP, but after being elected, she began to harness social events to her own causes. The smoking rooms and watering holes in and around the Palace of Westminster, important sites for informal politics, remained aggressively male territories long after the election of female MPs. Upper-class dinner hosting on the other hand was a predominantly female game. Nancy might not have been able to turn up at the smoking room, but she could make the smoking room turn up at St James's Square, and Cliveden. 'I was a terrific hostess in my day,' she later recalled, 'do you realise that, that's the thing I'm best at.' Nancy's parties were never frivolous. 'I never entertained without an object,' she said. 'I used to say to people I've got you here for a purpose, you see. Getting things done.'[2]

Nor did she discriminate, as many of the influential socialites of the day would have done, along party lines. When the first Labour government was elected in 1923, she invited not only the leading ministers from the administration, but also King George V and Queen Mary. The monarch hesitantly accepted the invitation, and on 9 March 1924, the king and queen dined at 4 St James's Square in the company of socialists – not to mention republicans. As ever, Nancy made great play of her Virginian heritage as an inspiration to her 'classless' ideals of hospitality: 'And therefore I can judge that it may be useful, as well as agreeable all round, for me to entertain dukes and even royal personages and members of the Labour Party on the same occasions,' she wrote. 'I know that they really like that sort of thing, forms and customs notwithstanding, and that it makes easier that expression of mental and political liberty which is one of the best things in England. And so, coming as I do from Virginia, I invite them all, and everything is well.'[3]

During the bitter, protracted labour disputes that followed the 1926 General Strike in the mining valleys of South Wales, Nancy and Waldorf managed to convene Welsh employers and trade-union leaders at Cliveden, with the intention of promoting a reconciliation. It was a typical expression of Nancy's belief that when 'opposing elements . . . meet each other, they generally make friends, and when they make friends they can find some of the solutions to their problems.'[4] They were the words of someone who had no time for materialist interpretations of history: in reply to those – including many of her closest friends, such as George Bernard Shaw and the Irish communist playwright Sean O'Casey – who saw protracted class conflict as an inevitable part of history working itself out, Nancy proposed that such conflict had arisen only from some kind of misunderstanding, from people not *talking* to each other. By assuming this role of arbiter in conflicts such as the miners' strike, Nancy was also implementing her notion that big property owners had a sort of paternalistic and quasi-magisterial responsibility for the working poor, an idea redolent of the Virginian culture in which she was raised. In this sense, Cliveden during the 1920s took on something of Mirador, and of the 'Big House' of the Old South.

As Nancy's children reached adolescence, the irascible and intolerant character of her father, Chillie Langhorne, came increasingly to govern her disposition. 'She became critical, sarcastic, and at times downright hurtful,' Edwin Lee observed.[5] The reason for the deterioration in Nancy's parenting skills was partly, as Michael Astor explained, to do with her ideal audience. 'With anything in between the age of innocence and a fully matured creature her performance often misfired,' he wrote.[6] Her intolerance of backchat did not sit well when pitched against the critical independence of young adults, and nor did her various fundamentalist views on drink, religion and sex. 'I don't like grown children,' she later admitted in a BBC Radio interview. 'I like children. It's quite a different thing when they grow up.'[7]

There were many occasions on which the children suffered from Nancy's swift and bewildering changes of mood. Harold Nicolson, one of the many critics of Nancy's mothering technique, described her as bringing up her children with 'stupidity', and David Astor later wrote that his three eldest siblings were 'shockingly treated' by their unpredictable mother, whose occasional expressions of kindness were punctuated with bouts of vindictiveness. Even when she was not in her most vitriolic moods, Nancy's conversation was barbed, and her own thick skin, which had been thickened further by years in the Commons, meant she failed to consider the damage that an insult or a put-down could wreak.

Opposition to Nancy's despotic domestic regime came from an unexpected source – her lady's maid Rose Harrison. Rose had originally been employed at Cliveden in the late 1920s as Wissie's maid, but it wasn't long before Nancy poached her. Nancy's acerbic nature had earned her the reputation of someone 'who couldn't keep a maid'. All of Rose's predecessors, floored by Nancy's capricious outbursts and cruel impersonations, had either handed in their notice or been dismissed. But Rose was different: after a period of being told regularly to 'shut up', she decided to stand her ground, calmly telling her mistress: 'My lady, from now on I intend to speak as I'm spoken to.'[8] She kept her word. Her straight-talking, no-nonsense Yorkshire temperament struck a chord with Nancy, and the two women went on to develop a remarkable mutual respect. The sheer ferocity of their exchanges baffled other members of the Astor family and Cliveden staff alike. Rose stayed in Nancy's service for 35 years, acting as stylist, hairdresser, seamstress, therapist and custodian of her vast jewellery collection – not to mention antagonist. Nancy often gave Rose items of jewellery and eventually bought her a large house on the Sussex coast. Rose, for her part, dedicated her life to Nancy, often working an 18-hour day, 7 days a week, and refusing even to take a holiday.

Despite her abiding loyalty, Rose was disapproving of Nancy's parenting style. Only Bobbie, who still occupied a sacred place in Nancy's affections, was spared her sadistic tirades. Bobbie possessed a rare ability to meet his mother on the gruesome battlefield of insult and counter-insult, and as a result became something of an idol to the Astor children. Nancy's affinity to Bobbie stood in stark relief to her feelings for Bill. 'Mr Billy was frightened of her, he would turn white when she came in the room,' Rose recalled. On one occasion, 'Mr Billy turned round to me and he said, "You know Rose I've never had my mother's love." I said, "Don't you talk so silly" . . . I knew it was the truth. She couldn't. I don't think she ever took them in her arms and held them, kissed them or gave them any affection.'[9]

For the only Astor girl, Wissie – highly strung and

insecure – it was always going to be hard to endure Nancy's brittle nature and withering put-downs. Nancy consistently undermined Wissie's confidence. Since their childhood in Virginia, the Langhorne sisters had been in the habit of sharing clothes with each other. In adulthood, their passion for new clothes, and Nora's in particular, was satisfied by Nancy through both monetary and sartorial loans – Nora's daughter Joyce remembered suitcases full of designer dresses arriving at her mother's flat in Chelsea. In this context, the apparently small matter of Nancy refusing to loan a pearl necklace had a devastating effect on Wissie's fragile ego. Rose Harrison interceded on Wissie's behalf and Nancy eventually handed over the necklace, though not before substantial harm had been done. For a brief moment in the late twenties Wissie's relationship with her mother showed some signs of improvement. 'Darling Mummie I know now exactly what I want for my birthday!' she wrote in 1928. 'In Truslove the Bookshop there is the most perfect set of Thackeray's works which I pine to collect. I have bought Queen Victoria's letters, which I believe are good.'[10] By the autumn of 1929, Nancy, who was not a very enthusiastic reader herself, had found a way of responding to her daughter's interests. 'O how kind of Bernard Shaw to give me his books. I am jibbering with excitement and pining to see them,' Wissie raved in a letter of thanks to her mother, who had clearly asked her close friend for the favour. Nancy even managed to find a kind word or two to say about her daughter. In a letter to Bill of 21 October 1929, she wrote: 'Mrs Strachey thinks she has got a job for Wissie. She wants her to learn library work. There are courses for it I think at Queen's. It will be interesting, and also she would be able to help collect libraries for people in distant parts later on. She looks much better, fitter and spryer.'[11]

Wissie's 'fitness and spryness' was not to last. On 12 December 1929, while hunting in Kelmarsh, Leicestershire, she suffered a nasty fall. Though the accident did not leave her in pain, and there was not any obvious damage, her hosts in Kelmarsh advised her to see a specialist, and called a Dr Whitling, who was experienced in treating hunting injuries. Whitling arrived from London with his portable X-ray machine, while Nancy hurried from Cliveden with a Christian Science practitioner. Whitling informed Nancy that her daughter's condition was serious, and that further treatment was urgently needed in order to prevent permanent damage. Wissie's injury posed an urgent challenge to Nancy's faith in the CS doctrine, which held that all bodily injuries were in some way chimerical, and could only be healed by divine intervention. Her solution to the dilemma was somewhat bizarre. After some manic floor-pacing and furious deliberation, Nancy conceded that Wissie could see a doctor, but insisted that it could only be Sir Thomas Crisp English, the abdominal surgeon who had treated her at Rest Harrow immediately before her conversion to CS. When Dr English arrived at midnight he 'flew into a rage', insisting that he 'knew nothing about spines'.[12] Eventually Nancy called an orthopaedic surgeon, but her prevarication meant that Wissie received treatment much later than she ought to have done. As a result, she was plagued by back pain for the rest of her life, a complaint for which she blamed her mother's fanaticism.[13] Nancy's response to Wissie's injury appalled her family.

Previously, they had characterised her devotion to Christian Science as somewhat comical and eccentric: in 1924 Bob Brand had written to Phyllis describing the idea of sending David to a CS prep school as 'mad' and narrating a story about a young pupil of Christian Science vomiting all over *Science and Health* as they sat on deck trying to conquer their seasickness with faith.[14] 'V. amusing letter', Phyllis had written on the envelope. After Wissie's fall, the unfunny side of the doctrine was strikingly clear.

Wissie's accident did not deter Nancy from her own thrill-seeking and sometimes dangerous antics. Out of fear for her safety, Waldorf had banned her from hunting shortly after their marriage, but he was powerless to stop an impromptu pillion ride or two on the motorbike of T. E. Lawrence. Lawrence, who had achieved great fame as 'Lawrence of Arabia' for his role in the Arab revolt against Ottoman rule during the First World War, was in the early 1930s living in the UK pseudonymously as 'Aircraftman Shaw'. During one visit to Cliveden he and Nancy were talking conspiratorially when 'suddenly both of them got up, rushed outside, jumped on his bike, her riding on the pillion, and drove off at top speed in a cloud of dust down the drive.' 'They were only away for a few minutes,' Rose recalled, 'but it seemed an eternity, and his lordship was beside himself with worry and embarrassment.' Nancy and Lawrence returned even faster than they had set out, coming to a halt in a skid across the gravel. 'We did a hundred miles an hour!' Nancy boasted, as she dismounted from Lawrence's Brough Superior SS100. She was not greeted with the enthusiasm she had expected. Enraged, Waldorf stalked off. It would not deter Nancy from future adventures. 'There was always a next time,' Rose wrote, 'and we knew there would be.'[15]

While Waldorf's 'embarrassment' says something about his careful, puritanical disposition, his 'worry' would have been shared by anyone. T. E. Lawrence was in the habit of riding his motorbike at terrifying speeds around the lanes near his Dorset home, and Nancy was not the sort to ask anyone to slow down. In the course of her own driving career she had several near misses, including one right by Parliament, in which she narrowly avoided ploughing through a marching band. Shortly after his joyride with Nancy, a similar 'near miss' would have fatal consequences for Lawrence: on 13 May 1935, he swerved to avoid two boys on bicycles on a country lane not far from his cottage at Cloud Hill, near Wareham. He was thrown over the handlebars of his bike and died in hospital six days later. Nancy had not even heard of his injury when Mr Lee brought her the news of Lawrence's death. She was entertaining at the time, and needed help leaving the room.[16] His funeral was a rare occasion for authentic solidarity between Nancy and Winston Churchill: 'As Mr Churchill was leaving afterwards she ran to him and caught hold of his hand, and they stood in silent understanding with tears falling from their eyes.' Lawrence's death was a key influence in the widespread adoption – and, later, the mandatory use – of motorcycle helmets: among the doctors who treated him was the young neurosurgeon Hugh Cairns, who was moved by the tragedy to research avoidable head injuries and deaths that could be prevented by head protection.

In the 1950s, the writer Richard Aldington would publish *Lawrence of Arabia: A Biographical Inquiry*, in which he made several controversial claims, one of which was that Lawrence had been gay. Writing ten years after the publication of Aldington's book, Rose Harrison said that 'her ladyship always treasured Mr Lawrence's memory, even after Richard Adlington besmirched him in his book. I didn't read it, but I'm told it was the truth. Even so, her ladyship refused to believe anything bad of him.'[17] Homosexuality definitely was, in Nancy's eyes, something 'bad' that she should 'refuse to believe' about a friend. In the late twenties and early thirties, this widely held prejudice would be tested in her precious relationship with her eldest son, the charming and irreverent Bobbie Shaw.

Chapter 8

CONVICTIONS

I n June 1929, Bobbie was reported drunk on duty, and decided to resign his commission from the Life Guards, the most senior regiment of the British army, rather than face a court martial. Given his mother's views on alcohol, this was embarrassing enough for Bobbie, but in fact the 'drunk on duty' version of events was a cover story concocted by Bobbie's commanding officer to disguise a larger taboo – a homosexual act with another officer. Nancy and Waldorf believed the commanding officer's account, and in the months following Bobbie's dismissal Nancy's main complaint against her son was that he spent all his time in cinemas and visiting friends, and had shown no inclination to get a new job. But Bobbie's situation was far more desperate than Nancy, in the remoteness of her disapprobation, could conceive of. His friendships and identity had all been tied up in his army life, and now, forced out of uniform, he began to drink heavily and have increasingly careless sexual encounters, picking up partners in familiar pubs near his old barracks in London.

It was not long before Nancy's illusions about her eldest son were shattered. After his resignation from the Guards, Bobbie was cautioned twice for propositioning guardsmen, and in July 1931, was warned by the police that he was going to be arrested for a homosexual offence. The idea behind the tip-off was that Bobbie would have a chance to leave the country; in most cases of this sort, the charges were dropped after a year or so, and it was possible to return. Self-imposed exile was the option chosen by many of those persecuted under the laws against gay sex. Bobbie decided he would rather face the prison sentence, and remained in London, at Brown's Hotel, waiting to be arrested. Nancy was informed of Bobbie's situation on a Monday night in July after returning from church. Unable to master her emotions, she wept openly and uncontrollably. Just before his arrest, Bobbie wrote his mother a heart-rending note, expressing a sense of relief at no longer having to conceal his struggle. In language redolent of the mentality of the time, he described his sexuality as 'a horrible disease', 'a tyranny', and 'what I have been up against'.[1]

Responses from family and friends often adopted a similar, medicalised terminology and, when they were supportive, attempted to offer advice to Bobbie in the struggle against his 'condition'. Bobbie's predicament fell easy prey to the paradigm of Christian Science, as Philip Kerr made clear in a letter to Nancy: 'It [jail] is really exactly what we have all known he needs – a period when he will have to work & be kept from idleness and false pleasures. It's just the charm of sensuality destroying itself. From the Science point of view it is a blessing for him & but preparation for healing. Scientifically you can rejoice in it.'[2] George Bernard Shaw's advice was rather more measured and enlightened: 'In this matter Mrs Eddy, bless her, is no use. The Bible, with its rubbish about Lot's wife, is positively dangerous' – in Genesis, Lot's wife is turned into a pillar of salt after she looks back at the city of Sodom while fleeing: the gesture of looking back had generally been taken as a sign that she regretted leaving the sinful city. 'A man may suffer acutely and lose his self respect very dangerously if he mistakes for a frightful delinquency on his part a condition for which he is no more morally responsible than for colour blindness.'[3]

The trial took place at Vine Street Magistrates' Court and lasted several hours; Bobbie was sentenced to four months in prison at Wormwood Scrubs. Nancy sobbed unremittingly throughout the hearing, traumatised by the sordid revelations. It was, however, her concern for Bobbie, not fears about personal defamation, that tortured her most during this darkest time. In fact, thanks to the Astors' far-reaching influence – Waldorf's ownership of the *Observer*, his brother John's controlling interests in *The Times*, and the Astors' familiarity with Lord Beaverbrook, owner of the Express Group – the press was effectively muzzled, and nobody's reputation was put widely at risk.

The day after Bobbie's conviction, Nancy was due to visit Russia with George Bernard Shaw, and whether to distract herself from the situation in England or simply because she had been looking forward to it, she insisted that she would still be making the trip. Shaw was famous internationally as an evangelist for socialism, and had been invited to Russia several times previously, but had always declined on the grounds that people were expecting too much of the Soviet state too soon. It was apparently Nancy's enthusiasm, rather than a change in his own feelings about the burden of expectation on the revolutionary project, that convinced Shaw to accept an invitation to Moscow in the summer of 1931. At 75, he was probably not going to get another chance to visit. Nancy would be a roistering companion: the two regularly clashed on the question of communism. George thought Nancy was incapable of maintaining a train of thought for longer than 60 seconds (he believed she had the potential to become a brilliant thinker if only she could focus); Nancy thought Shaw was in deep denial about the true conditions experienced by Russians under communist rule. There was some truth in both criticisms.

Shaw's hosts allowed him to bring a small group with him to Moscow, and in the end this included not only Nancy, Waldorf and their son David, but also Philip Kerr, a Christian Science friend called Charles Tennant, and Maurice Hindus, an expert on Soviet Russia. It was an outrageous gaggle to bring in tow: there were a handful of aristocratic titles, there was landed wealth, there were millionaires, there was religious faddism. And probably that was Shaw's intention: despite his admiration for Russian socialism, he conducted himself there, as elsewhere, with a mischievousness that knew no ideological bounds. Mrs Shaw did not make the journey, and in her absence it fell to Nancy to make sure George took care of his beard. She did this by washing it herself in Shaw's en-suite at the Hotel Metropole.[4]

Despite suffering intermittent panic attacks and an inner sense of despair that she had not experienced since her conversion to Christian Science, Nancy displayed stoic determination throughout the two-week expedition. She visited the Kremlin and shook hands with a 'neatly dressed' Stalin, and in the subsequent two-hour meeting grilled the Soviet leader on his questionable methods of quashing political opposition. According to an account by Waldorf, Stalin was charmed by the forthright Lady Astor and amused by her feistiness. When Nancy asked him how long he would continue to employ Tsarist methods of oppression, Stalin replied, 'Only so long as may be necessary in the interest of the State.' The dictator, wrote Waldorf, 'had quite a sense of humour'.[5]

A Professor Krynin at Yale University had written to Nancy and Shaw at the beginning of their trip begging for help to extricate his family from Russia. Some years previously, he had left Russia and, like all who failed to obey official summons to come back, was under sentence of death. His wife and children were trapped in Moscow and desperate to join him in America. Krynin believed that a request from high-profile figures such as Nancy and George Bernard Shaw might help his case. Nancy, hoping that publicity would force the hand of the Russian authorities, wasted no time in taking up the cause of the Krynin family. During a drinks party, she assailed Maxim Litvinov, the commissar for foreign affairs, and presented him with Krynin's telegram. The story made headlines for three consecutive days in America. Embarrassed by the media onslaught, the Soviet government placated Nancy, claiming it had no desire to keep a wife and children from their husband and father. On subsequent investigation, the journalist Eugene Lyons found Nancy's spirited intervention had landed the family in some secret exile, where they would never attract bad publicity for the government again.[6]

Two years later, Waldorf was asked to head a Christian

Science delegation to Germany, where adherents of the religion had been accused – rather improbably – of distributing Marxist propaganda. In September 1933, the delegates flew to Berlin and met the minister of the interior, William Frick, who assured them that Christian Scientists would not be harassed so long as they kept away from politics. Before his return to England, Waldorf was offered a meeting with Hitler. The pair spoke for 20 minutes, in which time the Führer managed to convince Waldorf that 'CS' had nothing to fear from Nazism. From 1931 onwards, Bob Brand was also in Berlin for long periods of time, working for Lazards as part of an international effort to save the German banking system. Neither Bob nor his colleague J. M. Keynes had become any more optimistic about the consequences of the Paris peace terms since the latter had proclaimed in 1919 that the vindictive peace was bound to start a new and terrible European conflagration.

The news Bob received from Phyllis was no more comforting than events in Berlin. Over in New York, David 'Winkie' Brooks, Phyllis's son from her first marriage, had developed a reputation for being a 'lady-killer and man about town', who was incapable of holding down a job. After a string of high-profile romances, in 1936 he married Adelaide Moffatt, who had achieved young fame by flouting the expectations of her oil-tycoon father to become a nightclub singer. The two married in a room at the Hotel Pierre and had a cake sent up by room service; Phyllis and the rest of the family only found out retrospectively. But there was worse news to come. In November that year, after a dance at the Hotel Pierre in New York, Winkie and Adelaide returned to their suite at the

Mayfair Hotel. Adelaide went to the bedroom to take off her coat and returned to the sitting room to find no trace of her husband, only the sight of a gaping window. She rushed down in the elevator and found Winkie's body on the pavement; he had been killed instantly on impact. It later transpired that Adelaide's father had sent Winkie a shovel in the post: a jibe at his failure to get a job that would support them both.[7]

Winkie's death destroyed Phyllis, who saw it as a reflection on her own parental failings. She spent Christmas at Cliveden with Nancy and the extended family, her behaviour alternating – according to Nora's daughter Joyce – between composure and paroxysms of grief. Soon after leaving Cliveden to return to Eydon Hall in Northamptonshire – which the Brands had bought in 1929 – Phyllis caught flu. After a few days it appeared that she was recovering, but at the end of the first week of January, following a hunt in particularly cold, wet weather, her condition worsened. Thankfully Bob was in London at the time, not Germany. He received a call at 4.30 in the morning, informing him that Phyllis had contracted pneumonia. Bob hurried up to Eydon. Nancy arrived shortly after with Rose Harrison and a Christian Science practitioner in tow. The Brands, however, opted for conventional doctors. Bob recounted Phyllis's last days with moving clarity. 'She said to me "Bob do you think I'm going to pass away?" I said "Of course not." But she knew the danger . . . And then she became delirious and it was too late . . . I never said what I wanted.'[8] Phyllis died shortly before dawn on Sunday 17 January 1937. Nancy and Bob were by her bedside in her final moments. Nancy had lost her 'soul mate'.

The chasm between their religious outlooks prevented Bob

and Nancy, the two people to whom Phyllis was closest, from offering each other the support they both craved in their bereavement. While Bob entered into a period of deep and depressive searching for a spiritual doctrine he could actually believe in, Nancy grieved with a combination of religious zeal and extrovert despair, 'crying and screaming and praying'. 'I went to her and hugged her,' Rose recalled. 'It was the only time I'd ever done that and I said "Now stop this my Lady, nothing on earth will bring Mrs Brand back. For goodness sake stop yelling and screaming." And she did. She did.'[9]

Bob Brand's depression following Phyllis's death was only exacerbated by his trips to Germany, where he began to get a clear and terrifying perspective on the brutality of the Nazi regime. One night in 1937, Bob took his seat at a concert at the Esplanade Hotel in Berlin where he was staying with some colleagues from Lazards. 'When we got in, to my surprise I saw within 20 feet of me in a box only just raised above floor level, Hitler, Goering and his wife, Goebbels and his wife, Blomberg and one or two more. I said to my young friend, "If I had a hand grenade I could get them all." I have often thought, "Would I, if I had had a grenade have thrown it?"' Soon after the concert, when he was back at Cliveden, Brand told David Astor that he regretted not having acted on his thoughts. 'He said a thing I've never heard anybody else say: "There's only one reason why I don't try to assassinate Hitler and why you and other people don't, and that's vanity. We have this ludicrous belief that there's something more valuable that we can do than give our lives in that effort but there's nothing more important."'[10]

Chapter 9

THE CLIVEDEN SET UP

O n 24 October 1937, Nancy hosted a lunch at Cliveden that would come to transform her own reputation and that of the house. Among the guests were the foreign secretary, Anthony Eden, and his wife; Sir Nevile Henderson, the newly appointed British ambassador to Berlin; Alec Cadogan, soon to take over as permanent under-secretary to the Foreign Office; Geoffrey Dawson, editor of *The Times*; Bob Brand and Philip Kerr. The prevailing topic of conversation, as was so often the case at Nancy's Cliveden, was politics.

In May 1937, Neville Chamberlain had taken over as prime minister from Stanley Baldwin; Eden and Chamberlain agreed that Britain should pursue a strategy of appeasement – responding to Hitler's expansionist programme with negotiation rather than military force. The Astors had been instrumental in supporting and developing the policy of appeasement. In June 1935, just two weeks after Germany had remilitarised the Rhineland, Nancy hosted a party at her London home attended by the German, American and Russian ambassadors. After dinner, she encouraged everyone to partake in a game of musical chairs. 'Some of the older ones stood by thinking, no doubt, that the English are mad, quite mad,' recalled her niece Joyce Grenfell. 'But they smiled benignly and were amused.' After the jovialities, more serious 'group conversations' took place.[1] The German ambassador, von Hoesch, was among the amused onlookers. If at this early meeting the Nazi representative can be discounted as just one of many at what was, by all accounts, an ecumenical gathering, the same cannot be said of the Astors' next contact with a Nazi diplomat, which took place a year later, in June 1936. Von Hoesch had died soon after the St James's party, and was succeeded in the post by von Ribbentrop, whose ambition was to broker a meeting between Hitler and Baldwin. To this end, he arranged several meetings with cabinet figures, first in Berlin with Thomas Jones, Baldwin's deputy secretary to the cabinet, and then – with Jones's help – in England, with Sir Thomas Inskip, the new minister for the coordination of defence.

The meeting took place at the Astors' house Rest Harrow in Sandwich, with Nancy Astor and Philip Kerr present. Waldorf was in Geneva on political business. At 5.10 on the afternoon of 2 June 1936, von Ribbentrop collected Jones from Tufton Court, a mansion block in Westminster, and drove him in a silver Mercedes-Benz to Sandwich, where they were met by Nancy, Philip Kerr and Thomas Inskip. After dinner they plunged into debate, with von Ribbentrop stressing the importance of collaboration between England and Germany. Together the two countries would form a new centre of European power around which the smaller states on the Continent would crystallise. He hinted that Germany was already receiving secret advances from some of these small states, and confirmed that a number of English trade unions were paying a private visit to Germany at that very moment. In return, Inskip expressed concerns about the persecution of the church in Germany, and Jones insisted that there was strong support for the League of Nations in Britain. The party 'talked till nearly midnight' and when the others had gone to bed, Philip Kerr and Jones retired to Waldorf's study to continue talks with von Ribbentrop until 12.45.[2]

The atmosphere the following morning was light-hearted, with Nancy teasing the German ambassador over breakfast about the 'bad company' he kept in England, namely her rival hostesses Lady Londonderry and Lady Cunard. Jones and von Ribbentrop then took a tour of the Roman fort at Richborough – where a rather overenthusiastic retired marine acted as their guide – before returning to London for a meeting with Geoffrey Dawson, editor of *The Times*.[3] While these meetings were covert, they were not kept secret from those in power. Stanley Baldwin was informed of the Sandwich discussions, and in a meeting with Thomas Jones several days later, said that he was in favour of meeting Hitler, and was prepared to go to Berlin to do it. The meeting, however, never took place.

The spirit of appeasement pervaded Nancy's Cliveden weekend of October 1937. There was a consensus among her guests sitting down to lunch on that blustery Sunday that Hitler could be handled, talked down, reasoned with. Compromise and concession, they believed, were a more palatable alternative to conflict, and nobody wished for another conflagration on the scale of the Great War. Nevile Henderson later wrote that his appointment to Berlin could 'only mean that I had been specially selected by Providence for the definite mission of, as I trusted, helping to preserve the peace of the world'.[4] Meanwhile, Philip Kerr, driven in part by his own sense of guilt, was convinced that every act of German antagonism could be traced back to the injustice of the Versailles Treaty. Kerr defended the policy of appeasement with vigorous perseverance, in the hope that leniency on Germany would, in some way, grant him absolution. Of all the guests, only Bob Brand was sceptical of appeasement. His visits to Berlin in the mid-1930s had given him an ominous insight into the nature of the Nazi regime and he believed that Britain would ultimately have to 'defend herself' from Hitler.

The next month, the International Hunting Exhibition was held in Berlin. Just as the Nazis had used the 1936 Munich Olympics to promote their racial ideology, so, under the direction of the Reichsjägermeister Hermann Goering, they would use the International Hunting Exhibition as a platform for various historical fantasies that informed the National Socialist project. There were medieval hunting horns and swords, a whole stuffed bison, and commemorative plates and medals that merged the iconography of Nazism with references to the mythological past of the *Nibelungenlied*. Among the attendees at the exhibition was Lutz Heck, who had been working on a programme to breed back the European auroch – a type of large wild cattle, extinct since the 17th century – so that Goering could reintroduce it to the Bialowieza Forest in Poland, and hunt it there. Also in attendance, looking rather out of place with his bowler hat, rangy figure and polka-dot tie, was

Lord Halifax, the British foreign secretary. A British Pathé newsreel shows him strolling through galleries full of hunting trophies, and paying particular attention to the head of a deer shot by the wife of George VI, before giving a brief speech about how much he had enjoyed himself.

But Halifax's visit was more than just a junket: both the British and Nazi governments intended to use it for diplomatic negotiations. After seeing the exhibition and going hunting with Goering, Halifax was escorted to Berlin, and then to Berchtesgaden where, on his arrival, he nearly caused a diplomatic incident by mistaking Hitler for a footman. 'As I looked out of the car window, on eye level, I saw in the middle of this swept path a pair of black trouser legs, finishing up in silk socks and pumps. I assumed this was a footman who had come down to help me out of the car and up the steps, and was proceeding in leisurely fashion to get myself out of the car when I hear von Neurath throwing a hoarse whisper at my ear of "Der Führer, der Führer". And it then dawned upon me that the legs were not the legs of a footman, but of Hitler. And higher up, the trousers passed into khaki tunic with swastika armlet complete.' Hitler greeted Halifax politely and led him up to his study, which was 'very overheated, but with a magnificent mountain view from immense windows'.[5]

Had it not been for the work of one journalist these two events – the October weekend at Cliveden and Halifax's November trip to Germany – would have remained distinct entities, forever unconnected in the public consciousness. Claud Cockburn had been editor, chief writer and printer of a mimeographed paper called *The Week* since 1933. The paper was muck-raking and strongly anti-appeasement, and the various scraps of information Cockburn had about the Astors, Cliveden and Berchtesgaden suggested to him an irresistible story. In a November edition of *The Week*, Cockburn cannily stitched Halifax's trip and Nancy's weekend together, alleging that the plan for the visit to Germany had been hatched at Cliveden during the weekend of 23–4 October. A sinister cabal, acting under the auspices of the Astors, had instructed Halifax to make a clandestine deal with the Führer, who had offered, among other things, a 10-year 'colonial truce to Great Britain in exchange for a free rein in central Europe'. It was a conspiracy of unrivalled proportions.

The first two issues of *The Week* that carried supposedly inside information on Halifax's visit to Berlin had very little impact. As Claud Cockburn himself put it: 'Absolutely nothing happened. It made about as loud a bang as a crumpet falling on a carpet.'[6] All this changed on 22 December 1937, when the paper developed its coverage of the 'Halifax coup' by restyling the villain of the story. Previously the Astors had appeared as 'the most important supporters of German influence here' and as people who commanded 'an extraordinary position of concentrated political power'; now, in the issue of 22 December, they appeared simply as the leaders of 'the Cliveden Set'. The term was not his own invention – it had first appeared in the 28 November edition of the Labour-leaning *Reynolds News*. But it was Cockburn whose fortunes would be transformed by the phrase. 'The consequences astounded me,' he wrote. The enigmatic, elitist ring of the new slur turned his campaign into an international sensation, and his tiny newspaper office in a

London attic into a journalistic shrine. Nancy was vilified in the national and international press, painted as a pro-German Machiavelli, fiendishly pulling the strings of the British government from her bunker at Cliveden. The left-wing press in particular pounced on the story, accusing her cabal of forcing Eden to resign as foreign secretary, and replacing him with their puppet, Halifax. David Low, the *Evening Standard*'s cartoonist, created his 'Shiver Sisters' series, in which Nancy, Kerr and Dawson were depicted as gargoyles of appeasement, their slogan 'Any Sort of Peace at Any Sort of Price'. In one Low cartoon, they appear dressed in tutus, dancing to the tune of a Nazi 'Foreign Policy' gramophone record, while Joseph Goebbels gleefully conducts.

Like most compelling stories, Cockburn's claim had a grain of truth in it. The Astors were pro-appeasement and remained in favour of the policy until the spring of 1939. Their position was shared by the *Observer* and *The Times*, though the assumption that, as owners, Waldorf Astor and John Astor directed the editorial policy of these organs was misguided. Nancy, Waldorf, Kerr and Dawson all felt to different degrees, and with various personal caveats, that eastern Europe was Germany's sphere of influence, or at least that British interests in the region were small enough that Nazi expansion was not worth another murderous conflict. Moreover, the Astors had played an active role in brokering negotiations between Nazi and British diplomats and politicians. Writing to Hitler at the end of 1937 about the prospects for Anglo-German relations, von Ribbentrop did not quite use the term 'Cliveden Set' but he did refer favourably to an 'Astorgruppe'.[7]

And yet the notion of a 'Cliveden Set' as a group of conspirators rather than a circle of like-minded people was, even by Cockburn's own admission, the product of fabrication and embellishment. Cockburn's brand of journalism purposefully relied on speculation, rumour and gossip as the basis of his stories, and *The Week* had made a name for itself thanks to his refusal to exercise any form of self-censorship. A consensus of opinion among the Astor circle did not mark these people out as a cabal. As Cockburn put it later in his autobiography: 'They would not have known a plot if you handed it to them on a skewer.' Support for appeasement extended far beyond the realms of Nancy's coterie. Neville Chamberlain was supported by most MPs, large sections of the press, and the majority of public opinion. As a Foreign Office report had it: 'Right or Left, everybody was for a quiet life.'[8] There was no need for a conspiracy in order to establish appeasement as the keystone of government foreign policy – it was already there.

On top of all this, the outline of the 'Cliveden Set' conspiracy was based on a number of provable errors. Cockburn's original account had Halifax visiting Cliveden on the weekend of 23–4 October and Eden absent, when in fact the opposite was the case; a subsequent meeting of the Cliveden Set was alleged to have happened in January 1938, but Nancy and Waldorf were in America that month, and Cliveden was empty. In response to the news that Eden had been at Cliveden on the weekend a plot was supposedly hatched against him, Cockburn claimed that the invitation had been made on purpose in order to incriminate the foreign minister – in his own downfall.

But then as now, the niceties of veracity did not prevent readers from lapping up a sensational story. The accusations made good copy, and the antics of the Cliveden Set gripped audiences across the world. Inevitably, the extensive coverage provoked some hot-headed responses; quantities of vindictive hate mail began to arrive at Cliveden and 4 St James's Square. These ranged from the poisonous – 'You blasted American whore of a chorus girl. Go back to your own country' – to the shrill – 'Resign! Pro-Germans are not wanted in a British Parliament' – to the amazingly jejune – 'Nancy had a Fancy Boy named Hitler. When's the baby arriving?' (this addressed to 'Mrs Judas').[9] In the Commons, Nancy was heckled when she spoke on foreign policy, and questioned about her interviews with German diplomats. The idea of a 'Cliveden Set' reinforced the suspicions of many Labour members that Nancy's politics were grounded in a plutocratic ignorance of the real world, and her more ill-considered interventions were met with increasingly short shrift, especially when they transparently related to her own limited life experience. On one occasion, wading into a debate on unemployment in Wales, she not only claimed authority to speak on the subject because she had visited the relevant area once in the last four years, but also went on to advance the argument that, in an imperfect world, there would always be people unemployed. She was met with an understandably righteous anger.

Rather than prompting her to reconsider her position or moderate her views, growing criticism only made Nancy more assertive and inflammatory, a tendency that was particularly evident in her pejorative use of the word 'Jew'. On 28 February

1938, after a heated meeting of the Foreign Affairs Committee, Harold Nicolson witnessed the following:

> In the corridor a friend of mine called Alan Graham (Conservative MP for the Wirral Division of Cheshire) came up to Nancy and said, 'I do not think you behaved very well.' She turned upon him and said, 'Only a Jew like you would dare to be rude to me'. He replied, 'I would much like to smack your face'. I think she is a little mad.[10]

When opposition came from the left, Nancy's habitual but increasingly rabid anti-communism made her all the more liable to respond in bad temper. After a council representing 30,000 Plymouth trade-union members expressed their concerns at the fascist sympathies of the 'Astor group of politicians', Nancy retorted: 'I notice that in spite of their democratic principles your members never send me resolutions of protest against the mass murder under Russian dictatorship; I wonder at their omission.'[11] Her two great prejudices did not exist independently of each other. In 1938, she rebuked the Jews for being 'anti-German' and warned them 'not to allow themselves to be got at by the Communists as has too often been the case in the past.'[12]

The previous summer, leaving New York for England, Nancy had complained to the press about 'the appalling anti-German propaganda here', and warned that 'if the Jews are behind it, they've gone too far. And it will react on them.'[13] Louise Wise, president of the Women's Division of the American Jewish Congress, wrote to Nancy: 'Dear Lady

Astor . . . If Jews in America are against Nazi Germany, it is because they conceive it to be their duty as Americans to battle for civilisation and humanity and therefore to stand against the crimes of Hitlerism . . . to render their country the service of making it aware of that monstrous iniquity – imperilling all that men hold dear in the political and spiritual world – of Nazism or Hitlerism.' Publicly, Nancy retracted the comments, claiming somewhat nebulously that she had spoken out because she wanted 'to help the Jews'. Yet in letters to Philip Kerr she continued to refer to 'the Jewish Communistic propaganda'.[14] The response of contemporaries and the press to these outbursts indicate that Nancy's anti-Semitism was fierce enough to stand out against the background noise of prejudice in thirties England. Guests at an English Speaking Union dinner found that Nancy's 'emotions about the Jews' had overcome her 'sense of fitness'; the *News Chronicle* asked, 'Is not this lady's spiritual home Berlin?' Nancy responded weakly to these charges, claiming, as many an anti-Semite had done before her, that they 'caused pain not only to me but to many of my friends who are themselves Jews'.[15]

On 4 March 1939, Nancy offered a more measured defence of herself in the *Saturday Evening Post*, in an article called 'Lady Astor Interviews Herself'. The outline of her argument was quite simply that Cockburn had got his facts wrong. On top of this, she advanced the important point that she had always invited to Cliveden a wide cross-section of people with varied political affiliations and social backgrounds, and that selective examination of the guest book could prove the existence of any number of 'Cliveden Sets'. She wrote:

We entertained Krassin not because we sympathised with Communists but because I sympathised with the starving children in Russia. Sokolnikoff, too, when Soviet ambassador to England, often came. He was intensely interesting. He had accompanied Lenin on his entry into Russia, in disguise, to overthrow Kerensky. Some time ago? Yes, certainly. But typical. It would be better called a Kremlin Set than a Cliveden Set, would it not? . . . My father once said in despair that I respected nothing but goodness – and this brings me to Gandhi. He came several times to St. James's Square, and he met strange company, including a crown prince who is as good as Gandhi. Those two had much in common. He also met Charlie Chaplin, but they didn't seem to click. This doesn't mean that I personally agreed either with Charlie Chaplin's belief in Douglas credit or with Gandhi's civil disobedience. But I liked both men.

There is another example. I had a little Cliveden Set all by myself with Lawrence of Arabia, when, as Aircraftsman Shaw, he was stationed near Plymouth. There was nothing political about it, though I suppose people who like imputing motives would have made certain I turned pro-Arab!

Her point was summed up by George Bernard Shaw: 'I could prove that Cliveden is a nest of Bolshevism, or indeed of any other bee in the world's bonnet.'[16] Shaw's articles in defence of Nancy were rebutted by Upton Sinclair, who on 22 April published 'An Open Letter to George Bernard Shaw About Lady Astor' in *Liberty*. By that time, however, the debate over the Cliveden Set had been outstripped by events: on 15 March the Nazi troops in the Czech Sudetenland, which had been ceded to Germany by the Munich Agreement of the previous autumn, crossed the border into Czechoslovakia, and Nancy's faith in appeasement began, at last, to falter. Philip Kerr had come to doubt the policy of appeasement several months earlier than his friend. The violent 'Kristallnacht' pogrom of 9–10 November had alerted him to the racist agenda of the Nazi regime. On 20 November, Kerr wrote an article in the *Observer* under the title 'Britain Awake!' in which he bemoaned the slowness of British rearmament, and argued for full military containment of Germany, in the hope that this would prevent the need for war. 'There is no time to lose. I doubt if most people yet realise how rapidly the next crisis of power may arise,' he warned, 'how formidable will be the threatened blow, and how much has still to be done in a very short time to organise our defences.'[17]

Once she had abandoned her hopes of peace with Germany, Nancy was apparently moved by the plight of German Jewish refugees, and responded to appeals from Lewis Namier and 'Baffy' Dugdale to help find Jewish academics places in British universities. Given the lamentable asylum policies of the British and American governments towards Jews fleeing Nazi persecution, she deserves some credit for this. She was involved in some of her own rescue missions too. In March 1938, when Dr Solomon Frankfurter was rounded up by the Nazis after the *Anschluss*, his nephew, the American legal scholar Felix Frankfurter (who had previously been a guest at Cliveden), appealed to Nancy for help. She spoke to the German ambassador in London, warning that if Dr Frankfurter was not released, she would go to Vienna herself and get him; Dr Frankfurter was released. But her subsequent correspondence with Felix Frankfurter was still marred by the same wild opinions about, for instance, a Jewish conspiracy of the press, a point on which Felix had to correct her, adding that if Nancy carried on like this, people would 'infer a sympathy on your part with Hitler's anti-Semitism', which 'I know to be untrue'.[18]

Rather than contradicting the prevailing evidence, instances such as these suggest that Nancy conformed to a familiar sort of bigotry whereby she was quite tolerant of individuals, but suspicious of the collective entities to which they belonged. Thus she was averse to the French, but also very fond of her French chef Monsieur Lamé; suspicious of communists, yet devoted to George Bernard Shaw and Sean O'Casey; and hostile to Jews, though friendly with Felix Frankfurter. It was this sort of prejudice, of course, that led to her describing Weizmann as 'the only decent Jew I have ever met'. How Nancy would have reacted to news that a Jewish family – my family – had acquired Cliveden just 50 years after her death is something best left to the imagination.

Chapter 10

CARTWHEELS IN
THE BUNKER

On 25 June 1940, France surrendered to Germany, and the Luftwaffe were able to fly unhindered from the French north coast to targets in the south of England. By the end of October, Nancy's beloved Plymouth had been battered by 21 bombing raids. The following month, an oil depot just outside Plymouth at Turnchapel was hit. The fire burned for five days, and was so hot that water from the fire hoses evaporated before it reached the flames; it illuminated the city by night, and marked it with a pillar of smoke by day.[1] Soon after the fire had been put out, bad news arrived from America. On 11 December, Philip Kerr had died of kidney failure, having refused the medical treatment that could have saved his life. Nancy maintained that given the tenets of Christian Science, his demise was not a cause for grief, but there is no doubt she was devastated by the loss.

The night of 20 March 1941 marked the first major attack on the densely populated heart of the city. That day, King George and Queen Elizabeth had visited, and had been met by crowds of Plymothians waving Union Jacks. The Royals toured the Virginia House Settlement, the welfare centre established by the Astors in 1925; there the king, flanked by Nancy and the queen, delighted in a rendition of 'All the Nice Girls Love a Sailor'.[2] As the royal train was about to depart for London, the air-raid sirens sounded. After some deliberation, it was decided that the royal couple should continue their journey despite the risk of being hit en route. Two hours later, the sirens blared again.

Nancy stood on the steps of 3 Elliot Terrace in her tin helmet and fur coat, her hands defiantly on her hips. She and the American journalist Ben Robertson, who was currently staying at the house, watched the enemy planes drone in over the Channel. Rose Harrison was one of the block's fire wardens. As the sirens went she donned her protective headgear 'and saw to it that we had buckets of water and stirrup pumps on every floor'.[3] Rose told Nancy and Robertson to go inside at once, but Nancy, acerbic as ever, barked her familiar 'shut up, Rose'. Eventually, an air warden ordered Nancy back into the house. As she entered the hall, a bomb dropped nearby, blowing in the glass on the front door and knocking her over in the blast. 'I helped my lady up,' Rose recalled, 'and we went to the shelter in the basement, with Mr Robertson sensibly following. As we were going down she was reciting the 23rd Psalm: "The Lord is my shepherd: therefore I can lack nothing" and when we were in the shelter she began on the 46th Psalm, "God is our hope and strength: a very present help in trouble . . ." She seemed serene as she sat there and quite without fear.' While the Luftwaffe pounded the city, Nancy chatted about her childhood days in Virginia, as Rose removed shards of glass from her mistress's hair.[4]

The next day, the Australian prime minister Robert Menzies arrived in town. When the bombing continued for a second night, he chose to go out and, 'regardless of danger', make a tour of the city, for which he was roundly praised in the national papers.[5] Nancy and Waldorf were out too, but did not get the same treatment in the nationals: perhaps this was because it was expected of them (on top of Nancy's constituency connection, Waldorf had been elected mayor at the start of the war), or else a sign that their reputation was still tarnished by the Cliveden Set allegations. While they were on their rounds, the Astors saw the end of Elliot Terrace burning, and mistakenly thought that their own house had been destroyed. Terrified that Rose had been crushed in the debris, Nancy rushed back, and upon seeing her maid alive, became uncharacteristically affectionate, crying: 'I'll never leave you again.'[6] Although the house had been spared a direct hit, the windows of Nancy's room had been smashed, the walls cracked, the ceiling partly brought down, and the bed and floor covered in glass. Rose did a superficial tidy-up, put Nancy to bed in her clothes, and then went up to the roof to watch the aftermath of the bombing. She 'stood there watching the city burn, seeing the flames from one house moving to the next and demolishing that, and eventually the whole row'. In the morning things looked even worse, 'skeletons of houses, twisted girders, wrecks of cars, the rubble that was once a home and possessions strewn across the street'.[7] Plymouth had been ravaged in two days of raids, 'wasting away in reddish trails of smoke'. The French writer André Savignon, who lived in Plymouth during the Blitz, described a cityscape enveloped by 'ashes, mud, dust . . . this poignant acrid smell . . . this effluvia of death'. As night fell, the town braced itself for further onslaughts. 'Those who were staying were snatching sleep before the bombers came,' Savignon wrote. 'Those who could were walking, or waiting silently for lorries, on the main roads out of town.'[8]

The Auxiliary Fire Service tried in vain to fight the blazes that engulfed the city centre, but it was soon evident that 'the fires were so numerous and so fierce' that tackling them all, especially given the shortage of equipment, was impossible.[9] The flames engulfed one street at a time, devouring churches, cinemas, hotels, shops and post offices. A bomb struck the maternity ward of the local hospital, instantly wiping out babies, mothers and nurses. To the diarist J. C. Trewin, the burning city was reminiscent of Pepys's description of London during the Great Fire. 'It was what Pepys, long ago, had called "a most horrid, malicious, bloody flame, not like the fine flame of an ordinary fire",' he wrote. Later, he again turned 'helplessly' to the 17th-century diarist to describe this very 20th-century carnage. 'The churches, houses, and all on fire,' he transcribed into his own journal, 'and flaming at once, and a horrid noise the flames made, and the cracking of houses at their ruin. So home with a sad heart.'[10] During the five nights of incessant raiding, all of which continued until well after midnight, 1,140 high-explosive bombs were dropped, and incendiaries by the thousand; 1,172 civilians were killed, with 4,448 civilian casualties overall.

Nancy picked through rubble, handed out food and clothing, rallied the residents with her dauntless energy. Now aged

61, she was still able to turn cartwheels in air-raid shelters 'to cause a diversion when things were at their worst'.[11] War once again brought out the best in Nancy. Faced with adversity, she summoned her unique brand of courage: 'not the "backs to the wall" stoic kind of British courage, but the flashing tempestuous rousing roistering courage of the Virginian . . . Not your sixty-one year old Nancy Astor, Lady of Cliveden, hostess to the aristocracy and member of Parliament, but Nannie the wild-eyed girl who rode unbroken horses'.[12]

Following the early raids, several unexploded bombs were thought to be buried near the house, and the Astors moved out of Plymouth to a nearby village. Three Elliot Terrace was tidied up and put to use as a mayoral office. After a while they moved further afield to Rock, and then back to Dartmoor to Bickham House, from which they could commute into the city more easily. 'Some people may criticise them for leaving the battleground when others couldn't,' wrote Rose, 'but commanders have to if they're to be in a fit condition to direct operations in the future, and in these circumstances I looked upon my two as generals.'[13] The Astors were certainly not unique in commuting: in heavily bombed towns all over the country, a large proportion of the urban population decamped nightly to the surrounding countryside and slept under hedges or in barns, or just in the open. Some 6,000–7,000 people trekked out of Plymouth every night, and returned to the city during the day to work.[14] On their way back to Bickham at night, the Astors' car was often packed with these 'nocturnal refugees'.[15]

As Lord Mayor, Waldorf oversaw the conversion of ruined

buildings into rest centres for the homeless, and came up with the idea of inviting a band to perform on the Hoe in the evenings. 'Now, when Plymouth lay battered across her hills, a dance band from the Army Pioneer Corps began to play on the Hoe for two hours in the light evenings of Double Summer Time,' J. C. Trewin wrote. 'Tired as they were, people crowded up through the ruins. On the promenade, itself free from bombing, Lady Astor often led the dance with a Serviceman. Hundreds, while the sun sank behind the Cornish hills, joined in as Plymouth had done during the wars of Napoleon . . . It grew into a custom, this laughing of a siege to scorn.'[16]

As MP to the embattled constituency, Nancy was responsible for more than leading dances on the seafront. In between trips up to Parliament – during which her outspoken criticism of the government's home-front policies became an increasing irritant to Winston Churchill – she applied her prodigious energy to meeting, rallying and aiding her constituents. 'We were always told to look for cases of individual hardship, for people who were too proud to ask for help, or who didn't know what was available for them,' Rose Harrison remembered.[17] In the summer of 1941, the entertainer Noël Coward visited Plymouth preparing 'accuracy of detail' for his upcoming film, the patriotic naval drama *In Which We Serve*. On his arrival, Coward drove 'through terrible devastation' to the Grand Hotel, where he had drinks with Dorothy the barmaid. The next morning he walked with Nancy around the town. 'A strange experience, Lady Astor very breezy, noisy and *au fond* incredibly kind, banging people on the back and making jokes The people themselves stoic, sometimes resentful of her b generally affectionately tolerant. The whole city a pitiful sight, houses that have held sailor families since the time of Drake spread across the road in rubble and twisted wood.' At lunch Nancy 'delivered tirade against Winston', and the pair discussed the appointment of the diplomat and secret agent Bruce Lockhart to the head of the Political Warfare Executive. Nancy argued that Lockhart could not really be a good appointment, as he had written a book discussing his travels around Europe with a mistress. 'This point of view baffling and irritating,' wrote Coward. 'How sad that a woman of such kindness and courage should be a fanatic.'[18]

There were, of course, limitations to the sort of assistance Nancy offered, and the ambivalence of some Plymothians towards her efforts (or their suspicion of her pose of solidarity) is hinted at in Coward's diary entry. The real benefits to the city arose from the combination of Nancy's flamboyant energy with Waldorf's methodical efficiency. As Harrison puts it: 'His lordship, while he wasn't so communicative, did things his own way. It was said at that time about the Astors that "she found out what needed doing, and he saw that it was done".'[19] But effective as their partnership might have been, there was, perhaps for the first time, real distance growing between the two. Hitherto, Nancy's viciousness had very rarely, if ever, been directed at Waldorf. One of her children recalled how, when Nancy went on the rampage, Waldorf would rest his hand on the scruff of her neck and rock her gently from side to side, whispering that she should ease off. Now he too fell victim to his wife's destructive impulses.

Florrie the housemaid described one of the early scraps to Rose Harrison. Waldorf had recently caught a cold, and Nancy had agreed to spend a short time with him at a hotel near Rock while he convalesced. In keeping with the strictures of Christian Science, he declined the care of doctors – but he insisted that Nancy be there to look after him. The day of their intended departure, they ate lunch at Elliot Terrace with some local dignitaries. Some sweets had arrived at the house from America, intended for the people of Plymouth. After lunch Nancy, who had always been partial to sugary treats, asked Waldorf to break open the stash for her. He refused, explaining that they were intended for those whose need was greater than hers. This was not the first occasion on which Nancy gave unreasonable priority to her own desires against a background of general deprivation: Rose Harrison admits that 'she did fiddle a few coupons', and in 1943 she would be arraigned at Bow Street Magistrates' Court after she asked a friend of hers in the Red Cross to bring some nylons over when he next came to Britain. This was probably a running irritation to the scrupulous Waldorf, but whatever his motivations at that moment, his refusal to hand over the sweets had disastrous consequences. 'She [Nancy] straightaway went into a tantrum, was rude and spiteful to him in front of the guests, and told him she wouldn't now go to Rock with him,' Rose recalled. 'His lordship left the room . . . When I went to his office I could see at once that he was in a dreadful state: he had difficulty with his breathing and his face was high-coloured. I thought he must have had a stroke, and to this day I'm convinced I was right.' Rose furiously confronted her mistress, warning her to accompany

Waldorf to Rock and threatening to tell the children of their mother's 'greed' and 'selfishness' if she did not comply. Nancy, looking 'meek and ashamed', backed down.[20] It was an explosive prelude to a gradual estrangement that would play out, for the most part, in distance and silence, as Waldorf's and Nancy's ways of looking at the world diverged irreversibly.

Chapter 11

FAREWELL TO BOTH
MY HOUSES

The row in 3 Elliot Terrace had clearly been about more than just sweets. Nancy resented having to spend time away from her constituency to accompany the increasingly ill Waldorf on convalescent trips to Rock, or to their house on the remote island of Jura in Scotland, and went to great lengths to express her displeasure. When asked if she was heading to Scotland, her standard response was: 'Yes, I'm going to Hell.'[1] She rebuked Waldorf for his failing body, invoking the tenets of Christian Science in a bid to make him feel that it was a weakness of mind that had induced his fragile state. Waldorf, meanwhile, took her complaints to heart, fervently apologising for irritating her and thinking up ways to compensate for his flagging energy. At Jura, he commissioned a special 'lighthouse' for Nancy, complete with a glass-walled office with panoramic views of the sea so she could work in peace. She remained unimpressed.

During Waldorf's extended absences from Plymouth, he applied himself to the question of the city's reconstruction. The post-war Plymouth of Waldorf's imagination was not the old city rebuilt, but a radically modern city planned for a more collective age. At Waldorf's behest, Plymouth council began recruiting urban planners in 1941, and in the autumn of that year *The Plan for Plymouth* was formally commissioned: at the head of the team producing the plan were James Paton Watson, the council's surveyor, and Patrick Abercrombie, who was at the time also working on his influential vision for the post-war capital, *The County of London Plan*. Addressing an American radio audience, Waldorf outlined the vision he and the planners shared for the city. 'What about Plymouth as a place to live in – the modern city, the Plymouth of the future? . . . We want, too, proper living space – for all the needs of citizens living in a modern town . . . so the plan offers us at Plymouth a City where the daily life of the ordinary man will be more spacious and dignified . . . The people of Plymouth have danced on the Hoe during the darkest days of the war. They will dance there again in peace – as they did after Waterloo – but the boys who come back from this war will dance on a Hoe which overlooks the building of a new city, a city which has been planned for them, for a wider, freer, healthier and more prosperous life.'[2] Despite her husband's nostalgic appeals, Nancy was not convinced by the plan. One of the most innovative aspects of Waldorf's regeneration project was the construction of a marketplace where the small shops, which had been destroyed in the Blitz or displaced by the development scheme, could operate alongside bigger stores. Nancy strongly objected to the idea, and whipped the small shopkeepers into a frenzy, warning them that their business risked being cannibalised by bigger competitors.

While Waldorf cautiously embraced the notions of collectivism and egalitarianism, Nancy's politics swung to the right. Her forthright criticism of the government's mismanagement of the home front had already alienated a swathe of the press and many of her parliamentary colleagues. 'The prime minister is a magnificent military leader, but we want a home front leader as well . . . I never wanted a government job until lately, but I have come to the conclusion that men are timorous animals,' she declared in May 1941. 'They are always passing the buck onto someone else. Women are not like that . . . There are plenty of women standing about idle when we have doddering old politicians in all parties that should have been buried long ago.'[3] In 1942 Nancy lost further support by denouncing the Soviet government at a time when Russia was a crucial ally in the war. In August that year, after a spring and summer of brutal fighting on the eastern front, Nancy told a United Nations rally: 'I am grateful to the Russians, but they are not fighting for us. They are fighting for themselves. In the Battle of Britain it was America who came to our aid. The Russians were allies of Germany. It is only now that they are facing German invasion that they have come into the fight. To hear people talk you would think that they came to us in our own dire need. Nothing of the kind.'[4] Nancy's tactless comments did not go down well. Her friend Thomas Jones, the diplomat who helped to arrange the meeting with von Ribbentrop at Rest Harrow in the late thirties, wrote her an excoriating letter. 'What an ungracious speech and at this moment. Do you think this is the way to increase sympathy for America? You achieve the exact opposite,' he fulminated. 'I have no reason to love the Bolsheviks but I hope I have some magnanimity and some pity left in me. You are the despair of your friends and we all deeply miss Philip's restraining hand.'[5]

Nancy's extremism also caused problems for her immediate family. Bill Astor had been elected to the Commons as Conservative MP for Fulham East in 1935; his role in the House had always to some extent been overshadowed by that of his mother, but during the war, as his colleagues became increasingly exasperated with Nancy's conduct, the proximity of their working lives became difficult. Even when Nancy was advocating important and progressive causes, such as the inclusion of more women within the Foreign Office, she had the tendency to digress lengthily, offering anecdotes of dubious relevance and prejudices of wearying predictability. In a Foreign Office debate that took place on 18 March 1943, it was 'Latins' who incurred her disapproval: 'The Foreign Office has been dominated by the Latin point of view,' she postulated. 'That is why the policy is dominated by France. Since the last war France has been a shell-shocked nation and everyone knows it but the Foreign Office. The Latin point of view is dangerous. What is wanted is the British point of view.' In a letter to his two sons, Harold Nicolson, who spoke after Nancy in the debate, described attempting to respond to her as 'like playing squash with a dish of scrambled eggs'.[6]

Nancy was also to become a thorn in the side of her younger son David. In February 1942 J. L. Garvin left the *Observer*, after Waldorf refused to renew his contract as editor. The natural candidate to fill the vacuum was David Astor, who had been wounded during a covert mission to make contact with the resistance in France, and since his return to London had been working for the *Observer* in his evenings and lunch hours. David, an intuitive and brilliant journalist, collaborated with his father to bring in Geoffrey Crowther of *The Economist* as a temporary editor. It was Crowther who introduced David to a number of influential writers, including the Marxist intellectual Isaac Deutscher, and Eric Blair, a.k.a. George Orwell, whom he would eventually employ.[7] When Bill Astor returned from his naval intelligence duties in the Middle East at the end of 1942 expecting to assume the editorship, he was dismayed by David's new pre-eminence at the paper. It was left to Waldorf to settle the dispute. While he admired David's incisive mind, he was aware that his younger son could be emotional and unpredictable at times. Bill was reliable and methodical, but his centre-right politics did not sit well with the direction of the newspaper.

In 1944, Waldorf found a solution by establishing an Observer Trust. This consisted of three or four trustees who would have the power to hire and fire editors and general managers, thus preventing a concentration of power within a proprietor-editor. The Trust was guided by several memos, which made it clear that while the *Observer* 'should not be a Party paper', it nevertheless had a clear political programme: 'The first task is to end the mad competition of nations by a world-wide organic control, a control not based on dictatorship but on the principles of representative authority and liberty. The second is to destroy the social injustices of an ill-balanced society without creating a sluggish conformity and a dull inertia.' He was equally clear about the roles he wished his sons to occupy. 'I hope that the trustees and directors will give David a main share in the control of the paper and that at some stage he will be appointed editor . . .' he stated. 'In general I support the political objectives that he has in mind . . . I have a high regard for his capacity, judgement, and public spirit . . . I have shown my confidence in Bill by giving him most of my British real estate. I have also looked to him largely for the supervision of my American property . . . As to the Observer, if he desires to have some connection . . . Then in my judgement he should be asked to assist on the business side . . . but not to the exclusion of David.'[8]

Nancy was in no uncertainty as to what this combination of instructions meant. The break from 'Party' was, more specifically, a departure from the broadly Conservative allegiance of the paper thus far, and the appointment of David was an endorsement of her son's 'leftish' politics. On 23 May 1944, David wrote to Thomas Jones about the conflict with his mother:

> I learn today re: the Observer and Bill . . . that part of the trouble is my mother. She apparently says (a) I am too 'Bolshie' and (b) she resents the way my father and I have got together to her exclusion. Egging Bill on and advising my father to take him into the Observer is apparently her reply.[9]

Henceforth, the *Observer* became one of what Nancy's family called her 'array of dragons' – things she would miss no opportunity to criticise, in public or private, often to the pain and embarrassment of those closest to her.

While Nancy's relationship with her family teetered

precipitously between froideur and outright animosity, the fate of Cliveden was also in jeopardy. In stately homes and on estates throughout the country, the great threat to the preservation of property was not enemy bombers, but the changing contours of British society. The erosion of landed privilege during the First World War and the rise of Labour politics in the interwar years had created a new political landscape in which country houses, like other kinds of big private asset, were prime targets for requisitioning. In the Second World War country houses such as Chatsworth, Longleat and Blenheim were used variously to accommodate evacuees, store treasures from national art collections and house schools. Others like Blickling, Alton Towers and Kedleston were used to house troops and airmen. Such was the fate of Evelyn Waugh's Brideshead, a fictional hybrid of Madresfield Court and Castle Howard, where Harriet, Duchess of Sutherland, grew up. By the end of *Brideshead Revisited*, the resident Marchmain family is confined to the upper floors. Downstairs has fallen prey to the philistine abuse of clerks and soldiers, who defile the historic furnishings and turn the grand fountain into a dumping ground for cigarette butts and sandwich crusts.

Cliveden was one of the lucky houses that did not endure the depredations that so horrified Waugh. The sculpted newel posts on the great staircase were not lopped off; the Fountain of Love remained clean and if anybody broke a window, it was likely to be Nancy, who enjoyed practising her golf drive down the length of the parterre. Though Cliveden did host soldiers, they were in no fit state to cause damage – in the Second World War, as in the First, the estate was used as a hospital by the

Canadian Red Cross. On 16 July 1940 a new hospital block, constructed in the grounds to the south-east of the main house, was ready to admit patients.[10]

Military usage, however, was a symptom rather than the cause of the decline of an aristocratic way of life that had its roots in complex social changes accelerated by the war. In the wake of the 1929 stock market crash, England had suffered an agricultural depression that ruined many landed families, with land prices falling to less than 10 per cent of their value 60 years previously. The Astors' dependence on urban rather than rural rents insulated them from this slump, but they had still felt the bite. In response, they laid off their casual staff and reduced the wages of the permanent staff. 'This will be fair,' reasoned Waldorf, 'as our wages are higher than those paid at Dropmore, Taplow Court and Hedsor.'[11] During the war, increases in income tax and death duties made it harder to maintain or inherit large stately homes without incurring financial ruin in the process. On top of these fiscal burdens, it was clear to fore-sighted owners like Waldorf that once the war ended, fewer people would want to return to the service jobs which they had left a few years earlier. The war was effecting a cultural shift away from old class-bound service roles: those who remained at the house after the war would increasingly be referred to as 'staff', rather than 'servants'.

Faced with these challenges, the owners of country houses increasingly turned, in the early 1940s, to the National Trust. The Trust had run a country-house programme since the 1930s, but there had been few donations during the early years. The war changed that, as James Lees-Milne, the diarist and secretary to the Country Houses Committee, explained: 'By 1942 owners had a future of a sort to look to, yet how were they to cope with their massive piles and possessions in the brave new world ahead? They guessed that it would be heavily weighted against the squirearchical system and way of life which, until hostilities broke out, had endured for centuries. Already they were contending with high taxation, lack of domestic staff and the disesteem of the *Zeitgeist*. Several returned and many turned to the National Trust for a discussion, if not a solution, of their problems. This explains how I was largely occupied during the last years of the war and the immediate post-war years.'[12]

While the acquisition of country houses was undertaken by the Trust in the interest of 'the nation', the programme also served – and in many cases saved – struggling owners. As Lees-Milne wrote in 1943, the scheme was 'first conceived *by owners* for their own benefit as well as of their historic houses'. It was the burden of death duties, and the impossibility of his heirs running the house with their post-tax inheritance, that convinced Philip Kerr to donate his Blickling Hall estate to the National Trust. And though Waldorf's politics were to the left of Kerr's, it was financial considerations rather than ideological commitments that led him to approach the National Trust in 1942, with the purpose of negotiating the house's donation. For precisely this reason, it was not long before the Country House Scheme became the subject of satire: a cartoon in *Punch* on 22 January 1947, for instance, showed two figures who appear to be father and son, standing in the cavernous Corinthian-columned library of a stately home. 'This is my last warning, Charles,' says the father. 'If you do not mend your ways I shall leave the estate to you instead of to the National Trust.'

When James Lees-Milne joined in 1942, the National Trust operated from West Wycombe Park in Buckinghamshire, the ancestral seat of Sir John and Lady Dashwood. Its staff consisted of the 'harassed secretary' Donald Macleod Matheson, and his assistant Eardley Knollys, plus female administrators. An indispensable asset to the Trust was a ramshackle Austin bequeathed by Hilda Matheson, who had worked as Nancy's political secretary in the twenties before moving to a job in the fledgeling BBC. She had died in the autumn of 1940, and her gift to the Trust saved Lees-Milne many long journeys by train, foot and bike.

The negotiations over Cliveden began on 11 May 1942 at St James's Square, where Lees-Milne met with Waldorf's private secretary Miss Davy. Davy, 'a dear lady, dressed in a well-tailored coat and skirt', announced to Lees-Milne Waldorf's decision to make over Cliveden to the National Trust with 'as little delay as possible': 'contents and grounds with an endowment of £200,000, and a hospital in the park, providing another £3,000 to £4,000 p.a.'[13] While the Trust was well-geared towards helping owners out of financial trouble, it could not take on properties without sufficient endowments to cover the cost of maintaining them. The next month, Lees-Milne met with the Chief Medical Officer to try to get an assurance that the Ministry of Health would rent the hospital after the war. Though he was assured that they would, he was not given a rental figure. Without a certain amount of rent guaranteed, he was unsure whether the endowment would be adequate. Meanwhile, at St James's Square, Waldorf was piling on the pressure: 'When I saw Miss Davy afterwards, she said that Lord Astor was adopting the attitude of "take it or leave it" (Cliveden). We must make up our minds at once. This is hardly fair, for the Trust cannot commit itself to accepting a property of such size without carefully weighing income and expenditure.'[14]

In fact, Waldorf's negotiation position was not very strong. Miss Davy, who soon became a sort of 'beloved, old-fashioned aunt' to Lees-Milne, had also confided to him that due to high tax rates 'Lord Astor in giving away £200,000 is actually losing only £150 a year'.[15] On top of this, in 1942 he was quite seriously ill, and it was clear that he wanted to dispose of Cliveden before he died, in order to avoid Bill having his inheritance decimated by death duties. For his part, Lees-Milne was interested in the house, but not so interested as to leave him at Waldorf's mercy. 'The site over the river is, as John Evelyn observed in the 17th century, superb,' he wrote after a trip there. 'The house too is well worthy of the trust. It illustrates the very end of the Palladian tradition. Barry conceived it with a real regard for architectural principles. It is heavy and majestical outside.' On the other hand, he thought that the interior commissioned from Pearson by William Waldorf had 'very little distinction', noted that the 'splendid gardens' were 'very unkempt', and thought that 'apart from a few Reynoldses and the Blenheim tapestries there is nothing much in the furniture line'.[16] Later, he would deny that the house had any exceptional architectural value, claiming that it was accepted 'ostensibly because of its majestic setting and grand garden above a stretch of the Thames', but 'virtually because of the handsome endowment offered'.[17]

While Nancy could see the necessity of donating the house in a time when tax 'left you sixpence in the pound', she was not so comfortable with the idea of it becoming a site of educational or touristic interest, as Lees-Milne learnt abruptly in a meeting at St James's Square. 'Lady Astor swept in and began rather offensively with, "Whatever you people do, I cannot have the public near the place", and before I had time to expostulate, corrected herself to the extent of adding, "At any rate their hours will have to be clearly defined." There is an insolence and a silliness about her. But how young and handsomely dressed she is.'[18]

The Trust acceded to Nancy and Waldorf's strict conditions of public access. The most important of these conditions was that the family be allowed to continue living at Cliveden for as long as they wished. Bill, who was to succeed Waldorf and Nancy at the house, was also to be given White Place Farm, and the surrounding paddocks. Given the financial problems the family would have inevitably come up against if they had not donated, it was a pretty generous deal. Too generous, many people thought. A friend of the National Trust, writing in November 1943, warned of 'the widespread and growing criticism of the country houses scheme . . . Briefly, the criticism is that the country houses scheme is a funk hole for death duty dodgers, and that the public has got by far the worst of the bargain inasmuch as it merely has the promise of some unknown amount of access – presumably, however, occasional and limited – in some unknown future.'[19] Similar criticism of the Trust's loose terms appeared in the left-leaning popular press, including the *Daily Herald* and the *Sunday Pictorial* (a forerunner of the *Sunday Mirror*). The latter berated the National Trust for taking on Gunby Hall with only limited public access. When Lees-Milne remonstrated over luncheon with Campbell Stuart, the paper's editor, he received a bruising lesson in the remoteness of his own ideas on architecture. Stuart 'thought Blenheim too ugly for words' and 'was surprised that the Trust should want to own any 18th-century buildings'. The luncheon, however, was not entirely fruitless: Lees-Milne took up Stuart's offer to publish a reply, in which he invited *Sunday Pictorial* readers to come up with their own ways of preserving country houses. The readers who accepted his invitation mooted a host of alternative uses, including 'a good beer house with dancing room'. It is hard to think of a use that would have more offended Nancy's sensibilities.

By late 1944, Nancy was ineffective and marginalised in Parliament, alienated by the politics of her family and defensive about the future of her home. But the worst was yet to come. The government had announced that once the fighting in Europe was done, a general election would be held. Unbeknown to Nancy, the chairman of her local Conservative Association had already advised Bill to dissuade his mother from standing. Aware of her deteriorating performance in the Commons and isolation within her own party, Waldorf took matters into his own hands, informing Nancy that neither he nor their sons would support her should she stand for re-election. The first of December marked the 25th anniversary of her election to Parliament, and the day's papers were full of the celebrations: a lunch was held in her honour at the Commons, as well as a dinner at the Grosvenor House Hotel, hosted by the British Federation of Business and Professional Women, of which Nancy had long been the president. Waldorf, the only man present, told *The Times*: 'When I married Nancy, I hitched my wagon to a star. And then when I got into the House of Commons in 1910, I found that I had hitched my wagon to a shooting star. In 1919, when she got into the House, I found I had hitched my wagon to a sort of V2 rocket. But the star which is represented by Nancy Astor will, I am sure, remain a beacon light for all with high ideals.'[20]

The following day, the papers carried news of her retirement. The Astors' letter to the press, written in the third person, offered Waldorf's deteriorating health as the reason, stating that 'he did not at his age feel physically able to go through the strain and stress of another contested election'. 'Lady Astor and he have fought seven elections together', the letter continued, 'and, including the period when he was MP for Plymouth, have supported each other actively in the political arena for 35 years. It would be difficult for Lady Astor to stand again without his help.'[21] Outside of the letter, Nancy spoke rather more candidly about her distress, and the real lead-up to her retirement:

> Today I have done a thing that has been terrible for me – one of the hardest things I have ever done in my life, but a thing that every man in the world will approve of. I have said that I will not fight the next election because my husband does not want me to. I have had twenty-five years in the House of

Commons, and I am bound to obey. Isn't that a triumph for
the men? But whether in or out of the House, I shall always
stand for what women stand for.[22]

Nancy's speech in Parliament on 14 June 1945, on the subject of fox hunting, marked the end of a 25-year career. It was
a loss she never came to terms with. 'Oh dear, oh dear, I never
knew that I could ever miss anything as much as the House of
Commons,' she once confessed to her son Michael.[23] Her
departure affected her as deeply as some of her life-defining
personal losses such as the death of her mother, and of Phyllis.
Nancy's final act as a Member of Parliament was to hire a train
that would transport the House of Commons staff and their
families to Taplow, for a day trip to her country estate. Once
again, Cliveden was playing the 'Big House' and Nancy the
benevolent hostess. It was an anachronistic gesture, but a
poignant finale for a woman whose house had nurtured her
political career and, latterly, cast a shadow over it.

The same year Nancy resigned her seat, a Gestapo 'black
list' emerged of 2,300 people who were to be arrested following
a German invasion of England. Nancy's name was on it. 'It is
the complete answer to the terrible lie that the so-called "Cliveden Set" was pro-Fascist,' she declared. Privately, she had
received a request from von Ribbentrop, currently in his cell at
Nuremberg, to stand as a witness in his trial. She quietly
declined. But even while she was trying to bury old controver-
sies, Nancy proved remarkably adept at creating new ones.
Soon after the war, she and Waldorf made their first trip to
America since the thirties. In Washington, she was invited to

address Dunbar High, a school for black pupils, where she explained how she, like many Southerners, had acquired an appreciation for black culture through her 'black mammy', Aunt Liza. She then warned against the temptations of drink and drugs in the black urban population of the day, pronouncing: 'No race can develop beyond its moral character.'[24] Nancy's patronising stance towards African Americans may not have attracted much media attention had it been aired in the 1910s or even the 1920s. But in the 1950s, the press – as well as the pupils – saw it as insulting. The incident recalled Rose Harrison's judgement on Nancy's treatment of Mirador's black staff, who 'were almost loved, although rather as a pet dog may be loved, in a superior, tolerant, patronising sort of way.'[25]

Public debates over the establishment of a Jewish state in Palestine offered plenty of further opportunities for Nancy to vent her opinions. In the face of growing public awareness of concentration camps and mass extermination, Nancy contended that more Christians had been displaced than Jews and that American money would be better channelled towards helping them. These and other pronouncements led to her being described as a 'vicious anti-Semite' by US Representative Emanuel Celler, who called for her not to be granted a visa to the USA in the future. If, as the *New York Times* claimed at the beginning of her visit to the States, Nancy was an 'extinct volcano', she still cast a pretty forbidding shadow over the surrounding country.

The politics of the *Observer* continued to provide an irresistible target, as well as a paranoiac springboard into her other hatreds: at the annual Cliveden office party in 1950, she described the paper as 'written by Germans for Blacks'. On another occasion, she accused an *Observer* staff member who was an anti-apartheid activist of 'turning the Observer into the Coon gazette'. Clearly her views on race were not just 'outdated': they were virulent. It upset her friends and family, and Bob Brand, whose charity towards Nancy apparently knew no bounds, ended up reaching out to David Astor on Nancy's behalf: 'Your Ma yesterday begged me to urge you to see more of her. She longs to see you but I fear might relapse into criticism of the Observer. Nevertheless she must not.'[26]

Her interventions into the lives of Bill and Jakie were often no more judicious or enlightened. Most of Jakie's affection for his mother had been lost in 1944 when he married an Argentinian woman – Ana, who bore the distinction of being both Latin and Catholic – and Nancy refused to attend the wedding. In reply to this insult, Jakie assured his mother that he would not be attending her funeral.[27] In 1950, Jakie stood as the Conservative candidate for Nancy's old Plymouth constituency; during the selection process he had promised to fight the seat without his mother's help, and once the campaign began the Plymouth Conservatives ensured that he stuck to that promise, warning him that Nancy's involvement would alienate those Conservatives who already opposed his selection as candidate. Jakie lost the 1950 contest, but subsequently held his mother's old seat from 1951 to 1959. The Conservative Association in Surrey East, Michael Astor's seat from 1945–51, was more relaxed about Nancy making a cameo appearance, and in 1950 Michael was encouraged by Waldorf to visit his mother at her new house at 35 Hill Street, Mayfair, and discuss what sort of speech she might make in his support. After reassuring Michael that she knew 'just how to handle an audience', she announced: 'I'm going to make a speech about you . . . I'll tell them you're just a lothario, an artist, and not a very good husband.' In fact, the speech was one of the more successful and moderate interventions she made during her later life. 'She was more demure than usual,' Michael wrote. 'And I was moved to see how proud she was to be appearing on my platform.' Not that there was any risk of her becoming soft in her old age: 'Now you just shut *up*,' she told an 18-year-old heckler.[28]

By the late 1940s, Nancy and Waldorf's marriage had broken down. She increasingly spent her time between Rest Harrow, Plymouth and their new London house, while Waldorf operated out of Cliveden. His asthma caused him breathing difficulties, and his mobility was limited. Nancy visited Cliveden only when her and Waldorf's joint presence was required. She certainly saw less of Waldorf than she saw of Bob Brand, who took a room at 35 Hill Street after returning from a period working in America. Although appalled by the intolerant lurch of her post-war politics, Brand maintained a sentimental affection for Nancy, believing that her growing extremism was, to some extent, a manifestation of stifled grief from the twin losses of Phyllis and Kerr.

One person who had reason to be glad at Nancy's absence from Cliveden was James Lees-Milne, who during 1946 and 1947 was still rushing around the country in the National Trust's battered old Austin, negotiating the donation of further houses, and trying to put the Trust's current portfolio in order. In large part, this meant installing attendants and guides – an 'inefficient lot', in his opinion.[29] At Cliveden his task involved preparing the grounds and a selection of the rooms for public viewing while Waldorf was still in residence. During one visit he examined the furniture that Lord Astor was giving to the Trust, or at least 'what we could find of it for it was so badly described'. Lees-Milne was not able to escape Nancy entirely – in September 1947, she summoned him to Hill Street to dispense advice on the upkeep not of Cliveden but of Blickling Hall. Once he was captive, she offered him some confessional advice too. 'As she advanced into the room she said: "Why are you a convert to that awful Catholicism. Do you not regret it?" I replied, "Not in the very least." She said, "My greatest fear and horror is Communism. Roman Catholicism breeds it." I replied, "Roman Catholicism is the only hope left in the world of combating Communism, which I too abominate." She said, "It is only Catholic countries that go Communist because of the poverty and discontent fostered by the priests. No Protestant countries become dictatorships."' In spite of this tirade, Lees-Milne was warming to this grande dame of British society with her 'white hair, healthy complexion and vital movements', concluding: 'She has dignity and deportment, in spite of her vulgarisms.'[30]

In 1950, Waldorf suffered a stroke that further impaired his mobility. He moved into the ground floor of Cliveden. To ease his breathing, the temperature was kept low and the windows left open. Nancy, fanatical about fresh air and still, in her seventies, partial to a cold bath in the morning, did not object. Her visits to Cliveden were becoming more frequent. As Waldorf approached his final days, the chill and distant relationship of the past decade appeared to be thawing. Waldorf suggested that they read and listen to music on the radio, 'because we could do this together'.[31] Finally, in the last months of her husband's life, Nancy was able to express some affection towards him. As Rose Harrison noted: 'By this time my lady's heart had relented towards him and she was able to be a deal of comfort to him until his death.'[32] Bill made frequent trips to Cliveden during Waldorf's illness, and was there in the September of 1952 when his father died. Waldorf's last words to his son were: 'Look after your mother.'[33] A letter from Nancy, written after Waldorf had passed away, captures something of their latter-day understanding, and of her sadness that rapprochement could only be induced by impending death: 'Glad he was like himself in the last ten days,' Nancy wrote, 'and oh how it makes me grieve of the years wasted . . . I just want to look back not forward, and thank God I had such a long and happy life and that Waldorf is now safe . . . No two people ever worked happier than we did.'[34] She subsequently confessed to a neighbour: 'You know, he was no good without me, and alas, I am no good without Waldorf.'[35]

Before his death, Waldorf had made clear to Nancy that if she wished to remain at Cliveden, she could run it for as long as she wanted. But unlike Harriet, Nancy did not wish to spend her widowhood at Cliveden, and departed after a few months, leaving the house to Bill. She loved Cliveden intensely, but in a rare moment of self-awareness, knew that her reign as queen of the house had run its course. The most irascible, uncompromising and fearless of Cliveden's mistresses, Nancy had redefined conceptions of female power for the 20th century and beyond. She had arrived at the house as pushy outsider, breathing life into its weary walls, reviving its mournful rooms and pioneering her own brand of hospitality before taking the halls of Westminster by storm. It was at Cliveden that she had evolved from Nancy Shaw, the Virginian divorcee, into the phenomenon that was Nancy Astor. In Nancy's interwar heyday, before the Cliveden Set story broke, Lord Curzon had described Cliveden in her absence as 'a church without a chancel, a nosegay without a flower, a wedding without a bride'.[36] Now that old age had eroded her splendour and grief had blunted her once-incisive mind, Nancy's departure seemed not only natural, but necessary. Over the coming years friends, family and household staff would go to great lengths to protect her fond memories of the house from desecration by a new, unprecedented scandal.

Chapter 12

SCHOOL FOR SCANDAL

B
ill Astor should have listened to his mother: Nancy had
steadfastly refused her children's pleas for an outdoor
pool at Cliveden, encouraging them instead to swim in
the Thames. 'No, no it's disgustin' I don't trust people in pools,'
she cautioned.[1] But in 1953, when Bill's horse Ambiguity won
the Oaks, he used the prize money to build an elegant
stone-flagged pool in the walled garden next to the house.[2] This
innocuous feat of home improvement was to have catastrophic
ramifications for both Cliveden and the Astor family. Bill had
unwittingly created the stage upon which one of the most salacious sex scandals in British political history would play out.

Three years after building the pool, Bill began renting
Spring Cottage to osteopath Stephen Ward. He had met Ward
in 1949, when Bobbie Shaw recommended him to treat a back
injury Bill had sustained while out riding, and subsequently
the two had become friends. By the 1950s, the course of the
natural springs had moved and Harriet's riverside house was
run-down, but Bill offered it to Ward for a nominal monthly
rent; access to the swimming pool came as part of the package.
Ward accepted. Socially ambitious, charming and urbane,

Ward had a penchant for courting the company of his rich and famous clients, as well as that of less well-known young women, whom he often drove to Cliveden from his studio flat in Notting Hill Gate. And so it was that he and Christine Keeler ended up in the pool on the night of 8 July, and Profumo saw Keeler climbing naked from the water, and the affair between minister and 'good-time girl' began.

Had it not also been for Keeler's encounter with Ivanov – which probably amounted to no more than a one-night stand – Profumo's secret would probably have been kept safe or, at most, relegated to a few lines in the gossip columns. But this was 1961, the height of Cold War paranoia, and MI5 were keeping close tabs on the movements of Ivanov. On 9 August, Profumo was informed of the liaison between Keeler and the Russian intelligence officer. Aware of the potentially explosive and embarrassing situation, Profumo dispatched a note to Keeler calling off all future contact. All was quiet until the following December when Keeler and her friend Mandy Rice-Davies hit the headlines after a scuffle at Ward's flat with Johnny Edgecombe, one of Keeler's former lovers. So far there had only been limited rumours of the brief affair between Keeler and Profumo and an oblique reference in the society magazine *Queen*, but in the aftermath of Edgecombe's arrest, Keeler sold her story, and the letter from Profumo ending their relationship, to the *Sunday Pictorial* for £1,000. Fearful of legal action, the *Pictorial* initially held back from publication.[3]

The consensus among Profumo's masters in the Conservative Party was that he should wait until an allegation emerged concerning his relationship with Keeler, and then sue for libel.

It wasn't long before *Westminster Confidential*, an influential newsletter with a small but powerful readership, broke the news. On 8 March 1963 they ran the headline: 'THAT WAS THE GOVERNMENT THAT WAS!' The article explained how Profumo and 'the Soviet military attaché' Ivanov were having an affair with the same 'call girl' at the same time. 'Who was using the call-girl to milk whom of information – the War Secretary or the Soviet military attaché – ran in the minds of those primarily interested in security,' wrote the paper.[4] The article confidently predicted that Profumo's foolish bedroom antics would bring down the government. Whether this turned out to be the case would be decided by the response of the main-stream press to the revelations, and in this respect, the augury of *Westminster Confidential* looked highly plausible. Prurience and sensationalism were not new to the press of the early 1960s, but with the advent of television news, they had become more prevalent. In a ferociously competitive market, editors were pressing their journalists to uncover titillating stories that could be illus-trated by attention-grabbing photographs. If there was any hope at all that the press would not pounce on the allegations, the Astors had one inveterate antagonist at hand who was determined to turn the story into a scandal.

Waldorf's relationship with Lord Beaverbrook, owner of the Express Group of newspapers, had never been particularly warm, but at the time of Bobbie's imprisonment in the early thirties, the two proprietors had been on sufficiently cordial terms that Beaverbrook was persuaded to withhold reporting on the court case. After David Astor assumed the editorship of the *Observer*, driving the politics of the paper to the left, the old

Astor–Beaverbrook rivalry had erupted into something like open war. In 1949 the *Observer* had published a withering profile of Beaverbrook in which his editorial policies were dismissed as 'political baby-talk', and during the 1950s, Beaverbrook's staff had dug back into Bobbie Shaw's case with the intention of serving revenge on the Astor family. In 1958 the editor of the *Sunday Express*, the arch-homophobe John Gordon, had gone as far as drafting a malicious revelation on Bobbie's sex life, but the article was held back at the last moment. In the Profumo allegations, Beaverbrook had found a story that was salacious enough to damage the Astors as well as being eminently justifiable in terms of public interest. While a revelation on Bobbie – who was currently affecting a 'working-class' life off the Fulham Road, smoking cheap cigarettes and speaking with a mild cockney accent – might have alienated readers through its sheer vindictiveness, revelations about misbehaving politicians ran no such risk.

On 15 March, a week after the *Westminster Confidential* story, Beaverbrook fired a warning shot at the Astors. His *Daily Express* ran the headline: 'WAR MINISTER SHOCK – Profumo: He asks to resign for personal reasons and Macmillan asks him to stay on', and next to it a story on Christine Keeler's disappearance during Edgecombe's trial, 'VANISHED – Old Bailey Witness'. The juxtaposition was, of course, deliberate, though only the cognoscenti would have recognised this. The same day, Bill and Bronwen Astor's London house in Upper Grosvenor Street was burgled, and a file of letters taken; their 11-year-old son's school locker was also broken into, and on 21 March Spring Cottage was ransacked. The intruders may have been working for the *Daily Mirror* or the *Daily Express*; a *News of the World* journalist admitted to having entered Spring Cottage once the door and window had been broken by someone else. By this point, knowledge of the Keeler–Profumo connection had spread, and when Profumo's wife Valerie returned home on 21 March she found her house in Chester Terrace surrounded by a crowd of journalists. At three in the morning, Profumo was summoned to the chief whip's room in the Commons. Drowsy from the sedatives he had taken to help him sleep through the journalistic racket outside his home, Profumo denied the allegations. The following morning he read a statement to the Commons, in which he admitted knowing both Ward and Ivanov and recalled having met Keeler 'on about half a dozen occasions', but denied anything further. 'Miss Keeler and I were on friendly terms,' he said. 'There was no impropriety whatsoever in my acquaintanceship with Miss Keeler.' He ended with a warning: 'I shall not hesitate to issue writs for libel and slander if scandalous allegations are made or repeated outside this House.'[5]

A few weeks later, Profumo sued the French and Italian magazines *Paris Match* and *Tempo Illustrato* for libel, and won minor damages. But on 5 April, Keeler confirmed her brief affair with Profumo to the police. Stephen Ward, meanwhile, fearing that he would be dragged down in the debacle, admitted to Macmillan's private secretary that Profumo was lying.[6] This information was leaked to Harold Wilson, the Labour leader, who was determined to use the affair as evidence that the Conservative administration had compromised national security. On 9 April, Wilson wrote to Macmillan advising him of rumours that Ward was somehow mixed up with MI5, and on 27 May he went to see Macmillan personally, to tell him that Ward was a 'tool of Russian Communism' and that the whole Profumo–Keeler incident might constitute a serious risk to national security.[7] On 4 June, after a meeting with the chief whip, Profumo resigned as both a minister and an MP, but by this point, resignation was not enough to end the matter. Four days later, Stephen Ward was arrested on the pretext of living off immoral earnings from Keeler and Rice-Davies, and was detained in Brixton prison.[8]

The Beaverbrook press focused especially – and vindictively – on Cliveden, and other newspapers followed the lead of the Express Group. In the summer, as press coverage burgeoned, any number of exotic variations were offered on the initial swimming-pool meeting. *News of the World* journalists paid Keeler for an account in which Astor and Profumo chased her naked round the pool. Other exaggerated reports had Bronwen Astor arriving at the pool in a tiara, and Ward turning on the floodlights to reveal Keeler as she emerged topless from the water. Many of the lurid details of the affair appear to have been inspired by offers of generous payment in return for stories. On 25 March, Keeler had been paid £2,000 for an interview with the *Daily Express*; in the summer, once the story had really blown up, the *News of the World* paid £24,000 for the 'Confessions of Christine', which came replete with absurd details, such as the claim that Ward once led her through Marylebone on a dog lead.[9]

Coverage of the scandal did not fall along the neat party-political lines that might have been expected. While there was some predictable partisan reportage – most notably from the Mirror Group, who used the scandal as a weapon in their ongoing crusade against the corrupt Conservative establishment – the paper most hostile to the Conservative government was the right-of-centre *Sunday Telegraph*. Meanwhile, David Astor's left-leaning *Observer* adopted a tone of restrained criticism, acknowledging that Profumo had been wrong to lie about his relationship with Keeler, but also pointing out that 'were it not for the conventional assumption that a politician's sexual morality is relevant to his public role, it is probable that Mr Profumo would not have felt it necessary to deny so explicitly that he had had an affair with Miss Keeler'.[10] The paper also editorialised that it would be foolish for Labour, who had already 'gained a large electoral advantage by the revelation of these scandals', to 'dress up the desire to exploit a political advantage as a concern for national security'.[11] David Astor was particularly keen to defend Cliveden from the lurid role it had been assigned by the popular press. In reply to the stories of tiaras, naked poolside chases, and lascivious floodlighting, he offered an image of the Cliveden pool as an altogether more salubrious and familial place. Among the guests previously hosted by Bill at Cliveden was the *Observer* photographer Jane Bown. She later recalled David's attempts to save his childhood home from infamy: 'He asked me if I had any pictures of my children in the swimming pool. He wanted it to look innocent, to show it in a good light.' When the Cliveden pool appeared in the *Observer* it came with Jane Bown's children splashing around in it.[12]

The costly and largely dubious confessions that dominated

coverage in the *Daily Express* and the *News of the World* were predictably absent from *The Times*'s coverage, though not simply out of family loyalty. John Jacob Astor had for some time been involved in a high-minded and reactionary movement against the voyeurism and lewdness of much press coverage, and was a founding member of the General Council of the Press, which met quarterly and issued reports that were openly critical of populist editorial policies, deploring, for instance, 'the unwholesome exploitation of sex by certain newspapers'. The paper's one major intervention in the scandal was a baldly sermonising editorial of 11 June, titled: 'It *Is* a Moral Issue'. William Haley began the piece by crediting Harold Wilson with being a 'shrewd politician' for stressing that Labour's concern was 'with security, not morals'; then he went on the offensive, arguing that 'morals have been discounted for too long' and that 'eleven years of Conservative rule have brought the nation psychologically and spiritually to a low ebb'. While he acknowledged that the *Washington Post*'s assessment of 'a picture of widespread decadence' emerging 'beneath the glitter of a wide section of stiff lipped society' may have been a caricature, he reminded readers that 'the essence of caricature is to exaggerate real traits'. In John Jacob Astor's view, the sensationalist coverage of other newspapers was just as much part of this 'low moral ebb' as the scandal itself.

The Profumo Affair became symbolic of the incompetence, moral laxity and security breaches that many said had plagued the Macmillan administration. On 21 June, in response to Harold Wilson's claim that 'there is clear evidence of a sordid underground network, the extent of which cannot be measured',

Macmillan asked Lord Denning to prepare a report on the 'security aspects' of the Profumo case.[13] Denning examined various rumours one by one and interviewed the hostesses of various bacchanalian Belgravia parties to which Keeler claimed Ward had taken her; the report concluded that Keeler had indeed attended 'perverted sex orgies', but was sceptical about the extent to which security had been compromised. The findings came too late for the Profumo Affair's ultimate victim, Stephen Ward.

The trial of Stephen Ward for living on the earnings of prostitution opened on 22 July. Although the charges were flimsy, the police were determined to uncover evidence, interviewing almost 140 people, and questioning Keeler alone on 38 separate occasions.[14] The proceedings were held at the Old Bailey, where crowds gathered to watch the witnesses arrive, and hundreds queued for the public gallery. They were regaled by stories of orgies, whippings and sexual perversion. Many of the testimonies were later discredited. On 30 July, after the first day of the judge's summing-up, Ward took an overdose of sleeping pills. He left a note: 'It is really more than I can stand – the horror, day after day at the court and in the streets . . . I am sorry to disappoint the vultures.' The next morning Ward was taken to hospital in a coma. At the Old Bailey, the trial continued, with the jury finding him guilty on two of five counts. He died several days later without regaining consciousness. In October 1963 Macmillan resigned, and a year later his party was defeated by Labour in the general election. The Conservatives would stay out of power for the rest of the decade.

The fact that Profumo and Keeler met at Cliveden, and that Stephen Ward lived in Spring Cottage and was one of

Bill's friends, meant that Bill himself was inevitably dragged into the coverage. In March 1963, as the scandal was beginning to unfold, Macmillan wrote in his diary of a second Cliveden Set: 'The old "Cliveden Set" was disastrous politically. The new "Cliveden Set" is said to be equally disastrous morally.'[15] Bill was interviewed by the police, and asked to provide a list of women he had slept with and whether he had paid them for sex. At the Old Bailey, Mandy Rice-Davies claimed to have had an affair with Bill, and responded to his denial with the line: 'He would, wouldn't he' – a phrase that would by the end of the next decade enter into the *Oxford Dictionary of Quotations*. Detectives soon discovered that Astor had once given Keeler a cheque to rent a flat in Barons Court, and erroneously extrapolated that he was profiting from some sort of sex enterprise. He was further shaken when police officers arrived at Cliveden to search for evidence of a brothel at Spring Cottage.[16] Although the charges were dropped, Bill was devastated by the inquisition. The reaction of his friends only worsened his plight: at Royal Ascot in June 1963, he was reduced to a social pariah, shunned and ostracised by the same people who, just two years previously, had rhapsodised over his lavish hospitality. A few weeks later, as Ward lay in a coma following his overdose, reporters were sent to Cliveden. John Gordon, editor of the *Sunday Express*, came armed with a message purportedly from Ward, which stated: 'Bill could have spoken up for me. His silence crucified me.'[17] Gordon speculated that, given the scandal, the National Trust might wish to reconsider its connection with Cliveden, and 'return the estate to Lord Astor bringing the shadow of future death duties back upon his family' as a form of 'popular retribution'.[18] In the wake of the Profumo Affair, Bill's health problems became chronic and in March 1966, at the age of 58, in no small part due to the stress of the scandal, he succumbed to a heart attack.

The enthusiasm with which the public consumed the sensational reporting of the poolside encounter was closely bound up with the idea of Cliveden in the collective consciousness – with what people believed could and did happen there. Despite the donation of the house to the National Trust, it continued to be associated – as it had sometimes been in previous decades, and centuries – with secrecy, conspiracy and opulence. This conception of Cliveden dates back to its very beginning and Alexander Pope's depiction of the house as 'The bower of wanton Shrewsbury and love', a 'proud alcove' in which Anna Maria and Buckingham could indulge their passion. In the 17th and 18th centuries, the word 'alcove' was used to describe not neutral or functional recesses, but places of intimacy: nooks in pleasure gardens, and, in houses, areas screened off for sleeping. Cliveden itself was, to Pope, a concupiscent nook that allowed and perhaps even encouraged 'love' and 'wantonness'. That Pope was wrong about Buckingham and Anna Maria using Cliveden in this way, or indeed about them ever being at Cliveden together, only goes to show what a romantic impression the house left on him. Having seen the house and read about the affair, he could not help thinking that one provided the setting for the other. The same idea of Cliveden expressed in his couplet – the notion of a luxurious estate that fosters conspiracy and misbehaviour – persisted through the centuries.

In some ways, the resilient myth of the 'proud alcove' arose self-consciously: in his memoirs, Ronald Gower expressed irritation at how many people, when they learnt where he grew up, quoted Pope's line at him. The more interesting part of its recurrence, however, was unintentional: the fanciful *News of the World* coverage of Keeler and Profumo's poolside introduction was not a homage to Pope – it was just an expression of people's genuine suspicions and fantasies about the way in which the wealthy and privileged disported themselves in remote 'alcoves' of luxury. The same suspicion had attended Frederick and Augusta's Cliveden-based 'counter-court' of the mid-18th century, and had stoked allegations of a 'Cliveden Set' in the 1930s. All of these episodes existed within bigger political and cultural shifts that made the house particularly eligible for criticism. Pope, a poet steeped in the classical tradition and a Whig writing on the far side of the Glorious Revolution, looked back on Restoration politics as a tawdry and unenlightened business, and by describing Cliveden as 'proud' cast it as the site of Buckingham's hubris – his nemesis being the 'worst inn's worst room' in which he died. Likewise, it was a certain political climate – as well as one big personal grudge – that attracted so much attention to Cliveden during the Profumo Affair. Six years of radical post-war Labour administration had been succeeded by eleven years of Conservative government. There was growing resentment against the vestiges of the aristocratic and interwar elites, and some suspicion that the Conservative establishment was incubating a new generation of corrupt and privileged administrators. In both the 18th and 20th centuries, Cliveden was not only a place where politics was conducted, but was also a pawn in bigger political struggles, a symbol of certain highly politicised forms of power and class and ideology.

When the Profumo Affair hit the headlines in 1963, Nancy was elderly and infirm, her mental faculties in steady decline. The family decided it would be best if she did not find out, and a series of complicated procedures were performed every day to ensure that she stayed ignorant: her butler at Eaton Square, Charles Dean, cut out all references to Profumo and Cliveden from the morning newspapers and arranged for friends to call at one o'clock and six o'clock every day, so she would be occupied when the news came on the radio.[19] One morning, when Nancy was staying with David Astor at Sutton Courtenay, she woke up early and got to the papers before Dean had managed to censor them. She asked to be driven to Cliveden straight away, but over the course of the journey forgot her reason for going, and never mentioned the affair again.[20]

Nancy had wanted to grow old like her own mother Nanaire, prized and doted on by her children. But she had never achieved the 'saintliness' she admired in her mother, and in her old age, her relationships with her children remained fractious. Even her relationship with Bobbie faltered. For most of his adulthood, Bobbie had idolised Nancy, but late in her life he realised that her love was tinged with narcissism. Nevertheless, Bobbie retained a special affection for Cliveden. He wrote to Nancy just before she left for a trip in the late 1950s: 'Just went over to Eton and I had such nostalgia for Cliveden as we have always known it, I thought I would die – the Hall, your boudoir with the sweet smells, I just broke down and wept. I can't believe it has gone. I just could not go up to Cliveden . . . I hope you will never be as unhappy as I am. I really don't know how I stand my existence. It is one unending hell. I will be pleased when you get back.'[21] Bobbie was sinking beneath the weight of a grave and hopeless depression. In 1964 he made his first serious suicide attempt, with pills and whisky, but was found early enough and revived at St Stephen's Hospital. Meanwhile, Nancy's feud with David continued, and he increasingly dealt with his mother's prejudices by avoiding her. Bob Brand, who had always been remarkably tolerant of Nancy's occasional cruelty, also began to tire of it. One day at Sandwich, Nancy pushed Bob too far with one of her caustic tirades about his materialism and cupidity, a favourite subject of hers after he took a job with Lazards in the 1910s. Refusing to hear another word, Bob threw down his napkin and retired to his room in disgust. It was the last time they met: in August 1963, while staying with family in East Sussex, Bob Brand died.

In spring 1964 Nancy went to stay with Wissie and her husband at Grimsthorpe Castle, their home in Lincolnshire. After her arrival, she had a stroke. Bobbie had recovered enough to come to visit her, along with her other children, nieces and nephews. Like Waldorf, she enjoyed a sort of 'Indian summer' in the last days of her life. David remembered her being 'happy, light and charming . . . It was a complete transformation, and it was delightful'.[22] Several decades previously, during her early years in Britain, she had written to Phyllis from Ross-shire expressing her longing to be back in Virginia: 'I wander around the wood humming "I'm going back to dixie" and that's as far as I get! It's a sort of . . . longing for Mirador – mother and father [and] all of "you all chillun".'[23] Now, according to David, she really did imagine herself to be back in the Virginia of her youth. She died in the early hours of 2 May 1964; she was 84. Nancy was buried next to Waldorf in the Octagon Temple at Cliveden. Six years later Bobbie ended his life with character-istic gentility, ringing David with the message: 'I'm terribly grateful and I'm just ringing to say goodbye.' When David begged him to see sense, Bobbie replied, 'You wouldn't be so unkind would you, to make me stay on?'[24]

Bill was the last person to run the house as a private resi-dence. The Astors had presided over a period in Cliveden's history which appeared to be a heyday at the time, but in retro-spect had actually been a dying glow. Previous generations of the house's residents had been fearful about its decline: Ronald Gower was horrified by the thought of Cliveden being run as a hotel, and the Duke of Westminster was widely thought to have 'redeemed' it from such a 'fate' when he bought the house from the Sutherlands. In the late 19th century, but even more so in the mid-20th, such attitudes misunderstood what the house was about. Though it was served by traditional domestic staff, Cliveden was not – and perhaps had never been – an exclusive family home. As Harold Macmillan replied when told the house was to become a hotel: 'My dear boy, it always has been.'[25]

NOTES

ARCHIVE ABBREVIATIONS

BL   British Library, London
BoL   Bodleian Library, Oxford
BR   Buckinghamshire Records Office, Aylesbury
DCO   Duchy of Cornwall Office Archives, London
DR   Devon Record Office, Exeter
HMC   Historical Manuscripts Commission
NLS   National Library of Scotland, Edinburgh
NLW   National Library of Wales (Llyfrgell Genedlaethol Cymru),
      Aberystwyth
NMM   National Maritime Museum Archive, Greenwich, London
NoR   Northumberland Record Office, Berwick-upon-Tweed
NR   Northamptonshire Record Office, Northampton
PWD   Plymouth and West Devon Record Office, Plymouth
SR   Staffordshire Record Office, Stafford
TNA   The National Archives, Kew
URSC University of Reading Special Collections, Reading
WL   The Women's Library @ LSE, London

INTRODUCTION

1   James Crathorne, *Cliveden: The Place and the People* (London: Collins & Brown, 1995), p.186.

2   Quoted in Dominic Sandbrook, *Never Had It So Good: A History of Britain from Suez to the Beatles* (London: Abacus, 2006), p.645.

PART I

1. THE DUEL

1   Pepys, *The Diary of Samuel Pepys*, 26 May 1667 (accessed online at www.pepysdiary.com).

2   Peter Ackroyd, *Thames: Sacred River* (London: Vintage, 2008), p.436.

3   Pepys, 17 January 1668.

4   Andrew Browning, ed., *Memoirs of Sir John Reresby* (London: Offices of the Royal Historical Society, 1991), pp.58–9; Pepys, 22 July 1667; Carl Niemeyer, 'Henry Killigrew and the Duke of Buckingham', *The Review of English Studies*, 12/47 (1936), pp.326–8.

5   Christine Phipps, ed., *Buckingham: Public and Private Man. The Prose, Poems and Commonplace Book of George Villiers, Second Duke of Buckingham* (New York and London: Garland Publishing, 1985), p.170.

6   Pepys, 17 January 1668.

7   Crathorne, *Cliveden*, p.13.

8   John Cockburn, *The History of Duels* (Edinburgh, 1888), p.205.

9   Charles II, *A Proclamation against fighting of duels*, 12 August 1660; quoted in Markku Peltonen, *The Duel in Early Modern England* (Cambridge University Press, 2003), p.206.

10   Thomas Hobbes, *Leviathan*, ed. Richard Tuck (Cambridge University Press, 1991), p.88.

11   Pepys, 17 January 1688; newsletters of Henry Muddiman, quoted in J. G. Muddiman, 'The Duel between Buckingham and Shrewsbury, 1668', *Notes and Queries*, 165 (1933), pp.22–3.

12   For accounts of the duel, see: Pepys, 17 January 1668; Anthony Hamilton, *The Memoirs of Count Grammont*, ed. Sir Walter Scott (London: George Routledge &

Sons, 1905), pp.360–1; newsletters of Henry Muddiman, quoted in Muddiman, 'Duel between Buckingham and Shrewsbury'.

13   Newsletters of Henry Muddiman, quoted in Muddiman, 'Duel between Buckingham and Shrewsbury'.

14   Pepys, 19 January 1668.

15   Bulstrode Papers, 16 & 18 March 1668, quoted in John Harold Wilson, *A Rake and His Times: George Villiers 2nd Duke of Buckingham* (London: Farrar, Strauss and Young, 1954), p.98.

16   Newsletters of Henry Muddiman, Thursday 19 March 1668, quoted in Muddiman, 'Duel between Buckingham and Shrewsbury'.

2. 'BEDS OF JEWELS AND RICH MINES OF GOLD'

1   Rachel Newport to Sir R. Leveson, 27 March 1658, in HMC, *Fifth Report* (London: H.M. Stationery Office, 1877), p.145.

2   Joan Wake, *The Brudenells of Deene* (London: Cassell and Company, 1953), p.115.

3   J. C. Gent, 'An epithalamium upon the auspicious nuptials of the Right Honorable the Earl of Shrewsbury and the vertuous Lady Anne Brudnel', 1658. Microfilm in University Library, Cambridge.

4   Edward J. Dent, *Foundations of English Opera: A Study of Musical Drama in England during the Seventeenth Century* (New York: Da Capo Press, 1965), p.106n.

5 Antonia Fraser, *King Charles II* (London: Phoenix, 2002), p.210.

6 Faramerz Dabhoiwala, *The Origins of Sex: A History of the First Sexual Revolution* (London: Penguin, 2013), pp.304–5.

7 Hamilton, *Memoirs of Count Grammont*, p.132n.

8 Pepys, 21 May 1662.

9 Ibid.

10 Dabhoiwala, *The Origins of Sex*, p.51.

11 'On the Ladies of the Court', lines 30–35, in *Court Satires of the Restoration*, ed. John Harold Wilson (Columbus: Ohio State University Press, 1976), p.4.

12 Charles Beauclerk, *Nell Gwyn* (London: Macmillan, 2006), p.87.

13 Hamilton, *Memoirs of Count Grammont,* p.225.

14 Ibid.

3. 'HE CAME, HE SAW AND CONQUERED'

1 Brian Fairfax, *Memoirs of the Life of George Villiers, Duke of Buckingham*, ed. Edward Arber (London, 1869), p.4.

2 Phipps, *Buckingham: Public and Private Man*, p.5.

3 Winifred Burghclere, *George Villiers, Second Duke of Buckingham, 1628–1687: A Study in the History of the Restoration* (London: John Murray, 1903), p.89.

4 Quoted in Burghclere, *George Villiers*, p.81.

5 Ian J. Gentles, 'Fairfax, Thomas, third Lord Fairfax of Cameron (1612–1671)', *Oxford Dictionary of National Biography* (Oxford University Press, 2004; online edn, Jan 2008, accessed 9 July 2014).

6 Hester W. Chapman, *Great Villiers: A Study of George Villiers, Second Duke of Buckingham, 1628–1687* (London: Secker and Warburg, 1949), p.89.

7 Quoted in Pierre Legouis, *Andrew Marvell: Poet, Puritan, Patriot* (Oxford: Clarendon Press, 1965), p.19.

8 Original: British Museum. Quoted in Chapman, *Great Villiers*, p.96.

9 Letter to a lady's confidante or servant, BL Add MS 27827, fols.1,2, quoted in Burghclere, *George Villiers*, p.6.

10 Fairfax, *Memoirs of the Life of George Villiers*, p.6.

11 Andrew Hopper, *'Black Tom': Sir Thomas Fairfax and the English Revolution* (Manchester: Manchester University Press, 2007), p.117.

12 George Villiers, 'To His Mistress', in Phipps, *Buckingham: Public and Private Man*, p.141.

13 Samuel Butler, *Posthumous Works* vol.2, p.72, quoted in Hamilton, *Memoirs of Count Grammont*, p.163n.

14 John Evelyn, *The Diary of John Evelyn*, ed. William Bray (London: Gibbings 1890), 19 September 1676.

15 George Villiers, *The Works of His Grace George Villiers Late Duke of Buckingham* (London, 1715), vol.1, pp.137–8.

16 Quoted in Chapman, *Great Villiers*, p.100.

17 Evelyn, *Diary*, 21 October 1671; Butler, *Posthumous Works* vol.2, p.72, quoted in Hamilton, *Memoirs of Count Grammont*, p.163n.

18 Pepys, 19 December 1666; Journal of the House of Lords, vol.12, 1666–75, pp.52–3.

19 See the account of Cosimo III of Tuscany, quoted in Edward Langhans, 'Post-1660 Theatres as Performance Spaces', in *A Guide to Restoration Theatre*, ed. Sue Owen (Oxford: Blackwell, 2001).

20 BL Harley MS 7005, fol.56; Niemeyer, 'Henry Killigrew and the Duke of Buckingham'.

21 HMC, *Seventh Report, Appendix*, (London: H. M. Stationery Office, 1879), p.486.

22 Countess Dowager of Roscommon to Mrs Frances Frescheville, quoted in Niemayer, 'Henry Killigrew and the Duke of Buckingham', p.327; Pepys, 22 July 1667.

23 Newsletter of Henry Muddiman, 19 September 1667. Quoted in Muddiman, 'Duel between Buckingham and Shrewsbury'.

24 Antoni Mączak, *Travel in Early Modern Europe* (Cambridge: Polity Press, 1995), p.49.

4. A LONDON LOVE TRIANGLE

1 Stuart Handley, 'Talbot, Charles, duke of Shrewsbury (1660–1718)', *Oxford Dictionary of National Biography* (Oxford: Oxford University Press, 2004; online edn 2008).

2 Dorothy H. Somerville, *The King of Hearts: Charles Talbot, Duke of Shrewsbury* (London: George Allen & Unwin, 1962), pp.17–19.

3 Calendar of State Papers, Domestic, vol.8 (November 1667–September 1668), p.192.

4 David C. Hanrahan, *Charles II and the Duke of Buckingham* (Stroud: Sutton Publishing, 2006), p.104.

5 Pepys, 6 February 1668.

6 Quoted in Burghclere, *George Villiers*, pp.196–7.

7 Burghclere, *George Villiers*, pp.154–5.

8 Roy Porter, *London: A Social History* (London: Hamish Hamilton, 1994) pp.87–8.

9 Evelyn, *Diary*, 7 September 1666.

10 Pepys, 14 September 1668.

11 Quoted in Alastair Bellany, 'The Embarrassment of Libels: perceptions and representations of verse libelling in early Stuart England,' in *The Politics of the Public Sphere in Early Modern England*, ed. Peter Lake and Steve Pincus (Manchester: Manchester University Press, 2007), p.154.

12 Vicomtesse de Longueville quoted in Chapman, *Great Villiers*, p.95.

13 Pepys, Friday 15 May 1668.

14 Brian Fairfax quoted in Chapman, *Great Villiers*, p.95.

15 Quoted in Fairfax, *Memoirs of the Life of George Villiers*, p.10.

16 Brett Dolman, *Beauty, Sex and Power: A Story of Debauchery and Decadent Art at the Late Stuart Court* (London: Scala, 2012), pp.94–5.

17 Butler, *Posthumous Works*, vol.2, p.72, quoted in Hamilton, *Memoirs of Count Grammont*, p.163n.

18 William Wycherley, *The Country Wife*, 5.4.116–17.

19 Kate Colquhoun, *Taste: the Story of Britain through its Cooking* (London: Bloomsbury, 2007); Joan Thirsk, *Food in Early Modern England: phases, fads, fashions 1500–1760* (London: Hambledon Continuum, 2007).

20 Hanrahan, *Charles II and the Duke of Buckingham*, p.129.

21 Hamilton, *Memoirs of Count Grammont*, pp.356–9.

22 Colbert to Lionne, 20 May 1669, quoted in Allan Fea, *Some Beauties of the Seventeenth Century* (London, 1907), p.234.

23 For other accounts of the incident, see HMC, *Twelfth Report, Appendix*, Part VII (London: H. M. Stationery Office, 1890), p.63; Pepys, 19 May 1669. Another attack on Killigrew is recorded in Hamilton, *Memoirs of Count Grammont*, pp.358–9.

24 Wilson, *A Rake and His Times*, p.124.

25 Nicholas Cross, *The Cynosura, or, a saving star that leads to eternity* (London, 1670), BoL.

26 Pepys, 19 May 1669.

27 Calendar of State Papers, Domestic, vol.10, 1670, p.390; Hanrahan, *Charles II and the Duke of Buckingham*, pp.119–20.

28 Wilson, *A Rake and His Times*, p.139.

29 Sir E. Harley to Lady Harley, 11 March 1671, in Historical Manuscripts Commission, *Manuscripts of his Grace the Duke of Portland preserved at Welbeck Abbey* (London: H. M. Stationery Office), vol.3, p.322; Sir Dernard Gascon to Williamson, 9 January 1674, *Calendar of State Papers, Domestic, November 1673–February 1675* (London: H. M. Stationery Office, 1904), p.98.

30 Pepys, 23 November 1668.

5. THE DRAMA OF POLITICS

1 Villiers, *The Works of His Grace George Villiers*, vol.1, p.132.

2 Wilson, *Court Satires*, p.19n.

3 Vicomtesse de Longueville quoted in Chapman, *Great Villiers*, p.95.

4 George Villiers, *The Rehearsal*, ed. A. G. Barnes (London: Methuen & Co., 1927), pp.11–13.

5 Quoted in Wilson, *A Rake and His Times*, p.126.

6 Montague Summers, *The Restoration Theatre* (London: Kegan Paul, 1934), p.293.

7 For a full account of the rivalry between Buckingham and

Dryden, see John Harrington Smith, 'Dryden and Buckingham: The Beginnings of the Feud', *Modern Language Notes*, 69/4 (1954), pp.242–5.

8 John Dryden, *Absalom and Achitophel*, ed. W. D. Christie (Oxford: Clarendon, 1946), lines 547–54.

9 Pepys, 28 June 1667.

6. CONCEPTION

1 Ackroyd, *Thames*, p.167.
2 Ibid., p.125.
3 Evelyn, *Diary*, 23 July 1679.
4 Crathorne, *Cliveden*, p.12; David Jacques, 'Garden Design in the Mid-Seventeenth Century', *Architectural History*, 44 (2001), p.365.
5 Charles Saumarez-Smith, 'Supply and Demand in English Country House Building 1660–1740', *Oxford Art Journal*, 11/2 (1998), pp.3–9.
6 Frank T. Melton, 'A Rake Refinanced: The Fortunes of George Villiers, Second Duke of Buckingham, 1671–1685', in *Huntington Library Quarterly*, 51/4, pp.301–2.
7 Ibid., p.310.
8 Ibid., pp.300–1.
9 Dryden, *Absalom and Achitophel*, lines 561–2.
10 Hanrahan, *Charles II and the Duke of Buckingham*, p.131.
11 Ibid.
12 Melton, 'A Rake Refinanced', pp.304–5.
13 Ibid.

14 William A. Pettigrew, *Freedom's Debt: The Royal African Company and the Politics of the Atlantic Slave Trade 1672–1752* (Chapel Hill: University of North Carolina Press, 2012), p.23.

15 'Goodchild vs. Villiers', TNA, C4/419/78, 1684.

16 Chapman, *Great Villiers*, pp.190–1.

17 'Goodchild vs. Villiers', TNA, C4/419/78, 1684.

18 'Winde, William (?–1722)' in Howard Colvin, *A Biographical Dictionary of British Architects, 1600–1840* (London: John Murray, 1978), pp.902–5.

19 Parklands Consortium, *Cliveden: Landscape and Archeology Plan* (unpublished report), vol.1, p.33.

20 Evelyn, *Diary*, 23 July 1679.

21 'Signior Dildo', lines 45–48, in Wilson, *Court Satires*, p.15.

7. BETRAYALS

1 HMC, *Ninth Report*, Part II: Appendix and Index (London: H. M. Stationery Office, 1884), pp.35–6.

2 Crathorne, *Cliveden,* p.26.

3 W. D. Christie, ed., *Letters Addressed from London to Sir Joseph Williamson while plenipotentiary at the Congress of Cologne in the years 1673 and 1674* (London, 1874), vol.2, pp.105–6.

4 Hanrahan, *Charles II and the Duke of Buckingham*, p.158.

5 Quoted in Burghclere, *George Villiers*, p.295.

6 Quoted in Burghclere, *George Villiers*, pp.299–301.

7 HMC, *Ninth Report*, Part II: Appendix and Index, pp.36–7.

8. 'YOUR MOST UNHAPPY MOTHER'

1 Joan Wake, *The Brudenells of Deene* (London: Cassell, 1953), p.178.

2 Anna Maria to Charles, NR, Buccleuch Collection, no.45, vol.1, letter 9.

3 Ibid.

4 Wilson, *Court Satires*, p.29n.

5 Charles to John Talbot, 27 November 1674, NR Buccleuch, no.45, vol.1, letter 26.

6 Ibid.

7 Charles to John Talbot, 27 March 1675, NR Buccleuch, no.45, vol.1, letter 28.

8 Charles Talbot to John Talbot, undated, NR Buccleuch, letter 31.

9 Charles Talbot to John Talbot, 27 November 1674, NR Buccleuch, no.45, vol.1, letter 26.

10 Charles to John Talbot, 22 June 1675, NR Buccleuch, no.45, vol.1, letter 33.

11 'Colin', lines 64–75, in Wilson, *Court Satires*, p.25.

9. CONSTRUCTION

1 Fairfax, *Memoirs of the Life of George Villiers*, p.8.

2 Hanrahan, *Charles II and the Duke of Buckingham*, p.184.

3 'Goodchild vs. Villiers', TNA C6/419/78, 1684.

4 Parklands Consortium, *Cliveden: Landscape and Archeology Plan* (unpublished report), vol.1, p.38.

5 Christine MacLeod, *Inventing the Industrial Revolution: the English Patent System, 1600–1800*, (Cambridge: Cambridge University Press, 1988), p.26.

6 Buckingham to Charles II, undated, BL Add MS 27872, fol.34.

7 'Goodchild vs. Villiers', TNA C6/419/78, 1684.

8 Estate vouchers, receipts and accounts, NLW, Cwmgwili Collection, nos. 838–49.

9 George Villiers, *The Lost Mistress*, in Phipps, *Buckingham: Public and Private Man*, p.147.

10 'Goodchild vs. Villiers', TNA C6/419/78, 1684.

11 Ibid.

12 John Fletcher, *Gardens of Earthly Delight: The History of Deer Parks* (Oxford: Windgather, 2011), p.182.

13 *Cliveden Garden* (National Trust, 2002), p.3.

14 *Cliveden* (National Trust, 1984), pp.8–9; Evelyn, *Diary*, 23 July 1679.

15 Andrea Wulf and Emma Giemen-Gamal, *This Other Eden* (London: Little, Brown, 2005), p.18.

10. THE LOST MISTRESS

1 Alexander Pope, *The Works of Alexander Pope* (London: Gall & Ingliss, 1881), vol.3, p.153; see also Arthur Mizener, 'Pope on the

Duke of Buckingham', *Modern Language Notes*, 53/5 (1938), pp.368–9.

2　'Commonplace Book', in Phipps, *Buckingham: Public and Private Man*, p.204.

3　Melton, 'A Rake Refinanced', p.299.

4　Nicholas Cross, *The Cynosura, or, a saving star that leads to eternity* (London, 1670), BoL.

5　Albert H. Tricomi, 'Counting Insatiate Countesses: The Seventeenth-Century Annotations to Marston's "The Insatiate Countess"', *Huntingdon Library Quarterly*, 64 (2001).

6　Burghclere, *George Villiers*, p.151.

PART II

1. FROM RICHMOND TO 'ROYAL WHORE'

1　Hester W. Chapman, *Mary II: Queen of England* (London: Jonathan Cape, 1953), p.96.

2　Jonathan Swift, *The Works of Jonathan Swift* (Edinburgh: Archibald Constable & Co., 1814), vol.3, p.103.

3　Samuel Johnson and Alexander Chalmers, eds., *The Works of the English Poets* (London, 1810), vol.6, p.22.

4　See John Cloake, *Richmond Palace: Its History and Its Plan* (London: Richmond Local History Society, 2000).

5　John Van der Kiste, *William and Mary: Heroes of the Glorious Revolution* (Stroud: The History Press, 2008), p.33.

6　Molly McClain, 'Love, Friendship and Power: Queen Mary II's Letters to Frances Apsley', *Journal of British Studies*, 47 (2008), pp.505–27.

7　Elizabeth Hamilton, *William's Mary: A Biography of Mary II* (London: Hamish Hamilton, 1972), p.19; Anne Somerset, *Queen Anne: The Politics of Passion* (London: Harper Press, 2012), pp.16–17.

8　Frances Harris, *A Passion for Government: The Life of Sarah, Duchess of Marlborough* (Oxford: Clarendon Press, 1991), p.15.

9　Benjamin Bathurst, *Letters of Two Queens* (London, 1924), p.44, p.49, p.58, p.60.

10　Somerset, *Queen Anne*, p.27.

11　'Diary of Dr Edward Lake' in *The Camden Miscellany* (London: Camden Society, 1847), vol.1, p.5, 6, 8, 10.

12　Ibid., p.12.

13　Van der Kiste, *William and Mary*, p.51.

14　Andrew Marvell, quoted in Simon Schama, *The Embarrassment of Riches: An Interpretation of Dutch Culture in the Golden Age* (London: Fontana, 1988), p.263.

15　Hamilton, *William's Mary*, p.51.

16　Van der Kiste, *William and Mary*, pp.72–5.

17　Quoted in ibid., pp.74–5.

18　Hamilton, *William's Mary*, pp.155–8; Van der Kiste, *William and Mary*, pp.81–2.

19 Benjamin Bathurst, *Letters of Two Queens* (London: Robert Holden, 1924), p.51.

20 Quoted in Chapman, *Mary II*, pp.101–2.

21 David Onnekink, *The Anglo-Dutch Favourite: The Career of Hans William Bentinck, 1st Earl of Portland, 1649–1709* (Aldershot: Ashgate, 2007), p.23.

22 Hamilton, *William's Mary*, pp.156–8.

2. THE END OF THE AFFAIR

1 Gilbert Burnet, 'Ill Effects of Animosities among Protestants in England Detected', quoted in Tim Harris, *Revolution: The Great Crisis in the English Monarchy, 1685–1720* (London: Allen Lane, 2006), pp.249–50.

2 Quoted in Harris, *Revolution*, p.272.

3 Quoted in Lisa Jardine, *Going Dutch: How England Plundered Holland's Glory* (London: Harper Perennial, 2009), p.6.

4 Jardine, *Going Dutch*, p.11.

5 Huygens, quoted in ibid., p.11.

6 Robert Beddard, *A Kingdom without a King* (Oxford: Phaidon, 1988), p.19.

7 Jardine, *Going Dutch*, p.14.

8 Quoted in ibid., p.18.

9 Huygens, quoted in Jardine, *Going Dutch*, p.18.

10 Huygens, quoted in Jardine, *Going Dutch*, p.18.

11 Robert Beddard, *A Kingdom without a King*, p.180.

12 Rudolf Dekker, *Family, Culture and Society in the Diary of Constantijn Huygens Jr.* (Leiden; Boston: Brill, 2013), p.125.

13 Marion Sharpe Grew, *William Bentinck and William III* (London: John Murray, 1924), pp.142–3.

14 Onnekink, *The Anglo-Dutch Favourite*, pp.87–8; Harris, *A Passion for Government*, p.57; Hamilton, *William's Mary*, pp.264–5. See also *A Dialogue between K. W. and Benting* (1694/5).

15 Quoted in Leo Damrosch, *Jonathan Swift: His Life and His World* (New Haven; London: Yale University Press, 2013), pp.65–6.

16 Quoted in Dekker, *Family, Culture and Society in Huygens Jr.*, p.127.

17 Dekker, *Family, Culture and Society in Huygens Jr.*, p.122.

18 Van der Kiste, *William and Mary*, p.164.

19 W. Whiston, *Memoirs of the Life and Writings of Mr. William Whiston containing Memoirs of several of his Friends also* (London, 1749), pp.113–14.

20 See Van der Kiste, *William and Mary*, p.181.

3. FAVOURS

1 Quane, 'Midleton School, Co. Cork', *The Journal of the Royal Society of Antiquaries of Ireland*, 82/1 (1952), p.4.

2   William Cox, ed., *The Private and Original Correspondence of Charles Talbot, Duke of Shrewsbury* (London, 1821), p.5.

3   For the letters between Elizabeth Villiers and Charles Talbot, see Cox, *Correspondence of Charles Talbot,* pp.19–21.

4   Jonathan Swift, *Remarks on the Characters of the Court of Queen Anne,* in Swift, *Works,* vol.10, p.315.

5   Jennings Churchill, Sarah (Duchess of Marlborough), *The Private Correspondence of Sarah, Duchess of Marlborough* (London: Henry Colburn, 1838), vol.1, p.322.

6   'Manfield vs. Duchess of Buckingham,' TNA C 6/298/72.

7   Crathorne, *Cliveden,* p.34.

4. REBUILDING

1   Edward Gregg, *Queen Anne* (New Haven: Yale University Press, 2001), p.231.

2   Orkney to Selkirk, 19 November 1705, NLS MS 1033, fol.7.

3   Quane, 'Midleton School', pp.9–10.

4   Ibid.

5   Orkney to Selkirk, NLS MS 1033, fols.7–11.

6   Ibid.

7   Orkney to Selkirk, 11 January 1706, NLS MS 1033, fol.14.

8   Orkney to Selkirk, 19 November 1705; Orkney to Selkirk, 11 January 1706, NLS MS 1033, fols.7–14.

5. 'THIS PLACE IS TOO ENGAGING'

1   Lord Archibald Hamilton to Lord Selkirk, 24 August 1708, NLS MS 1033, fol.52.

2   Ibid.

3   Elizabeth to Jonathan Swift in Swift, *Works*, vol.2, p.484.

4   Elizabeth to Selkirk, 26 July 1708, NLS MS 1033, fol.46.

5   Elizabeth to Ruglen, 19 July, NLS MS 1033, fols.167–8.

6   Vic Gatrell, *City of Laughter: Sex and Satire in Eighteenth-Century London* (London: Atlantic Books, 2006), p.25

7   Elizabeth to Selkirk, 26 July 1708, NLS MS 1033, fols.45–6.

8   Richard Holmes, *Marlborough: Britain's Greatest General* (London: Harper Perennial, 2009), p.300.

9   Orkney to his brother, 11 January 1706, NLS MS 1033, fols.12–14.

10 Orkney to Marlborough, 4 August 1704, BL Add MS 61474, fols.111–12.

11 Maynwaring to Marlborough, Nov/Dec. 1708, in Jennings Churchill, *Correspondence of the Duchess of Marlborough*, p.160.

12 Maynwaring to Marlborough, in ibid., p.161.

13 Ibid.

14 Ibid.

15 BL Add MS 61474, fols.114–15.

16 Somerset, *Queen Anne*, pp.415–16.

17 Ibid., p.411.

18 Orkney to Harley, 10 July 1710, in HMC, *Report on the Manuscripts of His Grace the Duke of Portland*

(London: H. M. Stationery Office, 1899), vol.4, p.549.

19 The National Trust, *Cliveden, Buckinghamshire* (National Trust, 2001), p.14.

6. 'THE WISEST WOMAN I EVER SAW'

1   Joseph Spence, *Observations, Anecdotes, and Characters of Books and Men, Collected from Conversation*, ed. James M. Osborn (Oxford: Clarendon, 1966), vol.1, p.52, quoted in Damrosch, *Jonathan Swift*, pp.25–6.

2   Jonathan Swift, 'The Journal to Stella' in *The Works of Jonathan Swift*, vol.2 (Edinburgh: Archibald Constable & Co. 1814), 15 September 1712.

3   Swift to Mary Pendarves, 29 Jan. 1736, in David Woolley, ed., *The Correspondence of Jonathan Swift* (Oxford: Peter Lang, 1999), vol.4, p.257; Woolley, *Correspondence*, vol.4, p.258n.

4   Orkney to Lady Harriet Harley, HMC *Portland*, vol.5, p.463.

5   Swift, 'Journal to Stella', 26 April 1713.

6   Ibid., 28 October 1712.

7   Ibid., 21 March 1713.

8   Ibid., 15 November 1712.

9   Ibid., 15 November 1712.

10 Ibid., 28 October 1712.

11 Ibid., 30 October 1712.

12 Ibid., 12 December 1712.

13 Ibid., 25 January 1713; 15 February 1713.

14 Swift to Mary Pendarves, 29 Jan. 1736, in Woolley, *Correspondence*, vol.4, p.257.

15 Jonathan Swift, *Of the Education of Ladies*, quoted in Damrosch, *Jonathan Swift*, p.428.

16 Quoted in Quane, 'Midleton School'.

7. 'I HAVE TIRED MYSELF WITH FRIGHT'

1   Orkney, quoted in Holmes, *Marlborough*, p.339.

2   Holmes, *Marlborough*, p.340.

3   Quoted in James Falkner, *Ramillies 1706: Year of Miracles* (Barnsley: Pen & Sword Military, 2006), p.98.

4   Orkney to Selkirk, 1 August 1708, NLS MS 1033, fols.47–8.

5   Ibid.

6   Letter from the Duke of Marlborough to Sarah, Duchess of Marlborough, quoted in Holmes, *Marlborough*, p.277.

7   Orkney to his brother, 3 April 1707, NLS MS 1033, fols.21–2.

8   T. M. Devine, *Scotland's Empire 1600–1815* (London: Allen Lane, 2003), pp.44–8; Michael Fry, *The Scottish Empire* (Edinburgh: Birlinn, 2001), p.20.

9   Orkney to his brother, 11 October 1707, NLS MS 1033, fols.34–5; Orkney to Selkirk, 15 May 1710, NLS MS 1033, fols.77–8.

10 Orkney to Selkirk, 15 May 1710, NLS MS 1033, fols.7–8.

11 Orkney to Selkirk, 11 October 1707, NLS MS 1033, fols.34–5; Orkney to Selkirk, 15 May 1710, NLS MS 1033, fols.77–8.

12 John Loveday quoted in Sarah Markham, *John Loveday of Caversham 1711–1798* (Salisbury: Michael Russell, 1984), p.177.

13 Colen Campbell, *Vitruvius Britannicus* (New York: Dover Publications, 2007), p.4.

14 Quoted in Markham, *John Loveday*, p.178.

15 Daniel Defoe, *A Tour through the Whole Island of Great Britain and Ireland 1724–1726*, ed. Nikolaus Pevsner (London, 1927), quoted in Rosemary Baird, *The Mistress of the House: Great Ladies and Grand Houses* (London: Phoenix, 2004), p.65.

16 Baird, *Mistress of the House*, p.66.

17 Quoted in Somerset, *Queen Anne*, p.454.

18 Holmes, *Marlborough*, p.301.

8. THE GREEN REVOLUTION

1 Harris, *A Passion for Government*, p.70.

2 Orkney to Selkirk, 2 February 1706, NLS MS 1033, fols.15–16.

3 Orkney to Selkirk, 11 January 1706, NLS MS 1033, fol.14.

4 Alexander Pope, *The Works of Alexander Pope* (London, 1776), vol. 4, p.267.

5 Orkney to Selkirk, 5 December 1723, NLS MS 1033, fols.159–60. See also Gervase Jackson-Stops, 'Formal Garden Designs for Cliveden: the work of Claude Desgots and others for the 1st Earl of Orkney', in *The National Trust Year Book 1976–77*, ed.

Gervase Jackson-Stops (London: Europa Publications, 1976).

6 Alexander Pope, 'Letters to and from Mr. Digby – Letter XVI', in *The Works of Alexander Pope, Esq. in verse and prose* (London, 1806), vol.8, p.88.

7 Lord Ronald Sutherland Gower, *My Reminiscences* (Boston: Roberts Brothers, 1884), vol.1, p.19.

8 Alexander Pope to the Earl of Orkney, 4 September 1736, NoR Craster Family Collection ZCR Box 9.

9 Orkney to Selkirk, 2 October 1723, NLS MS 1033, fol.157.

10 Orkney to Selkirk, 5 December 1723, NLS MS 1033, fol.159.

11 See Gervase Jackson-Stops, 'The Cliveden Album: drawings by Archer, Leoni and Gibbs for the 1st Earl of Orkney', *Architectural History* 19 (1976).

12 David Watkin, *The Classical Country House: from the archives of Country Life* (London: Aurum Press, 2010), p.66.

9. 'IT WAS AS IF HIS MAJESTY HAD LIVED HERE'

1 Ragnhild Hatton, *George I* (Yale University Press, 1978), p.205; J. M. Beattie, *The English Court in the Reign of George I* (Cambridge University Press, 1967), p.266.

2 HMC, *Portland*, vol.5, p.572.

3 Beattie, *The English Court in the Reign of George I*, p.275.

4 *Letters to and from Henrietta, Countess of Suffolk and her Second*

Husband, the Hon. George Berkeley (London: John Murray, 1824), vol.1, pp.350–2.

5 Quoted in Veronica Baker-Smith, *Royal Discord: The Family of George II* (London: Athena Press, 2008), p.21.

6 *Letters to and from Henrietta and her Second Husband*, vol.1, pp.350–2.

7 Ibid., vol.1, pp.350–2.

8 Baker-Smith, *Royal Discord*, p.51.

9 *Letters to and from Henrietta and her Second Husband*, vol.1, pp.350–2.

10. 'THE SHOCK IS GREATER THAN I EVER HAD IN MY LIFE'

1 Lawrence Stone, *The Family, Sex and Marriage in England, 1500–1800* (London: Penguin, 1979), p.57.

2 Lady Mary Wortley Montagu to Lady Mar, October 1727, in Robert Halsband, ed., *The Complete Letters of Lady Mary Wortley Montagu*, 3 vols. (Oxford: Clarendon, 1965), vol.2, p.85.

3 Elizabeth to John Boyle, 10 September 1732, BL R.P. 1109 Box 20 941D.

4 Ibid.

5 Orkney to John Boyle, 10 September 1732, BL R. P. 1109 Box 20 941D.

6 Sarah, Duchess of Marlborough to Somerset, 3 October 1723, DR Seymour MSS L18, 23/28, quoted in Harris, *A Passion for Government*, p.224.

7 Orkney to John Boyle, 10 September 1732, BL R. P. 1109 Box 20 941D.

PART III

1. 'RULE, BRITANNIA!'

1 Letter from Martin Madan to Judith Madan, quoted in Oliver J. W. Cox, 'Frederick, Prince of Wales, and the First Performance of "Rule, Britannia!"', *The Historical Journal*, 56/4 (2013), pp.931–3.

2 Simon Schama, *A History of Britain: The British Wars 1603–1776* (London: The Bodley Head, 2009), p.318.

3 See Schama, *A History of Britain*, vol.2, pp.318–19.

4 See Cox, 'Frederick and "Rule, Britannia!"', pp.931–3.

5 Alan D. McKillop, 'The Early History of "Alfred"', *Philological Quarterly*, 41/1 (1962), pp.311–12.

6 *Gloucester Journal*, 5 August 1729.

7 Household accounts of Frederick, Prince of Wales, referenced in Frances Vivian, *A Life of Frederick Prince of Wales* (Lewiston, NY: Edwin Mellen Press, 2006), p.271; *London Evening Post*, 29 September 1737; *London Evening Post*, 25 October 1737; see also George Lyttelton to the Duchess of Marlborough, 18 September 1737, BL Add MS 61467, fol.14.

8 Quoted in Cox, 'Frederick and "Rule Britannia!"'.

9   Percy A. Scholes, *The Oxford Companion to Music* (London: Oxford University Press, 1960), p.62.

10   *General Evening Post*, 31 July–2 August 1740.

11   Quoted in Sarah McCleave, *Dance in Handel's London Operas* (University of Rochester Press, 2013), p.116.

12   *London Evening Post*, 7 August 1740.

13   *London Daily Post and General Advertiser*, 5 August 1740.

14   Patricia Fara, 'Desaguliers, John Theophilus (1683–1744)', *Oxford Dictionary of National Biography* (Oxford University Press, 2004; online edn., May 2009).

15   *London Evening Post*, 7 August 1740.

2. RISE

1   Quoted in Lucy Worsley, *Courtiers: The Secret History of the Georgian Court* (London: Faber and Faber, 2010), p.196.

2   Quoted in Baker-Smith, *Royal Discord*, p.82.

3   See Andrew C. Thompson, *George II: King and Elector* (New Haven and London: Yale University Press, 2011), p.113.

4   Frances Vivian, *A Life of Frederick, Prince of Wales, 1707–1751: A Connoisseur of the Arts* (Lewiston, NY: Edwin Mellen Press, 2006).

5   Lady A. Irwin to Lord Carlisle, April 1736, HMC, *Fifteenth Report, Appendix*, Part VI: Manuscripts of the Earl of Carlisle (Norwich: H.M. Stationery Office, 1899), p.167.

6   John Walters, *The Royal Griffin: Frederick, Prince of Wales, 1707–51* (London: Jarrolds, 1972), p.113.

7   Lord Hervey, quoted in Worsley, *Courtiers*, p.189.

8   Quoted in Christopher Hibbert, *George III: A Personal History* (New York: Basic Books, 1998), p.3.

9   Hibbert, *George III*, p.3.

10   Quoted in Worsley, *Courtiers*, p.201.

11   Horace Walpole, *Memoirs of George II*, ed. John Brooke (New Haven: Yale University Press, 1985), vol.1, p.54.

12   Lord John Hervey, *Some Materials towards Memoirs of the Reign of George II*, ed. Romney Sedgwick (London: Eyre & Spottiswoode, 1931), vol.2, p.628.

13   Walpole, *Memoirs of George II*, vol.2, p.53.

14   Quoted in Walters, *The Royal Griffin*, p.113.

15   *St. James's Weekly Journal*, 31 October 1719.

16   Uriel Heyd, *Reading Newspapers: Press and Public in Eighteenth-Century Britain and America* (Oxford: Voltaire Foundation, 2012), p.95.

17   Quoted in Jeremy Black, *The English Press in the Eighteenth Century* (London: Croom Helm, 1987), p.116.

18   Black, *English Press*, p.148.

19 Ann C. Dean, 'Court Culture and Political News in London's Eighteenth-Century Newspapers', *English Literary History* 73/3 (2006), p.631.

20 Quoted in ibid., p.643.

21 *London Evening Post*, 24–7 April 1736.

22 *Grub Street Journal*, 29 April 1736.

23 *London Evening Post*, 24–7 April 1736.

24 Ibid.

25 Ibid., 27–9 April 1736.

26 *Grub Street Journal*, 29 April 1736.

27 Quoted in Hannah Smith, *Georgian Monarchy: Politics and Culture* (Cambridge: Cambridge University Press, 2006), p.118.

3. 'A PROFUSION OF FINERY'

1 The following account of the wedding is based on a report in the *London Evening Post*, 27–9 April 1736.

2 Thompson, *George II*, p.116.

3 Lord John Hervey, *Memoirs of the Reign of George the Second from his Accession to the Death of Queen Caroline*, ed. J. W. Croker (London: John Murray, 1848), vol.2, pp.114–15; Thompson, *George II*, p.116.

4 R. A. Roberts, ed., *Diary of Viscount Percival, afterwards first earl of Egmont* (London: H. M. Stationery Office, 3 vols., 1920–3), vol.2, p.264.

5 *London Evening Post*, 27–9 April 1736.

6 Ibid.

7 Ibid.

8 Thompson, *George II*, p.117.

9 Roberts, *Egmont Diary*, vol.2, pp.263–4.

10 Walters, *The Royal Griffin*, p.125.

11 Ibid., pp.114–15; Hervey, ed. Croker, vol.2, pp.302–5.

12 *London Evening Post*, 27–9 April 1736.

13 Nigel Arch and Joanna Marschner, *Splendour at Court: Dressing for Royal Occasions since 1700* (London: Unwin Hyman, 1987), p.37.

14 Ibid., p.40.

15 Ibid., p.41.

16 *London Evening Post*, 27–9 April 1736.

17 Ibid., 11 November 1738; Christine Gerrard, 'Queens-in-waiting: Caroline of Anspach and Augusta of Saxe-Gotha as Princesses of Wales', in Clarissa Campbell Orr, ed., *Queenship in Britain 1660–1837* (Manchester University Press, 2002), p.156.

4. A HANOVERIAN SOAP OPERA

1 Hervey, ed. Sedgwick, vol.2, p.556.

2 Ibid., pp.302–5.

3 Ibid.

4 Hervey, ed. Sedgwick, vol.3, p.757.

5 HMC, *Manuscripts of the Earl of Egmont: Diary of the 1st Earl of Egmont* (London: H. M. Stationery Office, 1923), vol.2, p.360.

6 Hervey, ed. Sedgwick, vol.3, p.758.

7   Ibid., p.758.

8   Ibid., p.759.

9   Ibid., p.761; ibid., p.763

10 Hervey, ed. Croker, vol.3, p.192.

11 Hervey, ed. Sedgwick,
    vol.3, p.820.

12 Hervey, ed. Croker, vol.3, p.286.

13 Walpole, *Memoirs of George II*,
    vol. 1, p.53.

14 *Read's Weekly Journal or British
    Gazetteer*, 6 August 1737.

15 Correspondence printed in *Letters
    in the Original, with
    Translations . . . That passed
    between the King, Queen, Prince,
    and Princess of Wales; on Occasion
    of the Birth of the Young Princess*
    (London, 1737), pp.23–30.

16 Ibid.

17 Ibid.

18 Ibid.

19 BL Stowe 308, fol.5, quoted in
    Smith, *Georgian Monarchy*, p.205.

20 Chesterfield, quoted in Arch and
    Marschner, *Splendour at
    Court*, p.35.

21 Worsley, *Courtiers*, p.226.

22 Hervey, ed. Sedgwick,
    vol.3, p.850.

23 Ibid., vol.3, p.268.

24 Ibid.

25 *Daily Gazetteer*, 7 June 1736.

26 See, for example, *Read's Weekly
    Journal or British Gazetteer*, 8 July
    1738; *Daily Post*, 21 June 1742.

5. THE QUEEN IS DEAD, LONG
LIVE THE QUEEN

1   Thompson, *George II*, p.122.

2   Hervey, ed. Croker, vol.3, p.299.

3   Ibid., vol.3, p.298.

4   Thompson, *George II*, p.123;
    Hervey, ed. Croker, vol.3, p.309.

5   Hervey, ed. Croker, vol.3, p.303.

6   Ibid., vol.3, p.308.

7   Hervey, ed. Sedgwick, vol.3, p.896.

8   Quoted in Thompson, *George II*,
    p.124.

9   Roberts, *Egmont Diary*, pp.458–9.

10 Quoted in Walters, *The Royal
    Griffin*, p.171.

11 Paul S. Fritz, 'The Trade in
    Death: the Royal Funerals in
    England, 1685–1830', *Eighteenth
    Century Studies*, 15:3 (1982), p.310.

12 Vivian, *A Life*, p.304.

13 *London Evening Post*, 25 October
    1737; *London Evening Post*,
    28 January 1738.

14 *London Evening Post*, 25 March
    1738.

15 *Read's Weekly Journal or British
    Gazetteer*, 22 July 1738.

16 *Common Sense or The
    Englishman's Journal*, 5 August
    1738.

17 Quoted in Worsley,
    Courtiers, p.306.

18 Vivian, *A Life*, p.316.

19 Ibid.

20 Lady Mary Wortley Montagu to
    Sarah Chiswell, *Letters of Lady
    Mary Wortley Montague, written
    during her travels in Europe, Asia
    and Africa* (Paris, 1822), pp.109–10.

21 Donald R. Hopkins, *The Greatest
    Killer: Smallpox in History*
    (University of Chicago Press,
    1983), pp.47–50

22 Veronica Baker-Smith, *Royal
    Discord: The Family of George II*
    (London: Athena Press,
    2008), p.129.

6. THE CHARMS OF SYLVIA

1 Frederick, Prince of Wales, 'The Charms of Sylvia', in Walpole, *Memoirs of George II*, vol.3, p.145; quoted in John L. Bullion, '"George, Be a King!": The Relationship between Princess Augusta and George III', in Stephen Taylor, ed., *Hanoverian Britain and Empire* (Woodbridge: The Boydell Press, 1998), p.180.

2 Vivian, *A Life*, p.308.

3 Ibid., p.307.

4 Ibid., p.323.

5 Walters, *The Royal Griffin*, pp.206–7.

6 David Coombs, 'The Garden at Carlton House of Frederick Prince of Wales and Augusta Princess Dowager of Wales. Bills in Their Household Accounts 1728 to 1772', *Garden History*, 25/2 (1997), pp.158–9.

7 Ibid., p.153.

8 Vivian, *A Life*, pp.271–2.

9 *Cliveden, Buckinghamshire* (National Trust, 1998), p.18.

10 Vivian, *A Life*, pp.271–2.

11 Kimerly Rorschach, 'Frederick, Prince of Wales (1701–51), As Collector and Patron', *The Volume of the Walpole Society*, 55 (1989/1990), p.34.

12 *London Evening Post*, 5 May 1743.

13 Ibid., 16 September 1740.

14 *London Daily Post and General Advertiser*, Tuesday 29 November 1743.

15 Vivian, *A Life*, p.318.

16 Ibid., p.320.

17 *The Diary of George Bubb Dodington* (London, 1828), 12 November 1749.

18 Quoted in Worsley, *Courtiers*, p.306.

19 Aubrey N. Newman, ed., 'Leicester House Politics, 1750–60, from the papers of John, Second Earl of Egmont', in *Camden Miscellany*, 23/7 (London: Royal Historical Society, 1969), p.195.

20 Walpole, *Memoirs of George II*, vol.1, p.50.

21 Quoted in Worsley, *Courtiers*, p.307.

22 Thompson, *George II*, p.208.

23 Ibid.

7. FALL

1 Walpole, *Memoirs of George II*, vol.1, pp.54–5.

2 Newman, 'Leicester House Politics', pp.198–9.

3 Walpole, *Memoirs of George II*, vol.1, pp.54–5.

4 Ibid., vol.1, p.55.

5 John Bullion, 'Augusta, Princess of Wales (1719–1772)', *Oxford Dictionary of National Biography* (Oxford: Oxford University Press, 2004; online edn, May 2009).

6 *Read's Weekly Journal or British Gazetteer*, 27 April 1751.

7 Walpole, *Memoirs of George II*, vol.2, pp.150–1.

8 Bullion, 'Augusta'.

9 'Vice triumphant over virtue, or Britannia hard rode', 1 August 1771, British Museum Satires 4877.

10 'The excursion to Cain Wood', 1771, British Museum Satires 4885.

11 Bullion, 'Augusta'.

12 Quoted in ibid.

13 *Daily Advertiser*, Tuesday 11 February 1772.

8. 'A SITE OF RUIN'

1 Edward Gibbon, *My Journal*, ed. D. M. Low (London: Chatto & Windus, 1929), pp.61–2.

2 *General Advertiser*, 3 October 1749.

3 *Gazetteer and New Daily Advertiser*, Thursday 3 October 1765.

4 *St. James's Chronicle or the British Evening Post*, 16–18 August 1764.

5 *London Evening Post*, 21–4 February 1778.

6 *St. James's Chronicle or the British Evening Post*, 16–19 May 1778.

7 *London Packet or New Lloyd's Evening Post*, 24–6 July 1780.

8 *The Gentleman's Magazine*, 102:1 (1832), p.79.

9 *St. James's Chronicle or the British Evening Post*, 9–11 September 1779.

10 Nigel Aston, 'Petty and Fitzmaurice: Lord Shelburne and his brother', in Nigel Aston and Clarissa Campbell Orr, ed., *An Enlightenment Statesman in Whig Britain* (Woodbridge: The Boydell Press, 2011), pp.40–1.

11 *Lloyd's Evening Post*, 22–5 May 1795.

12 Ibid.

13 *Star*, Saturday 23 May 1795.

14 *Lloyd's Evening Post*, 22–5 May 1795.

15 Emily J. Climenson, ed., *Passages from the Diaries of Mrs. Philip Lybbe Powys* (London: Longmans, Green and Co., 1899), pp.284–5.

16 Crathorne, *Cliveden*, p.71.

17 Ibid.

18 Charles Knight, *Passages of a Working Life during Half a Century: with a Prelude of Early Reminiscences*, 3 vols. (London: Bradbury and Evans, 1864–5), vol.1, pp.91–2.

PART IV

1. 'GOODBYE, CASTLE HOWARD!'

1 Walpole and Macaulay both quoted in Pevsner, *Yorkshire: The North Riding* (London: Penguin, 1966), pp.112–13.

2 Quoted in Maud Leconfield and John Gore, eds., *Three Howard Sisters: Selections from the writings of Lady Caroline Lascelles, Lady Dover and Countess Gower 1825–1833* (London: John Murray, 1955), p.3.

3 Georgiana, quoted in ibid., p.14.

4 See Leconfield, *Three Howard Sisters*, p.38.

5 Leconfield, *Three Howard Sisters*, p.39.

6 Lady Cavendish, quoted in Leconfield, *Three Howard Sisters*, pp.15–16.

7 Peter Mandler, *Aristocratic Government in the Age of Reform:*

Whigs and Liberals, 1830–1852 (Oxford: Clarendon Press, 1990), p.52.

8 Leconfield and Gore, *Three Howard Sisters*, pp.18–30.

9 George, quoted in Leconfield, *Three Howard Sisters*, p.21.

10 Lady Granville, quoted in Leconfield, *Three Howard Sisters*, p.31.

11 Ibid.

12 *Morning Post*, Thursday 29 May 1823.

13 *Hampshire Chronicle*, Monday 12 May 1823.

14 *Caledonian Mercury*, Saturday 14 June 1823.

15 Ibid.

16 *York Herald*, Saturday 31 May 1823.

2. REFORM AND REVOLUTION

1 Lady Granville, quoted in Leconfield and Gore, *Three Howard Sisters*, p.33.

2 Quoted in Leconfield, *Three Howard Sisters*, p.33.

3 Quoted in Leconfield, *Three Howard Sisters*, pp.34–5, p.37.

4 Quoted in Leconfield, *Three Howard Sisters*, pp.41–2.

5 Quoted in Leconfield, *Three Howard Sisters*, p.43.

6 Quoted in Leconfield, *Three Howard Sisters*, p.47.

7 Quoted in Leconfield, *Three Howard Sisters*, p.68, p.186.

8 Quoted in Leconfield, *Three Howard Sisters*, p.80.

9 Quoted in Leconfield, *Three Howard Sisters*, p.80, p.81.

10 Quoted in Leconfield, *Three Howard Sisters*, pp.130–1.

11 W. D. Rubenstein, *Britain's Century: A Political and Social History* (London: Arnold, 1998), p.31.

12 Quoted in Leconfield, *Three Howard Sisters*, p.150, p.152.

13 Ibid., p.143.

14 The following is summarised from a report in the *Spectator*, 18 September 1830.

15 *Spectator*, 18 September 1830.

3. FEAR IN A TIME OF CHOLERA

1 Harriet, quoted in Leconfield, *Three Howard Sisters*, p.157.

2 Harriet, quoted in Leconfield, *Three Howard Sisters*, p.171.

3 Rubenstein, *Britain's Century*, p.32.

4 Harriet, 7 November 1830, quoted in Leconfield, *Three Howard Sisters*, p.156.

5 Harriet, 6 March 1831, quoted in Leconfield, *Three Howard Sisters*, p.191.

6 Harriet, quoted in Leconfield, *Three Howard Sisters*, pp.212–13.

7 Harriet, quoted in Leconfield, *Three Howard Sisters*, pp.212–13.

8 Harriet, 15 November 1830, quoted in Leconfield, *Three Howard Sisters*, p.161.

9 Harriet, 17 November 1831, quoted in Leconfield, *Three Howard Sisters*, p.216.

10 Harriet, 10 August 1830, quoted in Leconfield, *Three Howard Sisters*, pp.135–6.

11 Harriet, 4 January 1832, quoted in Leconfield, *Three Howard Sisters*, p.233.

4. NORTH AND SOUTH

1   Harriet, 26 July 1832, quoted in Leconfield, *Three Howard Sisters*, p.235.
2   Harriet, quoted in Leconfield, *Three Howard Sisters*, p.236.
3   Christopher Hamlin, *Cholera: the biography* (Oxford University Press, 2009), p.158.
4   For the Highland clearances, see Eric Richards, *The Highland Clearances: people, landlords and rural turmoil* (Edinburgh: Birlinn, 2000); Eric Richards, *A History of the Highland Clearances: agrarian transformation and the evictions 1746–1886* (London: Croom Helm, 1982).
5   See R. W. Chapman, ed., *Johnson's Journey to the Western Isles of Scotland and Boswell's Journal of a Tour to the Hebrides with Samuel Johnson* (Oxford, 1924).
6   Quoted in Richards, *The Highland Clearances*, p.151.
7   Harriet, 18 Mary 1825, quoted in Leconfield, *Three Howard Sisters*, p.44.
8   Harriet, quoted in Leconfield, *Three Howard Sisters*, p.238.
9   Harriet, quoted in Leconfield, *Three Howard Sisters*, p.239.
10 Harriet, quoted in Leconfield, *Three Howard Sisters*, p.238.
11 Harriet, quoted in Leconfield, *Three Howard Sisters*, pp.240–3.

12 Jessica Rutherford, *A Prince's Passion: The Life of the Royal Pavilion* (Brighton: The Royal Pavilion, 2003), p.12.
13 Georgiana, 7 January 1833, quoted in Leconfield, *Three Howard Sisters*, p.250.
14 Harriet, 7 January 1833, quoted in Leconfield, *Three Howard Sisters*, p.261.
15 Georgiana, 11 January 1833, quoted in Leconfield, *Three Howard Sisters*, p.263.
16 Harriet, 7–8 January 1833, quoted in Leconfield, *Three Howard Sisters*, p.271.
17 Greville, quoted in Eric Richards, *The Leviathan of Wealth: The Sutherland Fortune in the Industrial Revolution* (London: Routledge & Kegan Paul, 1973), p.12.
18 Quoted in Leconfield, *Three Howard Sisters*, pp.279–80.

5. 'A LEVIATHAN OF WEALTH'

1   Ben Weinrib et al., *The London Encyclopedia* (London: Macmillan, 2008), p.473.
2   *Journals of Queen Victoria*, Friday 9 February 1838 [Lord Esher's typescripts, vol.4, pp.92–4] (accessed online at www.queenvictoriasjournals.org).
3   Quoted in Leconfield, *Three Howard Sisters*, pp.282–3.
4   Quoted in Leconfield, *Three Howard Sisters*, p.203.
5   *Spectator*, 23 August 1834.
6   Arthur Irwin Dasent, *The Story of Stafford House, Now the London*

Museum (London: John Murray, 1921), p.38.

7   Quoted in Leconfield, *Three Howard Sisters*, p.282.

8   George to his mother, quoted in Dasent, *The Story of Stafford House*, pp.41–2.

9   Quoted in Jeremy Paxman, *The Victorians: Britain Through the Paintings of the Age* (London: BBC Books, 2010), p.146.

10 Lawrence Stone, *The Road to Divorce: England 1530–1987* (Oxford: Clarendon, 1990), p.363.

11 Caroline Norton, *The Dream, and Other Poems* (London: Henry Colburn,1840).

12 Diane Atkinson, *The Criminal Conversation of Mrs Norton* (London: Preface, 2012), pp.300–1.

13 *Journals of Queen Victoria*, 1 July 1836; 9 July 1836; 27 April 1837.

14 Ibid., Monday 26 June 1837 [Lord Esher's typescripts, vol.3, p.72].

15 K. D. Reynolds, *Aristocratic Women and Political Society in Victorian Britain* (Oxford: Clarendon Press, 1998), pp.205–7.

16 Quoted in Stanley Weintraub, *Victoria* (London: John Murray, 1996), p.123.

17 Helen Rappaport, *Queen Victoria: A biographical companion* (Oxford: ABC-Clio, 2001), p.247.

18 *Journals of Queen Victoria*, 23 December 1837.

19 Ibid., 18 August 1839.

20 Ibid., Thursday 26 December 1839 [Lord Esher's typescripts, vol.13, pp.182–3].

6. CRISIS IN THE BEDCHAMBER

1   *Journals of Queen Victoria*, Tuesday 7 May 1839 [Lord Esher's typescripts, vol.10, p.164].

2   Ibid., Wednesday 8 May 1839 [Lord Esher's typescripts, vol.10, p.179].

3   K. Clark, *Peel and the Conservative Party, 1832–1841* (London: Frank Cass & Co., 1964), p.21; R. Livingstone Schuyler, 'The Life and Personality of Benjamin Disraeli. Review', *Political Science Quarterly* (1953): 295; D. Thompson, *Queen Victoria. Gender and Power* (London: Virago, 1990), p.30.

4   *Journals of Queen Victoria*, Thursday 9 May 1839 [Lord Esher's typescripts, vol.10, p.183].

5   John Doyle, 'Taking of Chusan', NMM HB Sketches No. 667.

6   Elizabeth Longford, *Victoria R. I.* (London: Pan, 1983), p.114.

7   R. F. Spall, 'The Bedchamber Crisis and the Hastings Scandal: Moral Politics and the Press at the Beginning of Victoria's Reign', *Canadian Journal of History*, 22/1 (1987), p.27.

8   Ibid., pp.37–8.

9   *Journals of Queen Victoria*, Wednesday 19 June 1839 [Lord Esher's typescripts, vol.11, p.75].

10 Ibid., Thursday 22 August 1839 [Lord Esher's typescripts, vol.12, p.70].

11 Ibid., Friday 11 October 1839 [Lord Esher's typescripts, vol.12, p.275].

12 Ibid., Saturday 28 August
    1841 [Princess Beatrice's copies,
    vol.12, p.115].

13 Ibid., Thursday 2 July
    1846 [Princess Beatrice's copies,
    vol.22, p.3].

14 Ibid., Sunday 20 May
    1849 [Princess Beatrice's copies,
    vol.27, p.180].

7. A MARRIAGE,
A DEATH AND A BLAZE

1   BR D92 18–33.

2   Gower, *My Reminiscences*,
    vol.1, p.11.

3   'An Inventory of the Effects of
    Cliefden House, Maidenhead,
    Berkshire', BR.

8. A RESURRECTION

1   Gower, *My Reminiscences*,
    vol.1, p.38.

2   Ibid., vol.1, p.29.

3   Ibid., vol.1, p.13.

4   Ibid.

5   Charles Barry to Harriet, 12 June
    1850, SR D593/P/20.

6   Cliveden Guest Books, BR D158/3.

7   Pamela Sambrook, *The Country
    House Servant* (Stroud: Sutton,
    1999), p.193.

8   Cliveden Inventory, SR
    D6578/14/11.

9   Richards, *Leviathan of
    Wealth*, p.293.

10 *Reading Mercury*, Saturday 31 July
    1858, p.4.

11 Jeffrey A. Auerbach, *The Great
    Exhibition of 1851: A Nation on
    Display* (New Haven: Yale
    University Press, 1999), p.9.

12 Labouchere, quoted in Auerbach,
    The Great Exhibition, p.26.

13 *Journals of Queen Victoria*,
    Thursday 21 February
    1850 [Princess Beatrice's copies,
    vol.29, pp.52–3].

14 *The Times*, 22 February 1850.

15 Auerbach, *The Great
    Exhibition*, p.66.

16 Ibid., p.60.

17 John Tallis, *Tallis's History and
    Description of the Crystal Palace*
    (London, 1851), vol.1, p.207.

18 Gower, *My Reminiscences*,
    vol.1, p.102.

9. 'THOU HYPOCRITE'

1   *The Standard*, Monday
    29 November 1852.

2   Ibid.; also in *The Times* of that date.

3   Evelyn L. Pugh, 'Women and
    Slavery: Julia Gardiner Tyler and
    the Duchess of Sutherland', *The
    Virginia Magazine of History and
    Biography*, 88/2 (1980), p.188.

4   Pugh, 'Women and
    Slavery', p.188.

5   Elizabeth Cady Stanton, *Eighty
    Years and More* (reprint of
    1898 edition, New York,
    1971), p.87, referenced in Pugh,
    'Women and Slavery', p.188;
    Reynolds, *Aristocratic
    Women*, p.122.

6   Pugh, 'Women and
    Slavery', p.186.

7   Quoted in David Herbert
    Donald, *Charles Sumner and the
    Coming of the American Civil War*
    (New York: Alfred A. Knopf,
    1994), p.69.

8 Joan D. Hedrick, *Harriet Beecher Stowe: A Life* (Oxford: Oxford University Press, 1994), p.245.

9 George Shepperson, 'Harriet Beecher Stowe in Scotland, 1852–3', *The Scottish Historical Review*, 32/113 (1953), pp.40–6.

10 Harriet Beecher Stowe, *A Reply to 'The Affectionate and Christian address of many thousands of women of Great Britain and Ireland, to their sisters, the women of the United States of America'* (London: Sampson Low, 1863), p.4.

11 'The Lady Abolitionists', *Spectator* XXV (4 December 1852).

12 *The Times*, 1 December 1852, p.8.

13 Pugh, 'Women and Slavery', p.191.

14 Ibid., p.192.

15 Quoted in ibid., p.194.

16 Quoted in Pugh, 'Women and Slavery', p.194.

17 *Boston Post* and *Richmond Dispatch* quoted in Pugh, 'Women and Slavery', p.196.

18 *Journals of Queen Victoria*, Tuesday 20 April 1854 [Princess Beatrice's copies, vol.37, pp.186–7].

10. 'WHAT A HOLD A PLACE HAS UPON ONE'

1 Duke of Sutherland to James Loch, quoted in Crathorne, *Cliveden*, p.96.

2 *Journals of Queen Victoria*, Friday 16 August 1839 [Lord Esher's typescripts, vol.12, pp.41–2].

3 Ibid., Saturday 3 April 1858 [Princess Beatrice's copies, vol.45, pp.138–9].

4 Lord Ronald Sutherland Gower, *Joan of Arc* (London, 1893).

5 Gower, *My Reminiscences*, vol.1, pp.20–3.

6 *Journals of Queen Victoria*, Saturday 3 April 1858 [Princess Beatrice's copies, vol.45, pp.138–9].

7 Translation from Crathorne, *Cliveden*, p.105.

8 Quoted in H. C. G. Matthew, *Gladstone, 1809–74* (Oxford: Clarendon Press, 1986), p.95.

9 M. R. D. Foot and H. C. G. Matthew, eds., *The Gladstone Diaries*, 22 April 1849 (Oxford: Clarendon Press, 1974), vol.4, p.117; 'out at all hours . . . path of danger' quoted in Richard Aldous, *The Lion and the Unicorn: Gladstone vs. Disraeli* (London: Pimlico, 2007), p.53.

10 Foot and Matthew, *Gladstone Diaries*, 13 May 1848, vol.4, pp.35–6.

11 Roy Jenkins, *Gladstone* (London: Pan, 2002), p.102.

12 See Gladstone's Diaries, 4–5/6/57; 4–6/7/57; 4–6/6/59; 13–14/8/59.

13 Gladstone's Diaries: 4/6/59; 13/8/59.

14 B. Coleman, '1841–46', in *How Tory Governments Fall: the Tory party in power since 1783* (London: Fontana, 1996), pp.135–6.

15 Jenkins, *Gladstone*, p.204.

16 Quoted in Jenkins, *Gladstone*, p.228.

17 Sutherland to Gladstone, BL Add MS 44325, fols.33–4.

18 Sutherland to Gladstone, BL Add MS 44325, fol.66.

19 *Journals of Queen Victoria*, Wednesday 27 February 1861 [Princess Beatrice's copies, vol.50, p.45].

20 Sutherland to Gladstone, BL Add MS 44325, fols.84–8.

21 Sutherland to Gladstone, BL Add MS 44325, fols.237–8.

22 Ronald Gower, quoted in Crathorne, *Cliveden*, p.97.

23 *Journals of Queen Victoria*, Monday 6 May 1861 [Princess Beatrice's copies, vol.50, pp.118–19].

I I. AN INDEPENDENT WIDOW

1 Sutherland to Gladstone, 16 April 1861, BL Add MS 44325, fol.105.

2 Cliveden Guest Books, BR D158/3.

3 Sutherland to Gladstone, 5 May 1861, BL Add MS 44325, fol.119.

4 Sutherland to Gladstone, 25 May 1861, BL Add MS 44325, fol.137.

5 Sutherland to Gladstone, 8 July 1861, BL Add MS 44325, fol.172.

6 Sutherland to Gladstone, 11 July 1861, BL Add MS 44325, fol.177.

7 Sutherland to Gladstone, 20 July 1861, BL Add MS 44325, fol.179.

8 Sutherland to Gladstone, BL Add MS 44325, fol.221.

9 Quoted in Christopher Hibbert, ed., *Queen Victoria in her Letters and Journals* (London: Murray, 1984), p.156.

10 Sutherland to Gladstone, 17 December 1861, BL Add MS 44325, fols.266–73.

11 Sutherland to Gladstone, BL Add MS 44325, fol.24.

12 Sutherland to Gladstone, 3 March 1862, BL Add MS 44326, fols.68–9.

13 Gladstone, *Diary*, Monday 5 May 1862.

14 Ibid., 2–5 May 1862.

15 See, for instance, Gladstone, *Diary*, 14 January 1862 and 20 January 1862.

16 Sutherland to Gladstone, 3 April [1862], BL Add MS 44326, fols.90–91.

17 Sutherland to Gladstone, BL Add MS 44326, fols.88–9; 90–1; 109–10.

18 Sutherland to Gladstone, BL Add MS 44326, fols.44–5.

19 Aldous, *The Lion and the Unicorn*, pp.137–8.

I 2. GARIBALDI-MANIA

1 Sutherland to Gladstone, 13 March 1864, BL Add MS 44328, fol.15.

2 Sutherland to Gladstone, BL Add MS 44325, fols.33–4.

3 D. M. Schreuder, 'Gladstone and Italian Unification, 1848–70: the Making of a Liberal?', *English Historical Review,* 85/366 (1970), p.478.

4 Sutherland to Gladstone, BL Add MS 44324, fol.91.

5 Sutherland to Gladstone, BL Add MS 44324, fol.96.

6   Lucy Riall, *Garibaldi: Invention of a Hero* (Yale University Press, 2007), pp.330–442.

7   Quoted in Riall, *Garibaldi*, pp.330–1.

8   Maura O'Connor, *The Romance of Italy and the English Political Imagination* (New York: St. Martin's Press, 1988), p.172.

9   Earl of Malmesbury, *Memoirs of an Ex-Minister* (London, 1885), pp.593–4.

10 *The Economist*, 26 June 1886, quoted in Ruth Dudley Edwards, *The Pursuit of Reason: 'The Economist' 1843–1993* (London: Hamish Hamilton, 1993), p.378.

11 *Norfolk Chronicle*, Saturday 30 April 1864.

12 *Leeds Mercury*, Monday 25 April 1864.

13 Quoted in Riall, *Garibaldi*, p.340.

14 Quoted in Riall, *Garibaldi*, p.340.

15 *Journals of Queen Victoria*, Tuesday 12 April 1864 [Princess Beatrice's copies, vol.53, p.157]; Friday 22 April 1864 [Princess Beatrice's copies, vol.53, p.166].

16 Sutherland to Gladstone, BL Add MS 44328, fols.70–1.

17 *Journals of Queen Victoria*, Sunday 10 July 1864 [Princess Beatrice's copies, vol.53, pp.270–1].

18 Queen Victoria to her daughter, quoted in Riall, *Garibaldi*, p.339.

19 Virginia Berridge and Griffith Edwards, *Opium and the People: Opiate Use in Nineteenth-Century England* (Allen Lane/St. Martin's Press, 1981), p.24.

20 Ibid., p.65.

21 Harriet Sutherland to Catherine Gladstone, 24 November, Glynne Gladstone Manuscripts 803, Flintshire Record Office.

22 BL Add MS 44328, fols.170–3.

23 Gower, *My Reminiscences*, vol.1, p.165.

24 Ibid., vol.1, p.186.

25 Sutherland to Gladstone, BL Add MS 44329, fol.98.

26 Sutherland to Gladstone, 4 June 1866, BL Add MS 44329, fols.91–2.

13. THE PUSHING STICK

1   *Journals of Queen Victoria*, Sunday 13 May 1866.

2   *Western Daily Press*, Monday 28 May 1866.

3   Quoted in Crathorne, *Cliveden*, p.113.

4   Sutherland to Gladstone, BL Add MS 44329, fols.82–3.

5   Sutherland to Gladstone, BL Add MS 44328, fols.250–1.

6   *Journals of Queen Victoria*, Tuesday 12 November 1867, Windsor Castle [Princess Beatrice's copies, vol.56, p.295].

7   Sutherland to Gladstone, BL Add MS 44329, fols.87–8.

8   Crathorne, *Cliveden*, pp.99–103.

9   Gower, *My Reminiscences*, vol.1, p.20.

10 Ibid., vol.1, p.270.

11 *Journals of Queen Victoria*, Tuesday 27 October 1868 [Princess Beatrice's copies, vol.57, pp.310–11].

12 Foot and Matthew, *Gladstone Diaries*, 28 October 1868, vol.6, p.632.

13 Ibid., 3 November 1868.

14 Quoted in Crathorne, *Cliveden*, p.118.

PART V

I. THE CHRONICLES OF CLIVEDEN

1 James Fox, *The Langhorne Sisters* (London: Granta, 1998), p.259; Nancy Astor, *Astor Story* (unpublished autobiography), p.122, URSC Nancy Astor Papers (hereafter 'Astor') MS 1416 1/6/86.

2 Fox, *The Langhorne Sisters*, p.239.

3 Ibid., p.259.

4 John H. Plumridge, *Hospital Ships and Ambulance Trains* (London: Seeley, Service & Co., 1975), p.105.

5 *Reading Mercury*, 23 January 1915; *The Times*, 10 March 1915.

6 'Emergency Military Hospital Construction', *Building News*, 17 (November 1915), p.554; Harriet Richardson, ed., *English Hospitals 1660–1948: A Survey of their Architecture and Design* (Swindon: Royal Commission on the Historical Monuments of England, 1998), p.99.

7 *The Times*, 30 March 1915.

8 Fox, *Langhorne Sisters*, p.240.

9 Christopher Sykes, *Nancy: The Life of Lady Astor* (St Albans: Granada Publishing, 1979), p.175.

10 Nancy Astor, *Astor Story* (unpublished autobiography), p.131, URSC Astor MS 1416 1/6/86.

11 Nancy Astor, *Astor Story*, pp.131–2, NA Papers Reading, MS 1416 1/6/86.

12 Fox, *Langhorne Sisters*, p.35.

13 Roy M. Anker, *Self-Help and Popular Religion in Modern American Culture* (London: Greenwood Press, 1999), p.39; Baker Eddy quoted in Fox, *Langhorne Sisters*, p.219.

14 Nancy Astor, *Astor Story*, p.13, URSC Astor MS 1416 1/6/86.

15 Fox, *Langhorne Sisters*, pp.158–9.

16 Quoted in Fox, *Langhorne Sisters*, p.166.

17 Fox, *Langhorne Sisters*, p.241.

18 Ibid., p.242.

19 Quoted in Fox, *Langhorne Sisters*, p.243.

20 Nancy to Phyllis, 12 November 1914, Nancy Astor Papers, University of Reading Special Collections, MS 2422/3.

21 Quoted in Fox, *Langhorne Sisters*, p.252.

22 Quoted in Fox, *Langhorne Sisters*, p.254.

23 Quoted in Fox, *Langhorne Sisters*, p.256.

24 Nancy Astor, *Astor Story*, p.129.

25 URSC Astor MS 1416/1/2/653, First World War Soldiers B2 1914–1921, Bell.

26 'Ward Notes', *Chronicles of Cliveden*, 1:10 (1917), p.6.

27 Fox, *Langhorne Sisters*, p.240.

28 Sykes, *Nancy*, p.176. The Women's Land Army (WLA) operated during the First and Second World Wars, providing

female agricultural labourers to replace the men who had been called up to fight. Women who worked in the WLA were known as Land Girls.

29 Sykes, *Nancy*, p.178.
30 Viscount Cranborne to Nancy Astor, 27 February 1915, URSC Astor MS 1416 1/2/16 (1915, A–C).
31 Viscount Cranborne to Nancy Astor, 26 April 1915, URSC Astor MS 1416 1/2/16 (1915, A–C).
32 Fox, *Langhorne Sisters*, pp.274–5.
33 [Nancy Astor Interview], BBC Radio 1962 (Interviewer: Kenneth Harris), BL Sound Archive.
34 E. Pankhurst to Mrs Waldorf Astor, 14 July 1915, URSC Astor MS 1416 1/2/18 (1915, M–Z).
35 E. Pankhurst to Nancy Astor, 4 July 1915, URSC Astor MS 1416 1/2/18 (1915, M–Z).
36 E. Pankhurst to Nancy Astor, 10 May 1915, URSC Astor MS 1416 1/2/18 (1915, M–Z).
37 'Viscountess Nancy Astor interviewed' BBC Radio 1954 (Interviewer: Stephen Black), BL Sound Archive; E. Pankhurst to Nancy Astor, 26 March 1915, URSC Astor MS 1416 1/2/18 (1915, M–Z).
38 Adrian Fort, *Nancy: The Story of Lady Astor* (London: Vintage, 2013), p.155.
39 Justin Kaplan, *When the Astors Owned New York: Blue Bloods and Grand Hotels in a Gilded Age* (New York: Plume, 2007), pp.52–3.
40 Quoted in Sykes, *Nancy*, p.199.
41 Nancy Astor to Jimmy Boyden, 19 November 1919, URSC Astor

MS 1416/1/2/653, First World War Soldiers B2 1914–1921.

2. THE THRILL OF THE CHASE

1 Quoted in James Fox, *Five Sisters: The Langhornes of Virginia* (Simon & Schuster, 2000), p.51.
2 Fox, *Langhorne Sisters*, p.54.
3 Quoted in Fox, *Langhorne Sisters*, p.55.
4 Quoted in Fort, *Nancy*, p.41.
5 Nancy Astor, *Astor Story*, quoted in Sykes, *Nancy*, p.60.
6 Ray Strachey, Manuscript notes for a life of Nancy Astor, WL 7BSH/5/1/1/1.
7 Quoted in Fort, *Nancy*, p.104.
8 Quoted in Fox, *Langhorne Sisters*, p.59.
9 Nancy Astor, *Astor Story*, pp.55–6, URSC Astor MS 1416 1/6/86.
10 Fox, *Langhorne Sisters*, p.66.
11 Nancy Astor, *Astor Story*, p.61; p.65, URSC Astor MS 1416 1/6/86.
12 Ibid., p.66.
13 Ibid., pp.66–7.
14 Ibid., p.68; p.70.
15 Quoted in Fox, *Langhorne Sisters*, p.80.
16 Quoted in Fox, *Langhorne Sisters*, pp.86–7.
17 Quoted in Fox, *Langhorne Sisters*, p.87.

3. THERE'S NO PLACE LIKE HOME

1 Fort, *Nancy*, p.84.
2 See Jackson-Stops, 'The Cliveden Album', p.5.

3　Nancy Astor, *Astor Story*, p.77, URSC Astor MS 1416 1/6/86.

4　Ibid., pp.77–8.

5　Nancy to Phyllis, 25 April 1907, URSC Astor MS 2422/1.

6　Quoted in Fort, *Nancy*, p.88.

7　Quoted in Fort, *Nancy*, p.106.

8　Quoted in Fox, *Five Sisters*, p.97.

9　Nancy's diary, 1907, URSC Astor MS 1416 1/6/77.

10　Quoted in Fox, *Langhorne Sisters*, p.100.

11　Quoted in Fox, *Langhorne Sisters*, p.97.

12　Quoted in Fox, *Langhorne Sisters*, p.105.

13　Nancy to Phyllis, 28 August, URSC Astor MS 2422/3.

14　Quoted in Fox, *Five Sisters*, p.94.

15　Nancy to Phyllis, 23 July 1908, URSC Astor MS 2422/1; quoted in Fox, *Langhorne Sisters*, pp.103–4.

16　Fort, *Nancy*, pp.109–10.

17　See Letter to Nancy Astor, 1 July 1932, URSC Astor MS 1416 1/6/110.

18　Nancy Astor, *Astor Story*, URSC Astor MS 1416 1/6/86.

19　Cliveden payroll notes, BR D158/49.

20　Nancy Astor, *Astor Story*, p.79, URSC Astor MS 1416 1/6/86.

21　Rose Harrison, *Gentlemen's Gentlemen: My Friends in Service* (London: Arlington Press, 1976), p.142.

22　Fox, *Langhorne Sisters*, p.120.

23　Quoted in Fox, *Langhorne Sisters*, p.128.

24　Quoted in Fox, *Langhorne Sisters*, p.131.

25　Nancy to Phyllis, undated, NA Papers Reading, MS 2422/3.

26　Quoted in Norman Rose, *The Cliveden Set: Portrait of an Exclusive Fraternity* (London: Pimlico, 2001), p.184.

27　Daisy, Princess of Pless, *My Diary*, entry for 24 July 1909; quoted in Fort, *Nancy*, p.120.

28　Nancy's diary, Tuesday 11 January 1910, URSC Astor MS 1416 1/6/78; quoted in Fox, *Langhorne Sisters*, p.148.

29　Quoted in Fort, *Nancy*, p.115.

30　Nancy Astor, *Astor Story*, p.88, URSC Astor MS 1416 1/6/86.

31　See URSC Astor MS 1416 1/6/87, for Nancy's account of her involvement in Waldorf's election campaign.

4. LIFE AMONG THE RUINS

1　Leo Amery, *The Times History of the War in South Africa* (1900) vol.6, p.147; see also Walter Nimocks, *Milner's Young Men: The 'Kindergarten' in Edwardian Imperial Affairs* (London: Hodder & Stoughton, 1970).

2　Quoted in Sykes, *Nancy*, p.106.

3　Michael Astor, *Tribal Feeling* (London: John Murray, 1964), p.54.

4　Quoted in Fox, *Langhorne Sisters*, p.224.

5　Quoted in Fox, *Langhorne Sisters*, p.225.

6　Quoted in Fox, *Langhorne Sisters*, p.226.

7　Fox, *Langhorne Sisters*, p.190.

8   Quoted in Fox, *Langhorne Sisters*, pp.190–1.

9   Quoted in Fox, *Langhorne Sisters*, p.198.

10 Quoted in Robert Skidelsky, *John Maynard Keynes: Hopes Betrayed, 1883–1920* (London: Macmillan, 1983), pp.370–1.

11 Correspondence between Philip Kerr and Nancy Astor, URSC Astor MS 1416 1/4/49.

12 Quoted in Fort, *Nancy*, p.160.

13 Quoted in Fort, *Nancy*, p.159.

14 Harrison, *Gentlemen's Gentlemen*, p.141.

15 Quoted in Karen J. Musolf, *From Plymouth to Parliament: A Rhetorical History of Nancy Astor's 1919 Campaign* (Basingstoke: Macmillan, 1999), p.20.

5. 'A LADY FOR PARLIAMENT'

1   Marquess of Salisbury to Nancy Astor, URSC Astor MS 1416 1/2/28.

2   Quoted in Fort, *Nancy*, p.161.

3   Quoted in Sykes, *Nancy*, p.220.

4   Musolf, *From Plymouth to Parliament*, p.35.

5   Quoted in Fort, *Nancy*, p.164.

6   Quoted in Sykes, *Nancy*, p.221.

7   [Nancy Astor Interview], BL Sound Archive.

8   Nancy frequently encouraged women to 'keep men in their place', or to 'keep the men down'. See, for example, Anna Louise Strong, 'Moscow News', 23 July 1931, in URSC Astor MS 1416/2/1, and [Lady Astor Interview], BL Sound Archive.

9   Quoted in Musolf, *From Plymouth to Parliament*, pp.42–3.

10 Musolf, *From Plymouth to Parliament*, p.45.

11 Barbara Strachey, *Remarkable Relations: The Story of the Pearsall Smith Family* (London: Victor Gollancz, 1980), p.287.

12 Quoted in Sykes, *Nancy*, p.225.

13 Quoted in Fox, *Langhorne Sisters*, p.318.

14 Quoted in Fort, *Nancy*, p.167.

15 Martin Pugh, 'Astor, Nancy Witcher, Viscountess Astor (1879–1964)', *Oxford Dictionary of National Biography* (Oxford University Press, 2004; online edn, Jan 2011, accessed 3 November 2014).

16 Ray Strachey, Manuscript notes for a life of Lady Astor, WL 7BSH/5/1/1/1.

17 Ibid.

18 Quoted in Sykes, *Nancy*, p.236.

6. 'A RATTLESNAKE IN THE HOUSE'

1   For Nancy's maiden speech, see *Hansard*, HC Deb 24 February 1920 vol.125, cc.1623–1632.

2   Diary of Sir Robert Sanders, Sunday 29 February 1920, BoL Special Collections, Dep. d. 752. Quoted in Fort, *Nancy*, p.178.

3   Strachey, *Remarkable Relations*, p.287.

4   [Nancy Astor Interview], BL Sound Archive.

5   Nancy often recounted this story: see, for example [Nancy Astor Interview], BL Sound Archive.

6   Fort, *Nancy*, p.180.

7   See Sykes, *Nancy*, pp.253–4.

8   Manuscript notes for a life of Lady Astor, WL 7BSH5/1/1/1.

9   Quoted in Fort, *Nancy*, p.181.

10 'Lady Astor at lunch, Feb. 15 1939', Manuscript notes for a life of Lady Astor, WL 7BSH/5/1/1/1.

11 Conan Doyle quoted in Sykes, *Nancy*, p.252; Fox, *Langhorne Sisters*, p.321.

12 Fox, *Langhorne Sisters*, p.321.

13 'Viscountess Nancy Astor Interviewed', BL Sound Archive.

14 Manuscript notes for a life of Lady Astor, The Women's Library @ LSE, 7BSH/5/1/1/1.

15 'Viscountess Nancy Astor interviewed', BL Sound Archive.

16 Sykes, *Nancy*, p.266.

17 'Second Woman M. P.', *The Times*, Saturday 24 September 1921, p.8.

18 Margaret Wintringham to Nancy Astor, 27 September 1921, Nancy Astor Papers, University of Reading Special Collections, MS 1416 1/2/2.

19 Quoted in Fox, *Five Sisters*, p.291.

20 Quoted in Fort, *Nancy*, p.184.

7. THE DOMESTIC DESPOT

1   Astor, *Tribal Feeling*, p.68.

2   'Viscountess Nancy Astor interviewed', BL Sound Archive.

3   Quoted in Fort, *Nancy*, p.215.

4   Quoted in Fort, *Nancy*, pp.114–15.

5   Harrison, *Gentlemen's Gentlemen*, p.133.

6   Astor, *Tribal Feeling*, p.68.

7   'Viscountess Nancy Astor interviewed', BL Sound Archive.

8   Rose Harrison, *The Lady's Maid: My Life in Service* (London: Ebury Press, 2011), p.114.

9   Quoted in Fox, *Langhorne Sisters*, p.385.

10 Wissie to Nancy, 1928, Nancy Astor Papers, University of Reading Special Collections, MS 1416 1/3/27.

11 Nancy to Bill, 21 October 1929, NA Papers Reading, MS 1416 1/3/27.

12 Harrison, *The Lady's Maid*, p.326.

13 John Grigg, *Nancy Astor: Portrait of a Pioneer* (London: Sidgwick and Jackson, 1980), p.128.

14 Bob Brand to Phyllis, NA Papers Reading, MS 2422/8.

15 Harrison, *The Lady's Maid: My Life in Service*, p.133.

16 Ibid., p.134.

17 Ibid.

8. CONVICTIONS

1   Quoted in Fox, *Langhorne Sisters*, p.424.

2   Quoted in Fox, *Langhorne Sisters*, p.427.

3   Quoted in Fox, *Langhorne Sisters*, p.428.

4   Eugene Lyons, *Assignment in Utopia* (London: G. G. Harrap & Co., 1938), p.429.

5   Waldorf Astor's diary, URSC Astor MS 1416/2/2.

6   Lyons, *Assignment in Utopia*, pp.431–2; Waldorf Astor's diary, 23 July 1931, URSC Astor MS 1416/2/2.

7   Fox, *Langhorne Sisters*, p.472.

8   Quoted in Fox, *Langhorne Sisters*, p.478.
9   Quoted in ibid., p.479.
10 Fox, *Langhorne Sisters*, pp.494–5.

9. THE CLIVEDEN SET UP

1   Quoted in Fort, *Nancy*, p.241.
2   Thomas Jones, *A Diary with Letters, 1931–1950* (London: Oxford University Press, 1954), 2 June, pp.214–16.
3   Ibid., 3 June, pp.216–17.
4   Nevile Henderson, *Failure of a Mission: Berlin, 1937–1939* (London: Hodder and Stoughton, 1940), p.13.
5   The Earl of Halifax, *Fulness of Days* (London: Collins, 1957), p.185.
6   Quoted in Sykes, *Nancy*, p.428.
7   Fort, *Nancy*, p.255.
8   Quoted in Fort, *Nancy*, p.252.
9   Quoted in Rose, *The Cliveden Set*, pp.181–2.
10 Quoted in Rose, *The Cliveden Set*, p.183.
11 Quoted in Fort, *Nancy*, p.261.
12 Anthony Julius, *Trails of the Diaspora: A History of Anti-Semitism in England* (Oxford: Oxford University Press, 2010), p.317.
13 Quoted in Sykes, *Nancy*, p.446.
14 Rose, *The Cliveden Set*, pp.182–3.
15 Ibid., p.183.
16 'GBS Hits Out in Defence of Lady Astor', *Sunday Graphic*, 5 March 1939.
17 Philip Kerr, 'Britain Awake!', *Observer*, 20 November 1938.
18 Quoted in Rose, *The Cliveden Set*, p.184.

10. CARTWHEELS IN THE BUNKER

1   Crispin Gill, *Plymouth: A New History* [vol.2]: *1603 to the Present Day* (Newton Abbot: David & Charles, 1979), p.194.
2   Fort, *Nancy*, p.278.
3   Harrison, *The Lady's Maid*, p.248.
4   Ibid., pp.249–50.
5   See, for example, *Manchester Guardian*, 23 March 1941.
6   Harrison, *The Lady's Maid*, p.253.
7   Ibid., pp.254–5.
8   Quoted in Gill, *Plymouth: A New History*, pp.195–6.
9   *Manchester Guardian*, 23 March 1941.
10 J. C. Trewin, *Portrait of Plymouth* (London: Hale, 1973), pp.166–7.
11 Harrison, *The Lady's Maid*, p.259.
12 Ibid.
13 Ibid., p.265.
14 Richard Overy, *The Bombing War: Europe 1939–1945* (London: Allen Lane, 2013), p.143.
15 Harrison, *The Lady's Maid*, p.269.
16 Trewin, *Portrait of Plymouth*.
17 Harrison, *The Lady's Maid*, p.257.
18 Quoted in Cole Lesley, *The Life of Noël Coward* (Harmondsworth: Penguin, 1978), p.219.
19 Harrison, *The Lady's Maid*, p.258.
20 Ibid., p.262.

11. FAREWELL TO BOTH MY HOUSES

1   Fort, *Nancy*, p.289.
2   'Blitzed Plymouth Plans a New City', broadcast by William Holt and Viscount Astor, transcript at

PWD 3642/1707; quoted in Fort, *Nancy*, p.290.

3   Quoted in Fort, *Nancy*, p.293.

4   Quoted in Fort, *Nancy*, p.294.

5   Quoted in Fort, *Nancy*, p.295.

6   Quoted in Sykes, *Nancy*, p.460, p.461.

7   Richard Cockett, *David Astor and the Observer* (London: Deutsch, 1991), p.94.

8   Quoted in Cockett, *Astor and the Observer*, pp.122–3, p.123.

9   Quoted in Cockett, *Astor and the Observer*, p.121.

10 *The Builder*, 15 January 1943, pp.62–7.

11 Quoted in Fort, *Nancy*, p.232.

12 James Lees-Milne, *Diaries, 1942–1945: Ancestral Voices and Prophesying Peace* (London: John Murray, 1995), pp.vii–viii.

13 Ibid., Monday 11 May 1942.

14 Ibid., Thursday 25 June 1942.

15 Ibid., 6 July 1942.

16 Ibid., Wednesday 19 May 1943; Wednesday 29 March 1944.

17 James Lees-Milne, *People and Places: Country House Donors and the National Trust* (London: Murray, 1992), p.14.

18 Lees-Milne, *Diaries*, Tuesday 20 July 1943. Nancy's hostility towards the idea of public access is reminiscent of Waldorf's father's: during his time at the house, he had banned boating parties from landing on the banks of the river beneath Cliveden and erected around the estate a wall topped with broken glass.

19 Quoted in Peter Mandler, *The Fall and Rise of the Stately Home* (New Haven, London: Yale University Press, 1997), p.324.

20 '25 Years in Parliament', *The Times*, 1 December 1944.

21 'Lady Astor to Retire', *The Times*, 2 December 1944.

22 Quoted in Sykes, *Nancy*, p.474.

23 Astor, *Tribal Feeling*, pp.204–5.

24 Quoted in Sykes, *Nancy*, p.487.

25 Harrison, *The Lady's Maid*, p.75.

26 Quoted in Cockett, *Astor and the Observer*, p.203.

27 Fort, *Nancy*, p.314.

28 Astor, *Tribal Feeling*, pp.204–5.

29 James Lees-Milne, *Caves of Ice* (London: Faber, 1983), p.81.

30 Ibid., pp.212–13.

31 Quoted in Fort, *Nancy*, p.318.

32 Harrison, *The Lady's Maid*, p.338.

33 Ibid.

34 Quoted in Fort, *Nancy*, pp.318–19.

35 Quoted in Crathorne, *Cliveden*, p.181.

36 Quoted in Fort, *Nancy*, p.319.

12. SCHOOL FOR SCANDAL

1   Quoted in Crathorne, *Cliveden*, p.182.

2   William Astor, 'William Astor: My father, his swimming pool and the Profumo scandal', *Spectator*, 11 January 2014.

3   Dominic Sandbrook, *Never Had It So Good* (London: Little, Brown, 2005), p.649.

4   *Westminster Confidential*, 8 March 1963; quoted in Sandbrook, *Never Had It So Good*, p.650.

5   Jack Profumo, 'Personal Statement', *Hansard* HC Deb 22 March 1963, vol.674, cc.809–10.

6   Sandbrook, *Never Had It So Good*, p.655.

7   Ibid.

8   Ibid., p.657.

9   'Sex and Politics', in the *Observer*, 9 June 1963, p.10.

10 Quoted in David Smith, 'Cliveden, the house of prime ministers and socialites', *Observer*, Sunday 12 March 2006.

11 'Sex and Politics', *Observer*, 9 June 1963, p.10.

12 David Smith, 'Cliveden, the House of Prime Ministers and Socialites', in the *Observer*, Sunday 12 March 2006.

13 Sandbrook, *Never Had It So Good*, p.660.

14 Sandbrook, *Never Had It So Good*, p.634.

15 Peter Catterall, ed., *The Macmillan Diaries, vol. II: Prime Minister and After, 1957–1966* (London: Pan Books, 2012), 22 March 1963, p.552.

16 Richard Davenport-Hines, *An English Affair: Sex, Class and Power in the Age of Profumo* (London: HarperPress, 2013), pp.305–6.

17 Ibid., p.327.

18 Quoted ibid., p.327.

19 Harrison, *My Life in Service*, pp.175–7.

20 See Sykes, *Nancy*, p.611. Rose Harrison has a slightly different story: that when he was drunk, Bobbie told Nancy about Profumo; she asked to call Cliveden but Rose and Charles managed to put her off the scent by calling their own phone line instead, so it appeared that 'Cliveden' was engaged. Rose was adamant that Nancy never knew anything about it: 'I am firmly convinced that she never knew anything about what had happened. If she had she would most certainly have spoken to me about it.' See Harrison, *My Life in Service*, pp.175–7.

21 Quoted in Fox, *Langhorne Sisters*, p.539.

22 Quoted in Fox, *Langhorne Sisters*, p.546.

23 Nancy to Phyllis, undated letter, URSC Astor MS 2422/3.

24 Quoted in Fox, *Langhorne Sisters*, p.546.

25 Quoted in David Smith, 'Cliveden, the House of Prime Ministers and Socialites', *Observer*, Sunday 12 March 2006.

SELECT BIBLIOGRAPHY

All five parts of the book are indebted to *Cliveden: The Place and the People*, by James Crathorne (London: Collins & Brown, 1995), to the National Trust guides *Cliveden, Buckinghamshire* (NT, 2001) and *Cliveden Garden* (Jonathan Marsden and Oliver Garnett; NT, 2002) and to unpublished gazetteers and archaeological plans prepared in 2012 by the Parklands Consortium Ltd.

The newspapers quoted in Parts I–III are from the British Library's *Burney Collection Database*; those in Part IV are from the *Nineteenth-Century British Library Newspaper Database* and *The Times Digital Archive*; and those in Part V from *The Times Digital Archive*, *The Sunday Times Digital Archive*, and *Proquest Historical Newspapers (The Guardian and The Observer)*.

Part III benefited greatly from the *Enlightened Princesses* symposium held at Hampton Court Palace in July 2014; of particular help were papers given by Cassandra Albinson, Wolf Burchard, Mark Laird, Lee Prosser and Cynthia Roman. The accounts of Langhorne family relations in Part V are indebted to James Fox's *The Langhorne Sisters* (London: Granta, 1998).

PART I

ARCHIVAL SOURCES

Bodleian Library, Oxford

G 7.3 Th., *The Cynosura*, dedicated to Anne, Countess of Shrewsbury by Nicholas Cross in 1670, with manuscript notes by Thomas Barlow.

Bruce Christopher Yardley, 'The political career of George Villiers, 2nd Duke of Buckingham (1628–87)' unpublished DPhil dissertation, University of Oxford, 1989.

SELECT BIBLIOGRAPHY

British Library

Add MS 5821, recounting the selling of Bletchley Park by Buckingham, 1671

Add MS 15903, a relation of the Duke of Buckingham's entertainment in France, 1672

Add MS 18914, inventory of 'hangings of arras, tapistry, and other hangings, plate, jewells, aggats, pictures, statues, household stuff, goods, chattells, rings, and other things', assigned to George Villiers, 2nd Duke of Buckingham

Add MS 29553, letter to Lord Hatton

Add MS 46458, letter from Charles II granting parts of Holland, Lincolnshire to the Earl of Shrewsbury in 1664

Egerton MS 3330, letter from Anna Maria, Countess of Shrewsbury, to Lord Danby

Harley MS 6862, Brian Fairfax's life of Buckingham

Stowe MS 755, signature of Anna Maria, Countess of Shrewsbury

London Metropolitan Archive

MS 15818, accounts of 2nd Duke of Buckingham, 1660–70

Acc/382, leasing of Buckingham house, 1664

The National Archives, Kew

C6/419/78, '1684, Goodchild vs. Villiers, Court of Chancery'

National Library of Wales, Aberystwyth

Cwmgwili 838–49, Cliveden estate vouchers, receipts and accounts

Northamptonshire Record Office

Buccleuch Collection 45 Vol I, correspondence of Charles Talbot

Journal of Charles Talbot, 1702–1705

Buccleuch Collection 65 Vol XXI, journal of the Duke of Shrewsbury 1700–1706

PUBLISHED SOURCES

Ackroyd, Peter, *London: The Biography* (London: Vintage, 2001).

—— *Thames: Sacred River* (London: Vintage, 2008).

SELECT BIBLIOGRAPHY

Beauclerk, Charles, *Nell Gwyn* (London: Macmillan, 2006).

Browning, Andrew (ed.), *Memoirs of Sir John Reresby* (London: Offices of the Royal Historical Society, 1991).

Bucholz, Robert O., and Ward, Joseph P., *London: A Social and Cultural History* (Cambridge: Cambridge University Press, 2012).

Burghclere, Lady Winifred, *George Villiers, Second Duke of Buckingham, 1628–1687: A Study in the History of the Restoration* (London: John Murray, 1903).

Chapman, Hester W., *Great Villiers: A Study of George Villiers Second Duke of Buckingham, 1628–1687* (London: Secker & Warburg, 1949).

Crathorne, James, *Cliveden: The Place and the People* (London: Collins & Brown, 1995).

Dabhoiwala, Faramerz, *The Origins of Sex: A History of the First Sexual Revolution* (London: Penguin Books, 2013).

Dolman, Brett, *Beauty, Sex and Power: A Story of Debauchery and Decadent Art at the Late Stuart Court* (London: Scala, 2012).

Dryden, John, *Absalom and Achitophel*, ed. W. D. Christie (Oxford: Clarendon, 1946).

Evelyn, John (ed. William Bray), *The Diary of John Evelyn* (London: Gibbings, 1890).

Fairfax, Brian (ed. Edward Arber), *Memoirs of the Life of George Villiers, Duke of Buckingham* (London, 1869).

Fisher, John, and others, *The A to Z of Restoration London* (London Topographical Society, 1992).

Fraser, Antonia, *King Charles II* (London: Phoenix, 2002).

Girouard, Mark, *Life in the English Country House: A Social and Architectural History* (New Haven and London: Yale University Press, 1978).

Hamilton, Anthony (ed. Sir Walter Scott), *The Memoirs of Count Grammont* (London: George Routledge and Sons, 1905).

Hanrahan, David C., *Charles II and the Duke of Buckingham* (Stroud: Sutton Publishing, 2006).

[Historical Manuscripts Commission], *Fifth Report* (London: H.M. Stationery Office, 1877)

—— *Seventh Report* (London: H. M. Stationery Office, 1879).

—— *Ninth Report*, Part II (London: H. M. Stationery Office, 1884).

—— *Twelfth Report* (London: H. M. Stationery Office, 1890).

Hopkins, Graham, *Nell Gwynne: A Passionate Life* (London: Robson Books, 2003).

McFadden, George, 'Political Satire in "The Rehearsal" ', *The Yearbook of English Studies* 4 (1947): 120–8.

Melton, Frank T., 'A Rake Refinanced: The Fortunes of George Villiers, Second Duke of Buckingham, 1671–1685', *Huntington Library Quarterly* 51/4 (1988): 297–381.

Marston, John, and others, *The Insatiate Countess*, ed. Giorgio Melchiori (Manchester: Manchester University Press, 1984).

Muddiman, J. G., 'The Duel between Buckingham and Shrewsbury, 1668', *Notes and Queries* 165 (1933): 22–3.

Niemeyer, Carl, 'Henry Killigrew and the Duke of Buckingham', *The Review of English Studies* 12/47 (1936): 326–8.

Peltonen, Markku, *The Duel in Early Modern England: Civility, Politeness and Honour* (Cambridge: Cambridge University Press, 2003).

Pepys, Samuel, *The Diary of Samuel Pepys* (accessed online at www.pepysdiary.com).

Pettigrew, William A., *Freedom's Debt: the Royal African Company and the Politics of the Atlantic Slave Trade 1672–1752* (University of North Carolina Press, 2012).

Phipps, Christine, ed., *Buckingham: Public and Private Man. The Prose, Poems and Commonplace Book of George Villiers, Second Duke of Buckingham (1628–1687)* (New York and London: Garland Publishing, 1985).

Pope, Alexander, *The Works of Alexander Pope* (Edinburgh; London: Gall & Ingliss, 1881).

Pritchard, Allan, 'A Defence of His Private Life by the Second Duke of Buckingham', *Huntington Library Quarterly* 44/3 (1981): 157–71.

Saumarez-Smith, Charles, 'Supply and Demand in English Country House Building, 1600–1740', *Oxford Art Journal* 11/2 (1988): 3–9.

Schama, Simon, *A History of Britain: The British Wars 1603–1776* (London: The Bodley Head, 2009).

Smith, John Harrington, 'Dryden and Buckingham: The Beginnings of the Feud', *Modern Language Notes* 69/4 (1954): 242–5.

Somerville, Dorothy H., *The King of Hearts: Charles Talbot, Duke of Shrewsbury* (London: George Allen & Unwin, 1962).

Villiers, George, *The Works of His Grace George Villiers, Duke of Buckingham*, 2 vols. (London, 1715).

—— (ed. A. G. Barnes) *The Rehearsal* (London: Methuen & Co., 1927).

Wake, Joan, *The Brudenells of Deene* (London: Cassell and Company, 1953).

Wilson, John Harold, *A Rake and His Times: George Villiers 2nd Duke of Buckingham* (London: Farrar, Strauss and Young, 1954).

—— *Court Satires of the Restoration* (Columbus: Ohio State University Press, 1976).

PART II

ARCHIVAL SOURCES

British Library

Add MS 4804, Swift correspondence

Add MS 4806, Swift correspondence

Add MS 22627, Elizabeth Orkney to Mrs Howard

Add MS 28894, Elizabeth Orkney to J. Ellis

Add MS 36228, settlement of estate at Cliveden and Taplow, 1720

Add MS 61162, Lord Orkney, military correspondence with Marlborough

Add MS 61294, Lord Orkney, military correspondence

Add MS 61299, Lord Orkney, military correspondence

Add MS 61474, Marlborough correspondence

Add MS 61605, Elizabeth Orkney to Lord Sunderland

Add MS 61628, Lord Orkney to Lord Sunderland

R. P. 1109 Box 20 941D, Boyle correspondence

Stowe 247, Lord Orkney, letters

National Archives, Kew

C6/298/72, 'Manfield vs. Duchess of Buckingham'

Will of Lord Orkney 11/682/48, last will and testament of Lord Orkney

SELECT BIBLIOGRAPHY

National Archives of Scotland, Edinburgh

GD406/1, correspondence of the dukes of Hamilton, 1563–1712

National Library of Scotland

MS 1033, Correspondence of Earl Selkirk

Northamptonshire Record Office

Buccleuch Collection 51 Vol VII, letters from and to Mrs Villiers and Mrs Lundee 1693.

Craster Family Collection ZCR Box 9, Alexander Pope to the Earl of Orkney.

PUBLISHED SOURCES

Baird, Rosemary, *Mistress of the House: Great Ladies and Grand Houses* (London: Phoenix Press, 2004).

Baker-Smith, Veronica, *Royal Discord: The Family of George II* (London: Athena Press, 2008).

Bathurst, Benjamin, *Letters of Two Queens* (London, 1924).

Beattie, J. M., *The English Court in the Reign of George I* (Cambridge: Cambridge University Press, 1967).

Bisgrove, Richard, *The National Trust Book of the English Garden* (London: Penguin Books, 1992).

Campbell, Colen, *Vitruvius Britannicus* (New York: Dover Publications, 2007).

Chisholm, Kate, *Wits & Wives: Dr Johnson in the Company of Women* (London: Pimlico, 2012).

Claydon, Tony, *William III* (London: Longman, 2002).

Cox, William (ed.), *The Private and Original Correspondence of Charles Talbot, Duke of Shrewsbury* (London, 1821).

Damrosch, Leo, *Jonathan Swift: His Life and His World* (New Haven; London: Yale University Press, 2013).

Dekker, Rudolf, *Family, Culture and Society in the Diary of Constantijn Huygens Jr.* (Leiden; Boston: Brill, 2013).

Devine, T. M., *Scotland's Empire 1600–1815* (London: Allen Lane, 2003).

Gatrell, Vic, *City of Laughter: Sex and Satire in Eighteenth-Century London* (London: Atlantic Books, 2006).

—— *The First Bohemians: Life and Art in London's Bohemian Age* (London: Allen Lane, 2013).

Gregg, Edward, *Queen Anne* (New Haven: Yale University Press, 2001).

Grew, Marion Sharpe, *William Bentinck and William III* (London: John Murray, 1924).

Halsband, Robert (ed.), *The Complete Letters of Lady Mary Wortley Montagu*, 3 vols. (Oxford: Clarendon, 1965).

Hamilton, Elizabeth, *William's Mary: A Biography of Mary II* (London: Hamish Hamilton, 1972).

Harris, Frances, *A Passion for Government: The Life of Sarah, Duchess of Marlborough* (Oxford: Clarendon Press, 1991).

Harris, Tim, *Revolution: The Great Crisis in the English Monarchy, 1685–1720* (London: Allen Lane, 2006).

[Historical Manuscripts Commission], *Report on the Manuscripts of His Grace the Duke of Portland*, vols.4 & 5 (London: H. M. Stationery Office, 1899).

Holmes, Richard, *Marlborough: Britain's Greatest General* (London: Harper Perennial, 2009).

Jennings Churchill, Sarah (Duchess of Marlborough), *The Private Correspondence of Sarah, Duchess of Marlborough* (London: Henry Colburn, 1838).

Jackson-Stops, Gervase, 'The Cliveden Album: drawings by Archer, Leoni and Gibbs for the 1st Earl of Orkney', *Architectural History* 19 (1976): 5–16 & 77–88.

Jardine, Lisa, *Going Dutch: How England Plundered Holland's Glory* (London: Harper Perennial, 2009).

McClain, Molly, 'Love, Friendship and Power: Queen Mary II's Letters to Frances Apsley', *Journal of British Studies* 47 (2008): 505–27.

Musson, Jeremy, *How to Read a Country House* (London: Ebury Press, 2005).

Onnekink, David, *The Anglo-Dutch Favourite: The Career of Hans William Bentinck, 1st Earl of Portland, 1649–1709* (Aldershot: Ashgate, 2007).

Palladio, Andrea, *The Four Books of Architecture* (New York: Dover Publications, 1965).

Pincus, Steve, *1688: The First Modern Revolution* (New Haven and London: Yale University Press, 2009).

Pope, Alexander, *The Works of Alexander Pope, Esq. in Verse and Prose* (London, 1806).

Quane, 'Midleton School, Co. Cork', *The Journal of the Royal Society of Antiquaries of Ireland* 82/1 (1952): 1–27.

Schama, Simon, *The Embarrassment of Riches: An Interpretation of Dutch Culture in the Golden Age* (London: Fontana, 1988).

Somerset, Anne, *Queen Anne: The Politics of Passion* (London: Harper Press, 2012).

Suffolk, Henrietta Countess of, *Letters to and from Henrietta, Countess of Suffolk and her Second Husband, the Hon. George Berkeley*, 2 vols. (London: John Murray, 1824).

Swift, Jonathan, *The Works of Jonathan Swift*, 19 vols. (Edinburgh: Archibald Constable & Co., 1814).

Tillyard, Stella, *Aristocrats: Caroline, Emily, Louisa and Sarah Lennox 1740–1832* (London: Vintage, 1995).

Van der Kiste, John, *William and Mary: Heroes of the Glorious Revolution* (Stroud: The History Press, 2008).

Walpole, Horace, *The Works of Horatio Walpole, Earl of Orford* (London, 1798).

Wharncliffe, James Archibald Stuart (ed.), *The Letters and Works of Lady Mary Wortley Montagu* (London: R. Bentley, 1837).

Woolley, David (ed.), *The Correspondence of Jonathan Swift* (Oxford: Peter Lang, 1999).

Willis, Peter, *Charles Bridgeman and the English Landscape Garden* (Newcastle upon Tyne: Elysium Press Publishers, 2002).

PART III

ARCHIVAL SOURCES

British Library

Add MS 32417, Ludwig von Schrader to Casper Wettstein

Add MS 61467, Marlborough correspondence

SELECT BIBLIOGRAPHY

British Museum

BM Satires 4877 (museum number 1618,0808.9971), 'Vice triumphant over virtue, or Britannia hard rode', 1 August 1771

BM Satires 4885 (museum number Y,4.578), 'The excursion to Cain Wood', 1771

PUBLISHED SOURCES

Arch, Nigel, and Marschner, Joanna, *Splendour at Court: Dressing for Royal Occasions since 1700* (London: Unwin Hyman, 1987).

Baker-Smith, Veronica, *Royal Discord: The Family of George II* (London: Athena Press, 2008).

Black, Jeremy, *The English Press in the Eighteenth Century* (London: Croom Helm, 1987).

Brooke, John, *King George III* (London: Constable, 1972).

Bullion, John L., 'Augusta, Princess of Wales (1719–1772)', *Oxford Dictionary of National Biography* (online edition; accessed May 2014).

Campbell Orr, Clarissa (ed.), *Queenship in Britain 1660–1837* (Manchester and New York: Manchester University Press, 2002).

Coombs, David, 'The Garden at Carlton House of Frederick Prince of Wales and Augusta Princess Dowager of Wales: Bills in Their Household Accounts 1728 to 1772', *Garden History* 25/2 (1997): 153–77.

Cox, Oliver J. W., 'Frederick, Prince of Wales, and the First Performance of "Rule, Britannia!"', *The Historical Journal* 56/4 (2013): 931–54.

Dean, Ann C., 'Court Culture and Political News in London's Eighteenth-Century Newspapers', *English Literary History* 73/3 (2006): 631–49.

Fritz, Paul S., 'The Trade in Death: the Royal Funerals in England, 1685–1830', *Eighteenth Century Studies* 15/3 (1982): 291–316.

Gerrard, Christine, 'Queens-in-waiting: Caroline of Ansbach and Augusta of Saxe-Gotha as Princesses of Wales', in Clarissa Campbell Orr (ed.), *Queenship in Britain 1660–1837* (Manchester and New York: Manchester University Press, 2002).

Goff, Moira; Goldfinch, John; Limper-Herz, Karen; and Peden, Helen, *Georgians Revealed: Life, Style and the Making of Modern Britain* (London: The British Library, 2013).

Hervey, Lord John (ed. J. W. Croker), *Memoirs of the Reign of George the Second from his Accession to the Death of Queen Caroline*, 2 vols. (London: John Murray, 1848).

—— (ed. Romney Sedgwick), *Some Material towards Memoirs of the Reign of George II*, 3 vols. (London: Eyre & Spottiswoode, 1931).

Heyd, Uriel, *Reading Newspapers: Press and Public in Eighteenth-Century Britain and America* (Oxford: Voltaire Foundation, 2012).

Hibbert, Christopher, *George III: A Personal History* (New York: Basic Books, 1998).

[Historical Manuscripts Commission], *Fifteenth Report* (Norwich: H. M. Stationery Office, 1899).

—— *Manuscripts of the Earl of Egmont: Diary of the 1st Earl of Egmont* (London: H. M. Stationery Office, 1923).

McKillop, Alan D., 'The Early History of "Alfred"', *Philological Quarterly* 41/1 (1962): 311–24.

Marschner, Joanna, *Queen Caroline: Cultural Politics at the Early Eighteenth-Century Court* (New Haven and London: Yale University Press, 2014).

Newman, Aubrey N. (ed.), 'Leicester House Politics, 1750–60, from the Papers of John, Second Earl of Egmont', *Camden Miscellany* 23/7 (London: Royal Historical Society, 1969).

Ribeiro, Aileen, *Facing Beauty: Painted Women & Cosmetic Art* (New Haven and London: Yale University Press, 2011).

Roberts, R. A. (ed.), *Diary of Viscount Percival, afterwards First Earl of Egmont*, 3 vols. (London: H. M. Stationery Office, 1920–3).

Schama, Simon, *A History of Britain* [vol.2]: *The British Wars 1603–1776* (London: The Bodley Head, 2009).

Smith, Hannah, *Georgian Monarchy: Politics and Culture* (Cambridge University Press, 2006).

Thompson, Andrew C., *George II: King and Elector* (New Haven and London: Yale University Press, 2011).

Vivian, Frances, *A Life of Frederick, Prince of Wales, 1707–1751: A Connoisseur of the Arts* (Lewiston, NY: Edwin Mellen Press, 2006).

Walpole, Horace (ed. John Brooke), *Memoirs of George II*, 3 vols. (Yale University Press, 1985).

Walters, John, *The Royal Griffin: Frederick, Prince of Wales, 1707–51* (London: Jarrolds, 1972).

Worsley, Lucy, *Courtiers: The Secret History of the Georgian Court* (London: Faber and Faber, 2010).

PART IV

ARCHIVAL SOURCES

British Library

Add MS 44324–44329, correspondence between Harriet, Duchess of Sutherland, and William Gladstone, 1860–8.

Buckinghamshire Record Office

D/BASM/74/35, documents related to Taplow

D/X/1174/1, The Children's Journal

D92/18–33, house conveyances and legal documents

D11/9/1c, 'Her Majesty's stay at Cliveden', 1866

D158/1, 'An Inventory of the Effects of Cliefden House, Maidenhead, Berkshire', 1849

D158/3, Cliveden guest books

Flintshire Record Office

Glynne Gladstone MS 803

National Maritime Museum

HB Sketches no.667, 'The Taking of Chusan'

The Royal Archives

Queen Victoria's journals, accessed via http://www. queenvictoriasjournals.org/home.do.

Staffordshire Record Office

D593/K/1/3/43, Cliveden accounts

D593/P/20, Sutherland correspondence

SELECT BIBLIOGRAPHY

D593/R/3/2/7, J. Fleming's vouchers concerning Cliveden

D593/R/3/2/9/14, plate and wine at Cliveden, 1868

D593/R/2/41, Duchess of Sutherland, receipts

D868/11–12, Sutherland correspondence

D6578/14/11, Cliveden Inventory, 1861

D6578/15/1–14, Sutherland correspondence

D6579/22/1–99, Sutherland correspondence

D6579/73/1–3, Sutherland correspondence

D6579/74/1–16, Sutherland correspondence

D6579/75/1–50, Sutherland correspondence

D6579/80/1–39, Sutherland correspondence

D6579/83/1–48, Sutherland correspondence

D6579/84, Duchess of Sutherland, commonplace book

D6579/85/1–13, Sutherland correspondence

PUBLISHED SOURCES

Aldous, Richard, *The Lion and the Unicorn: Gladstone vs. Disraeli* (London: Pimlico, 2007).

Atkinson, Diane, *The Criminal Conversation of Mrs Norton* (London: Preface, 2012).

Auerbach, Jeffrey A., *The Great Exhibition of 1851: A Nation on Display* (New Haven: Yale University Press, 1999).

Barry, Alfred, *The Life and Works of Sir Charles Barry, R. A., F. R.S.* (London: John Murray, 1867).

Beales, Derek, 'Garibaldi in England: the politics of Italian enthusiasm', in Davis, John A., and Ginsborg, Paul (eds.), *Society and Politics in the Age of the Risorgimento* (Cambridge: Cambridge University Press, 1991).

Beem, Charles, 'The Lioness Roared: the problems of female rule in English history', PhD thesis, University of Arizona.

Cannadine, David, *The Decline and Fall of the British Aristocracy* (London: Pan Books, 1990).

Dasent, Arthur Irwin, *The Story of Stafford House, Now the London Museum* (London: John Murray, 1921).

Evans, Siân, *Life Below Stairs in the Victorian & Edwardian Country House* (London: National Trust Books, 2011).

Fleming, John, *Spring and Winter Flower Gardening; Containing the System of Floral Decoration as Practised at Cliveden, the Seat of Her Grace Harriet Duchess of Sutherland* (London: Journal of Horticulture and Cottage Gardener, 1864).

Foreman, Amanda, *Georgiana: Duchess of Devonshire* (London: HarperCollins, 1999).

Gladstone, William (ed. Foot, M. R. D., and Matthew, H. C. G.), *The Gladstone Diaries*, vols.3–4 (Oxford: Clarendon Press, 1974).

Gower, Lord Ronald Sutherland, *My Reminiscences*, 2 vols. (Boston: Roberts Brothers, 1884).

Hedrick, Joan D., *Harriet Beecher Stowe: A Life* (Oxford: Oxford University Press, 1994).

Hunting, Penelope, 'Henry Clutton's Country Houses', *Architectural History* 26 (1983): 96–104; 176–80.

Jackson-Stops, Gervase, 'The Cliveden Album II: Nineteenth-Century and Miscellaneous Drawings', *Architectural History* 20 (1977): 65–70 & 102–116.

Jenkins, Roy, *Gladstone* (London: Pan, 2002).

Leconfield, Maud and Gore, John (eds.), *Three Howard Sisters: Selections from the writings of Lady Caroline Lascelles, Lady Dover and Countess Gower 1825–1833* (London: John Murray, 1955).

Longford, Elizabeth, *Eminent Victorian Women* (Stroud: The History Press, 2008).

Longford, Elizabeth, *Victoria* (London: Abacus, 2011).

Mandler, Peter, *Aristocratic Government in the Age of Reform: Whigs and Liberals, 1830–1852* (Oxford: Clarendon Press, 1990).

Matthew, H. C. G., *Gladstone 1809–1874* (Oxford: Clarendon Press, 1986).

Musson, Jeremy, *Up and Down Stairs: The History of the Country House Servant* (London: John Murray, 2010).

Norton, Caroline, *The Dream, and Other Poems* (London: Henry Colburn, 1840)

O'Connor, Maura, *The Romance of Italy and the English Political Imagination* (New York: St. Martin's Press, 1998).

Paxman, Jeremy, *The Victorians: Britain Through the Paintings of the Age* (London: BBC Books, 2010).

Philips, Melanie, *The Ascent of Woman: A History of the Suffragette Movement* (London: Abacus, 2004).

Pugh, Evelyn L., 'Women and Slavery: Julia Gardiner Tyler and the Duchess of Sutherland', *The Virginia Magazine of History and Biography* 88/2 (1980): 186–202.

Reynolds, K. D., *Aristocratic Women and Political Society in Victorian Britain* (Oxford: Clarendon Press, 1998).

Riall, Lucy, *Garibaldi: Invention of a Hero* (Yale University Press, 2007).

Richards, Eric, *The Leviathan of Wealth: The Sutherland Fortune in the Industrial Revolution* (London: Routledge & Kegan Paul, 1973).

—— *The Highland Clearances: people, landlords and rural turmoil* (Edinburgh: Birlinn, 2000).

Rubenstein, W. D., *Britain's Century: A Political and Social History* (London: Arnold, 1998).

Sambrook, Pamela, *The Country House Servant* (Stroud: Sutton, 1999).

Schreuder, D. M., 'Gladstone and Italian Unification, 1848–70: the Making of a Liberal?', *The English Historical Review* 85/336 (1970): 475–501.

Shepperson, George, 'Harriet Beecher Stowe in Scotland, 1852–3', *The Scottish Historical Review* 32/113 (1953): 40–46.

Spall, R. F., 'The Bedchamber Crisis and the Hastings Scandal: Moral Politics and the Press at the Beginning of Victoria's Reign', *Canadian Journal of History* 22/1 (1987): 19–39.

Stowe, Charles Edward, *Life of Harriet Beecher Stowe* (London: Sampson Low & Co., 1889).

Stowe, Harriet Beecher, *A Reply to 'The Affectionate and Christian address of many thousands of women of Great Britain and Ireland, to their sisters, the women of the United States of America'* (London: Sampson Low & Co., 1863).

Weintraub, Stanley, *Victoria* (London: John Murray, 1996).

PART V

ARCHIVAL SOURCES

British Library

[Nancy Astor Interview], BBC Radio 1962 (Interviewer: Kenneth Harris), British Library Sound Archive.

[Nancy Astor Talking], BBC Radio, British Library Sound Archive.

'Viscountess Nancy Astor interviewed', BBC Radio, 2 August 1954. (Interviewer: Stephen Black), British Library Sound Archive.

[Lady Astor Interview] Interviewer: Kenneth Harris, BBC, 1962, British Library Sound Archive.

'Work at Cliveden as Under-Butler for the Astors, Charles Dean', National Trust Sound Archive, 1/1/1997, and British Library Sound Archive.

Buckinghamshire Record Office

D158/6/1, agreement for private wire into a post office, 1906

D158/6/2, agreement for a telephone installation at Cliveden, 1907

D158/6/3, additional flex, telephone (Cliveden), 1914

D158/29, servants' payroll, Cliveden

D158/49, payroll notes, Cliveden

Reading University Archive (Special Collections, Nancy Astor Papers)

MS 1416 1/1/1635, Palestine problem, 1947

MS 1416 1/2/28, General Correspondence 1919

MS 1416/1/2/653, First World War Soldiers B2 1914–1921

MS 1416/1/3/1, letters from the Earl of Ancaster

MS 1416 1/3/25, correspondence concerning Wissie

MS 1416 1/3/27, correspondence concerning the Astor children

MS 1416 1/3/30 [1927], letters from Wissie

MS 1416 1/3/32, scrap books & moments

MS 1416 1/3/35, interviews

MS 1416 1/4/49, letters from Philip Kerr 1916–1919

SELECT BIBLIOGRAPHY

MS 1416 1/6/77, Nancy Astor's diary

MS 1416 1/6/86, 'Astor Story' (unpublished autobiography of Nancy Astor)

MS 1416 1/6/110, servants

MS 1416/1/6/100, dinner invitations and responses

MS 1416 1/7/84 Jul–Jul 1945–49, British Press Cuttings

MS 1416 1/7/85 Jul–Oct. 1949–50, British Press Cuttings

MS 1416 1/7/87 Jan–May 1960–64, British Press Cuttings

MS 1416 1/7/89 May 1964, British Press Cuttings on Nancy Astor's death

MS 2422/1–3, letters of Nancy, Viscountess Astor, to members of her family

The Women's Library @ LSE

9/31/21: Nancy Astor to various, December 1919

3AMS/B/02/08: General Election: correspondence with parliamentary candidates

7BSH/5/1/1/1: Manuscript notes for a life of Lady Astor

7MGF/A/1/210: Nancy to Mrs Fawcett [Millicent Garret Fawcett], 15 July 1920

8SUF/B/122–123c: Interview with Barbara Strachey about Ray Strachey

PUBLISHED SOURCES

Amery, Leo, *The Times History of the War in South Africa* (1900).

Anker, Roy M., *Self-Help and Popular Religion in Modern American Culture* (London: Greenwood Press, 1999).

Astor, Michael, *Tribal Feeling* (London: John Murray, 1964).

Baker Eddy, Mary, *Manual of the Mother Church* (Trustees of Mary Baker G. Eddy, 2006)

Bartley, Paula, *Emmeline Pankhurst* (Routledge, 2002).

Billington, David P., *Lothian: Lord Kerr and the Quest for Global Order* (2006).

Butler, J. R., *Lord Lothian* (1960).

Catterall, Peter (ed.), *The Macmillan Diaries, vol. II: Prime Minister and After, 1957–1966* (London: Pan Books, 2012).

Cockburn, Claud, *Crossing the Line* (London: MacGibbon & Kee, 1958).

Cockett, Richard, *David Astor and the Observer* (London: Deutsch, 1991).

Davenport-Hines, Richard, *An English Affair: Sex, Class and Power in the Age of Profumo* (London: HarperPress, 2013).

Fort, Adrian, *Nancy: The Story of Lady Astor* (London: Vintage, 2013).

Fox, James, *The Langhorne Sisters* (London: Granta, 1998).

—— *Five Sisters: The Langhornes of Virginia* (New York: Simon & Schuster, 2000).

Gilbert, Martin, and Gott, Richard, *The Appeasers* (London: Phoenix Press, 2000).

Gill, Crispin, *Plymouth: A New History* [vol.2]: *1603 to the Present Day* (Newton Abbot: David & Charles, 1979).

Grigg, John, *Nancy Astor: Portrait of a Pioneer* (London: Sidgwick & Jackson, 1980).

Halifax, Earl of (Edward Frederick Lindley Wood), *Fulness of Days* (London: Collins, 1957).

Harrison, Rosina, *Gentlemen's Gentlemen: My Friends in Service* (London: Arlington Press, 1976).

—— *The Lady's Maid: My Life in Service* (London: Ebury Press, 2011).

Ishiguro, Kazuo, *The Remains of the Day* (London: Faber & Faber, 2005).

Jarvis, David, 'Mrs Maggs and Betty: The Conservative Appeal to Women Voters in the 1920s', *Twentieth-Century British History* 5:2 (1994): 129–52.

Jones, Thomas, *A Diary with Letters, 1931–1950* (London: Oxford University Press, 1954).

Julius, Anthony, *Trails of the Diaspora: A History of Anti-Semitism in England* (Oxford: Oxford University Press, 2010).

Kaplan, Justin, *When the Astors Owned New York: Blue Bloods and Grand Hotels in a Gilded Age* (New York: Plume, 2007).

Lees-Milne, James, *Caves of Ice* (London: Faber, 1984).

—— *Diaries, 1942–1945: Ancestral Voices and Prophesying Peace* (London: John Murray, 1995).

—— *People and Places: Country House Donors and the National Trust* (London: Murray, 1992).

Lovin, Clifford R., *A School for Diplomats: the Paris Peace Conference of 1919* (University Press of America, 1997).

Lyons, Eugene, *Assignment in Utopia* (London: G. G. Harrap & Co., 1938).

MacMillan, Margaret, *Peacemakers: The Paris Peace Conference of 1919 and its attempt to end war* (London: John Murray, 2001).

Mandler, Peter, *The Fall and Rise of the Stately Home* (New Haven; London: Yale University Press, 1997).

Musolf, Karen J., *From Plymouth to Parliament: A Rhetorical History of Nancy Astor's 1919 Campaign* (Basingstoke: Macmillan, 1999).

Nimocks, Walter, *Milner's Young Men: The 'Kindergarten' in Imperial Affairs* (London: Hodder & Stoughton, 1970).

Orbell, John, 'Baring, John, second Baron Revelstoke (1863–1929)', *Oxford Dictionary of National Biography* (Oxford University Press, 2004; online edn., May 2006).

Overy, Richard, *The Bombing War: Europe 1939–1945* (London: Allen Lane, 2013).

Pakenham, Thomas, *The Boer War* (London: Weidenfeld & Nicolson, 1979).

Richardson, Harriet, ed., *English Hospitals 1660–1948: A Survey of their Architecture and Design* (Swindon: Royal Commission on the Historical Monuments of England, 1998).

Rose, Norman, *The Cliveden Set: Portrait of an Exclusive Fraternity* (London: Pimlico, 2001).

Sandbrook, Dominic, *Never Had It So Good: A History of Britain from Suez to the Beatles* (London: Abacus, 2006).

Schama, Simon, *A History of Britain* [vol.3]: *The Fate of Empire 1776–2000* (London: The Bodley Head, 2009).

Shotwell, James T., *At the Paris Peace Conference* (New York: Macmillan, 1937).

Sinclair, David, *Dynasty: The Astors and their Times* (London: Onslow Books, 1983).

Skidelsky, Robert, *John Maynard Keynes: Hopes Betrayed, 1883–1920* (London: Macmillan, 1983).

Stanford, Peter, *Bronwen Astor: Her Life and Times* (London: HarperCollins, 2000).

Strachey, Barbara, *Remarkable Relations: The Story of the Pearsall Smith Family* (London: Gollancz, 1980).

Sykes, Christopher, *Nancy: The Life of Lady Astor* (St Albans: Granada Publishing, 1979).

Thane, Pat, 'The Impact of Mass Democracy on British Political Culture, 1918–1939', in Gottlieb, Julie V., and Toye, Richard, eds., *The Aftermath of Suffrage: Women, Gender, and Politics in Britain, 1918–1945* (Palgrave Macmillan, 2013).

Trewin, John Courtenay, *Portrait of Plymouth* (London: Hale, 1973).

Tyack, Geoffrey, 'Service on the Cliveden Estate between the Wars', *Oral History* 5/1 (1977): 63–87.

Wilson, Derek, *The Astors, 1763–1992: Landscape with Millionaires* (London: Weidenfeld & Nicolson, 1993).

PICTURE CREDITS

PICTURE CREDITS

SECTION 2

p.1   Portrait of Harriet Howard, Duchess of Sutherland, Franz Xavier Winterhalter ©National Trust Collections

p.2   George Granville Sutherland-Leveson-Gower (1786–1861), 2nd Duke of Sutherland, KG, DCL (after John Partridge), William Corden II ©National Trust Collections

p.3   The Duchess of Sutherland's assembly at Stafford House in honour of Garibaldi, English School (19th century) / Private Collection / © Look and Learn / Bernard Platman Antiquarian Collection / Bridgeman Images

p.3   © National Portrait Gallery, William Ewart Gladstone, Sir John Everett Millais, 1st Bt, 1879, Transferred from Tate Gallery, London, UK, 1957, Primary Collection NPG 3637

p.4   Nancy Astor (1879–1964) 1906, John Singer Sargent / Cliveden, Buckinghamshire, UK / National Trust Photographic Library / John Hammond / Bridgeman Images

p.5   Nurses and patients at the New Brunswick Ward of the Duchess of Connaught's Canadian Red Cross Hospital at Cliveden (Imperial War Museum Q53611)

p.5   Front cover of *Chronicles of Cliveden* (June 30th 1917) with thanks to the National Library of Australia

p.6   Lady Astor, Charlie Chaplin, Amy Johnson and George Bernard Shaw (Photo by Time Life Pictures / Mansell / The LIFE Picture Collection / Getty Images)

p.6   1941: Nancy Witcher Astor (Photo by Tunbridge / Tunbridge-Sedgwick Pictorial Press / Getty Images)

p.7   Photo by Hans Wild / The LIFE Picture Collection / Getty Images

p.8   Cliveden from the parterre, courtesy of Cliveden House Hotel

INDEX

INDEX

INDEX

ACKNOWLEDGEMENTS

Books, like houses, need strong foundations and I would like to thank the following for their unrelenting support throughout the challenges of the building phase:

My editor, Jocasta Hamilton, for her astute advice, warmth and humour, and my agent, Jonny Geller, for taking a punt on a first-time writer.

Professor David Reynolds, my former supervisor at Christ's College, Cambridge, who has been as extravagantly generous with his time as he has with his wisdom. Without his faith and guidance this book would not have happened.

My formidable team of researchers – Tom Evans, Miranda Critchley, Andrea Cobern and Harriet Lyon – for their meticulous work, brilliance and enthusiasm, even when the sheer volume of archive material seemed overwhelming. I could not have completed this book without their help and have learned so much from them.

Much appreciation is also due to Ellen Leslie for imparting her boundless knowledge of art and architecture, and to my mentor and friend Catherine Ostler for her kindness, encouragement and endless patience. My thanks, too, to the wonderful Kate Weinberg for offering invaluable advice on the writing process and a shoulder to cry on when the words failed to flow.

A special thank you to my family: my parents Ann and Howard, for their love, inspiration and unswerving support – and to my sisters Caroline and Laura.

ACKNOWLEDGEMENTS

Thanks also to Caroline Carr for her wise counsel and unwavering friendship, and to Katie Cowell for bearing with me during the dizzy highs and lows of book writing. I am also hugely grateful to Richard Dennen for giving me the confidence to write the story of the Mistresses.

Above all, I owe thanks and eternal gratitude to the three loves of my life: my husband, Ian, and my daughters Grace and Alice – who make everything worthwhile.